POLITICS OF SECURITY

OXFORD HISTORICAL MONOGRAPHS

The *Oxford Historical Monographs* series publishes some of the best Oxford University doctoral theses on historical topics, especially those likely to engage the interest of a broad academic readership.

Politics of Security

British and West German Protest Movements and the Early Cold War, 1945–1970

HOLGER NEHRING

For Hartmut —

with many thanks for your excellent supervision — and intellectual and moral support.

Holger
October 2013

OXFORD
UNIVERSITY PRESS

OXFORD

UNIVERSITY PRESS

Great Clarendon Street, Oxford, OX2 6DP,
United Kingdom

Oxford University Press is a department of the University of Oxford.
It furthers the University's objective of excellence in research, scholarship,
and education by publishing worldwide. Oxford is a registered trade mark of
Oxford University Press in the UK and in certain other countries

© Holger Nehring 2013

The moral rights of the author have been asserted

First Edition published in 2013
Impression: 1

Published in the United States of America by Oxford University Press
198 Madison Avenue, New York, NY 10016, United States of America

British Library Cataloguing in Publication Data
Data available

Library of Congress Control Number: 2013936237

ISBN 978–0–19–968122–8

As printed and bound by
CPI Group (UK) Ltd, Croydon, CR0 4YY

For my parents, and for Julia

Acknowledgements

This book has been long in the making, and its journey has been a transnational one. Accordingly, I have accrued many debts over the last few years. My study of the protests against nuclear weapons originates in an Oxford D.Phil. thesis. For making my move to the UK possible, I would like to thank the Rhodes Trust for its generous financial, but also moral and communal support during my time at Oxford. University College provided an ideal community of scholars, and its Old Members' Travel Fund very generously supported many of my research trips to German and British archives. My D.Phil. supervisors, Martin Ceadel and Hartmut Pogge von Strandmann, provided intellectual support as the project was taking shape: I have learned a great deal from Martin's intellectual rigour and quest for analytical precision, and Hartmut has been a true *Doktorvater*, whose tolerance and openness for approaches other than his own are a model for scholarship. Ross McKibbin's support for my work, his unrivalled knowledge of Labour Party politics, and his keen interest in comparative perspectives have also been an important influence. My D.Phil. examiners, Jane Caplan and Pat Thane, pushed me to turn the thesis into a real book by encouraging me in subtle ways to think about some of my original assumptions about the protests. Patrick Major, who subsequently outed himself as one of the anonymous reviewers for the Press, also made a number of very astute suggestions that were very helpful in improving the text.

Over the course of the gestation of this book, I have learned a great deal by presenting my work to a number of audiences at conferences and workshops and by discussing aspects of it with a number of scholars and friends: Julia Angster, Stefan Berger, Paul Betts, Frank Biess, Tom Buchanan, Jodi Burkett, Kathleen Canning, Rita Chin, Eckart Conze, Belinda Davis, Tom Dowling, Geoff Eley, Moritz Föllmer, Martin Geyer, Michael Geyer, Jose Harris, Sir Brian Harrison, Corinna Hauswedell, Matthew Hilton, Jon Lawrence, Josie McLellan, Klaus Naumann, Molly Nolan, Andrew Oppenheimer, Ari Reimann, Dieter Rucht, Tony Shaw, George Steinmetz, Peggy Somers, the late Klaus Tenfelde, Nick Thomas, Stephen Tuck, Till van Rahden, Bernd Weisbrod, Marilyn Young, and Oliver Zimmer. Lawrence Goldman and Mark Whittow, with their legendary hospitality and generosity, were ideal colleagues when I held a junior research fellowship at St Peter's College. Carole Fink deserves special thanks because she made an extremely productive visit to the Mershon

Center for International Security Studies possible. Likewise, I am extremely grateful to Bernd Greiner for arranging a stay at the Hamburg Institute of Social Research, the centre of cold war social history in Germany.

Geoff Eley has taken an interest in my work from early on, and he has been a generous supporter and intellectual interlocutor ever since. For this—and for enabling me to spend two very productive months at the Eisenberg Institute for Historical Research at the University of Michigan during which I was able to put the finishing touches to this manuscript—I am very grateful. The Department of History at the University of Sheffield has provided an intellectual home since March 2006, and I would like to thank subsequent heads of Department, Bob Shoemaker, Mike Braddick, Bob Moore, and Mary Vincent for bearing with me during the long gestation period of this book. My first academic mentor, Anselm Doering-Manteuffel, and the excellent atmosphere he created at his chair at Tübingen first exposed me to the practice of contemporary history, and I am deeply grateful for the experience. I must also thank the editors of this series, in particular Joanna Innes, for their patience and support in seeing this manuscript to press, as well as the team at the Press—Stephanie Ireland, Cathryn Steele, Emma Barber, and my meticulous copy-editor Hilary Walford—for the excellent care they have provided.

Historical research depends on the use of libraries and archives, and the commitment of the archivists, librarians, and their assistants: the Archiv der sozialen Demokratie, Bonn (and here especially Michael Schneider), Reinhart Schwarz and Wolfgang Hertle at the archives of the Hamburg Institute of Social Research, and Mieke Ijzermans at the archives of the International Institute for Social History in Amsterdam deserve to be singled out for special thanks for their generosity, as do the unrivalled librarians at the Bodleian Library. Some of the former activists generously gave up time to discuss their experiences with me: the late John Saville was especially welcoming, and information from the late Dorothy Thompson and from Peter Worsley was also very helpful. In Germany, Helga and Hans-Konrad Tempel and Klaus Vack in particular provided great assistance to a young researcher, and the late Carl Amery, Andreas Buro, Arno Klönne, and Erdmann Linde also generously shared their experiences with me.

Last, but not least, I owe an enormous debt of gratitude to the four people who have read all or some sections of the manuscript, sometimes even in several incarnations: Christopher Dowe, Julia Moses, Nick Stargardt, and Benjamin Ziemann have generously shared their astute intellectual engagement and scholarly commitment with me ever since my days as a D.Phil. student. Julia has been with me almost as long as my work on this project and has reminded me of what really matters. Our dog Fritz contributed not only by giving some real bite to subsequent printouts of the typescript, but also by providing a loyal companion who listened to my rambling without caring to comment. My parents have been extremely supportive of my academic career, and they have taken a keen interest in my work that goes far beyond what I could expect. For all they have done, I could not be more grateful. This book is dedicated to them, and to Julia.

Sheffield
First Sunday of Advent

Contents

List of Figures

Abbreviations

AdsD	Archiv der sozialen Demokratie, Bonn
AEU	Amalgamated Engineering Union
APOA	Archiv APO und soziale Bewegungen, Free University Archives, Berlin
BAK	Bundesarchiv, Koblenz
BA–MA	Bundesarchiv–Militärarchiv, Freiburg
BCPV	British Council for Peace in Vietnam
BJL	Brynmor Jones Library, University of Hull
BLPES	British Library for Political and Economic Science, London
BStU	Die Behörde des Bundesbeauftragten für die Unterlagen des Staatssicherheitsdienstes der ehemaligen DDR
C100	Committee of 100
CARD	Campaign against Racial Discrimination
CC	Central Committee
CCND	Christian Campaign for Nuclear Disarmament
CDU	*Christlich Demokratische Union Deutschlands* (Christian Democratic Union)
CND	Campaign for Nuclear Disarmament
CPGB	Communist Party of Great Britain
CND	Campaign for Nuclear Disarmament
CPSU	Communist Party of the Soviet Union
CSU	*Christlich-Soziale Union in Bayern* (Christian Social Union)
DAC	Direct Action Committee
DGB	*Deutscher Gewerkschaftsbund* (German Trade Union Federation)
DFG	*Deutsche Friedensgesellschaft* (German Peace Society)
EF	European Federation against Nuclear Weapons
EKiD	*Evangelische Kirche in Deutschland*
EZA	Evangelisches Zentralarchiv, Berlin
FDP	Free Democratic Party
FDP	*Freie Demokratische Partei* (Free Democratic Party)
FCGB	*Freier Deutscher Gewerkschaftsbund* (Free German Trade Union Federation)
FDJ	*Freie Deutsche Jugend* (Free German Youth)
GDR	German Democratic Republic
GVP	*Gesamtdeutsche Volkspartei* (All-German People's Party)
HIS	Hamburger Institut für Sozialforschung
HStAD	Hauptstaatsarchiv Düsseldorf
HWR	Hans Werner Richter papers, Stiftung Archiv Akademie der Künste, Berlin
ICDP	International Confederation for Disarmament and Peace
IdK	*Internationale der Kriegsdienstgegner—Deutscher Zweig* (War Resisters' International, German branch)
IfZ	Institut für Zeitgeschichte, Munich

IISG	Internationaal Instituut voor sociale Geschiedenis, Amsterdam
IMG	International Marxist Group
KdA	*Kampagne Kampf dem Atomtod* (Campaign against Atomic Death)
KPD	*Kommunistische Partei Deutschlands* (Communist Party of Germany)
LAB	Landesarchiv Berlin
LHASC	Labour History Archive and Study Centre, Manchester
LSE	London School of Economics and Political Science
MALSU	Manchester Archives and Local Studies Unit
M-OA	Mass Observation Archive, University of Sussex, Falmer, Brighton
MRC	Modern Records Centre, University of Warwick, Coventry
NATO	North Atlantic Treaty Organization
NCANWT	National Committee for the Abolition of Nuclear Weapons Tests
NEC	National Executive Committee
NLR	*New Left Review*
NUR	National Union of Railwaymen
PolArchAA	Politisches Archiv des Auswärtigen Amtes, Berlin
PPE	Politics, Philosophy and Economics
PPU	Peace Pledge Union
RSSF	Revolutionary Socialist Students' Federation
SAPMO-BArch	Sammlung Archiv Partei- und Massenorganisationen im Bundesarchiv, Berlin
SB	*Sozialistisches Büro* (Socialist Bureau)
SDS	*Sozialistischer Deutscher Studentenbund* (Socialist German Student Federation)
SDS	Students for a Democratic Society
SED	*Sozialistische Einheitspartei Deutschlands* (Socialist German Unity Party)
SPD	*Sozialdemokratische Partei Deutschlands* (Social Democratic Party of Germany)
TGWU	Transport and General Workers' Union
TNA	The National Archives, Public Record Office, Kew
TUC	Trades Union Congress
ULR	*Universities & Left Review*
UNA	United Nations Association
UNRRA	United Nations Relief and Rehabilitation Administration
USDAW	Union of Shop, Distributive and Allied Workers
VK	*Verband der Kriegsdienstverweigerer* (Association of Conscientious Objectors)
VSC	Vietnam Solidarity Campaign
WCML	Working Class Movement Library, Salford
WPC	World Peace Council
WRI	War Resisters' International

Introduction

In January 1959, the philosopher Günther Anders defined Hiroshima, the city on which the US air force dropped the first atom bomb on 6 August 1945, as 'a world condition'. He elaborated in his 'Theses for the Atomic Age', which he gave at a student conference against nuclear weapons in West Berlin: 'Any given place on our planet, and even our planet itself', he argued, could now be transformed 'into a Hiroshima'.[1] What made the cold war a war, rather than a mere battle on the level of ideologies and representations, was precisely this condition of the nuclear arms race and what it meant for politics, societies, and culture. Turning Karl Marx's dictum about human agency on its head, Anders regarded the 'atomic age' as an existential condition: 'It is not enough to change the world. We do this anyway. And it mostly happens without our efforts, regardless. What we have to do is interpret this change so we in turn can change it, so that the world doesn't go on changing without us—and not ultimately become a world without us.'[2]

This is a book about what international politics meant to people in Britain and West Germany from the end of the Second World War into the late 1960s, from the beginnings of the nuclear arms race to the first signs of détente between the two superpowers. It aims to make the cold war comprehensible as war by focusing on the nuclear arms race as its core element and to demonstrate its profound impact on politics during this time period. Unlike Anders, however, I am interested in how people acted within the context of the cold war. I examine how people

<hr />

[1] Günther Anders, 'Theses for the Atomic Age', *Massachusetts Review*, 3/3 (1962), 493–505, here 505. On Anders's conceptual importance, see Benjamin Ziemann, 'Situating Peace Movements in the Political Culture of the Cold War. Introduction', in Ziemann (ed.), *Peace Movements in Western Europe, Japan and the USA during the Cold War* (Essen, 2007), 13–38, here 12–15, and Michael Geyer, 'Der kriegerische Blick: Rückblick auf einen noch zu beendenden Krieg', *SoWi*, 19 (1990), 111–17.

[2] Günther Anders, *Die Antiquiertheit des Menschen*, ii. *Über die Zerstörung des Lebens im Zeitalter der dritten industriellen Revolution* (Munich, 1980), 5 (epitaph). On the historicization of Anders's ideas, see Holger Nehring, 'Technologie, Moderne und Gewalt: Günther Anders, Die Antiquiertheit des Menschen (1956)', in Habbo Knoch et al. (eds), *Klassiker modernen Denkens neu gelesen* (Göttingen: Wallstein, 2011), 238–47.

became aware of the arms race as the core of the cold war, how they sought to challenge their respective governments to end the arms race, and how they wrote their own experiences and memories into the cold war. Not least, this book seeks to show how, on the basis of these contestations, activists discovered political and social causes that led them away from regarding the nuclear arms race as the primary and fundamental problem in international relations.[3]

This study therefore focuses on what I call the 'politics of security'. 'Security' in its incarnation of 'national security' is often regarded as a hegemonic concept during the cold war. Historians and political scientists usually deploy it to describe governmental policies and politics. It normally signifies a general orientation towards stability, the status quo, safety, the avoidance of risks, and therefore the avoidance of utopian schemes. But the precise meaning of 'security' is not clear: there exists a wide variety of definitions of 'security'; it is an 'essentially contested concept'.[4] 'Security' is not merely out there. It is the product of the ways in which societies define which dangers threaten their governments, way of life, and values.[5] Discussions about security thus evoked political feelings and emotions that were inversely related to discussions about fear.[6] By focusing on the *politics* of security, I want to suggest that 'security' merely offered a common discursive terrain from which defence and foreign policy could be debated and contested. This concerned the question of the reference point for discussions of security (what Christopher Daase called its 'reference dimension'), the question of how exactly 'security' should be defined (the 'issue dimension'), as well as the 'geographical scope' and the kinds of dangers that formed part of the discussions.[7] Its

---

[3] Cf. the pathbreaking attempt at a social history of the cold war by Paul Steege, *Black Market, Cold War: Everyday Life in Berlin, 1946–1949* (Cambridge, 2007).

[4] Christopher Daase, 'Die Historisierung der Sicherheit. Anmerkungen zur historischen Sicherheitsforschung aus politikwissenschaftlicher Sicht', *Geschichte und Gesellschaft*, 38, 3 (2012), 387–405; Emma Rothschild, 'What is Security?', *Daedalus*, 124 (1995), 53; Barry Buzan, *People, States and Fear: An Agenda for International Security Studies in the Post-Cold War Era* (Boulder, CO, 1991), 3–5.

[5] David M. Goldstein, 'Toward a Critical Anthropology of Security', *Current Anthropology*, 51 (2010), 487–99; Ole Wæver, 'Securitization and Desecuritization', in Ronnie D. Lipschutz (ed.), *On Security* (New York, 1995), 46–86; for a critique of the latter approach as 'anti-political', see Matt McDonald, 'Securitization and the Construction of Security', *European Journal of International Relations*, 14 (2008), 563–87.

[6] On framing such debates as discussions about fear, see the pathbreaking research by Frank Biess, 'Feelings in the Aftermath: Toward a History of Postwar Emotions', in Frank Biess and Robert Moeller (eds), *Histories of the Aftermath: The Legacies of the Second World War in Europe* (New York, 2010), 30–48.

[7] Christopher Daase, 'National, Societal, and Human Security: On the Transformation of Political Language', *Historical Social Research*, 35/4 (2010), 22–37.

significance was that of 'an ambiguous symbol': like the sýmbolon of ancient cultures, it is a sign for something else, and its meanings are politically and socially embedded.[8]

'Security' was one of the key words in Britain and West Germany from the end of the Second World War into the cold war, as it symbolized the challenges of political, social, and moral reconstruction after the mass violence of that conflict, but it also referred to security from a future military confrontation. It served as a code that bridged the gaps between social, economic, foreign, and defence policy.[9] By discussing 'security', people therefore also evoked its opposites: danger and fear. Debates about 'security' evoke key issues of governance and government: political and social theorists since the early modern period have designated the guarantee of the security of a country's population the core function of good government and governance. And yet policy-making, especially in defence and foreign policy, was part of the machinery of both countries' 'secret states'.[10] Discussions about 'security' therefore always involved debates about the legitimacy of what Michael Mann has called states' 'geopolitical privacy'.[11]

Specifically, this book considers the British and West German protests against nuclear weapons during the early phase of the cold war as well as their predecessors and their successors. I seek to undercut the 'comfortable dichotomies of power and resistance' that have characterized most of the historical scholarship on social movements.[12] Such approaches have reified the distance between oppositional cultures and movement organizations, on the one hand, and mainstream politics, on the other hand. They have thus provided interpretations that read organizations as the

---

[8] Arnold Wolfers, ' "National Security" as an Ambiguous Symbol', *Political Science Quarterly*, 67 (1952), 481–502.

[9] Eckart Conze, 'Sicherheit als Kultur: Überlegungen zu einer "modernen Politikgeschichte" der Bundesrepublik Deutschland', *Vierteljahrshefte für Zeitgeschichte*, 53 (2005), 357–80 and Conze, *Die Suche nach Sicherheit: Eine Geschichte der Bundesrepublik Deutschland von 1949 bis in die Gegenwart* (Berlin, 2009); Hans Braun, 'Das Streben nach "Sicherheit" in den 50er Jahren: Soziale und Politische Ursachen und Erscheinungsweisen', *Archiv für Sozialgeschichte*, 18 (1978), 279–306.

[10] Peter Hennessy, *The Secret State: Preparing for the Worst 1945–2010* (Harmondsworth, 2010); Arnulf Baring, *Außenpolitik in Adenauers Kanzlerdemokratie: Westdeutsche Innenpolitik im Zeichen der Europäischen Verteidigungsgemeinschaft* (Munich, 1971); on the genealogies of secrets of state, cf. Bernhard W. Wegener, *Der geheime Staat: Arkantradition und Informationsfreiheitsrecht* (Göttingen, 2006).

[11] Michael Mann, *States, War and Capitalism* (Oxford, 1988), 32.

[12] Paul Steege, Andrew Stuart Bergerson, Maureen Healy, and Pamela E. Swett, 'The History of Everyday Life: A Second Chapter', *Journal of Modern History*, 80 (2008), 358–78, here 370. Cf. also Ingrid Gilcher-Holtey, *'Die Phantasie an die Macht'. Mai 68 in Frankreich* (Frankfurt/Main 1995).

structural embodiments of counter- or subcultures.[13] Instead, I aim to
demonstrate the dialectical and dialogical processes by which social movement activists engaged with their societies by highlighting how activists in
the British Campaign for Nuclear Disarmament (CND) and the West
German 'Campaign against Atomic Death' and 'Easter Marches of
Nuclear Weapons Opponents' challenged, developed, but also appropriated languages and practices of security in manifold ways. This book seeks
to make the anti-nuclear-weapons protesters in both countries comprehensible as 'strangers at the gates' 'who operate on the boundaries of
the polity', but are nonetheless connected with it.[14] Both movements
challenged elements of their societies, but they were also part of those
very societies. Opposition against nuclear weapons mobilized substantial
popular movements across the world. In 1959, between 20,000 and
25,000 people took part in the final rally of the second annual British
protest march against nuclear weapons between the nuclear weapons
establishment in Aldermaston, Berkshire, and central London. For 1960,
the estimates for the final rally on Trafalgar Square vary between 60,000
and 100,000 participants. In 1961, between 40,000 and 50,000 people
participated.[15] In the Federal Republic, campaigns against nuclear weapons enjoyed a similar popularity. By 1964 more than 100,000 in the
whole of the Federal Republic took part. Similarly, in the United States,
in Scandinavia, and in Japan, people took their opposition to nuclear
armaments to the streets.[16] The anti-nuclear-weapons movements in both
countries were the largest of their kind in Europe, mobilizing hundreds of
thousands of people during their peak period in the late 1950s and early
1960s and relying on the more silent consent of public opinion of many
more.

Treating both movements in one study also helps us to take account
of the fact that British and West German history had become deeply
entangled in the twentieth century during and in the wake of two world

[13] Cf. Francesca Polletta, ' "Free Spaces" in Collective Action', *Theory and Society*, 28 (1999), 1–38, here 13 and 20; Marc W. Steinberg, 'The Talk and Back Talk of Collective Action: A Dialogic Analysis of Repertoires of Discourse among Nineteenth-Century Eng-lish Cotton Spinners', *American Journal of Sociology*, 105 (1999), 736–80, here 741–2.
[14] Sidney Tarrow, *Strangers at the Gates: Movements and States in Contentious Politics* (Cambridge, 2012), 3.
[15] Cf. Richard Taylor, *Against the Bomb: The British Peace Movement 1958–1965* (Oxford, 1988), 42, 57, 77 n. 16.
[16] Lawrence S. Wittner, *Resisting the Bomb: A History of the World Nuclear Disarmament Movement 1954–1970* (Stanford, CA, 1997), 220, and Hans Karl Rupp, *Außerparlamentar-ische Opposition in der Ära Adenauer: Der Kampf gegen die Atombewaffnung in den fünfziger Jahren. Eine Studie zur innenpolitischen Entwicklung der Bundesrepublik* (Cologne 1970), 130–43.

wars as well as the cold war. As Susan Pedersen has noted, 'the struggle with Germany shaped Britain in the twentieth century as deeply as the struggle with France did in the eighteenth', and Britain was one of the three main occupying powers in cold war West Germany.[17] The movements in both countries came to be closely intertwined and developed a mutual awareness of their position at the same historical conjuncture of the cold war arms race. They shared in some of the same historical processes, while at the same time remaining firmly anchored in local and national political contexts, not least because the similar experiences and arguments could have completely different resonances.

In order to take account of this constellation, my book combines comparative history with a transnational optic. It highlights the networks between the movements and how mutual observations among activists themselves informed a 'comparative imagination'.[18] My conception of transnational history therefore goes beyond one that focuses on inter- or cross-cultural transfers and relies on rather straightforward models of diffusion.[19] Instead, I seek to highlight how the transnational and national levels were mutually intertwined. My objective is not to develop a clear set of criteria that explain specific outcomes. Rather than focusing on origins and thus reifying nationalism methodologically, my interest lies in using this approach to highlight historical specificities, ambiguities and paradoxes and thereby stress the interaction of 'distinctive processes, their complex imbrication, their differing temporalities, their territorially uneven application, and their unanticipated outcomes.'[20]

This is, then, a book about 'lives lived out on the borderlands, lives for which the central interpretative devices of the culture don't quite work', and I seek to highlight 'the complexity of people's relationship to the situation they inherit'.[21] This implies trying to combine attention to the eventfulness of activism with an awareness of the longer political–cultural patterns in which the protests were embedded. This is an attempt to steer clear of both master narratives of long-term social–cultural

[17] Susan Pedersen, 'Roundtable: Twentieth-Century British History in North America', *Twentieth Century British History*, 21/3 (2010), 375–418, here 393.
[18] George M. Fredrickson, *The Comparative Imagination: On the History of Racism, Nationalism and Social Movements* (Berkeley and Los Angeles, 2000).
[19] See, conceptually, Sidney Tarrow, *The New Transnational Activism* (Cambridge, 2005), 32; Sean Scalmer, 'Translating Contention: Culture, History, and the Circulation of Collective Action', *Alternatives*, 25 (2000), 491–514.
[20] Simon Gunn and James Vernon, 'Introduction', in Gunn and Vernon (eds), *The Peculiarities of Liberal Modernity in Imperial Britain* (Berkeley and Los Angeles, 2011), 1–18, here 13.
[21] Carolyn Kay Steedman, *Landscape for a Good Woman* (London, 1986), 5, 19.

changes, on the one hand, and an inward-looking protest history, on the other.[22]

I do this by taking inspiration from more recent research on social movements in the social sciences and developing it further by incorporating the importance of international relations for the formation of domestic social relations. Social scientists have moved away from structuralist or individualist explanations of social action and have come to highlight how it is possible to create order in conditions of uncertainty. They have shown that social movements do not have the organizational capacities that political parties or trade unions have, but they nonetheless constitute more than a series of protest events.[23]

This book investigates the role the cold war arms race played in accounting for how 'the unstable ordering of multiple possibilities' within societies became 'temporarily fixed in such a way as to enable individuals and groups to behave as a particular kind of agency', how 'people [became] shaped into acting subjects'.[24] I seek to highlight how activists' engagement with the cold war nuclear arms race enabled them to think of themselves as members of a *movement*, and to be considered as such by observers. My emphasis is, therefore, on the cognitive frames that activists developed as part of their politics of security, their forms of activism, as well as their practices within the context of tangible social networks.[25] 'Frames' are schemata of interpretations that individuals rely on to understand and respond to events, and establishing a set of shared interpretations is key for the emergence and sustainability of social movements.[26]

While the movements' names and the salience of the topic in domestic politics gave the campaigns some coherence and endowed them with a clear beginning and end, they never possessed fixed collective identities.[27]

[22] For differently accentuated attempts, see Nick Thomas, 'Challenging Myths of the 1960s: The Case of Student Protest in Britain', *Twentieth Century British History*, 13, 3 (2002), 277–97, and Lucy Robinson, *Gay Men and the Left in Post-War Britain: How The Personal Got Political* (Manchester, 2007).
[23] Andreas Pettenkofer, *Radikaler Protest: Zur soziologischen Theorie politischer Bewegungen* (Frankfurt/Main, 2010); Sidney Tarrow, *Power in Movement: Social Movements and Contentious Politics* (Cambridge, 1998).
[24] Geoff Eley, 'Is All the World a Text? From Social History to the History of Society Two Decades Later', in Terrence J. McDonald (ed.), *The Historic Turn in the Human Sciences* (Ann Arbor, 1996), 193–243, here 220.
[25] David E. Snow and Robert Benford, 'Master Frames and Cycles of Protest', in Aldon Morris and Carol McClurg Mueller, (eds), *Frontiers in Social Movement Theory* (New Haven, 1992), 133–55, here 137.
[26] David A. Snow, et al., 'Frame Alignment Processes, Micromobilization, and Movement Participation', *American Sociological Review*, 51 (1986), 464–81.
[27] For a critique of the term 'identity', see Rogers Brubaker and Frederick Cooper, 'Beyond "Identity"', *Theory and Society*, 29 (2000), 1–47; and Lutz Niethammer, *Kollektive Identität: Heimliche Quellen einer unheimlichen Konjunktur* (Reinbek, 2000), esp. ch. 1.

Instead, I stress the variety and diversity of activists' views and experiences in order to place them in their concrete historical contexts.[28] This book aims to uncover the political processes during which protesters' manifold experiences converged within the movements without ever being identical with them. Rather than being founded on 'identity', these processes involved identifications: the ways in which the protesters came to identify nuclear armaments as an issue of concern, the identification of solutions to these concerns, the protesters' identification with what became 'the movement', and the creation of boundaries between them and the society surrounding them.[29]

This was not merely a constellation of challenge and reaction. Rather, in what Marshall Sahlins has called the 'structure of the conjuncture', 'a set of historical relationships' at once reproduced 'the traditional cultural categories' and gave them 'new values': the actual practices of framing themselves produced novelty.[30] We therefore do not encounter pure or authentic movement activists and their experiences.[31] I am instead interested in highlighting the extent to which some dominant discourses of the age were internalized and negotiated and, through that, created activism. Conflicts are social relationships that the actors involved tend to reify, as they struggle for the same symbolic or material resources. They nonetheless still share the same field of action, but merely interpret it in different ways.[32]

The notable absence of women and female voices in most of my story underlines this ambiguity. It is therefore important to note at the outset that their absence was a constant presence that ran as the *basso continuo* throughout the politics of security. A highly gendered division of labour was a constant presence in both movements, with predominantly male front-line activists and women who were channelled away to the more informal leadership level or backroom duties, such as typing and cooking. Despite this gendered division, the movements still provided

---

[28] Cf. Robert Gildea and James Mark, 'Introduction: Voices of Europe's '68', *Cultural and Social History*, 8/4 (2011), 441–8. On the problems of conceptualizing 'experience' as a historical category, see Harold Mah, 'The Predicament of Experience', *Modern Intellectual History*, 5 (2008), 97–119.

[29] Charles Tilly, 'Social Boundary Processes', *Philosophy of the Social Sciences*, 34 (2004), 211–36.

[30] Marshall Sahlins, *Islands of History* (Chicago, 1985), pp. vii, 72, 125 (quotation).

[31] Conceptually important: Kathryn Gleadle, *Borderline Citizens: Women, Gender and Political Culture in Britain, 1815–1867* (Oxford, 2009), and Carolyn Kay Steedman, *Master and Servant: Love and Labour in the English Industrial Age* (Cambridge, 2007), 26, 219–24.

[32] Alberto Melucci, *Challenging Codes: Collective Action in the Information Age* (Cambridge, 1996), 355–6; Ron Eyerman and Andrew Jamison, *Social Movements: A Cognitive Approach* (Cambridge, 1991), 3–10.

female activists with openings to challenge those very conditions.[33] Not least, some of the languages that male and female activists employed, such as languages of sensibility and suffering and of experiences, and the heroic form that some of the stories of male activists took is itself difficult to think through without specifically female experiences and knowledges.[34]

Because of this dialectic relationship, the study of social movements can offer valuable insights into broader trends within cold war politics, society, and culture. Social movements crossed boundaries: they challenged existing political, social, and cultural practices as well as norms and beliefs. They quite literally crossed borders by regarding themselves as both local and global actors. Yet, at the same time, they still related their activism to more mainstream politics.[35] Social movements therefore bring into sharp relief the very concept of the political—namely, the forces and factors that open or close down what is perceived to be possible in politics. Analyzing them allows us insights into the transformations of such political imaginaries.[36] Pierre Bourdieu has argued that knowledge and politics are inextricably linked: politics is ultimately about perception and legitimate definitions of reality. This happens primarily by drawing boundaries that help to classify what is regarded as legitimate.[37] This process is complicated further because society has to be imagined before it can take place: 'politics works on this imaginary field by seeking to make stable and unitary sense of what is going on.'[38]

This was especially true for foreign and defence policy during the cold war. Policy-making itself went on in secret, and the arms race itself could be grasped only indirectly through armaments statistics, radiation measurements, or the simulation of war in nuclear weapons tests. The core of cold war politics was, therefore, a contest over specific representations of the reality of the nuclear weapons and the arms race: did they merely pose risks that could be managed and controlled like risks of any other technology? Or did nuclear weapons, as the protesters claimed, pose

[33] Sheila Rowbotham, *Promise of a Dream: Remembering the Sixties* (Harmondsworth, 2000); Robinson, *Gay Men and the Left*; Belinda Robnett, 'African-American Women in the Civil Rights Movement, 1954–1965: Gender, Leadership, and Micromobilization', *American Journal of Sociology*, 101 (1996), 1661–93, here 1667.

[34] Carolyn Kay Steedman, 'Weekend with Elektra', *Literature and History*, 6 (1997), 17–42.

[35] Cf. conceptually Guobin Yang, 'The Liminal Effects of Social Movements: Red Guards and the Transformation of Identity', *Sociological Forum*, 15 (2000), 379–406.

[36] Cornelius Castoriadis, *The Imaginary Institution of Society* (Cambridge, MA, 1998).

[37] Pierre Bourdieu, *Language and Symbolic Power* (Cambridge, 1992), 171–202; Bourdieu, *Soziologische Fragen* (Frankfurt/Main, 1993), 51–2, 83–90.

[38] Geoff Eley and Keith Nield, *The Future of Class in History: What's Left of the Social?* (Ann Arbor, 2007), 169.

dangers that were precisely outside the realm of efficient control and management?[39] I am therefore interested in exploring, through the lens of the politics of security, the 'wider set of political dispositions—codes of conduct, values, assumptions, identifications, and contests that characterize the relationship between citizens and the political system of governance' in both countries.[40] In particular, I wish to find out how and when specific cultural assumptions about 'security' became politicized.[41]

My approach has implications for the selection and use of archival sources: any archive is made from selected and consciously chosen documents, and that is especially true for the study of social movements—it is in their very nature, as networks of activists, initially not to develop a sense of their organizational coherence. Many archives are, therefore, personal collections of pamphlets, papers, diaries, letters, and photographs—some have ended up in public and even state archives, others are still in private collections. Their existence, or their lack of coherence, are themselves expressions of the constantly evolving notions of the political in the two countries. It is telling that, of the social movements under consideration here, only the *SPD*-led 'Campaign against Atomic Death' and the British CND as well as the pressure groups in the orbit of the West German Easter Marches, such as the War Resisters' International and the German Peace Society, had their own archival collections. It is important, then, to realize that in this case, perhaps even less than in other cases, there is no real sovereignty of the archive, but there are many loose ends that historians need to accept and interpret rather than challenge.[42]

This book builds upon and seeks to braid together in productive ways four strands of research on post-1945 European history. Through its comparative nature and its awareness for transnational relations and mutual observations, it seeks to bring together the histories of two countries under one conceptual rubric.[43] Their histories and historiographies have, because of the by and large national orientation of most historical

[39] Ziemann, 'Situating Peace Movements in the Political Culture of the Cold War', 19.
[40] Kathleen Canning, 'Introduction: The Politics of Symbols, Semantics, and Sentiments in the Weimar Republic', *Central Eurpean History*, 43 (2010), 567–80.
[41] Margaret Somers, *Genealogies of Citizenship: Markets, Statelessness, and the Right to Have Rights* (Cambridge, 2008), 171–210; Karl Rohe, 'Politische Kultur und ihre Analyse: Probleme und Perspektiven der politischen Kulturforschung', *Historische Zeitschrift* 250 (1990), 321–46. The pathbreaking historical study is Detlef Siegfried, *Time Is on my Side: Konsum und Politik in der westdeutschen Jugendkultur der 60er Jahre* (Göttingen, 2006).
[42] Carolyn Steedman, *Dust: The Archive and Cultural History* (Manchester, 2002), 68.
[43] On the methodological nationalism of European historiography, see Stefan Berger, 'A Return to the National Paradigm? National History Writing in Germany, Italy, France and Britain from 1945 to the Present', *Journal of Modern History*, 77 (2005), 629–78.

scholarship, been written apart from one another, although they unfolded within the same historical conjuncture of post-war reconstruction and cold war politics. Comparing the histories of British and West German anti-nuclear-weapons activists is, therefore, also an opportunity to bring the existing historiographies in conversation with one another.

Through its focus on debates about the political, this book takes issue with linking social movements directly to processes of social and cultural change during the 1950s and 1960s that some have conceptualized as 'liberalization', and others have interpreted as the transformation of socio-cultural values or generational changes.[44] In such explanations, social movements tend to become either the mouthpieces of anonymous social structures, or the expression of novel social values. They appear as the direct outcomes, or even products, of rising affluence, and the growth of 'permissiveness', so that their protests are ultimately written into the mainstream and become part of more general processes of 'liberalization', or the 'peacetime revolutions' of post-war societies.[45] Such stories, however, neglect the ambiguities and ambivalences of the political and societal transformations that characterized post-war societies, and they forget to account for 'the continuing force and adaptability of nineteenth-century cultural forms' within the context of affluent societies.[46] But it would be equally problematic to regard the protest movements in Britain only as expressions of the *longue durée* of British radicalism.[47] This book

[44] For Britain, see the pathbreaking study by Lawrence Black, *Redefining British Politics: Culture, Consumerism and Participation, 1954–70* (Basingstoke, 2010) and Caroline Hoefferle, *British Student Activism in the Long Sixties* (London, 2012); on research on 1968, see Martin Klimke and Joachim Scharloth (eds), *1968: Handbuch zur Kultur- und Mediengeschichte der Studentenbewegung* (Stuttgart, 2007); Martin Klimke and Joachim Scharloth (eds), *1968 in Europe: A History of Protest and Activism* (New York, 2008); Detlef Siegfried, 'Furor und Wissenschaft. Vierzig Jahre nach "1968"', *Zeithistorische Forschungen/Studies in Contemporary History*, online edn, 5 (2008) <http://www.zeithistorische-forschungen. de/16126041-Siegfried-1-2008>. (accessed 14 July 2010).

[45] Paul Addison, *The Peacetime Revolutions of Post-War Britain* (Oxford, 2010); Ulrich Herbert (ed.), *Wandlungsprozesse in Westdeutschland. Belastung, Integration, Liberalisierung 1945–1980* (Göttingen, 2002). For an attempt to overcome this: Christina von Hodenberg and Detlef Siegfried (eds), *Wo '1968' liegt: Reform und Revolte in der Geschichte der Bundesrepublik* (Göttingen, 2006). For Britain cf. the overview by Mark Donnelly, *Sixties Britain* (Harlow, 2005).

[46] Frank Mort, 'The Ben Pimlott Memorial Lecture 2010: The Permissive Society Revisited', *Twentieth Century British History*, 22 (2011), 269–98, here 272; Nick Thomas, 'Will the Real 1950s Please Stand up? Views of a Contradictory Decade', *Cultural and Social History*, 5 (2008), 227–36; Adrian Bingham, *Family Newspapers: Sex, Private Life, and the British Popular Press 1918–1978* (Oxford, 2009). On 1968, see Gerd-Rainer Horn, *The Spirit of '68: Rebellion in Western Europe and North America, 1956–1976* (Oxford, 2007).

[47] Brian Harrison, *Seeking a Role: The United Kingdom 1951–1970* (Oxford, 2009), 95–100, 448–51.

highlights, by contrast, that tradition is not a stable and static relationship to the past. Rather, focusing on traditions means considering the manner in which past experiences are passed on through webs of personal relationships.[48] At the same time, it seeks to take account of the eventfulness of the age, the importance of real contestations for the developments.

This book, therefore, speaks directly to, and thereby historicizes, the debate about the 'the peculiarities of the English'. In that debate, E. P. Thompson and Perry Anderson, both involved in activism at the time, discussed the role of the dynamics of contention in English political culture and reflected on the importance of 'traditions' for the stability of British class society.[49] What enables this move from stories of origins to genealogies is the second historiographical theme in this book. Although it has been one of the main fields of investigation in the contemporary history of West Germany, this topic has been relegated to the sidelines in studies of the recent British past: understanding the history of post-1945 from the viewpoint of post-*war* history.[50] The boundary between pre-1945 violence and post-1945 peace and affluence is far less clearly drawn than often presumed. Following cues from Frank Biess, Svenja Goltermann, and Bob Moeller, this work brings into view the 'multifaceted consequences of the war' within societies that seemed to be increasingly peaceful.[51] Post-war history, as Frank Biess has put it, 'focuses not so much on what societies became, but [rather on] from what they emerged'. This book, therefore, seeks to uncover the hidden and not so hidden traces of war in both post-war societies and to identify the specific linkages between war and post-war.[52] This book demonstrates how the experiences and memories of the Second World War were crucial in making the cold war comprehensible. Well into the 1960s, West German and British activists

---

[48] Craig Calhoun, *Roots of Radicalism: Tradition, the Public Sphere and Early Nineteenth-Century Social Movements* (Chicago, 2012), 289–90.

[49] Perry Anderson, 'Origins of the Present Crisis', *New Left Review* 23 (1964), 26–53; Tom Nairn, 'The English Working Class', *New Left Review* 24 (1964), 43–57; E. P. Thompson, 'The Peculiarities of the English', *Socialist Register*, 2 (1965), 311–62.

[50] Geoff Eley, 'Finding the People's War: Film, British Collective Memory, and World War II', *American Historical Review*, 106 (2001), 818–38; Matthew Grant, *After the Bomb: Civil Defence and Nuclear War in Britain* (Basingstoke, 2009).

[51] Frank Biess, *Homecomings: Returning POWs and the Legacies of Defeat in Postwar Germany* (Princeton, 2006), 1; Svenja Goltermann, *Die Gesellschaft der Überlebenden: Deutsche Kriegsheimkehrer und ihre Gewalterfahrungen im Zweiten Weltkrieg* (Munich, 2009); Bob Moeller, *War Stories: The Search for a Usable Past in the Federal Republic of Germany* (Berkeley and Los Angeles, 2001).

[52] Frank Biess, 'Histories of the Aftermath', in Biess and Bob Moeller (eds), *Histories of the Aftermath: The Legacies of the Second World War in Europe* (New York, 2010), 1–10, here 1; Paul Betts and Greg Eghigian (eds), *Pain and Prosperity: Reconsidering Twentieth-Century German History* (Stanford, CA, 2003).

imagined the cold war arms race as a constant pre-war situation; they viewed a potential nuclear war through the lens of their own experiences and memories of the Second World War. Their protests therefore appear as direct enactments of the memory of the Second World War.[53] Civil defence played a relatively limited role, compared with other matters of concern, in movement debates at the time. Given the existence of a number of studies that analyse these debates from a comparative perspective, this book will not discuss them in greater detail.[54] For the same reason, the role of nuclear war in popular culture is discussed here only in so far as it had direct repercussions for the ways in which protesters framed their activities.[55]

The histories of the British and West German anti-nuclear-weapons movements during the time period covered by this book has already been the subject of several studies.[56] Yet, with the important exception of James Hinton's book on the role of nationalism in the history of British peace activism, most of this work argues primarily from an organizational perspective and therefore tends to ignore the manifold ways in which protest practices and cognitive frameworks were tied to more general debates in West German and British political cultures.[57] The under-

[53] This follows conceptually from Alon Confino and Peter Fritzsche, 'Introduction: Noises of the Past', in: Confino and Fritzsche (eds), *Work of Memory: New Directions in the Study of German Society and Culture* (Urbana, IL, 2002), 1–21, here 6–7; Alon Confino, 'Collective Memory and Cultural History: Problems of Method', *American Historical Review*, 102/5 (1997), 1386–403.

[54] Grant, *After the Bomb*, 130–6, 176–80, and Frank Biess, ' "Everybody Has a Chance." Civil Defense, Nuclear *Angst*, and the History of Emotions in Postwar Germany', *German History*, 27/2 (2009), 215–43.

[55] Jonathan Hogg and Christoph Laucht, 'Introduction: British Nuclear Culture', *British Journal for the History of Science*, 45/4 (2012), 479–93; Tony Shaw, *British Cinema and the Cold War: The State, Propaganda and Consensus* (London, 2000).

[56] James Hinton, *Protests and Visions: Peace Politics in 20th Century Britain* (London, 1989); Richard Taylor, *Against the Bomb*; Frank Parkin, *Middle Class Radicalism: The Social Bases of the British Campaign for Nuclear Disarmament* (Manchester, 1968); Rupp, *Außerparlamentarische Opposition*; Karl A. Otto, *Vom Ostermarsch zur APO: Geschichte der ausserparlamentarischen Opposition in der Bundesrepublik 1960–1970* (Frankfurt/Main and New York, 1982); Marc Cioc, *Pax Atomica:: The Nuclear Defense Debate in West Germany during the Adenauer Era* (New York, 1988); Lawrence S. Wittner, *One World or None. A History of the World Nuclear Disarmament Movement through 1953* (Stanford, CA, 1993); Wittner, *Resisting the Bomb*; Wittner, *Toward Nuclear Abolition: A History of the World Nuclear Disarmament Movement: 1971 to the Present* (Stanford, CA, 2003); Kate Hudson, *CND—Now More than Ever: The Story of a Peace Movement* (London, 2005).

[57] Exceptions are the wide-ranging comparison, on the basis of secondary literature, by Benjamin Ziemann, 'A Quantum of Solace? European Peace Movements during the Cold War and their Elective Affinities', *Archiv für Sozialgeschichte*, 49 (2009), 351–89, the analysis of images of peace by Benjamin Ziemann, 'The Code of Protest: Images of Peace in the West German Peace Movements, 1945–1990', *Contemporary European History*, 17 (2008),

lying reason for this is that they are based on a specific vision of what politics is and should be about, mainly organized through interest group or party politics. However, they neglect that the very creation of social formations is in itself highly contested and political, and that definitions of the boundaries of political activity are always in flux.[58] Thus, only because she argues through the narrow and static optic of interest-group politics can Helen McCarthy come to the striking conclusion that the idea of democratized international relations had no salience after 1945: she infers from recognizing the decline and demise of the specific *form* of pressure group politics in the League of Nations Union after 1945 that the topic as a whole was no longer relevant for British politics.[59] Conversely, social-movement scholars have often presupposed a deinstitutionalized understanding of politics rather than actually delineating specific political genealogies.

Some of these conceptual problems also have an impact on the fourth field to which this book seeks to contribute: the importance of the cold war for domestic political cultures, including social activism, which has often been written from the perspective of challenge and response. Jeremi Suri's path-breaking work has opened up a whole field for investigation by developing an argument about the relationship between social and cultural change, activism around the world, and the politics of détente in international relations.[60] Martin Klimke has provided us with a profound archivally grounded study of the multiple connections between American and West German activists, and the ways in which their respective

---

237–61, and the intellectual histories by Meredith Veldman, *Fantasy, the Bomb, and the Greening of Britain: Romantic Protest, 1945–1980* (Cambridge, 1994), and Jodi Burkett, 'Re-Defining British Morality: "Britishness" and the Campaign for Nuclear Disarmament 1958–1968', *Twentieth Century British History*, 21 (2010), 184–205. Conceptually important: Matthew Hilton, 'Politics is Ordinary: Non-Governmental Organisations and Political Participation in Contemporary Britain', *Twentieth Century British History*, 22 (2011), 230–68; Nick Crowson, Matthew Hilton, and James McKay (eds), *NGOs in Contemporary Britain: Non-State Actors in Society and Politics since 1945* (London, 2009); Geoff Eley, *Forging Democracy: The History of the Left in Europe, 1850–2000* (Oxford, 2002).

[58] Belinda Davis, 'What's Left? Popular Participation in Postwar Europe', *American Historical Review*, 113 (2008), 363–90; Detlef Siegfried, 'Demokratie und Alltag: Neuere Literatur zur Politisierung des Privaten in der Bundesrepublik Deutschland', *Archiv für Sozialgeschichte*, 46 (2006), 737–50.

[59] Helen McCarthy, *The British People and the League of Nations: Democracy, Citizenship and Internationalism, c.1918–1945* (Manchester, 2011); McCarthy 'Democratising British Foreign Policy: Rethinking the Peace Ballot, 1934–5', *Journal of British Studies*, 49/2 (2010), 358–87.

[60] Jeremi Suri, *Power and Protest: Global Revolution and the Rise of Détente* (Cambridge, MA, and London, 2005).

government assessed them as 'the other alliance' over the course of the 1960s.[61]

In a powerful critique of these approaches, Quinn Slobodian has emphasized forms of internationalism that cannot find their expression in symbolic alliances and their links to the politics of the past. Instead, he has conceptualized them as lived in and through agency and interactions in concrete works of solidarity with those projects of political transformation and national liberation that could be found beyond Europe and the North Atlantic in Africa, America, and Asia. The importance of this work is that it alerts us powerfully to the importance of the many concrete ways of feeling and interacting in the history of activism around 1968. It thus offers a way of engaging with the *global* nature of the cold war and what this implied for local conceptions of pluralism and feelings of belonging among West German activists.[62] My own study further develops this approach by emphasizing the complexities of transnational protests in the early cold war as the direct result of the active production and reproduction of contestations over the changing shape of the political, and by highlighting the multiple forms of protest and belonging that emerged within the movements. This will allow me to write a history of these social movements that does not follow the traditional modernist-functionalist paradigms of 'left' and 'right' and of organized politics.

In line with trying to highlight the dynamic character of the movements and the multiple genealogies, I do not seek to tell the parallel and interconnected stories of the British and West German activists in a process of temporal revelation. Instead, I have chosen to arrange my material in a mixture of chronological and thematic chapters. This also means that, at times, British or West German activists can be heard more loudly, or that connections are foregrounded at some points, but a more implicit presence at others. The politico-cultural transformations that are the subject of this book generated many inconclusive and ambiguous outcomes. The first chapter seeks to highlight the ways in which British and West German activists gained an awareness of the problems of the nuclear arms race. This was fundamentally the story of how the British and West German activists gained an awareness of sharing a common historical conjuncture.

[61] Martin Klimke, *The Other Alliance: Student Protest in West Germany and the United States in the Global Sixties* (Princeton, 2009).
[62] Quinn Slobodian, *Foreign Front: Third World Politics in Sixties West Germany* (Durham, NC, 2012); cf. also Andrew Oppenheimer, 'Conflicts of Solidarity: Nuclear Weapons, Liberation Movements, and the Politics of Peace in the Federal Republic of Germany, 1945–1975' (unpublished Ph.D. thesis, University of Chicago, 2010).

The second and third chapters trace the ways in which activists from very different backgrounds in both countries found their ways into the social movements. Frustrated with the strictures that the bipolarity of cold war thinking imposed on their own milieux, they saw that the movements could provide them with multiple openings to think through the politics of security as a form of politics that went beyond the cold war. The fourth chapter highlights the role movement organization played in forging the movements. The next two chapters highlight the key frames that emerged within the movements: understandings of the nation in the context of international relations; and the protest marches themselves and the emotions they created.

The last three chapters trace the divergent paths of transformation of the politics of security in both countries over the course of the 1960s: how, on the basis of these discussions, the movements provided an opening for wider discussions about the relationship between politics and culture; the emergence of a politics of solidarity; and the development of grass-roots politics in the late 1960s and early 1970s. Fundamentally, the movements not only contributed to the politics of security by making specific policy proposals but also helped generate inter-personal security among the activists through providing them with a community. By forming social links and networks, the activists managed to generate a feeling of belonging as well as the impression among observers that the movements were indeed the unitary political actors they purported to be. These feelings of belonging were, in the end, a way of dealing with the complexities of political communication in societies that appeared to be increasingly insecure. It is mainly due to this interaction that we can now write their history as not merely a history of protest events, but rather a history of movement.

1

From War to Post-War: Security
Lost and Found

At the beginning was the end. The end of war provided the central reference point for the politics of security that British and West German
peace activists advanced in the post-war period. As the philosopher
Günther Anders pointed out in the early 1950s, 'the moment at which
the bomb appeared was...the least convenient that could have been
chosen from the point of view of someone wishing to direct a film. For
it was precisely that moment towards the last phase of the war, during
which the present fear that war and dictatorship had brought began to
relax.'[1] There was already some reflection on the changing character of
war in the light of these experiences. In Britain, there was now an awareness that 'our island [was] no longer a detached participant', sharing in
wars 'only through the adventures of masculine youth', vulnerable as it
had become to bombing raids from elsewhere.[2] But there was very little
explicit reflection on the nature of the threat that the new weapons
brought. The predominant feeling in Britain and West Germany was,
however, one of relief, relief that the war was finally over.[3] The dropping
of two nuclear bombs on the Japanese cities Hiroshima and Nagasaki
on 6 and 9 August 1945 therefore received only scant attention in both
countries.

This chapter traces the ways in which British and West German peace
campaigners developed an awareness of the repercussions of what came
to be known as the 'atomic age', how they responded to it, and why they
responded in the ways they did. The period from the mid-1940s to the
mid-1950s saw the transition from a politics of peace to a politics of
security. In 1945, most Britons and West Germans thought that they had

---

[1] Günther Anders, 'Über die Bombe und die Wurzeln unserer Apokalypse-Blindheit', in
Anders, *Die Antiquiertheit des Menschen: Über die Seele im Zeitalter der zweiten technischen
Revolution* (2 vols; Munich, 1956, 1980), i. 265–6.
[2] Vera Brittain, *England's Hour* (London, 1941), p. xiii.
[3] Richard Bessel, *1945. From War to Peace* (London, 2009), 246–78; David Kynaston,
Austerity Britain 1945–1951 (London, 2007), 60–83.

lost all their security. During this time period from 1945 to the mid-1950s, discussions about the nuclear arms race and the nuclear age became an opportunity to discuss losses, but also hopes for a better future, that were borne out of the experiences of violence and death in the Second World War. This happened as British and West German peace campaigners and their governments embarked on a multitude of ways to find security again. Peace activists had problems addressing these issues head-on, however: bombing war and nuclear weapons had destabilized exisiting languages of peacemaking, and pacifist organizations had problems addressing these issues within the framework of post-1945 politics. The ideological cold war between Soviet peace campaigns and the Western emphasis on freedom came to constrain their activities further. Thus, whereas the politics of peace had contained notions of moving towards a better and often utopian future, the politics of security sought to generate movement not by referring to utopian ideals, but by conjuring up hopes for stability and the status quo as an essential ingredient of peacemaking. The late 1950s saw the convergence of a number of attempts at finding security in the nuclear age that fundamentally differed from that sought by governments: instead of separating issues of material and military security, they advanced a holistic politics of security through networks and activism from below, building on, but also transcending, the peace activism of the traditional pacifist organizations.

The story that this chapter tells was at once a shared history of common perceptions, fears, and hopes, and a history of fundamental differences in their resonances. We can also detect many transnational connections through mutual observations and direct personal contacts. Both British and German societies were connected to each other: first on opposite sides of the aerial bombings of the Second World War; then together in the 'Western' camp of the cold war and its nuclear arms race. But, whereas British society had to deal with reconstructing the country economically, socially, and culturally, West German 'reconstruction' remained conjoined with the racial violence of the Nazi regime and carried with it a fundamental moral problem. This meant that talking directly about violence obtained a particularly strong stigma in West Germany in the post-war years.[4] It was first an occupied, and then a semi-sovereign and divided nation, so the politics of security gained a significance in Germany that differed fundamentally from that in Britain.

---

[4] Michael Geyer, 'The Stigma of Violence, Nationalism, and War in Twentieth-Century Germany', *German Studies Review*, 15 (1992), 75–110.

AUGUST 1945: HIROSHIMA AND NAGASAKI IN BRITAIN AND GERMANY

Britons and Germans perceived '1945' as a 'zero hour', as a point of time in history where they had the opportunity to start afresh, from which to look back and gaze forward and to remake their countries and their lives. Everyone in their own individual way experienced the end of war as 'one of those rare moments in which history's continuum became shattered in the most spectacular fashion'.[5] Remembering the end of war thus became a way of establishing distance from those events that were characterized by existential fears for survival, radical moral and emotional uncertainty, but also the opportunity for new beginnings. Ideas of 'reconstruction' that were tied to this moment were therefore related to a multitude of political projects that had been borne out of the experiences of fear and violence of the war years. Fundamentally, this was about coping with 'man-made mass death'.[6] The means Britons and Germans found of un-making death was to depoliticize and to anonymize its causes by attribut-ing it to machines and technology rather than to individuals. Early interpretations of 'the bomb' therefore turned the new weapon into an anonymous technological force with its own agency, an agency from which people could not escape. Often, Britons and Germans discussed the bombs as they would have discussed natural disasters. Comparisons with earthquakes and volcanic eruptions were especially frequent.[7]

In Britain, '1945' and the victory of the Labour Party that year served as markers for a barrier to the hunger, poverty, and want that many Britons had been experiencing during the economic depression and the war years. This meant, though, that people's hopes for a better future were conjoined with images of death and destruction; hopes for prosperity and security linked to fears of pain. This gave the manifold projects for creating less violent, better, and more hopeful futures in the immediate post-war their particu-lar valency. The end of the war did not immediately bring the desired security, but rather more uncertainty. Pain was cordoned off so as not to be able to pollute the future that Britons and Germans wanted to build for

---

[5] Geoff Eley, 'A Disorder of Peoples: The Uncertain Ground for Reconstruction in 1945', in Jessica Reinisch and Elizabeth White (eds), *The Disentanglements of Populations: Migration, Expulsion and Displacement in Post-War Europe, 1944–1949* (Basingstoke, 2011), 291–314, here 305, and Mark Mazower, 'Reconstruction: The Historiographical Issues', *Past & Present*, suppl. 11 (2011), 17–29.

[6] Edith Wyschogrod, *Spirit in Ashes: Hegel, Heidegger, and Man-Made Mass Death* (New Haven, 1990).

[7] 'Atombombenexplosion in der Wüste von Neu-Mexiko', *Wochenschau Welt im Film* 19/7 (September 1945); 'Die Atombombe', *Frankfurter Rundschau*, 11 August 1945.

themselves.[8] The moral repercussions of such attempts of anonymizing and depoliticizing the war were particularly problematic in Germany: the extreme violence of the last months of fighting and the fundamental rupture between the ideology of the German *Herrenmenschen* and the feeling of moral bankruptcy that dawned upon the war's losers endowed '1945' with a significance there that it did not have in Britain.[9]

British and German histories of pain and prosperity were intricately and intimately connected. The air forces of both countries had bombed each other's cities and towns; and Britain's role as an occupying power in Germany after the National Socialists' unconditional surrender on 8 May 1945 connected the politics of both countries further. People's expectations for the post-war period were framed by the assumption that the end of war would bring security—in both countries, fear and anxiety had been regarded as detrimental to the war effort. Not least, there was a general Western sentiment that put a high premium on security and was highly critical of fear that applied to both Nazi Germany and wartime Britain. 'Freedom from fear', US President Franklin Delano Roosevelt had stated in his State of the Union address in January 1941, became one of the war aims and subsequently became part of the UN Declaration of Human Rights.[10] For British and West German peace activists after the war, Roosevelt's ideas for a novel international order, based upon a functioning and united international organization with effective mechanism for the peaceful settlement of international disputes and connected with an agenda of harnessing individual economic and social well-being, provided the central template and reference point for thinking about issues of international order.[11] Post-war peace activists measured their political successes and disappointments against this yardstick. It was this desire for an undivided and indivisible world that initially guided their critique of the American government's use of nuclear weapons as a bargaining chip in the emerging conflict with the Soviet Union over the geostrategic implications of the post-war order.[12]

[8] Monica Black, *Death in Berlin: From Weimar to Divided Germany* (Cambridge, 2010), 229–70; Pat Jalland, *Death in War and Peace: A History of Loss & Grief in England* (Oxford, 2010), 157–75.

[9] For this and the preceeding argument, see Michael Geyer, 'Die eingebildete Heimkehr: Im Schatten der Niederlage', in Daniel Fulda et al. (eds), *Demokratie im Schatten der Gewalt: Geschichten des Privaten im deutschen Nachrkieg* (Göttingen, 2010), 72–96, here 76.

[10] Peter Stearns, *American Fear: The Causes and Consequences of High Anxiety* (London, 2006), 14.

[11] James Hinton, *Protests and Visions: Peace Politics in 20th Century Britain* (London, 1989), 139.

[12] See the document issued by the Federation of American Scientists: Dexter Masters and Katharine Way (eds), *One World or None: A Report on the Full Meaning of the Atomic Bomb* (New York, 1946).

It was in this context that British and German peace campaigners read about—and watched on newsreels—the bombings by US bombers of the Japanese cities of Hiroshima and Nagasaki on 6 and 9 August 1945 respectively. They struggled to make sense of these issues, as their conceptualization of 'peace' was still framed by either utopias of a non-violent social order, the remits of liberal internationalism, or socialist ideas of peace through social justice that sat uneasily with the individualist language of human rights that was emerging and that stressed not social progress, but individual safety and security. British and German peace campaigners were part of two societies that could yet make little sense of what had happened: very few people in Britain and Germany realized the full significance and implications of the events. Little concrete information on the implications of the new technology was available. There was also little or no awareness of the dangers stemming from radiation. Pictures of the disfigured, the dying, and the dead had been censored. And the newsreels and newspapers showed rubble landscapes that looked very similar to what Britons and Germans knew from their own countries.[13]

In Britain, which continued to fight with the allied powers in Asia, the war continued until Japan's unconditional surrender on 15 August 1945. Hence, the initial debates about nuclear weapons emerged in the context of discussions about the usefulness of the bombs for ending a war, a war that most had seen as a 'good war', fought as it was against National Socialism, fascism, and Japanese imperialism. But perceptions were not at all clear at the time, and the author of the *Manchester Guardian*'s editorial published two days after the Nagasaki bombing wondered whether this really meant that Britain had reached the 'brink of peace'.[14] Some even hoped that the new weapons, precisely because they were so strong and horrific, would be able to put an end to war as such, as no government would dare launch war if threatened with the new superweapon.[15]

So, when Britons recorded their reactions, fear and uncertainty characterized the first responses to the dropping of atomic bombs. In Britain, most contemporaries phrased their reactions in terms of both hopes for a better future and threats of a new war. One male participant in the British *Mass Observation* surveys wrote in his diary that 'such hideous destruction seems to knock the moral bottom out of life... Ideals, hopes

[13] 'Der Mensch und die Atomenergie', *Herder-Korrespondenz*, 1/6 (1947), 306.
[14] 'The Brink of Peace?', *Manchester Guardian*, 11 August 1945, 4.
[15] Ilona Stölken-Fitschen, 'Der verspätete Schock: Hiroshima und der Beginn des atomaren Zeitalters', in Michael Salewski and Ilona Stölken-Fitschen (eds), *Moderne Zeiten: Technik und Zeitgeist im 19. und 20. Jahrhundert* (Stuttgart, 1994), 139–55, here 143.

and principles seem to fade to nothingness.'[16] A 15-year-old boy wrote: 'I don't think I'll put my name down for hop-picking now—it's not worth while.'[17] *The Times*'s diplomatic correspondent, by contrast, high-lighted the weapon's character as both a source for evil and a source for good, a trope that would determine debates well into the 1960s. He pointed to the bomb's 'wider and fearful possibilities' that were 'as yet undisclosed'. And, the next day, the paper diagnosed that 'the world stands in the presence of a revolution of earthly affairs at least as big with potentialities of good and evil as when the forces of steam or electricity were harnessed'.[18]

British intellectuals who discussed the politics of the new weapons highlighted the repercussions their development and use would have to questions of the morality of the British war effort, especially with regard to aerial bombing. Such issues had already agitated some peace campaign-ers, left-wing politicians, and clergy in the context of the night bombing of German cities during the war. These debates were framed primarily within the context of 'just war' theory and discussed specifically the ques-tion whether a war that was fought against the civilian population could still be called 'just', however just its cause.[19] They now rehearsed similar arguments and applied them to what this meant for the transition from war to peace. At the request of an angry Victor Gollancz, the left-wing publisher, Revd John Collins, then Dean of Oriel College, Oxford, and later a founder member of the Campaign for Nuclear Disarmament (CND), rang his friend Sir Stafford Cripps (who had just become the President of the Board of Trade in the new Labour government). The purpose of the phone call was to gain reassurances that, at the very least, no more of these new bombs would be used against Japan. Collins also tried to ring the Archbishop of Canterbury, Geoffrey Fisher, but he did not answer the phone, so Collins was left discussing the matter with a chap-lain: in light of the discussions of the war years, Fisher found the problem too tricky to address it head-on.[20] George Bell, the bishop of Chichester, who had been one of the main Anglican voices against bombings of German cities during the war, was more outspoken. He called the destruc-tion of Hiroshima 'a crime against humanity' that should be punished in ways similar to the war crimes trials against Nazi leaders that were being

---

[16] Mass Observation Archive (M-OA), University of Sussex, FR 2272, 'Public Reactions to the Atomic Bomb', 1.

[17] M-OA, FR2272, 'The Atomic Bomb', 2.

[18] Editorial, *The Times*, 7 August 1945; Editorial, *The Times*, 8 August 1945.

[19] Andrew Chandler, 'The Church of England and the Obliteration Bombing of Germany in the Second World War', *English Historical Review*, 108 (1993), 920–46.

[20] L. John Collins, *Faith under Fire* (London, 1966), 98–9.

contemplated at the time.[21] Highlighting the particularly cruel nature of the attacks, C. C. Thicknesse, the dean of St Albans, refused to ring the bells in the Abbey tower, and did not give permission for a service of thanksgiving in the Abbey to mark the end of the war, causing a national controversy: 'I cannot honestly give thanks to God', he wrote in an open letter, 'for an event brought about by the wrong use of force, by an act of wholesale indiscriminate massacre, which is different in kind from all the acts of open warfare hitherto'.[22]

This mixture of fear and hope that Britons recorded when they heard about the bombings of Hiroshima and Nagasaki resonated fundamentally differently in occupied Germany. Given the situation most Germans were in, few were interested in discussing the direct political implications of the new weapons. If politics mattered, it was primarily in the context of hopes for reconstruction rather than with regard to distant Japan. While Germans also discussed the promising features of nuclear energy (rather than nuclear weapons as a source for another war), the aerial bombings and fire storms that had ravaged Hamburg in late July and August 1943, and Dresden on 13/14 February 1945, were still very present in people's minds.[23] While the majority of German bombing raids against British cities had occurred during the first phase of the war in the early 1940s, most of the German war deaths, both on the battlefields and through allied bombing raids, had occurred in the second half of the war. Many Germans, moreover, had an uncanny feeling that nuclear weapons had been developed to be used against them in the first place:

We Germans feel a bit detached [*abseits*] from this question of humankind, and we almost register our relief. We have something behind us that has made us awfully tired. We are glad that our hands do not have to shake when enjoying our luck, for what we have experienced was already a first example of applying the smashing of atoms—against us.[24]

Such connections between nuclear issues and wartime experiences meant that the 'atomic question' was crowded out by issues of social and economic reconstruction in the immediate post-war years. Soon, Germans and Britons lost interest in the atom bomb question. George Orwell remarked laconically in October 1945 that, 'considering how likely we all

---

[21] Letter to the editor, *The Times*, 14 August 1945, 1.

[22] *Daily Herald*, 16 August 1945, 3, and the responses in *Daily Express*, 16 August 1945, 1; *Daily Mail*, 16 August 1945, 1; *Daily Telegraph*, 16 August 1945, 5; *Manchester Guardian*, 16 August 1945, 5; *The Times*, 16 August 1945, 2.

[23] 'Die Welt atmet auf', *Kölnischer Kurier*, 14 August 1945.

[24] 'Atombombe', *Rhein-Neckar-Zeitung*, 27 October 1945; 'Harter Doppelschlag gegen Japan', *Kölnischer Kurier*, 10 August 1945; 'Die Atombombe', *Berliner Zeitung*, 9 August 1945.

are to be blown to pieces by it within the next five years, the atomic bomb has not roused so much discussion as might have been expected.'[25] Veteran liberal internationalist Leonard Woolf's assessment even regarded the discussions as part of a frenzy caused by the mass media. The atomic bomb, he argued in 1946, was typical of those ' "sensations", whose depth is measured by the height of sales of evening papers' but that were 'of their nature short-lived and in effect transient and abortive. They pass away with the last Derby or last scandal leaving much the same kind of mark on human history.'[26] For most British peace campaigners, as oriented towards educated middle-class ideas of culture and civility as Woolf, the issue of nuclear weapons came as an afterthought to more general debates about the status of civilization in the wake of war.

This lack of interest or understanding was at least partly a function of the international climate: only those interested in the high politics of negotiations for a deal to prevent the proliferation of nuclear weapons after the war and those who, like Orwell, had an acute sense for the political importance of the atom bomb in the context of the growing geostrategic competition between the Soviet Union and the United States were able to develop some basic understanding of the role the bomb might play in international politics. But, even for public intellectuals such as Orwell, the dimensions of the nuclear arms race that would unfold between the United States and the Soviet Union after the first successful Soviet test were hard to fathom in the context of the immediate post-war years. The fact that most of the discussions took place within the secrecy of the governmental bureaucracy re-enforced this trend further.[27] In Germany, nuclear weapons were simply a non-issue, as conventional, let alone nuclear, rearmament seemed beyond reach in the destroyed and occupied country.

ORGANIZING FOR PEACE IN POST-WAR SOCIETY

The British and West German peace campaigners who wished to organize their activities not only had to make sense of the new technology in the light of their war experiences but were also constrained by the nature of

---

[25] George Orwell, 'You and the Atom Bomb', in Sonia Orwell and Ian Angus (eds), *The Collected Essays, Journalism and Letters of George Orwell*, iv. *In Front of your Nose, 1945–1950* (London, 1968), 6.

[26] Leonard Woolf, 'Britain and the Atom Bomb', *Political Quarterly*, 17 (1946), 14.

[27] Matthew Grant, *After the Bomb: Civil Defence and Nuclear War in Britain, 1945–1968* (Basingstoke, 2010), 10.

politics at the time. The re-emergence of pacifist organizations was part of a 'transnational moment of change' in 1945 that affected continental Europe as well as British politics.[28] In the UK, this was a continuation of the pluralism that had characterized British political culture before and during the war. On the political left, it was particularly closely linked to some strands of Methodism and left-wing Anglicanism. A similar pluralism had also characterized German politics before the rise of the National Socialists to power in 1933.[29] In Germany, its re-emergence was a direct consequence of the complete breakdown of political structures and the structured revival of party-political organizations within the four occupation zones. As in Britain, it was often linked to activism of the churches. Protestantism—and especially those sections of the German Protestantism that had belonged to the Confessing Church, which had been critical of some aspects of the Nazi regime—was particularly relevant for peace campaigns.[30]

This blossoming of non-governmental activism and campaigning was very narrowly circumscribed, however, so that pacifist organizations were unable to tap the yearnings for security from within the framework of their old pacifist organizations. The reasons for this were organizational and sociocultural. In occupied Germany, grass-roots organizing was quite popular, and the emergence of anti-fascist organizations across the country highlighted the dynamics for social transformations. Likewise, there was a plethora of voluntary organizations that populated the politics in the British occupation zone in particular and that reintroduced Germans to middle-class models of organizations that revitalized popular politics: the most notable activities were those by the Quakers and other Christian groups that provided material relief and were not satisfied with the top-down planning of relief efforts that the United Nations Relief and Rehabilitation Administration (UNRRA) provided.[31] It was through these efforts that British and German peace campaigning came to be connected for the first time after the war. Quakers did not only bring European aid to Germany; they also brought with them their ways of thinking and campaigning. It was through Quaker groups' advocacy of non-violent

---

[28] Gerd-Rainer Horn and Padraic Kenney (eds), *Transnational Moments of Change: Europe 1945, 1968 and 1989* (Lanham, MD, 2004); Geoff Eley, 'Legacies of Antifascism: Constructing Democracy in Postwar Europe', *New German Critique*, 67 (1996), 73–100.

[29] Helen McCarthy, 'Parties, Voluntary Associations, and Democratic Politics in Interwar Britain', *Historical Journal*, 50 (2007), 891–912; Diethart Kerbs and Jürgen Reulecke, eds., *Handbuch der deutschen Reformbewegungen 1880–1933* (Wuppertal, 1998).

[30] Christoph Kleßmann, *Die doppelte Staatsgründung: Deutsche Geschichte 1945–1955* (Bonn, 1991), 121–55.

[31] Jessica Reinisch, 'Internationalism in Relief: The Birth (and Death) of UNRRA', *Past and Present*, suppl. 6 (2011), 258–89.

means of conflict resolution and through the attempts of Quakers to help with the education of young German people to democratic citizens that many of the later anti-nuclear weapons activists first came in touch with British pacifists. It was a little ironic that it was the Quakers, criticized before for their direct involvement in the war effort as paramedics on the various fronts, who now imported new ways of thinking about peace to Germany.[32] For the British and West German Quakers, for the related activities at the youth camp on an estate near the north German town of Vlotho, the seat of the Council of British Societies for Relief Abroad, and the centre for youth contacts that was set up in the town of Bücke-burg, this amounted to an experience of conversion. It acquainted them with the British Peace Pledge Union (PPU), founded in 1936 with an agenda of personal discipline and non-violence, and meant that 1945 was both an end and a beginning for them.[33]

But the general outlook for peace campaigning was bleak. Germany had been divided into four occupation zones, governed by US, British, French, and Soviet authorities respectively. The material situation was dire, as those who had stayed at home competed for scarce resources with returning soldiers and refugees. Unlike their British counterparts, Ger-man peace campaigners could not tap images of a 'peaceable kingdom'. They still had to face prejudices in a society that had been mobilized for racial warfare. The National Socialists had dismantled all peace organiza-tions and many pacifists had to go into exile, often to Britain, but also to the United States. Many had died there or committed suicide; some of those who had remained in Germany had ended up in concentration camps. Yet there was still a community of peace activists who tried to revitalize their organizations and campaigns, buoyed by the belief that the war experience would have bolstered their position within society.

With this in mind, the German Peace Society (*Deutsche Friedensgesell-schaft* (*DFG*)) was re-established in November 1946. It was still dominated by those age cohorts who had been active in the 1920s.[34] In particular, a more radical pacifist wing around Fritz Küster drove the discussions and continued to argue for a centralized and disciplined movement that would oppose any governmental efforts to create 'peace', as it argued that

[32] Matthew Frank, 'Working for the Germans: British Voluntary Societies and the Ger-man refugee Crisis, 1945–50', *Historical Research*, 92 (2009), 157–75.

[33] Helga Tempel and Hans-Konrad Tempel, 'Anfänge gewaltfreier Aktion in den ersten 20 Jahren nach dem Krieg', *Gewaltfreie Aktion. Sonderband* (Berlin, 1997), 63–88 ; Gerhart Schöll, 'Zur politischen Bildung im Jugendhof Vlotho 1946–1960', *Mitteilungen des Landesjugendamtes Westfalen Lippe*, 139 (1999), 43–58.

[34] 'Aus der Friedens-Bewegung', *Die Friedens-Warte* (1946), 120, 155–9; 'Die deutschen Pazifisten der Vorkriegszeit', *Die Friedens-Warte* (1946), 392–3.

governments were prone to becoming militaristic.[35] The *DFG*'s revival
was part of the rebirth of a plethora of political and cultural organizations
and institutions that sought to revive primarily bourgeois modes of
organization and the culture of the educated middle class as a bulwark
against the revival of National Socialism. More broadly, the *DFG* was
part and parcel of efforts to create a democracy from below that would
anchor democratic thoughts and practices more strongly in the German
population. They wanted to create a new democratic future for Germany
by reviving ideas from past pacifist thought and activism, primarily looking back to the 1920s as an era of fruitful democratic engagement.[36]

DFG activists argued that a change of hearts and minds was fundamental to establishing peace after the war: they pointed out that the war had
become possible only because of the acceptance of positive ideas about the
military in German society. Hence, political renewal could occur only
once the German mind had been disarmed, and the 'belief in the power of
the sword' had been replaced by alternative modes of social interaction.[37]
Crucially, this implied that peacemaking was a national German problem
and thus required national solutions.[38] Neither peace activists nor the general German population considered themselves citizens of the world and
continued to highlight the importance of their 'fatherland'.[39] Efforts at
peace campaigning across borders were therefore very limited. There were
small-scale attempts, for example, by the World Organization of Mothers
of All Nations (WOMAN), which aimed to transcend national boundaries
by appealing to essentialist conceptions of mothers as representatives of a
global moral conscience.[40] And there were those who revived ideas of liberal internationalism or world government from the interwar period.[41]

---

[35] *Programm und Aufgaben der Deutschen Friedensgesellschaft: Bericht über den Zonentag in
Bielefeld am 8. November 1946* (Hanover, 1946). On the background, see Helmut Donat,
'Die radikalpazifistische Richtung in der deutschen Friedensbewegung (1918–1933)', in
Karl Holl und Wolfram Wette (eds), *Pazifismus in der Weimarer Republik. Beiträge zur histor-
ischen Friedensforschung* (Paderborn, 1981), 27–45.

[36] Gabriele Clemens (ed.), *Kultur und Kulturpolitik im besetzten Deutschland 1945–1949*
(Stuttgart 1994).

[37] 'Erste Tagung des Landesverbands Schleswig-Holstein der Deutschen Friedensgesellschaft (24–26 August 1946)', *Die Friedens-Warte* (1946), 392.

[38] See for this argument: Andrew Oppenheimer, 'Extraparliamentary Entanglements.
Framing Peace in the Federal Republic of Germany, 1945–1974', in Hara Kouki and
Eduardo Romanos (eds), *Protest beyond Borders: Contentious Politics in Europe since 1945*
(New York, 2011), 15–31.

[39] Stefan Appelius, *Pazifismus in Westdeutschland. Die Deutsche Friedensgesellschaft
1945–1968* (2 vols; Aachen, 1999), i. 165.

[40] Irene Stoehr, 'Der Mütterkongreß fand nicht statt. Frauenbewegungen, Staatsmänner
und Kalter Krieg 1950', *WerkstattGeschichte*, 17 (1997), 66–82.

[41] Karl Holl, *Pazifismus in Deutschland* (Frankfurt/Main, 1988), 221.

British peace campaigners did not see themselves in a much better position than their German counterparts. But they were able to appeal to a political culture that prided itself on its civility. They could proudly look back to the campaigns of the 1930s that had opened up governmental foreign and defence policy decisions to democratic scrutiny.[42] Experiences of the anti-fascist popular front activities that had campaigned against the fascist occupation of Abyssinia in 1935 and had taken an active role in mobilizing significant sections of the British left in a campaign to aid Republican Spain against Franquist forces from 1936 to 1939 were still highly resonant in the immediate post-war period.[43]

Yet British peace campaigners were also the victims of the relative popularity of their general beliefs in British society. The campaigns of the 1930s had left a heritage of political divisions. There still existed fundamental disagreements that stemmed from the debate between those who had advocated appeasement, those who had argued in terms of collective security arrangements within the League of Nations, and those (primarily in the PPU) who saw personal experiences of conversion and asceticism as the key to creating peace through the practice of non-violence. These had already limited the political reach of pacifist organizations in the 1930s, and they continued to cause schisms after 1945.[44]

Moreover, peace campaigners' particular political recommendations raised many eyebrows. Now, after 1945, many campaigners—be they non-violent pacifists, more moderate advocates of non-intervention, or mere critics of governmental policies—were faced with accusations from outside their circles that they were fellow travellers of the Nazi regime who had made appeasement against Hitler in the 1930s possible and that they had indirectly supported the Nazi war effort when campaigning against the night-time aerial bombing against German cities during the war.[45] As late as March 1945, Vera Brittain, herself active in the Bombing Restriction Committee, had complained against publicizing news of Nazi death camps in the British media as a way of 'divert[ing] attention from the havoc produced in German cities by Allied obliteration bombing' and thus implied, too, that it had been only through war, rather than through a political programme of annihilation,

---

[42] McCarthy, *The British People and the League of Nations*, 15–45.

[43] Tom Buchanan, *Britain and the Spanish Civil War* (Cambridge, 1997), 189; Lewis Mates, *The Spanish Civil War and the British Left: Political Activism and the Popular Front* (London, 2007).

[44] See Martin Ceadel, *Pacifism: The Defining of a Faith* (Oxford, 1980); Martin Pugh, 'Pacifism and Politics in Britain, 1931–1935', *Historical Journal*, 23 (1980), 641–56.

[45] Hinton, *Protests and Visions*, 100–17.

that the Holocaust had become possible.[46] The discovery of the Nazi camps and an increasing awareness of the Holocaust seemed to have dealt peace activism a vital blow. Pacifism, John Middleton Murry observed in summer 1945, 'assumes an irreducible minimum of human decency...which no longer exists'.[47] An editorial in *Peace News* was therefore at pains to deny 'the assumption...that pacifists are, as a body, sceptical of Nazi depravity'.[48]

The fundamental challenge that British and German peace campaigners faced in 1945 did not have to do with organizational questions or political issues. It had to do with the kinds of problems and issues they faced and how they were able to respond to them within the framework of their concepts of peace. This was a question of how they engaged with, contributed to, and thus reforged the sociocultural context in which they campaigned. In both countries, the debates of how to master the transition from war to peace took place against the backdrop of the thorough mobilization for war of British and German societies that had shifted the focus away from utopias of peace towards an emphasis on security.[49] Hence, the meanings of 'peace' in political culture had changed as a consequence of war experiences. Peace campaigners were now able to voice their claims for a novel international order within languages of patriotism: peace, popular involvement in politics, and nationhood thus became part and parcel of the same policy.[50] In Britain, this revitalization of agency and hopes for popular involvement were connected to the revival of ideas of anti-fascism connected with the Spanish Civil War when it had been a lingua franca for large parts of the liberal, social-democratic, socialist, and communist left. The post-war society that emerged in Britain was, therefore, emphatically 'the people's peace' in that it signified these hopes and aspirations, although it was initially far from clear what 'peace' meant.[51]

---

[46] Vera Brittain, *Testament of a Peace Lover: Letters*, ed. Winifred Eden-Green and Alan Eden-Green (London, 1988), 254.

[47] *Herald of Peace*, 22 June 1945, 2.

[48] *Peace News*, 4 May 1952, 2.

[49] Penny Summerfield and Corinna Peniston-Bird, *Contesting Home Defence: Men, Women and the Home Guard in the Second World War* (Manchester, 2007), and Bernd Lemke, *Luftschutz in Großbritannien und Deutschland 1923 bis 1939: Zivile Kriegsvorbereitungen als Ausdruck der staats- und gesellschaftspolitischen Grundlagen von Demokratie und Diktatur* (Munich, 2005).

[50] Geoff Eley, 'When Europe was New: Liberation and the Making of the Post-War Era', in Monica Riera and Gavin Schaffer (eds), *The Lasting War: Society and Identity in Britain, France and Germany after 1945* (Basingstoke, 2008), 17–43, here 36.

[51] Kenneth O. Morgan, *The People's Peace: British History 1945–1989* (Oxford, 1990); Eley, *Forging Democracy*, 278–98.

In the wake of rising tensions between the United States and the Soviet Union, utopias of peace and social justice soon lost even more currency in mainstream political discussions, as they came to be tied to efforts by the Soviet Union to destabilize Western societies. Hence, 'peace'—and the notions of progress and reordering of society that the term implied—was soon replaced by 'security' as the key word of the time. This shift from peace to security was, in both countries, encapsulated by the slogan 'Never again': the term established distance from the violence as well as from the economic and social crisis of the 1930s and the first half of the 1940s, and used that as a source for political and social transformation. It would therefore be wrong to conclude that the shift towards a politics of security implied a general apathy, as this shift also entailed different emphases and a transformation of the forms of politics.[52] Whereas concepts of 'peace' were about opening up opportunities for political and societal change and offered utopias of a better world, the emphasis on 'security' as it emerged in British and West German political cultures potentially emphasized the limiting of choice and the closure of opportunities for choice. While peace was about movement, security concerned stability.[53]

The tension between 'peace' and 'security' that peace campaigners faced was a direct outcome of the war years. The 'people's community' in Nazi Germany and the interpretation of the war effort as a good 'people's war' as responses to the challenges of aerial bombardment had created a language of political empowerment.[54] Moreover, the war experiences in both countries, albeit with entirely different connotations and meanings, meant that the pull went away from diversity towards unity of purpose. In Britain, even pacifists had been part of this development. Most preferred to 'serve their fellow citizens than to defy their state'.[55] Such sentiment led to the revival of humanitarian projects, such as the Friends Ambulance Unit, in order to assist the war effort.[56] Ironically, therefore,

[52] Mass Observation, *Peace and the Public* (London, 1947), 44, but see Ross McKibbin, *Parties and People. England 1914–1951* (Oxford, 2010), 129, and Angus Calder, *The People's War: Britain 1939–1945* (London, 1969), 524–86.

[53] See Paul Betts and David Crowley, 'Introduction', *Journal of Contemporary History*, 40 (2005), 213–36.

[54] Dietmar Süß, *Tod aus der Luft: Kriegsgesellschaft und Luftkrieg in Deutschland und England* (Munich, 2011), 25, 62–3, and Malte Thießen, *Eingebrannt ins Gedächtnis: Hamburgs Gedenken an den Luftkrieg und Kriegsende 1943 bis 2005* (Munich, 2007), 45–55; Susan R. Grayzel, *At Home and under Fire: Air Raids and Culture in Britain from the Great War to the Blitz* (Cambridge, 2012).

[55] Martin Ceadel, *Semi-Detached Idealists: The British Peace Movement and International Relations, 1854–1945* (Oxford, 2000), 397.

[56] L. Smith, *Pacifists in Action: The Experience of the Friends Ambulance Unit in the Second World War* (New York, 1998), 4–6. For the use of the word 'humanitarian', see *Peace News*, 8 September 1939, 1.

peace organizations were those that perhaps profited least from the blossoming of non-governmental activities at the war's end. Their position at the margins of efforts for reconstruction therefore highlights a general paradox of the aftermath of mobilizations for war in both societies: that 'large-scale democratic breakthroughs' depend on 'processes and conjunctures that massively *strengthen* state power'.[57]

This paradox explains why the flourishing of non-governmental organizations in both countries did not imply a sustained 'movement away from party'. This movement would have offered an alternative mode of political organization and was what many of the British extra-parliamentary bodies and movements that campaigned for peace and, as they claimed, 'for the country' rather than for personal interests had desired.[58] But parties were swiftly recreated in occupied Germany, and the resilience of party organizations during wartime highlights the continued importance of party-political organizing in Britain.[59] War experiences meant that popular campaigning from below struggled to find a permanent place in the politics of security in Britain and West Germany. There continued to be a general expectation of political change through governmental intervention in both societies. Expectations of popular involvement in politics always remained part and parcel of an endorsement of state intervention: 1945 was not a libertarian moment *tout court*.[60] Governmental 'planning'—as opposed to the 'fellowship' promoted by pacifist organizations—was the order of the day.[61]

PEACE AS SECURITY

As they strove to address and contribute to the broader processes of the reconfiguration of the politics of peace in the wake of the Second World War, peace campaigners had to find new languages of campaigning that

---

[57] Geoff Eley, 'War and the Twentieth-Century State', *Daedalus*, 14 (1995), 155–74, here 164.

[58] See G. R. Searle, *Country before Party: Coalition and the Idea of 'National Government' in Modern Britain, 1885–1987* (London, 1995).

[59] Andrew Thorpe, *Parties at War: Political Organization in Second World War Britain* (Oxford, 2009), 276–88, against Stephen Fielding, 'The Second World War and Popular Radicalism: The Significance of the "Movement away from Party"', *History*, 80 (1995), 38–58.

[60] McKibbin, *Parties and People*, 117–28, 140, 146–7; Matthew Hilton and James McKay, 'The Ages of Voluntarism: An Introduction', in Hilton and McKay (eds), *The Ages of Voluntarism* (Oxford, 2011), 1–26; Süß, *Tod*, 336–7, 485–6.

[61] For this shift from 'fellowship' to 'planning' in Britain, see Ben Jackson, *Equality and the British Left: A Study in Progressive Political Thought* (Manchester, 2007), 228.

addressed the challenges of the sociocultural shifts that the war years had brought. The response of the executive committee of one of the main British pacifist organizations, the PPU, was indicative of this shift. It resolved that not the bombing of Hiroshima and Nagasaki, but the 'Save Europe Now' campaign that sought to address hunger and want on the continent, 'was the most important form of activity'. This also had implications for how both societies might relate to each other: while Germans had already begun to portray themselves as victims of war and of Hitler's National Socialist state, Britons' engagement in humanitarian war efforts helped reify this German sense of victimhood by casting them as hungry, dishevelled people in need of help.[62]

Another response was to revive thinking in terms of world government and international order and to adapt it to the United Nations.[63] British peace campaigners in particular tried this route and wanted to revive their efforts from the 1920s and 1930s to campaign for a working international government. But these efforts soon ran up against the realities of international politics in the early cold war. The United States and the Soviet Union failed to come to an agreement in the United Nations disarmament committee over the proliferation of nuclear weapons and there were growing tensions over the future of the European and global geostrategic order between the Soviet Union, on the one hand, and the United States, Britain, and their allies, on the other.[64] Thus, in 1947, the annual report of the United Nations Association (UNA), the successor of the League of Nations Union of the interwar period, pointed out that the cold war made its work for world government within the United Nations 'unbelievably difficult'.[65] Murry had feared this as early as 1945: 'Visibly the United Nations are not united...To the short-term vision the prospects of future peace look as black as human imagination can conceive.'[66] Some former peace campaigners had even gone so far as to request the construction of world government by force, and by atomic bombing. Victor Gollancz, the publisher and founder of the Left Book Club as well supporter of many popular causes in the 1930s, praised the bomb for

[62] *Peace News*, 28 September 1945, 1. On the genealogy, see Matthew Frank, 'The New Morality: Victor Gollancz, "Save Europe Now" and the German Refugee Crisis', *Twentieth Century British History*, 17 (2006), 230–56; Atina Grossman, 'Grams, Calories, and Food: Languages of Victimization, Entitlement, and Human Rights in Occupied Germany, 1945–1949', *Central European History*, 44 (2011), 142–3.

[63] Cecelia Lynch, *Beyond Appeasement: Interpreting Peace Movements in World Politics* (Ithaca, NY, 1999), 208.

[64] See Wittner, *One World or None*, 80–8.

[65] United Nations Association, *Annual Report 1947*, 3.

[66] John Middleton Murry, *The Third Challenge* (NPC Peace Aims pamphlet, 3) (London, 1945), 3.

ending the war quickly.[67] The illusions British campaigners harboured
about world government is even more evident from the ways in which
they tied it to the issue of nuclear weapons. John Middleton Murry and
Bertrand Russell even mused about an attack against the Soviet Union to
prevent a nuclear arms race.[68] Proposals such as this still relied on the
assumption of Britain's status as a world power. But the economic and
financial constraints highlighted to many activists in the UNA that
the fundamental assumption behind this argument had broken away.[69] By
the early 1950s, few British peace campaigners still regarded liberal internationalism as a viable basis for a peace campaign, especially because the
division of the world into a Soviet and a 'Western' camp appeared to have
been even more entrenched.

Likewise, German peace campaigners' emphasis on developing utopias
of 'peace' ran up against the twin obstacles of economic reconstruction
and the cold war: after the currency reform of the western zones of occupation had been accomplished in June 1948, interests shifted towards the
generation of economic and social security rather than towards utopian
ideas of peace. In Germany, at the front line of the geopolitical conflict,
the cold war constrained pacifists' field of action even more than in Britain. Peace campaigners had to take account of a cold war conception of
'peace' that thought in terms of stability and international security, rather
than in terms of movement and utopias of self-fulfilment. Crucially, official cold war readings of 'peace' stressed that individual freedom had to be
created as a precondition for peace—and that that freedom, in good
Hegelian manner, could be had only in the context of a strongly armed
state that was willing to defend freedom against its enemies.[70]

In the late 1940s, British and West German peace campaigners were
faced with cold war ideological divisions even more acutely, as 'peace'
became a propaganda tool for the Soviet government and thus discredited
many peace campaigns and campaigners in mainstream political culture.
In Britain, the parameters of subsequent debate about maintaining peace
during the emerging cold war drew a firm line between those who were in
favour of disarmament efforts generally, but refused to cooperate with any
Soviet efforts, and those who regarded cooperation across the blocs itself
as a symbol for the removal of tensions. The Stockholm Peace Petition,

---

[67] Ruth Dudley Edwards, *Victor Gollancz: A Biography* (London, 1987), 405.
[68] *Peace News*, 17 August 1945, 1, 4.
[69] Helen McCarthy, 'The League of Nations, Public Ritual and National Identity in
Britain, c.1919–56', *History Workshop Journal*, 70 (2010), 109–32, here 127.
[70] Irene Stoehr, 'Feministischer Antikommunismus' und weibliche Staatsbürgerschaft in der
Gründungsdekade der Bundesrepublik', *Feministische Studien*, 16 (1998), 86–94, here 90.

issued by a number of internationally prominent public intellectuals in August 1950 and the Soviet-sponsored World Peace Council (WPC), therefore found an extremely mixed reception among British peace campaigners. The same was true for the Second World Peace Congress that the WPC wished to stage in Sheffield in November of that year, but that failed to materialize as the British government prevented the delegates from entering the country. It also affected the ways in which the churches and nonconformist groups, during the war years divided but normally at least lukewarm supporters of pacifist causes, were able to conduct these debates.[71]

In Germany, in 1949, the *DFG* was banned in the Soviet zone of occupation, as the traditional pacifist organization stood for 'reactionary bourgeois pacifism' rather than for the movement for a state-sponsored peace that the East German regime of the Socialist Unity Party (*Sozialistische Einheitspartei Deutschlands* (*SED*)) wanted to see. This was also why, paradoxically, 'peace' soon became associated with communist subversion of 'Western' values, which made campaigning for peace in Germany extremely complicated.[72] This meant that protests for disarmament and peace in West Germany always involved a direct competition with East German peace campaigns for the legitimacy of the politics of peace. More generally, they concerned the boundaries between what could legitimately be said and done in West German public affairs.

The German communist party (*Kommunistische Partei Deutschlands* (*KPD*)) did indeed try to capitalize on this competition. It highlighted what it regarded as the inverse relationship between armament and economic growth, and there was a perception among the British occupation authorities that this contributed to attitudes against rearmament and fears of a new war.[73] Within the new West German state, extra-parliamentary protests offered one of the few avenues for asserting its aims, as all other political parties shunned them. Reviving ideas about 'peace and socialism' from the 1920s and wishing to capitalize on the general public mood in the Federal Republic, 'peace' campaigns appeared to communist organizers to be especially promising, and several peace conferences were

---

[71] Philip Deery, 'The Dove Flies East: Whitehall, Warsaw and the 1950 World Peace Congress', *Australian Journal of Politics and History*, 48 (2002), 449–68; Bill Moore, *Cold War in Sheffield* (Sheffield, 1990).

[72] Anselm Doering-Manteuffel, 'Im Kampf um "Frieden" und "Freiheit": Über den Zusammenhang von Ideologie und Sozialkultur im Ost-West-Konflikt', in Hans Günter Hockerts (ed.), *Koordinaten deutscher Geschichte im Zeitalter des Ost-West-Konflikts* (Munich, 2003), 29–48.

[73] TNA FO1013/1326. Land Commissioner NRW, Monthly Report, February 1952.

supposed to generate a mass movement towards a socialist peace, combined with German reunification. Many of the meetings ended in violent
clashes with the police, most famously the 'youth caravan' in Essen in
May 1952 during which the police shot dead a young protester.[74] Yet,
although many *KPD* activists still participated in genuinely communist
ventures of launching local peace committees and events in factories,
the level of motivation began to decline. In reality, however, it signified
a desire to maintain stability. Hence, many *KPD* activists preferred the
mainstream protests to the militant traditions of marching in columns
that the *KPD* organized.[75]

The *KPD* had misread the yearnings for security in West German society as an indication for a mood of societal transformation. The particular
ways in which British and West German societies dealt with the heritage
of violence and loss that the Second World War left meant, however, the
majority of the West German and British public defined 'peace' in terms
of 'stability'. In the late 1940s and early 1950s, these feelings were not
expressed directly and publicly, but they were part and parcel of private
experiences. Opinion polls reveal this privatized history of mass death and
the yearnings for security. In West Germany, such feelings were especially
pronounced, and it is telling that British pollsters did not even care to ask
the relevant questions. The US opinion pollsters Anna and Richard Merritt, working on behalf of the US military government in West Germany,
diagnosed 'highly anti-militaristic views' amongst Germans in the 1950s,
while Britons still thought about the role of the military for the defence of
the realm in essentially the same ways as they had done before the Second
World War.[76] Such fears became especially acute during the debates about
German rearmament that started when plans by the Adenauer government to promote the creation of a West German army became public.
One opinion poll found that 75 per cent considered it 'wrong' to serve as
soldiers—or for their husbands and sons to serve. Only 7 per cent were

---

[74] See the reports in Hauptstaatsarchiv Düsseldorf (HStAD), NW 34/9 and NW 34/10;
for later events: 'Tumult bei KP-Versammlung', *Hannoversche Allgemeine Zeitung*, 20 July
1953.
[75] Public Safety Department, Western District to PSD, Land NRW, 11 October 1950:
TNA FO 1013/2063.
[76] Anna J. Merritt and Richard L. Merritt (eds), *Public Opinion in Semisovereign Germany: The HICOG Surveys, 1949–1955* (Urbana, IL, 1980), 19. My argument here follows
Michael Geyer, 'Cold War Angst: The Case of West-German Opposition to Rearmament
and Nuclear Weapons', in Hanna Schissler (ed.), *The Miracle Years: A Cultural History of
West Germany, 1949–1968* (Princeton and Oxford, 2001), 376–408. Geyer also uses some
of the same source material. For the visual framing of these debates, see Benjamin Ziemann,
'The Code of Protest: Images of Peace in the West German Peace Movements, 1945–1990',
Contemporary European History, 17 (2008), 237–61, here 247–8.

undecided.[77] While the Adenauer government used imagery of the Russian threat, often harking back to National Socialist iconography, the propaganda did not have the desired effect of mobilizing the West German population, although the majority agreed that there existed an imminent threat of war in the early 1950s.[78]

These sentiments reflected the fundamental fact that most Germans saw a trade-off between social and economic reconstruction and military security.[79] They were often connected to conjuring up the material security of the Nazi regime during which the 'people's community' had created a sense of belonging.[80] Germans still liked the *notion* of conscription and a standing army, however—they had not suddenly become pacifists. An overwhelming majority still regarded the Nazi *Wehrmacht* as an honest army that should not be judged badly by anyone—and they still cherished it as a 'people's army', but not as a military organization.[81] This paradox—a dislike of conscription, but an approval of the idea of conscription—reveals the central elements of the West German politics of security, as opposed to a politics of peace that emerged with the debates about rearmament.

Discussions about the new army stressed that the military would not be a German organization, but integrated into either a European or a NATO force—for many, a non-German army was not worth having. Fundamentally, there existed a distrust of the state as an institution that protected personal safety and security—Germans had seen the violence a state could mete out. Germans' refusal to contemplate conscription—the key connection between citizenship and statehood—illustrates this sense of

---

[77] Bundesarchiv-Militärarchiv (BA–MA), BW9/764: Presse- und Informationsamt der Bundesregierung, EMN-12/52, 12 December 1952, 2; Bundesarchiv, Koblenz (BAK), B145/4220: Institut für Demoskopie Allensbach, 'Die Stimmung im Bundesgebiet', no. 1 (November 1950), table 1.

[78] BA–MA, BW21/28: Institut für Demoskopie Allensbach, 'Die jungen Männer: Interessen, Neigungen, Verhalten: Rohergebnisse einer Umfrage unter den Geburtsjahrgängen 1927–1934' (March 1952); BAK, B145/4222: Institut für Demoskopie Allensbach, 'Los vom Westen', 28 August 1952. On the background, see David Clay Large, *Germans to the Front: West German Rearmament in the Adenauer Era* (Chapel Hill, 1996).

[79] For a similar argument with regard to Japan, see: Toshihiro Higuchi, 'An Environmental Origin of Antinuclear Activism in Japan, 1954–1963: The Government, the Grassroots Movement, and the Politics of Risk', *Peace & Change*, 33 (2008), 333–67.

[80] BAK, B 145/4221: Institut für Demoskopie Allensbach, 'Das politische Klima: Ein Bericht über die Stimmung im Bundesgebiet 1951'; BAK, B 145/422: Institut für Demoskopie Allensbach, 'Die wichtigste Frage—die beste Zeit', November 1951.

[81] Quote: Geyer, 'Cold War Angst', 384. BAK, B145/4223: Institut für Demoskopie Allensbach, 'Meinung über Hitler', 20 January 1953; BAK B145/4221: 'Im Ernstfall: Kriegsdienstverweigerung' (November 1951); BAK B145/4227: Institut für Demoskopie Allensbach, 'Wehrfragen', 10 December 1956.

'injured citizenship' particularly well. The new West German state did not
seem to honour their experience by trying to take a national defence force
away from them; whereas the Nazi regime, according to perceptions visible in a number of opinion polls, had exposed them to unimaginable
dangers.[82] It meant that Germans were willing to trust the state again only
if it guaranteed them some form of security. And they tried to achieve this
by keeping themselves busy by pursuing material and social security.[83]
This was aided further by the cold war context of the divided Germany:
welfare policy—and security policy more generally—was Chancellor Konrad
Adenauer's version of Bismarck's late-nineteenth-century *Sammlungspoli-*
tik (policy of integration) that the Social Democratic Party, itself burnt by
what it perceived as the betrayal of communists in the final days of the
Weimar Republic, could not ignore.[84]

Contemporaries framed this mood as one of 'without me' ('Ohne mich').
But it was really a movement that should be called 'in favour of me' ('für mich')
that argued for personal security that was supposed to protect an 'unpolitical
space of action for economic achievements and private successes'.[85] This mood
found its political expression in the debates about German rearmament that
became virulent when Chancellor Konrad Adenauer made public his wishes
for participating in the Western defence alliance by building up a West German army. Supported by a number of organizations, ranging from Christian
groups, to traditional pacifists, and sections of the Free Democratic (*Freie*
Demokratische Partei (*FDP*)) and Social Democratic (*Sozialdemokratische*
Partei (*SPD*)) parties, this critique of official defence policies was also linked to
the emergence of a form of political neutralism that wished to maintain Germany's status as an unarmed and neutral country in central Europe and thus
keep the possibility for national unification open.[86] The Protestant politician Gustav Heinemann, who resigned from the Adenauer government in

[82] Quote and general argument: Geyer, 'Cold War Angst', 386. See, e.g., the report on
a public meeting on rearmament, Frankfurt/Main, 19 October 1949, Dr. Pollmann:
BA–MA BW9/740.

[83] Hannah Arendt, 'A Report from Germany: The Aftermath of Nazi Ideology', *Commentary* (October 1950), 342–53. On the background, see Braun, 'Das Streben nach
"Sicherheit" in den 50er Jahren'.

[84] Eric Weitz, 'The Ever-Present Other: Communism in the Making of West Germany',
in Hanna Schissler (ed.), *The Miracle Years. A Cultural History of West Germany, 1949–1968*
(Princeton, 2001), 219–32, here 222.

[85] Michael Geyer, *Deutsche Rüstungspolitik 1860–1980* (Frankfurt/Main, 1984), 181;
Lutz Niethammer and Ulrich Borsdorf, 'Traditionen und Perspektiven der Nationalstaatli-
chkeit', in *Außenpolitische Perspektiven des westdeutschen Staates*, ii (Munich, 1972), 32.

[86] Klaus von Schubert, *Wiederbewaffnung und Westintegration: Die innere Auseinandersetzung um die militärische und außenpolitische Orientierung der Bundesrepublik 1950–1952*
(Stuttgart, 1970).

protest against the policy of rearmament and who founded the 'Emergency Community for Peace in Europe' *(Notgemeinschaft für den Frieden Europas)* and later the 'All-German People's Party' (*Gesamtdeutsche Volkspartei* (*GVP*)), was probably the most famous representative of this line of argument. Martin Niemöller, the Protestant Church President of Hesse-Nassau, was another famous protagonist.[87]

The West German debates about rearmament established some of the networks around which the campaigns against nuclear weapons would gather later on. More importantly, they also made available a new language for the politics of security—a language that stressed the rationality of the claims, emphasized the control of emotions, and argued in terms of the control of the future rather than the multitude of possibilities. This development was especially striking for women's peace campaigners who took part in the campaigns and who had propagated programmes for peace as part and parcel of an agenda for a thorough societal transformation. They employed maternalist images of victimhood (rather than active female agency) from mainstream commemorations of the war years to make their case. Moreover, they articulated their claims as part of a discourse of emotional control. They voiced their wartime experiences only as long as they could be expressed with rational arguments.[88] By the mid-1950s, mainstream public discourses, by contrast, had begun to move away from the emphasis on death and destruction and imaginings of disaster and moved towards an engagement with the reality of the emerging consumer society and the beginnings of affluence in the context of an ideological conflict between the Eastern and Western bloc.[89] The structure of the paradox of security that emerged during this time period can therefore be glimpsed only from the margins.

This paradox behind the politics of security—playing material security out against military security—can be gleaned particularly well from local commemorative practices in West German towns and cities that had been subject to aerial bombardment. In Kassel, which had been subjected to a massive air raid in October 1943, the local campaign against rearmament played on this trade-off, using the slogan 'Never again!' to signal the distance that the Kassel population had already gained by rebuilding parts of

---

[87] Michael Werner, *Die 'Ohne mich'-Bewegung: Die bundesdeutsche Friedensbewegung im deutsch-deutschen Kalten Krieg* (Münster, 2006), 189–230.

[88] Irene Stoehr, 'Kriegsbewältigung und Wiederaufbaugemeinschaft: Friedensorientierte Frauenpolitik im Nachkriegsdeutschland, 1945–1952', in Karen Hagemann and Stefanie Schüler-Springorum (eds), *Heimat-Front: Militär und Geschlechterverhältnisse im Zeitalter der Weltkriege* (Frankfurt/Main, 2002), 326–44, here 330–2.

[89] This is highlighted by Axel Schildt, *Zwischen Abendland und Amerika: Studien zur westdeutschen Ideenlandschaft der 50er Jahre* (Munich, 1999), 16.

the city, while warning of what the protesters regarded as the remilitariza-
tion of public life and deepen the division of Germany. These issues were
especially acute for Kassel: the city had hosted a garrison before 1945, and
the stationing of soldiers there would expose the city, which was no more
than 50 kilometres west of the border with the GDR, again to an enormous risk in a new war.[90]

A similar rejection of direct involvement in armaments and the military, while still emphasizing material security, also existed in Britain. As
in Germany, the welfare state—and the material security it provided—
were used by both Labour and Conservative governments as a way of
making Britain safe against communist subversion.[91] This paradox
between the desire to rely on the state in some areas related to material
security, but to reject its grip in others related to military security, had
already affected the salience of British peace movements, such as the
Union of Democratic Control, during the First World War. They were
content to support the state as an actor in social and welfare policy, while
opposing military conscription as a sign of the kind of authoritarian
statehood that Britons were fighting.[92] It had only been after Nazi Germany's occupation of the whole of Czechoslovakia in the wake of the
Munich conference in 1938 that many peace campaigners and their
sympathizers in the 1930s accepted that military intervention could be
justified under certain circumstances, although they continued to warn
of the dangers that Britain could itself become a 'voluntary totalitarian
state', as Aneurin Bevan called it at the 1937 Labour Party conference.[93]
This conflict was resolved when most peace campaigners established a
direct link between their campaigns and British nationhood by highlighting the essential Britishness of peace and civility. This meant that
references to nationhood and 'patriotism' became essential ingredients
for any political campaign that wished to appeal to more than fringe
groups within the population, and the Labour Party especially, non-
governmental groups in its direct orbit, as well as communists managed
to portray themselves, in these circumstances, successfully as representatives of the 'ordinary Briton'.[94]

---

[90] Jörg Arnold, *The Allied Air War and Urban Memory: The Legacy of Strategic Bombing
in Germany* (Cambridge, 2011), 132.

[91] Harriet Jones, 'The Cold War and the Santa Claus Syndrome: Dilemmas in Conservative Social Policy Making, 1945–1957,' in Martin Francis and Ina Zweiniger-Bargielowska
(eds), *Conservatives and British Society, 1880–1990* (Cardiff, 1996), 240–54.

[92] Martin Ceadel, *Thinking about Peace and War* (Oxford, 1987), 118–19.

[93] Labour Party, *Proceedings of the 30th Annual Conference* (Bournemouth, 1937), 209.

[94] Paul Ward, 'Preparing for the People's War: Labour and Patriotism in the 1930s',
Labour History Review, 67 (2002), 181; Hinton, *Protests and Visions*, 118–32.

When the war was over, some peace campaigners, together with social-ists and left-wing Labour politicians, sought to oppose the symbolic con-nection between military statehood and 'the people' that had been forged during the Second World War. They argued for the abolition of conscrip-tion in March 1947, and, still appealing to a socialist variant of British patriotism, they sought to establish the UK as a leader in European and international reconstruction.[95] Yet they ran up against the significantly weaker position of the UK in the international system, owing to its lack of financial and economic strength as well as of political clout, vis-à-vis the United States and the Soviet Union.[96] The specific balance between material and military security continued to cause significant problems into the early 1950s: in 1951, Aneurin Bevan resigned from Prime Min-ister Clement Attlee's Labour government in protest against Hugh Gaitskell's successful proposal to introduce certain charges and reduce some free services in the National Health Service to help finance a hugely expanded arms budget.[97] The debate's salience differed, however, funda-mentally from its importance in German society. While we can see how the memory of war came to be connected with notions of a community of active citizens during the Blitz that elided the social, political, and racial exclusions of that community, there was no sense of injury.[98] In British political culture, the war appeared as a 'good' conflict that had been fought against the 'right' enemy in a society that regarded itself as a 'peaceable kingdom'.[99]

Interestingly, however, the connection between sovereignty and the nuclear arms race led to structurally similar interpretations of the role of the United States in the cold war. In Britain, both critics and supporters of government policy linked nuclear weapons directly with the need to remain independent from US hegemony and to maintain British sover-eignty in world politics and to overcome the experience of the 'American occupation of Britain' during the Second World War.[100] The conservative

[95] See Holger Nehring, 'Towards a Transnational Social History of "a Peaceable King-dom": Peace Movements in Post-1945 Britain', *Mitteilungsblatt des Instituts für soziale Bewegungen*, 32 (2004), 21–47.

[96] Paul Weiler, *British Labour and the Cold War* (Stanford, CA, 1988); Martin Francis, *Ideas and Politics under Labour 1945–1951* (Manchester, 1997), 227.

[97] Kenneth O. Morgan, *Labour People: Leaders and Lieutenants, Hardie to Kinnock* (Oxford, 1987), 204–19.

[98] Sonya O. Rose, *People's War? National Identity and Citizenship in Wartime Britain 1939–1945* (Oxford, 2003), 285–93.

[99] Geoff Eley, 'Finding the People's War: Film, British Collective Memory, and World War II', *American Historical Review*, 106/3 (2001), 818–38.

[100] David Reynolds, *Rich Relations: The American Occupation of Britain, 1942–1945* (London, 2001).

government under Prime Minister Harold Macmillan preferred nuclear weapons as the cheaper alternative to a conventional army to keep Britain's role on the world state intact; critics, by contrast, with the exception of diehard pacifists who opposed all armaments *tout court*, pointed out that a conventional standing army would offer a far safer alternative. Experiences of aerial warfare during the Second World War offered a central reference point in these debates. But both positions were carried by a more or less fundamental mistrust of the intentions and rationality of US foreign and defence policies.[101] These debates were played out in the various debates about foreign policy in Britain during the 1950s, often, as in the case of the debates over the British intervention at Suez in 1956, with rather odd alliances between ultra-conservatives and non-violent pacifists.

In West Germany, the situation was much more acute: while the successive Adenauer governments sought to use armaments policies as a means of regaining sovereignty within the context of the Western alliance, the population remained fundamentally sceptical. The visible presence of US forces in occupied and semi-sovereign Germany was, together with the threat coming from the Soviet army on German soil, singled out as the source for insecurity: in West German self-perceptions, the aerial bombardment of Dresden (often incorrectly attributed to the United States) and the dropping of atomic bombs on Hiroshima and Nagasaki differed little. As opinion pollsters registered it, memories of mass death influenced perceptions of the possibility of an impending nuclear 'annihilation' of Germany that could ultimately be traced back to the responsibility of the United States. In 1954, nearly half of the West German population felt that way.[102]

These similar developments had their root in the general context of international defence policy as it emerged over the course of the early 1950s. The military command structure had been internationalized within NATO under US hegemony. The consequences of warfare were no longer restricted to soldiers. Rather, the violence and destruction of a future war would be felt by societies as a whole—the trend for the socialization of violence that had already been a reality for those cities affected by the bombing raids of the Second World War would be completed in the scenario of an all-out nuclear exchange.[103] Britain was almost as affected by

---

    [101] Lawrence S. Freedman, *The Evolution of Nuclear Strategy*, 3rd edn (Basingstoke, 2003).
    [102] Michael Geyer, 'Amerika in Deutschland:. Amerikanische Macht und die Sehnsucht nach Sicherheit', in Frank Trommler and Elliott Shore (eds), *Deutsch-Amerikanische Begegnungen: Konflikt und Kooperation im 19.und 20. Jahrhundert* (Stuttgart and Munich, 2001), 155–87, here 157 and 170.
    [103] Geyer, *Deutsche Rüstungspolitik*, 171–6.

this development as semi-sovereign Germany. At first, Britain had no legal arrangements in place that regulated the presence of US troops when they returned to bases in East Anglia in 1948, and the Visiting Forces Act of 1952 granted them more extra-territorial rights than any other country, with the exception of occupied Germany. Nonetheless, Britain maintained some direct say in policymaking by maintaining its own arsenal of nuclear weapons, precisely in order to avoid being entirely at the whim and will of US defence policy. The military, and the government in its wake, regarded society as an object of planning. According to this scheme of thinking, it was the state as an abstract unit that endowed society with security. In West Germany, in particular, this had a special resonance: as those former officers who planned the creation of a German army under democratic auspices formulated it in their 'Himmerod Memorandum' (October 1950), it had been the state that had given German society back its 'concept of freedom', a concept of freedom that could be protected only by the military; German society therefore had to learn to re-engage with the role of the military in society.[104]

CAMPAIGNING FOR SECURITY: EMBRACING THE ATOMIC AGE

The issues of nuclear energy and nuclear weapons were uniquely suited to debates about the role of nationhood, community, and society in the post-war world that had remained under the surface since the mid- to late 1940s: like no other available issues, they encapsulated the contradictions between material and military security and the role of states vis-à-vis societies. 'Atomic energy' soon became a source of hope in British and West German discussions, even among peace campaigners, and a symbol for the end of the immediate post-war period and for economic reconstruction. A source of cheap and enormous energy, the new energy offered a healing balm that could cover up the wounds of war and help build a new technical age on Europe's ruins.[105] Given the experience of post-war reconstruction in Germany, this binary opposition between the experiences of pain and hopes for prosperity was more pronounced there than in Britain. It meant that the distinction between either 'curse' or 'blessing'

---

[104] Hans-Joachim Rautenberg and Norbert Wiggershaus, *Die 'Himmeroder Denkschrift' vom Oktober 1950: Politische und militärische Überlegungen für einen Beitrag der Bundesrepublik Deutschland zur westeuropäischen Verteidigung* (Karlsruhe, 1977), 36.

[105] 'Die Geschichte der Atombombe', *Ruhr-Zeitung*, 15 August 1945; 'Der zündende Gedanke. Erfindungen und ihre Zeit', *Die Zeit*, 22 August 1946.

that nuclear energy could bring was a much more powerful means of political communication in West Germany than in Britain.[106]

But before the campaign for security in the nuclear age could emerge that could turn this paradox of security into a political issue, the international context had to change. One precondition was the brief opening in East–West politics that Soviet leader Krushchev's admission of Stalin's crimes created, especially among the members of the British left, who could now realistically claim that an end to the cold war division of Europe had become conceivable, especially when set against the backdrop of the short period of détente between the superpowers in 1955 and the emergence of what appeared to be a poweful movement of non-aligned countries around the world. The debate about Krushchev's 'secret speech' in which the Soviet leader admitted Stalin's crimes, about the British intervention in Suez in 1956, and about the nuclearization of the new West German army created the concrete occasions at which networks of activists first coalesced and developed new agendas for a politics of security that sought to overcome the strictures of pacifist activism, while relying on similar personal connections and modes of campaigning.[107]

The nascent anti-nuclear-weapons campaigns in both countries were connected through the same international context in which they emerged: the proliferation of nuclear weapons in world politics, which turned into an arms race between the United States and the Soviet Union in the early 1950s. In October 1949, the Soviet Union successfully tested its first nuclear bomb. In October 1952, Britain tested its first nuclear device in the Monte Bello Islands. On 1 November 1952, the United States performed the first test of a thermonuclear weapon that was heralded as the new superweapon. From the end of 1953, the United States started to deploy smaller-scale, short-range nuclear weapons in West Germany in order to support the conventional forces stationed there, while the negotiations for German rearmament continued. These years saw the first campaign against these weapons in Germany, led primarily by Protestant clergy. They linked the 'new Wild West morality' of the US way of warfare with the continuation of the 'mass bombing of West Germany' from the Second World War.[108]

[106] See Ilona Stölken-Fitschen, *Atombombe und Geistesgeschichte: Eine Studie der fünfziger Jahre aus deutscher Sicht* (Baden-Baden, 1995), 18–30.
[107] For the importance of '1956' as a watershed, see Eley, *Forging Democracy*, 329–36.
[108] Open Letter by Hermann Sauer, 29 April 1954, printed in *Kirchliches Jahrbuch* (1954), 67–9.

These developments, culminating in the adoption of nuclear deterrence as the cornerstone of British defence policy together with the abolition of conscription in Britain in 1957 and the nuclearization of defence policies in the Federal Republic (albeit under Allied control), were part and parcel of a trade-off between material and national security that the British and West German governments wanted to introduce. In response to the bungled Suez intervention, the British government sought to introduce a more cost-efficient way of guaranteeing its great power status that imposed a lighter burden on British citizens than a conventional army. Likewise, the nuclearization of West German forces was a direct response to recruitment problems as well as an attempt by the Adenauer government to become a more fully fledged and sovereign member of the Western alliance system and to prevent an American withdrawal from German territory.[109] These moves aroused the suspicions of the Soviet Union. Settling these issues without the outbreak of war and the construction of a post-war international order in Europe could occur only in the wake of a number of crises—the two Berlin crises of 1958 and 1961, as well as the Cuban missile crisis of 1962 chief among them—that were fundamentally about the status of Germany and nuclear weapons in international relations and that brought the world repeatedly to the brink of nuclear war between the Soviet Union and the United States.[110]

More generally, then, these concerns had their origins in the changing configurations of the cold war and, in particular, the role that governments assigned to nuclear weapons in trying to achieve peace and stability in the international system. In December 1954, NATO shifted its strategic emphasis from conventional armaments to nuclear weapons, as its members, most importantly the United States and Great Britain, believed that only nuclear armaments could provide a financially sustainable and politically justifiable defence of Western Europe. Yet this created the inexorable dilemma for the West European front in the cold war that the use of nuclear weapons in defence might well result in the complete destruction of Europe. The parameters of security had shifted towards a very dramatic image of future warfare and an all-embracing conflict between

---

[109] Hans-Peter Schwarz, 'Adenauer und die Kernwaffen', *Vierteljahrshefte für Zeitgeschichte*, 37/4 (1989), 567–93.

[110] Marc Trachtenberg, *A Constructed Peace. The Making of the European Settlement 1945–1963* (Princeton, 1999), 398–402, and Bruno Thoß, 'Bündnisintegration und nationale Verteidigungsinteressen: Der Aufbau der Bundeswehr im Spannungsfeld zwischen nuklearer Abrüstung und nationalen Verteidigungsinteressen', in Frank Nägler (ed.), *Die Bundeswehr 1955 bis 2005: Rückblenden—Einsichten—Perspektiven* (Munich, 2007), 13–38.

the 'Western' and 'Eastern' political, social, and cultural systems. Defence planning now threatened to place political systems and societies under the shadow of planning for a devastating war.[111]

The United States, because of its geographical distance from the Soviet Union, at first remained shielded from the potential effects of these policies until intercontinental missiles had been developed in the late 1950s and early 1960s. However, the nuclearization of NATO strategy had more immediate and far-reaching implications for the defence policies of all West European nations. Its impact was particularly pronounced in Britain and West Germany. American short- (so-called tactical) and medium-range nuclear weapons were stationed in Britain and the Federal Republic from late 1953 onwards. Successive British governments sought to acquire independent nuclear weapons capabilities by testing hydrogen bombs and by placing the main strategic emphasis on the 'nuclear deterrent'.[112]

West Germany had hardly regained partial sovereignty after the Second World War with its admission to NATO and the remit to build up conventional forces, when, in late 1957 and early 1958, it planned to adapt to international strategic developments by acquiring nuclear-capable launching pads, used under a dual-key arrangement with the American NATO forces. Yet, even more than was the case for Britain, what might have been in the Federal Republic's foreign political interest, also turned central Europe into a potential nuclear battlefield.[113] Both the British and West German governments also regarded nuclear weapons as a key marker for political sovereignty and modern government: for them, nuclear weapons were essentially about leaving the post-war world behind, whereas those sceptical of nuclear armaments regarded nuclear weapons as the continuation of the war by other means. For the movement activists, the post-war period felt less and less like the order and stability they had yearned for after the ravages of the Second World War. They began to experience the cold war as a 'cruel peace'.[114] Nuclear weapons tests, in particular, were the focus of the first campaigns: they made visible the dangers stemming from nuclear weapons by highlighting the destruction

[111] 'MC 48', in *NATO Strategy Documents, 1949–1969*, ed. Gregory W. Pedlow (Brussels, 1997), 229–50; Beatrice Heuser, *NATO, Britain, France and the FRG: Nuclear Strategies and Forces for Europe, 1949–2000* (Basingstoke and London, 1998).

[112] Martin S. Navias, *Nuclear Weapons and British Strategic Planning, 1955–1958* (Oxford, 1991) and Lawrence Freedman, *Britain and Nuclear Weapons* (London and Basingstoke, 1980).

[113] Bruno Thoß, *NATO-Strategie und nationale Verteidigungsplanung: Planung und Aufbau der Bundeswehr unter den Bedingungen einer massiven atomaren Vergeltungsstrategie 1952–1960* (Munich, 2006); Hans-Peter Schwarz, 'Adenauer und die Kernwaffen'.

[114] Fred Inglis, *The Cruel Peace: Everyday Life and the Cold War* (New York, 1991).

that a future nuclear war would mean. They were essentially simulations of nuclear warfare.[115]

During this time period, British and West Germans peace campaigners developed a growing sense of the implications of nuclear energy. They used their perceptions to develop a politics of security around the issue of the 'atomic age'. The development of this awareness was itself tied to the international context. The American 'Atoms for Peace' campaign that President Dwight D. Eisenhower had launched in a speech before the United Nations General Assembly on 8 December 1953 was meant to accompany the testing of new powerful hydrogen bombs sought to promote this image of modernity. In his speech, Eisenhower warned the public of the grave dangers stemming from nuclear weapons, but called for a programme that would harness 'atoms' 'for peace' and involve the internationally controlled use of nuclear energy.[116] Celebrations of the power of nuclear energy in conjunction with items of consumer culture (such as the bikini) in both countries attest to this.[117] Already in 1947 'atom trains' had travelled Britain in order to educate the general public about the new 'atomic age', sometimes accompanied by scientists such as Joseph Rotblat, who had been involved in the Anglo-American bomb-building efforts during the war and who was later one of the most prominent peace campaigners in the scientific community.[118]

Thus, the science writer Ritchie Calder, later the Campaign for Nuclear Disarmament's vice-chairman, could still write enthusiastically, in an article entitled 'The Atom Goes to Work for the Housewife' about the opening of the Calder Hall reactor at Windscale in Cumberland in October 1956, that it was 'a historic and symbolic act—Britain's entry, in the forefront of all the nations, into the Atomic Age, with the atom tamed for domestic and industrial purposes'.[119] Similar interpretations were true for West Germany as well, where, in addition to signifying modernization

---

[115] Thomas Brandstetter, 'Wie man lernt die Bombe zu lieben: Zur diskursiven Konstruktion atomarer Gewalt', in Günther Friesinger, Thomas Ballhausen, and Johannes Grenzfurthner (eds), *Schutzverletzungen: Legitimation medialer Gewalt* (Berlin, 2010), 25–54.

[116] Printed in Joseph F. Pilat et al. (eds), *Atoms for Peace after Thirty Years* (Boulder, CO, 1985), 283–8.

[117] Eckhard Siepmann, Irene Lusk, and Jürgen Holtfreter (eds), *Bikini: Die fünfziger Jahre. Kalter Krieg und Capri- Sonne. Fotos, Texte, Comics, Analysen* (Reinbek, 1983).

[118] Christoph Laucht, 'Atoms for the People: The Atomic Scientists' Association, the British State and Nuclear Education in the Atom Train Exhibition, 1947–1948', *British Journal for the History of Science*, 45 (2012), 591–608; Bryce Halliday, 'Professor Rotblat and the atom train', in Peter Rowlands and Vincent Attwood (eds), *War and Peace: The Life and Work of Sir Joseph Rotblat* (Liverpool, 2006), 139–44.

[119] Ritchie Calder, 'The Atom Goes to Work for the Housewife', *News Chronicle*, 17 October 1956.

and an end to wartime restrictions, dreams of generating electricity through nuclear energy also served as symbols for gradually regaining sovereignty.[120]

But there also developed a growing sense of the dangers of nuclear weapons. With the increase of tensions in the emerging cold war, highlighted by the crisis over the reconstruction of Greece in the first half of 1947, the emergence of communist governments in Poland and Czechoslovakia in the second half of the same year, the crisis over access to Berlin in 1948–9, and the creation of two German states in autumn 1949, British and German peace campaigners began to reflect on their time period as the 'atomic age'. Over the course of the 1950s, there emerged a growing scientific and popular knowledge of the dangers of radioactivity for human bodies. In September 1949, the director-general of the World Health Organization had written in *Peace News* that nuclear weapons were 'child's play compared to biological weapons' because there was 'a product in existence which if spread extensively can kill on contact or if breathed in'. By the mid-1950s few but the most enthusiastic supporters of nuclear weapons would lack an awareness of the invisible dangers of radioactivity.[121]

The 'atomic age' had fundamentally different resonances in Britain and West Germany. The war in divided Korea that started in June 1950 and ended with the permanent division of the country in July 1953 was a turning point for perceptions in Germany, whereas it failed to have a major impact on British discussions on nuclear energy. Many Germans feared that Germany could soon be a 'second Korea' and that a war over Germany would be waged with nuclear weapons.[122] For Germans in both government and society more generally, the Korean war helped turn the cold war into experiences of a constant pre-war situation, imagined by drawing on images of the aerial bombardment of German cities in the Second World War. 'Aviators were above the city, birds evoking disaster. Landing and take-off, rehearsals of death, a hollow roar, shaking, memories in ruins. The planes' bomb shafts were still empty. The augurs smiled. No one looked skywards.'[123] Thus opens Wolfgang Koeppen's 1951 novel *Pigeons in the Grass*. In the wake of the Korean war, this knowledge of

[120] Peter Fischer, *Atommacht und staatliches Interesse: Die Anfännge der Atompolitik in der Bundesrepublik Deutschland 1949–1955* (Baden-Baden, 1994).

[121] *Peace News*, 16 September 1946, 1. On general perceptions in Britain, see Adrian Bingham, ' "The Monster"? The British Popular Press and Nuclear Culture, 1945–Early 1960s', *British Journal for the History of Science*, 45 (2012), 609–24.

[122] Hans-Peter Schwarz, *Die Ära Adenauer: Gründerjahre der Republik 1949–1957* (Wiesbaden, 1981), 104.

[123] Wolfgang Koeppen, *Tauben im Gras*, in *Gesammelte Werke*, ed. Marcel Reich-Ranicki et al. (Frankfurt, 1990), ii. 11.

material destruction was directly connected to the issue of nuclear testing and the invisible dangers stemming from nuclear radiation. Nuclear weapons tests became, for Germans much more than for Britons, projection screens for their own annihilation, as one observer put it. The mass-market cinema and newsreel as well as the new medium, television, made these experiences directly available to viewers.[124]

The West German and British governments played a part in creating this awareness as part of their efforts to educate their societies for the threats of the nuclear age. Most households obtained basic information about 'the Bomb' through civil defence efforts and civil defence drills—and they also acquainted them with the discourse that was required to address the threat: not fear, but rationality was required to respond adequately to the challenges of the new age.[125] The official Home Office civil defence pamphlet, published in 1957, advised Britons that cleanliness and good hygiene were the best answers to the threat of radioactivity: 'Radioactive dust on the body could be washed off with soap and water, particular attention being given to the nails and hair.' Washing machines should be avoided, as radioactive particles might stick to the drum, whereas 'a bucket or tub would be better'.[126] In West Germany, public civil defence efforts were a bit slower to take hold, given that state agencies still had to be rebuilt in the semi-sovereign setting of an occupied country. But when they discussed these issues, civil defence planners suggested similarly everyday measures for protection, such as using a briefcase to cover one's head in the event of a nuclear strike.[127]

While the increased testing had led to a growing awareness of the dangers of radiation from nuclear tests, it was an incident involving a Japanese shipping vessel that led to the emergence of the first sustained campaigns for security in the 'atomic age'. When the crew of the Japanese fishing vessel *Lucky Dragon* was exposed to severe radiation from a US hydrogen bomb test in 1954, it had become clear to many peace activists that they needed to find a novel language beyond traditional patterns of liberal internationalism and non-violent pacifism to address the dangers of nuclear weapons testings as a simulation of a future nuclear war for

---

[124] Werner Friedmann, 'Die Wolke über uns', *Süddeutsche Zeitung*, 10 April 1954; see also 'Atomexplosion—von Soldaten erlebt, am Fernsehgerät gesehen', *Die Neue Zeitung*, 24 April 1954.

[125] Melissa Smith, 'Architects of Armageddon: The Home Office Scientific Advisers' Branch and Civil Defence in Britain, 1945–68', *British Journal for the History of Science*, 43 (2010), 149–80; Biess, ' "Everybody Has a Chance" '.

[126] *The Hydrogen Bomb*, Home Office pamphlet (London, 1957).

[127] Nicholas J. Steneck, 'Eine verschüttete Nation? Zivilschutzbunker in der Bundesrepublik Deutschland 1950–1965', in Inge Marszolek and Marc Buggeln (eds), *Bunker: Kriegsort, Zuflucht, Erinnerungsraum* (Frankfurt/Main, 2008), 75–87.

which traditional pacifist paradigms no longer sufficed. In Britain, which ran its own tests, there now emerged a new set of organizations that used 'direct action' and that focused on the radiation coming from tests as well as the brittle nature of the arms race. The BBC's Panorama programme broadcast a special programme on the *Lucky Dragon* incident that involved the philosopher and mathematician Bertrand Russell and the scientist Joseph Rotblat.[128] While some, like the Labour defence policy expert and nuclear scientists P. M. S. Blackett, argued that nuclear weapons had 'abolished total war', peace activists and intellectuals pointed to the warlike character of the arms race: the dangers stemming from radioactive radiation from tests as essential part of this arms race and from the febrile nature of international relations at the time.[129]

The first of these reconfigurations of more traditional peace activism in Britain was *Operation Gandhi*, organized by a few activists with a PPU background. It sought to protest through sit-downs at Whitehall offices and military installations. The second important venture was the 'Hydrogen Bomb National Campaign' that aimed at supporting a parliamentary motion, brought in by a Labour MP, for a multilateral arms control treaty. The socialist Methodist Revd Dr Donald Soper chaired the campaign; John Collins, now Canon of London's St Paul's Cathedral, was also involved. The campaign was soon torn apart, however, by the old rifts between traditional pacifists, Labour and socialist internationalists, and UN supporters. The attention these campaigns received led to more local iniatives that campaigned for an end to testing and that further popularized knowledge on the dangers stemming from nuclear weapons through leaflets and screening of films such as *Children of Hiroshima*.[130]

The second impulse for campaigns against nuclear weapons testing came from scientists who were dissatisfied with the political messages attached to the 'Atoms for Peace' programme. The combination of thermonuclear threat and hopes for a more stable international system that would control nuclear weapons effectively led to a joint venture by several Western scientists that came to be known as the Russell–Einstein Manifesto. In the public presentation of their programme for peace in the nuclear age on 9 July 1955, the analytical philosopher and mathematician Bertrand Russell and the Nobel prize-winning physicist Albert Einstein declared that only a general cognisance of the fate of 'humanity' ('remember your humanity, and forget the rest') should guide foreign policies

---

[128] Jack Harris, 'Joseph Rotblat and Pugwash', in Rowlands and Attwood (eds), *War and Peace*, 195.

[129] P. M. S. Blackett, *Nuclear Weapons and East–West Relations* (Cambridge, 1956).

[130] Christopher Driver, *The Disarmers: A Study in Protest* (London, 1964), 25–7.

in East and West and lead to a rapprochement between the two blocs: 'we now know . . . that nuclear bombs can gradually spread destruction over a much wider area than had been supposed . . . the best authorities are unanimous in saying that a war with H-Bombs might quite possibly put an end to the human race.'[131] Shortly before, in April 1954, the Nobel peace prize-winning missionary and theologian Albert Schweitzer had published an open letter in the London *Daily Herald* that urged politicians to take the dangers of hydrogen weapons seriously. Both statements show that Hiroshima as a reference point had almost entirely lost its importance. Instead, the debate now focused on the present dangers stemming from nuclear weapons.

While these efforts received a significant level of attention in the British media as both the *Lucky Dragon* incident and Eisenhower's speech were still fresh in people's minds, it was in West Germany that they had a fundamental impact on the ways in which peace activists discussed the dangers of nuclear weapons. This was directly related to the specific salience of technological 'progress' and material security in West German political culture as a way of dealing with the consequences of war, violence, and man-made mass death. Thus, the Nobel prize-winning chemist Otto Hahn, a veteran of the Nazi atomic bomb project, gave a lecture on the north-west German radio station NWDR on 'Cobalt 60—danger or blessing for mankind' that was subsequently translated into English.[132] Accordingly, the main thrust for the renewed awareness did not come from the general public or non-governmental organizations. Rather, scientists who discussed the dangers of radioactivity in the context of hydrogen bomb tests prompted a more far-reaching debate. Many of the German scientists who had been previously involved in nuclear weapons programmes published a declaration on the island of Mainau in Lake Constance after a gathering of mainly German Nobel laureates in July 1955. Outlining the risk of self-destruction, the statement warned in stark terms of the dangers that the nuclear arms race posed and called on all governments and nations 'to come to the decision voluntarily to renounce the use of force as the last resort of politics'.[133]

---

[131] Sandra I. Butcher, 'The Origins of the Russell–Einstein Manifesto', *Pugwash History Series*, 1 (2005), 7–8.

[132] Elisabeth Kraus, *Von der Uranspaltung zur Göttinger Erklärung: Otto Hahn, Werner Heisenberg, Carl Friedrich von Weizsäcker und die Verantwortung des Wissenschaftlers* (Würzburg, 2001), 155–7.

[133] 'Mainauer Kundgebung', *Nachrichten aus Chemie und Technik*, 4/8 (April 1956), 112–13; Cathryn Carson, *Heisenberg in the Atomic Age: Science and the Public Sphere* (Cambridge, 2010), 318–19.

As a result, the 'atomic age' became a term used to describe contemporary society in all its shapes and forms. Images of poverty and images of
economic growth and paradise of plentiful consumption came to be
linked to this description. In West Germany in particular, challenges of
democratic government and planning also came to be linked to the
nuclear age, as Germans discussed the nature of technology in contemporary society more generally.[134] Activists began to use one of this age's
elements—the one denoting material security, peaceful governmental
planning, and programmes of modernization that aimed at hiding the
heritage of war and violence—to expose the other key element of the
atomic age: the danger of all-out destruction, a danger that activists now
imagined by drawing on the repository of experiences they had gained in
the Second World War.

The early discussions about nuclear testing, civil defence, and the role
of standing armies in the context of the cold war were rehearsals for the
more pronounced and explicit debates about the role of nuclear weapons
in national and international politics in the late 1950s and early 1960s.
They involved a discussion about the fundamentals of the cold war international order in the light of experiences of the Second World War in
general and aerial bombing in particular. At their core, they were one
attempt of many, situated at the borderlands of the cold war in British
and West German societies, to find security again after it had been lost.
Inititially, peace activists trying to revive their campaigns from the interwar period had problems engaging with the new context. Gradually, however, they found a language of security that moved away from an emphasis
on nationalism as a cause for international strife towards one that incor-
prorated an awareness of the social structure of peace, and its ideological
dimensions between East and West in the cold war. While, in line with
their efforts from the interwar years, peace activists continued to look for
supranational solutions to the problem of war and peace, they rejected the
particular international order that the cold war had made.

In both countries, peace activists in the 1950s lacked, however, the
organizational platforms that were appropriate for communicating these
ideas to a broader public. Moreover, their assessments initially lacked
resonance as they grappled with reconciling existing concepts of peace
with the new realities of the 'atomic age'. Crucially, they also did not have
an awareness of the democratic and social implications of this way of
organizing military affairs: British and West German activists as well as

---

[134] Bernhard Moltmann, *Das Atomzeitalter: Zur Gegenwart einer unaufgeklärten Vergangenheit* (HSFK Standpunkte, 4/1999) (Frankfurt/Main, 1999).

the general populations and the respective governments debated the relationship between the internationalization of military command structured within NATO and the fact that the impact of a future war would not only (or even primarily) be borne by soldiers alone, but that military violence was now potentially something that would involve society as a whole, continuing trends from the ways in which the Second World War had been waged.

Hence, while the memories of the Second World War lost their immediacy from the mid-1950s onwards, they never disappeared. They undergirded the ways in which contemporaries thought about and publicly discussed the dangers posed by nuclear weapons.[135] 'The world the Cold War made'[136] contained within it traces of the destruction that the Second World War had wrought. But it also contained the seeds of hope for political, social, cultural, and moral transformation that had characterized the 1945 moment. This moment was characterized by 'complex motives, diverse intentions, and turbulent circumstances', especially with regard to the heritage of the Second World War in these societies and the legacies of anti-fascism.[137]

The debates of the late 1940s and 1950s therefore involved more than discussions about the precise shape and size of the military commitments. They were about 'fundamental questions of constitution of politics and society on the whole'.[138] While providing the central reference point for discussions about nuclear weapons and the role of the military in both countries, 'security' in post-war Britain and West Germany never simply and only implied a status quo oriented policy. Its definitions were contested, and the concept had the potential to be used for the critique of defence and foreign policy, just as the British and West German governments used it for purposes of legitimation. The protests against nuclear weapons that emerged in the late 1950s did just that. And they did so in a form and with a way of campaigning and with broader languages of contestations that managed to transcend the structural constraints that traditional pacifists had faced from 1945 to the late 1950s, while still drawing, in new contexts, on the languages of popular political identifications of the immediate post-war period.

---

[135] This is highlighted for the local level by Arnold, *Allied Air War*, and Thießen, *Eingebrannt*.

[136] James E. Cronin, *The World the Cold War Made* (London, 1996).

[137] Melvyn P. Leffler, 'The Cold War: What do "We now Know"?', *American Historical Review*, 104 (1999), 501–24, here 519.

[138] Arnulf Baring, *Außenpolitik in Adenauers Kanzlerdemokratie: Bonns Beitrrag zur Europäischen Verteidigungsgemeinschaft* (Munich, 1969), 20.

Debates about 'the atom' became key sites at which the memories of
the Second World War, the experiences of the cold war, and hopes for the
future met, not only in Britain and West Germany, but across the Western world after 1945.[139] The general structural similarities of the debates
in both countries are surprising. Britain possessed its own nuclear weapons, while the content, if not the rhetoric, of the West German debate
centred around the stationing of tactical and medium-range nuclear missiles on West German soil and on the equipment of the Federal Army
with nuclear-capable equipment. Also, Britain had already opened its first
nuclear reactor—also used for producing weapons-grade plutonium—
in Windscale in 1950. A research reactor was already operational at
Harwell.[140] In 1953, a carbon-dioxide gas-cooled reactor opened at Calder Hall as the first British reactor devoted to the generation of electricity
only.[141] Under Allied statutes, nuclear research in the early Federal Republic was severely restricted, and the Federal Republic was banned from
possessing its own nuclear weapons. The West German government created a Ministry for Atomic Affairs only in 1955 after some restrictions
upon sovereignty had been lifted as part of the Federal Republic's accession to NATO in 1955. The first research reactor opened in Garching
near Munich in 1956 shortly before the foundation of the European
Atomic Community in March 1957, which allowed for research collaboration between France, Italy, Belgium, Luxembourg, the Netherlands,
and the Federal Republic.[142]

For the protesters in both countries, conjuring up apocalyptic images
of nuclear war meant, albeit to different degrees and in different forms,
reliving their experiences of warfare and violence of the previous years.
Imagining the apocalypse was, therefore, the flipside of the ways in which
the protesters on the marches regarded themselves as 'pilgrims' and 'victims'. Yet, for the majority of activists, the apocalypse was no longer
religious and transcendental.[143] Although the concept still evoked strong

---

[139] J. P. Delzani and C. Carde, 'Approche psychologique de l'évolution du theme
nucléaire à partir d'un quotidian populaire de 1950 à 1970', in Maurice Tubiana (ed.),
Colloque sur les implications psycho-sociologiques du développement de l'industrie nucléaire
(Paris, 1977), 354–74; Spencer R. Weart, *Nuclear Fear: A History of Images* (Cambridge,
MA, 1988), 387.

[140] Ministry of Supply (ed.), *Harwell, the British Atomic Energy Research Establishment,
1946–1951* (London, 1952).

[141] Margaret Gowing, *Independence and Deterrence: Britain and Atomic Energy, 1945–1952*
(2 vols, London, 1974).

[142] 'Die ersten Forschungsreaktoren in der Bundesrepublik', *Die Atomwirtschaft*, 2
(1957), 215–55; Michael Eckert, 'Die Anfänge der Atompolitik in der Bundesrepublik
Deutschland', *Vierteljahrshefte für Zeitgeschichte*, 37 (1989), 115–43.

[143] For the original religious *locus*, cf. Rev. 6: 12–14.

Christian feelings about the 'end of the world' and the final Revelation, for most protesters it had come to sit in the real world.[144] Through their marches and through their binary rhetoric of 'apocalypse or prosperity', the movements both expressed and created a feeling of accelerated time. But it was precisely in this situation that the future appeared as something that could be influenced and moulded through clear political decisions.[145]

The question was not 'if', but 'when', one would be blown up.[146] The protests were, therefore, the 'last chance' to save the world.[147] West German protesters pointed out that they lived 'in a global state of emergency'.[148] One West German protester even resorted to eugenic language to justify his claims: whoever wanted someone else to adopt his own ideology by force had not understood the realities of the nuclear age and was, therefore a 'parasite of the community' ('Gemeinschaftsschädling'), because existence of the whole of mankind was at stake.[149] Given the dangers of nuclear weapons, 'clear decisions' were necessary from everyone. Ambivalence, by contrast, had to be avoided at all costs, as this was a life-or-death matter.[150] Murder and the dominance of fear through nuclear weapons stood against progress through economic and technological developments.[151]

Activists in both countries based their assessments on the same body of information about nuclear tests and the impact of nuclear weapons when assessing the impact of nuclear war on the respective national territories. Particularly important were the widely publicized results of NATO's *Battle Royal* combat exercise in 1954. NATO powers had used ten imaginary nuclear weapons in order to throw back a Soviet tank division on an 80-kilometre front. Some 2,000 square kilometres of German soil would

[144] Hans Magnus Enzensberger, 'Zwei Randbemerkungen zum Weltuntergang', *Kursbuch*, 52 (1978), 1.

[145] Martin Niemöller, 'Kirche und Gesellschaft an der Schwelle einer neuen Zeit', *Stimme der Gemeinde*, 12/9 (1960), cols 265–72, here col. 266; *Peace News*, 13 November 1959, 2; *Peace News*, 28 June 1961, 4; *Peace News*, 15 September 1961, 4.

[146] *Peace News*, 4 August 1961, 1; *Peace News*, 8 September 1961, 10; poster at Easter March, *pläne* no. 9/1962, no pagination.

[147] Gustav W. Heinemann, 'Christus ist für uns alle gestorben', *Friedensrundschau*, 12/3 (1958), 16–22, here 18.

[148] 'Briefwechsel zwischen Erich Kuby und dem Präsidenten des Deutschen Bundestages', *Frankfurter Hefte*, 13/7 (1958), 453–7, here 454.

[149] Hamburger Institut für Sozialforschung (HIS), WOL, folder 'Anti-Atombewegung/ Luftschutzkampagne': 'Rettet die Freiheit!', appeal by the *Kampfbund gegen Atomschäden* [*c*.1960].

[150] Heinz Theo Risse, 'Die Gefahren atomarer Versuchsexplosionen', *Frankfurter Hefte*, 12/10 (1957), 685–96; BAK, ZSg. 1–262/1: 'Ostermarsch 1963', brochure, n.d.

[151] BAK, ZSg. 1-E-70: Kampagne Kampf dem Atomtod, brochure, n.d. [*c*. March 1958], 13.

have been contaminated.[152] The second important reference point was the 1955 NATO combat exercise *Carte Blanche*: 335 hypothetical nuclear bombs were dropped on Germany on more than 100 targets; 1.7 million mock deaths of civilians were counted; and 3.5 million were wounded. This was more than three times the number of German civilian casualties of the Second World War. And casualties from fallout had not even been computed. One commentator put it bluntly: 'Germany would become a desert', and the NATO exercise *Lion Noir* in March 1957, shortly before the deployment of some Allied missile battalions to the Federal Republic, seemed to confirm this.[153] A third important reference point was the *Fallex 62* combat exercise, which showed that West German forces were unable to counter a Soviet attack without causing severe damage to German territory by resorting to nuclear weapons.[154] British protesters believed that nuclear weapons had once and for all destroyed the protection that the island had provided in previous wars, and they felt that the results of combat exercises on the Continent were immediately relevant to them.[155] The combat exercise received particular attention in the Federal Republic, as the magazine *Spiegel* published confidential information on the disastrous death toll among Germans that the exercise had revealed and the Secretary of Defence, the Christian Social Union (*CSU*) politician Franz Josef Strauß, had the responsible journalist and the magazine's editor Rudolf Augstein arrested for treason. The Easter Marches played an important role in organizing the public protests.[156]

The 'clock of doom', depicted on each issue of the American *Bulletin of Atomic Scientists* since 1947, formed a further transnational reference point. In addition, public opinion in Britain could draw on the publication of a detailed report by the British mission in Hiroshima and Nagasaki, although the questions in the House of Commons at the time were primarily about the effects of the bombing on wildlife.[157] When

---

[152] Marc Cioc, 'Abschreckung und Verteidigung: Die Kontroverse über die Atombewaffnung in der Ära Adenauer, 1949–1963', in Ludolf Herbst et al. (eds), *Vom Marshallplan zur EWG* (Munich, 1990), 507.

[153] Elisabeth Noelle and Erich P. Neumann (eds), *The Germans: Public Opinion Polls 1947–1966* (Allensbach, 1967), 594; Thoß, *NATO-Strategie*, 332–54.

[154] 'Bedingt abwehrbereit', *Der Spiegel*, 10 October 1962, 9; *Peace News*, 30 November 1962, 5.

[155] Hull University Archives, Brynmor Jones Library (BJL), JS-106: Hull CND leaflet [1958]; British Library for Political and Economic Science, London (BLPES), CND/7/15: Oxford CND leaflet [1958]; *Peace News*, 9 September 1961, 9; 'FallEx '63', *Sanity* (November 1963), 3.

[156] Jürgen Seifert (ed.), *Die Spiegel Affäre* (2 vols, Freiburg, 1963).

[157] *The Effects of Atomic Bombs at Hiroshima and Nagasaki: Report of the British Mission to Japan*, published for the Home Office and Air Ministry (London, 1946).

transferring this knowledge to their protest announcements, the activists pointed out that they dealt with 'objective physical danger[s]'.[158]

Whereas British protesters gradually moved towards assessing the problems of technological developments and faults in bureaucratic decision-making as causes for nuclear war, West German activists continued to see international politics as the main source for nuclear war. West German protesters, by contrast, had at once a more abstract and more immediate vision of catastrophe that led to a spatial conception of security: nuclear destruction would happen because of a war above and on German soil. The first air combat exercise in Europe in 1955 had demonstrated that 268 bombs, two-thirds of the total payload, had been dropped on the territory of the Federal Republic, and the scenario envisaged that 1.7 million Germans had died, with 3.5 million wounded.[159]

Unlike in Britain, the location of the future war appeared to coincide with that of the last war. Characteristic for British visions of the apocalypse was Nevil Shute's 1963 novel *On the Beach*: after a Third World War had wiped out all life in the northern hemisphere, Australians tried to carry on with their normal lives, but died through radiation blown to them by the wind. Shute had already written invasion-scare novels during the 1930s, mainly concerned with a possible breach of British air defence by Nazi stealth bombers.[160] Rather than depicting violence or looting, Nevil Shute's novel emphasized the role of the nuclear war survivor as a wretched victim.[161]

Interestingly, Shute's novel did not feature in West German movement discussions at the time. It seems that Germans' own memories of violence were so close that German activists did not need to externalize them to faraway territories. Indeed, what was striking about the arguments put forward by West German protesters was the extent to which they depopulated the apocalypse. West German activists drew on the same scientific data on the impact of nuclear weapons, and they conveyed their opinions by using similar charts. One commentator used Berlin as an example and argued that the whole area of the city, 'except

[158] Kurt Vogel, 'Ostermarsch der Atomwaffengegner', *Wir sind jung*, 2 (1961), 5–7, here 5.

[159] 'Über 1.7 Millionen Deutsche wären getötet worden', *Westdeutsches Tagblatt*, 18 July 1955; '1959—Jahr der Entscheidung', *Neue Politik*, 4/1 (1959), 5–6; Biess, ' "Everybody Has a Chance" ', 226.

[160] Martin Ceadel, 'Popular Fiction and the Next War, 1918–1939', in Frank Glover-smith (ed.), *Class, Culture and Social Change* (Brighton, 1980), 161–84.

[161] Nevil Shute, *On the Beach* (London, 1957); Alan Lovell, 'On the Beach', *Peace News*, 25 December 1959, 8.

perhaps Spandau and Köpenick, would be in a zone where buildings would collapse immediately.[162]

Yet theirs was an end to the world without any people, but it nonetheless revealed an 'uncanny knowledge of what total annihilation was'.[163] While the West German activists spoke of their nightmares, these visions, in line with the general memory of the bombing war in the Federal Republic, contained only lunar landscapes of buildings in Cologne, in Hamburg, and across the Iron Curtain in Dresden. Most pictures still depicted depersonalized images of destruction; many even depicted conventional fighting.[164] Often, brochures showed anonymous people from far away, walking past bombed-out buildings.[165] The victims were inanimate, devoid of life. Buildings and things had become historical subjects and victims of both the National Socialist leadership and allied bombing.[166] Alternatively, the victim the West German activists invoked, following the language of the Nuremberg War Crimes Tribunal, was 'humanity'.[167] As it had happened at Auschwitz, planning for nuclear war signified a complete dehumanization.[168] Echoing arguments within the German Protestant Church immediately after the Second World War, activists framed their own time as that of a 'dehumanized humanity' and of 'bloody confusion'.[169]

Not only had the German apocalypse lost its transcendence, it had also lost its actors. The title of CND's exhibition 'No Place to Hide' had, when it moved through the Federal Republic, the far more dramatic title 'Keiner kommt davon' ('No one will be able to escape'), drawn from Hans Hellmut Kirst's novel on bombing in the Second World War.[170] The links

---

[162] Gerd Burkhardt, 'Die Veränderung der Welt durch die Atomwaffen', *Frankfurter Hefte*, 14/9 (1959), 635–50, here 642.

[163] Quote and interpretation: Geyer, Angst, 398; BAK, B145/4230: IfD, Stimmung no. 357, 'Die KZ Prozesse', 27 October 1958; BAK B145/5481: EMNID, 'Einstellung der Öffentlichkeit (1958)'; Detlef Bald, *Die Atombewaffnung der Bundeswehr: Militär, Öffentlichkeit und Politik in der Ära Adenauer* (Bremen, 1994), 124.

[164] *Wir sind jung*, 17/3 (1964), 11.

[165] *pläne*, 9 (1962), no pagination.

[166] SAPMO-BArch, DY30-IV 2-10.02-120: 'Auszüge aus den Reden auf den Ostermarsch-Kundgebungen 1962'.

[167] Martin Niemöller, *Martin Niemöller zu atomaren Rüstung: Zwei Reden* (Darmstadt, 1959), 13.

[168] Archiv der sozialen Demokratie, Bonn (AdsD), PVAM/000017: Dr. Arno Klönne to Campaign against Atomic Death, n.d. [c. summer 1961]; Heinemann, 'Christus', 20.

[169] *pläne*, 6–7 (July 1962), cover; Günther Anders, 'Der Sprung: Betrachtungen zur atomaren Situation', *Blätter für deutsche und internationale Politik*, 5 (1958), 597–605, here 597, 601.

[170] AdsD, 2/PVAM000044: John Brunner to Walter Menzel, 19 September 1959; John Brunner, 'Travelogue of an A-bomb exhibition', *Peace News*, 20 November 1959, 5. For the novel, see Hans Hellmut Kirst, *Keiner kommt davon: Bericht von den letzten Tagen Europas* (Munich, 1957).

between Hiroshima and German cities were often very abstract, but expressed uncertainty about the future: 'Hiroshima 1945—Munich?'[171] The possible Third World War appeared to continue a trail of violence in twentieth-century Germany that had started in 1914.[172]

While apocalyptic scenarios were not absent from CND's rhetoric, the West German campaign emphasized the inevitability of destruction in much more drastic terms.[173] In 1965, the Easter March played on this theme ironically, by staging the 'Action People's Coffin' (*Aktion Volkssarg*) (see Figure 1). Although there were campaigns against the lack of efficient civil defence efforts, it is hard to imagine that British organizers would have chosen such a language of death to communicate their aims.[174]

For one speaker at the Easter March in Hesse and the northern Palatinate, war had burnt itself internally into the Mainz cityscape: 'We could already see the new truths on 27 February 1945. Then, this city, Mainz, burnt for 12 hours. They [the new truths] have become even clearer through the bombs on Hiroshima and Nagasaki, the tests at the Bikini Atoll and at Nowaya Semlya.'[175] The German cold war thus turned into a 'terrorism of fear' and the root of the future 'hot war and its mass murder'.[176] Accordingly, West German activists characterized nuclear weapons, evoking memories of post-war German experiences, as a form of 'naked violence, the rape itself'.[177]

Hiroshima achieved a much greater symbolic significance in West German protesters' arguments about the apocalypse than in those of the British activists. Both British and West German protesters argued that Auschwitz and Hiroshima could be equated. Yet the concrete *location* of this memory differed substantially. When West German protesters mentioned Hiroshima, they moved away from their own past. What had

[171] *pläne*, 9 (1962), no pagination; AdsD, 2/PVAM000021: Fritz von Unruh, 'Mächtig seid Ihr nicht in Waffen!', enclosure to letter by W. Peters to Walter Menzel, 2 May 1958.
[172] Ossip K. Flechtheim, 'Von Sarajewo über Auschwitz und Hiroshima nach…?', *Stimme der Gemeinde*, 16/17 (1964), cols 521–6, here col. 526; AdsD, DGB, Abt. Organisation, 24/2182: Georg Reuter to Willi Richter, 17 March 1958.
[173] Cf. *Peace News*, 24 April 1959, 1; *Peace News*, 31 May 1963, 6, with '300 Luftschutzsirenen heulen in Frankfurt zum gemeinsamen Atomtod', *Stimme der Gemeinde*, 12/10 (1960), cols 291–2.
[174] Arno Klönne, 'Nach zwei Weltkriegen: Die politische und geistige Situation in Deutschland', *Wir sind jung*, 17/3 (1964), 8–9, 12–13; *Peace News*, 10 May 1957, 1; *Peace News*, 7 April 1961, 4; *Peace News*, 8 September 1961, 9.
[175] Herbert Faller's speech at the 1964 Easter March in Mainz, *Wir sind jung*, 17 (1964), 5.
[176] 'Wie gewinnen wir den Frieden? Friedensthesen von Heinrich Vogel', *Junge Kirche*, 20 (1959), 603–5.
[177] 'Resignation vor den Atomwaffen', *Atomzeitalter*, 8 (August 1959), 93–4, here 94. AdsD, ASAF000177: Lecture by Eckart Heimendahl, 15 July 1959.

Figure 1. Peace protest, demonstrating with cars: 'Atomic armaments turn Germany into a graveyard. Mothers think about your children. Atomic war is threatening. If you don't want to listen find out the hard way.' (Image courtesy of Deutsches Historisches Museum, Berlin, F 59/371)

remained a neutral void in the memories of German bombing sites became graphic when they invoked Hiroshima as the geographical location of the apocalypse.

The perceptions of the dangers of nuclear weapons were highly gendered. Female activists in both countries made similar arguments about the nuclear threat by pointing to their responsibilities as mothers for the future of their children and by claiming that male politicians acted irresponsibly.[178] In both countries, such interpretations resonated with more mainstream discourses about primarily female and young victims of war; they were not significantly different from general discourses that

---

[178] Quoted in Midge Decter, 'The Peace Ladies', *Harper's*, 226 (March 1963), 48–53; Modern Records Centre, University of Warwick, Coventry (MRC), MSS 181/4: Marghanita Laski, Naomi Mitchison, Ella Hunter, and a Doctor, *Survivors: Fiction based on Scientific Fact*, ed. Dr Antoinette Pirie [n.d.]; *Tomorrow's Children* [n.d., c. 1961], 5–6; *Sanity* (December 1962), 3; Jonathan Howard, 'How Nuclear Tests Affect Tomorrow's Children', *Sanity* (Easter Sat. 1962), 2; BLPES, CND/1/62: CND leaflet on the dangers from nuclear radiation [c.1959].

highlighted the importance of the nuclear family for post-war social and moral reconstruction.[179]

Because of different war experiences and the different geostrategic position in the cold war, British images of the apocalypse did not have a concrete location in Britain's geography. Increasingly, the emphasis was on accidents that might trigger catastrophe in Britain, but that so far had happened elsewhere. History appeared to provide guidance in this respect. As A. J. P. Taylor argued in his books and CND pamphlets, both the First and the Second World wars had been started by accidents.[180] CND pamphlets regularly mentioned the seven crashes of new B-47 bombers under Strategic Air Command, especially the incident in March 1958 when a nuclear bomb accidentally fell from a bomber on South Carolina, a news item that reached the general public in April, but that was registered by the pacifist press in Britain.[181] Images of mad generals were also far more widespread in Britain than in West Germany.[182]

The dangerous present that the activists faced created its own problem for the activists. As Rolf Schroers, an activist and former *Wehrmacht* officer who had been involved in the war against partisans in Yugoslavia and who was therefore well aware of the conditions for social bonding in wartime, pointed out: 'The future cannot produce a present community of suffering'—trying to realize it would only mean chaos today in order 'to prevent tomorrow's catastrophe'.[183] West German activists solved this problem by thinking of both the present and future together and interpreting the politics of security as one of a dramatic choice between unmitigated death and disaster should nuclear armaments continue, and a prosperous and affluent future if nuclear armaments were stopped and 'the atom' be used 'peacefully' in order to create nuclear energy.[184] Exploiting the non-military uses of nuclear energy was, from this perspective, a 'blessing', while using 'the atom' militarily was a curse.[185]

---

[179] See Ziemann, 'Code of Protest', 252–3, for this argument.
[180] A. J. P. Taylor, *The Origins of the Second World War* (London, 1961); A. J. P. Taylor, 'Accident Prone, or What Happened Next', *Journal of Modern History*, 49, 1 (1977), 1–18.
[181] *New York Times*, 19 April 1958, 1, 4; *Peace News*, 25 April 1958, 5.
[182] Peter Bryant [Peter Bryan George], *Two Hours to Doom* (London, 1957).
[183] AdsD, ASAF0000110: Rolf Schroers, 'Generalstreik', *CrP Infodienst*, June 1958.
[184] Gerhard Gollwitzer, 'Globales Hiroshima oder globale Entspannung', *Blätter für deutsche und internationale Politik*, 4 (April 1958), 433–7, here 433 *Peace News*, 13 June 1958, 1; *Peace News*, 27 June 1958, 4; *Peace News*, 3 April 1959, 2; *Peace News*, 28 April 1961, 6.
[185] Werner A. Uhlig, *Atom, Angst oder Hoffnung? Die Lehren des ersten Atommanövers der Welt*, 2nd edn (Munich, 1956), 3; Uhlig, 'Atom-Angst und Wirklichkeit', *Die Politische Meinung*, 3 (1956), 52–63; *Peace News*, 13 December 1957, 8; BLPES, CND/1/62: CND pamphlet, CND Scientists' group [1961]; on the condensation of this in the image of the

These two options have to be read together in order to make sense, as they represented the framing with which protesters addressed their audience. Günther Anders's idea about the 'atomic age' as an existential condition that required not human action, but phenomenological analysis and intellectual engagement in order to prolong the time that was left had remarkably little resonance within the movements. Activists still made sense of their cold war by reading the presence of the nuclear arms race through the past of the Second World War.[186] Nonetheless, movement discussions in both countries perceived their present as an 'atomic age' in a non-existentialist fashion. The *SPD*'s campaign even had a journal called *Atomic Age* (*atomzeitalter*). Its purpose was not primarily to warn the population of the dangers of nuclear energy, but to introduce them to a 'rational dealing' with these matters.[187]

Accordingly, the perceptions and arguments about an impending apocalypse were not 'anti-modern' or 'romantic'.[188] One can, therefore, not make sense of the activists' arguments if interpreting these images of the apocalypse in isolation. They were, very much in line with those of the general public at the time, directly connected to a wholehearted endorsement of technological progress in general.[189] Protest against nuclear power was minimal and remained restricted to neighbours of the relevant sites, not resulting in larger social networks.[190] No one protested when the first West German research reactor in Garching, just outside Munich, celebrated the completion of the roofing on 12 January 1957 and the owners served an 'atomic menu', including 'uranium sticks' (Bavarian *Weißwürste*), 'fat isotopes' as the unspecified desert, with

mushroom cloud, see Gerhard Paul, ' "Mushroom Clouds": Entstehung, Struktur und Funktion einer Medienikone des 20. Jahrhunderts im interkulturellen Vergleich', in Gerhard Paul (ed.), *Visual History* (Göttingen, 2006), 243–64.

[186] Günther Anders, *Frankfurter Allgemeine Zeitung*, 13 July 1957.

[187] On the history of the journal under the editorship of Claus Koch, cf. AdsD, PVAM000012: Claus Koch (KdA) to Georg Breuer (Wien), 11 December 1962; *Atomzeitalter*, 1 (January 1960), 11; *Peace News*, 24 October 1958, 8; Jodi Burkett, 'The Campaign for Nuclear Disarmament and Changing Attitudes towards the Earth in the Nuclear Age', *British Journal for the History of Science*, 45 (2012), 625–39.

[188] The ambivalence of this framing is especially obvious from a film used by the Campaign Atomic Death: Key to Hell (Schlüssel zur Hölle), Cassiopeia Film, 16mm, b/w, 12 min, n.d. [1958]; I would like to thank Benjamin Ziemann for making a copy of the film available to me. Cf., by contrast, Veldman, *Fantasy, the Bomb, and the Greening of Britain*.

[189] Cf. the polls, which show hopes and fears to sit side by side: *DIVO-Pressedienst*, May I—1958, 13–14; August I—1960, 10–11; October I—1961, 8–10; January II—1962, 13; George H. Gallup (ed.), *The Gallup International Public Opinion Polls, Great Britain, 1937–1975* (2 vols, New York, 1976), i. 458.

[190] Ute Hasenöhrl, *Zivilgesellschaft und Protest: Eine Geschichte der Naturschutz- und Umweltbewegung in Bayern 1945–1980* (Göttingen, 2011), 232.

'cooling water' (beer) to drink.[191] In Britain, likewise, early exhibitions of nuclear energy more or less ignored the military uses, although the 'Atom Train' that toured Britain in the late 1940s at least carried one carriage that alerted the population to the dangers connected with the military uses of nuclear energy.[192]

The activists' enthusiasm for science served as a powerful argument at a time when the movements were accused of contributing to public hysteria. But it also had its source in the declining strength of cultural pessimism and in the rise of a more empirical analysis of society, which manifested itself in a veritable euphoria for democratic planning in both countries.[193] There was agreement that 'the atom' had, for better or for worse, become the signature of a new period in human history. While the general public discourses in both countries came, from the early 1960s onwards, to be increasingly euphoric about the peaceful uses of nuclear energy, the sceptical and euphoric interpretations continued to sit side by side within the British and West German movements against nuclear weapons.[194]

While the military use of 'the atom' would result in the impossibility of all planning, using nuclear energy peacefully could contribute to the more rational ordering of societies and thus to the efforts to overcome the legacies of war and destruction. This emphasis on the peaceful uses of atomic energy was linked to the changing cold war climate of détente. The proponents of this view did not regard arms and military developments as the most important area of battle between East and West, but emphasized the areas of technology and culture instead.[195] The distinction between peaceful and military uses of 'the atom' was especially welcome for activists on the political left represented in the movement: it allowed them to combine thinking about progress with social utopias and could be linked to the conviction that the future could be designed and planned.[196]

---

[191] Hasenöhrl, *Zivilgesellschaft*, 204.

[192] Sophie Forgan, 'Atoms in Wonderland' Laucht, 'Atoms for the People', *History and Technology*, 19 (2003), 177–96.

[193] Cf. Francis Rona, 'Atomic Energy for Life and Progress', *Peace News*, 18 October 1957, 3; Bernd-A. Rusinek, ' "Kernenergie, schöner Götterfunken!" Die "umgekehrte Demontage": Zur Kontextgeschichte der Atomeuphorie', *Kultur & Technik*, 4 (1993), 15–21.

[194] Cf. Stölken-Fitschen, *Atombombe und Geistesgeschichte deutscher Sicht*, 166–7.

[195] Robert Jungk, 'Wenn der Frieden ausbricht', *Atomzeitalter*, 1 (January 1961), 3–6; BJL, JS-108: Ralph [Samuel] to Edward P. Thompson, n.d. [c.1957/8].

[196] BJL, JS-51: E. P. Thompson to Stuart Hall and John Saville [1959]; *Peace News*, 8 September 1961, 5; Eugen Kogon, 'Demokratischer Staat—Moderne Technik', *Atomzeitalter*, 7 (July 1961), 147–51.

The knowledge of the dangers of the cold war and the pitfalls and opportunities of the 'atomic age' that peace activists heard about and discussed in and through the mass media created the political reality that the anti-nuclear-weapons activists of the late 1950s used to develop a politics of security that challenged, but also replicated, key features of governmental conceptions of military and material security.

2

Identifying the Protests and the Protest-Makers

It was only in the late 1950s that the British and West German publics became aware of the importance of the nuclear arms race for the cold war. This constellation provided the ground from which the various campaigns could conceive of their scattered activities as movements. And it linked the British and West German protests together in the same historical conjuncture. This chapter analyses the most basic processes of identification of the movements by examining the campaigns' origins, their socio-structural composition as well as the ways in which contemporary observers made sense of them. Its purpose is to provide a broad overview of the campaigns' histories and to lay the ground for a more detailed investigation of activism. While the social structures of the supporters of both movements appear to have been remarkably similar, the campaigns acquired very different political resonances.

THE DEVELOPMENT OF THE
ANTI-NUCLEAR-WEAPONS CAMPAIGNS

In 1956, the National Council for the Abolition of Nuclear Weapons Tests (NCANWT), founded by a group of non-violent pacifists inspired by Gandhi's campaigns in 1930s' India, first galvanized public scepticism towards nuclear weapons in general and the acquisition of British hydrogen bombs in particular.[1] It concentrated on lobbying, but never became a movement. In spring 1957, an Emergency Committee for Direct Action against Nuclear War (the Direct Action Committee (DAC)) was founded to support pacifist Harold Steele's attempt to sail into the Pacific in protest against British H-bomb tests.[2] The DAC also developed plans for

[1] TNA CAB 128/72, C(54): 'Memorandum on Fall-Out from the Minister of Defence', 9 December 1954; Driver, *The Disarmers*, 31.
[2] *Manchester Guardian*, 12 April 1957, 3.

further protests, such as a march between the Atomic Weapons Research Establishment, Aldermaston, and London.[3] Its roots lay in the divisions within the ailing Peace Pledge Union (PPU) and attempts since the late 1940s and early 1950s to give pacifism a new meaning by reviving Gandhian traditions of non-violent direct action.[4] In the Federal Republic, a group of scientists from Göttingen University pointed out the dangers of nuclear weapons by criticizing Chancellor Konrad Adenauer's use of language. He had, following NATO terminology, compared tactical nuclear weapons to an advanced and 'modern' form of artillery and had justified the possible equipment of the West German army with the need to keep the young armed forces up to date.[5]

The year 1958 saw the emergence of movements in both countries that formulated security policies that differed from that of the governments. In January 1958, a number of political, religious, and literary intellectuals came together in the flat of Canon John Collins of London's St Paul's Cathedral and discussed ways to prevent the 'universal apocalypse' that the writer J. B. Priestley had predicted in an article in the *New Statesman* in November 1957.[6] The article had generated an overwhelming response by *New Statesman* readers, to which two specific factors had contributed. First, Aneurin Bevan, the standard bearer of the Labour Left, had just abandoned the unilateralist camp of the Labour Party, which argued that the decisive gesture of Britain's nuclear disarmament could guarantee national security. Bevan now supported multilateral disarmament through the United Nations framework, which ultimately depended on Soviet consent at international conferences. After the Labour Left had lost its strongest champion, the chances that the Party—and indeed any party in Britain—would represent unilateral disarmament as its official defence policy at a general election had, therefore, become rather slim.[7]

The second factor that prompted the meeting was that the American foreign-policy expert and former ambassador to Moscow George F. Kennan had advocated nuclear disarmament in Europe in his BBC Reith lectures: this had given the topic further resonance.[8] Not least, in the subsequent time period, with the obsolescence of Britain's V-bomber force in an age

---

[3] Hugh Brock, 'The Evolution of the Aldermaston Resistance', *Peace News*, 9 January 1959, 6.
    [4] Cf. the articles by Esme Wynne Tyson and Gene Sharp in *Peace News*, 6 January 1956, 6–7; *Peace News*, 3 January 1958, 4; Richard Taylor, *Against the Bomb*, 117–18, 120.
    [5] Cf. the letters from the population to the Federal Ministry for Atomic Energy: BAK, B138/100 (2); *Der Spiegel*, 17 April 1957, 8.
    [6] J. B. Priestley, 'Britain and the Nuclear Bombs', *New Statesman*, 54, 2 November 1957, 554–6.
    [7] *Proceedings of the 57th Annual Conference of the Labour Party* (Brighton, 1957), 10.
    [8] George F. Kennan, *Russia, the Atom, and the West* (London, 1958).

of intercontinental missiles, the cancellation of the *Blue Streak* and Anglo-American *Skybolt* programmes and the signing of a contract to acquire the submarine-based nuclear missile *Polaris* from the United States, it became clear that what the Macmillan government claimed was Britain's 'independent deterrent' was in fact quite dependent on American technology and expertise.[9]

On 28 January 1958, this group of intellectuals named themselves the 'Campaign for Nuclear Disarmament' or CND. There now existed a campaign that expressed the manifold fears of the British population about nuclear war. The DAC had never been able to gain much support within the British population, as its spectacular forms of attracting attention were not to most people's liking. By contrast, the response to CND was staggering. When the Campaign went public on 17 February 1958 with a meeting in Methodist Central Hall, Westminster, the room could not hold everyone who had gathered, and overflow facilities had to be organized.[10] People's experiences of the nuclear age had now, for the first time in Europe, been translated into a political movement.[11] Apart from staging many local protests, the supporters came together, from 1958, at the annual marches between the Atomic Weapons Research Establishment, Aldermaston (in Berkshire), and London. The idea for such a march had come from the DAC, and there had been considerable debate among CND's organizers whether the Campaign should participate in such a march. Ever since, however, the marches have become fixed dates in the annual calendar of political events in Britain, although they were suspended for some time from the mid-1960s into the 1970s. While differing in nuances, all these supporters fundamentally agreed that the security of the British people could be guaranteed only if their government unilaterally renounced its nuclear weapons.

On 12 October 1960, a group with links to the DAC split off from CND. Its focus was no longer on the Labour Party and pressure-group politics. Instead, the activists propagated the use of mass non-violent disobedience and direct action in order to communicate security issues. The new group called itself the Committee of 100 after 'the Guelphs and Ghibellines with their Council of 100'.[12] Its symbol and figurehead was

---

[9] Cf. Nigel Ashton, *Kennedy, Macmillan and the Cold War: The Irony of Interdependence* (Basingstoke and New York, 2002).

[10] MRC, MSS 181: National Executive, minutes, 27 February 1958.

[11] MRC, MSS 181: National Executive, minutes, 2 January 1959.

[12] Ronald William Clark, *The Life of Bertrand Russell* (London, 1975), 576; Internationaal Instituut voor sociale Geschiedenis, Amsterdam (IISG), C100 papers, unsorted folder: C100 minutes, 22 October 1960. On the general history, cf. Frank E. Myers, 'British Peace Politics: The Campaign for Nuclear Disarmament and the Committee of 100, 1957–1962' (Columbia Univ. PhD thesis, 1965) and Myers, 'Civil Disobedience and Organizational Change: The British Committee of 100', *Political Science Quarterly*, 86 (1971), 92–112.

the philosopher Bertrand Russell, who resigned from his CND presidency after a public row with Canon Collins.[13] Although C100 never had a large support base, it attracted significant media attention through its unconventional campaigns, such as the occupation of military bases.[14]

Across the Channel, in the Federal Republic, experiences of the nuclear age and the desires for security also found their expression in a new political movement. A smaller-scale movement emerged in the mid-1950s, but never had any major prominence. The *Kampfbund gegen Atomschäden* (Fighting League against Atomic Damages) was founded by the head consultant of the Detmold hospital, Dr Bodo Manstein, and was a curious assembly of ex-National Socialists and left-wing national-neutralists. It maintained close links with existing veterans' organizations, such as the *Verband der Kriegsbeschädigten, Kriegshinterbliebenen und Kriegsrentner* and the *Deutsche Volksgesundheits-Bewegung*, and launched its own journal, *Das Gewissen* (The Conscience), in mid-1956, edited by the former left-wing Social Democrat, Communist, and Dachau inmate Wolfgang Bartels.[15]

After a parliamentary debate on nuclear weapons on 23 January 1958, the opposition Social Democratic Party (*Sozialdemokratische Partei Deutschlands* (*SPD*)) decided to organize a general campaign 'to enlighten the public' about the dangers nuclear weapons posed for the security of the whole German nation.[16] As the Christian Democrats had an absolute majority in the *Bundestag*, the West German parliament, and an effective opposition in parliament was therefore difficult, the *SPD*'s executive moved into the extra-parliamentary arena in order to mobilize what they thought was the silent majority of the German population. Unlike in Britain, the first extra-parliamentary protests in West Germany depended on the organizational capacities and legitimacy of a political party. While the movement issued its first public announcements in late February and early March 1958, the first public meeting took place in Frankfurt deliberately on 23 March 1958, the anniversary of Hitler's Enabling Act and the date for another parliamentary debate on nuclear weapons.[17] The Campaign against Atomic Death (*Kampagne Kampf dem Atomtod* (*KdA*)) was born. After this event, the local party organizations founded branches across the Federal Republic as regional and local committees were set up, by and large under the auspices of the *SPD* and the Federation of German

[13] Cf. the material in BLPES CND 1–15.
[14] Richard Taylor, *Against the Bomb*, 22.
[15] Rupp, *Außerparlamentarische Opposition*, 70–1.
[16] AdsD: Parteivorstand, minutes, 20 November 1957.
[17] AdsD 2/PVAM00005: 'Kampf dem Atomtod', brochure, 23 March 1958.

Trade Unions (*Deutscher Gewerkschaftsbund* (*DGB*)). There were no central protest events as in Britain, but the many local and regional committees organized their own protests in close coordination with the *KdA*'s Bonn headquarters.[18] Vigils and demonstrations took place across the country in spring and early summer 1958. In May, the *SPD* launched a campaign for state-level plebiscites against the purchase of nuclear-capable equipment for the German army. Prompted by the *SPD*'s campaign, the Munich writer and essayist Hans Werner Richter set up an independent Committee against Atomic Armaments (*Komitee gegen Atomrüstung*), which attracted the support of the local educated bourgeoisie and came to function as the Bavarian branch of the Campaign against Atomic Death.[19]

Yet the *SPD* soon abandoned the campaign, after the Federal Constitutional Court had ruled its plans for plebiscites incompatible with the Basic Law and after its hopes for electoral gains in the state elections of North Rhine Westphalia in July 1958 had not paid off.[20] Although the movement continued to exist on paper, it no longer planned and staged major protests.[21] But the issue of nuclear weapons had become no less pressing, and observing the British example kept the West German movement alive. A small group of pacifists from the Hamburg area who had attended the 1959 Aldermaston March decided to look for a German Aldermaston. On Easter Friday 1960, some hundred people marched from different locations in northern Germany to the British weapons base Bergen Hohne, close to the site of the Bergen Belsen concentration camp. The 'Easter Marches of Nuclear Weapons Opponents' were born and, from 1961, took place all over the Federal Republic.[22] Like in Britain, it was mainly through media reports that the protest events turned into a seemingly coherent protest movement.

Throughout, the British and West German movements maintained their momentum by adapting to developments in foreign policy and

[18] AdsD, Menzel papers: circular by the *SPD*'s *Kommunalpolitische Zentralstelle*, 17 March 1958; Parteivorstand, minutes, 25 April 1958; Minutes of the meeting of the *DGB*'s executive committee, 4 March 1958, in Klaus Schönhoven and Hermann Weber (eds), *Quellen zur Geschichte der deutschen Gewerkschaftsbewegung im 20. Jahrhundert*, xii. *Der Deutsche Gewerkschaftsbund 1956–1963* (Bonn, 2005), 263–5.

[19] Archiv Stiftung Akademie der Künste, Berlin, Hans Werner Richter papers (HWR), 72.86.512: Hans Werner Richter to Siegfried Bußjäger, 26 February 1960.

[20] AdsD 3/BEAB000557: minutes, SPD Berlin, 13 October 1958; *Parlamentarisch-Politischer Pressedienst*, 1 August 1958; *Bulletin des Presse- und Informationsamtes der Bundesregierung*, 14 June 1958, 1065–6, 1068.

[21] AdsD: Präsidium, minutes, 23 January 1961, 3; AdsD, DGB Archives, Abt. Organisation, 24/9006: 'Pressemitteilung der SPD, betr.: Ostermarsch-Bewegung', 7 November 1963.

[22] Hamburger Institut für Sozialforschung (HIS), TEM 400,01: Central committee, minutes, 6/7 May 1961.

international relations: while the movements were initially concerned with rather narrow issues of national defence and foreign policy, they came to broaden their approach. With the announcement by the United States and by the Soviet Union to stop atmospheric nuclear tests in 1959, this issue fell out of view. Both movements staged protests when France began atmospheric testing in the Sahara in 1960, when the USSR resumed atmospheric nuclear testing in 1961, and when the USA followed with a resumption of its nuclear weapons tests in 1962.[23]

The Cuba crisis in autumn 1962 was a particular turning point for CND.[24] It led to a reformulation and clarification of the CND programme as 'Steps towards Peace': the crisis had shown that 'Great Britain was inevitably involved in any nuclear crisis', with its commitments to NATO and its nuclear bases. On the one hand, the new programme was presented as a move away from more radical proposals towards disarmament and towards programmes of controlling the arms race. On the other hand, CND continued to advocate Britain's immediate unilateral nuclear disarmament and now included a call for the withdrawal from 'nuclear alliances'.[25] The official West German Easter March announcements regarded the Cuba crisis as a reaffirmation of their goal of halting the proliferation of nuclear weapons and of creating nuclear-free zones, not only in Europe, but all over the world. In the end, 'reason had won: but what kind of reason is it which was born only out of fear of mutual annihilation?'[26] Like the crises over Berlin in winter 1958–59 and in August 1961, Cuba had shown that additional efforts towards atomic armaments in areas close to the superpowers brought not more security but 'catastrophic insecurity'.[27]

THE SOCIAL STRUCTURES OF SUPPORT

The historian who approaches the movements will find that diversity was their main feature. And, indeed, the movements stressed that they represented 'people from all walks of life'.[28] Activists and supporters came

[23] *Peace News*, 17 January 1958, 1; 5 December 1958, 4; 5 June 1959, 4.
[24] Hilary Bourne, 'In Fleet Street', *Sanity* (October 1962), 3.
[25] BLPES, CND/1/4: 'Press statement', 27 November 1962.
[26] Institut für Zeitgeschichte, Munich (IfZ), ED 702–7: 'Entwurf eines Rundschreibens an die Jugendorganisation des Ortsausschusses München', n.d. [c. summer 1963].
[27] IfZ, ED 702, 2: Arno Klönne, 'Ostermarsch—Zentraler Ausschuß, Einige Argumente für's Bonner Lobby', n.d. [c.1963].
[28] AdsD 2/PVAM00005: 'Volksbewegung Kampf dem Atomtod', leaflet (April 1958); Hamburger Institut für Sozialforschung (HIS), TEM 200,06: 'Ostermarsch der Atomwaffengegner', pamphlet, 1961; BLPES, CND/1/3: Flyers for the 1958 and 1959 Aldermaston Marches.

from groups that are usually not regarded as having features in common: atheist or agnostic socialists and Christians, communists and nationalists, pacifists, anarchists, and trade-union leaders and generally liberally minded citizens. And there were almost as many different reasons for people joining as there were activists. In fact, it was only when confronted with the question of nuclear weapons that the activists came to assert their experiences explicitly with reference to what they regarded as their main social reference points. At the same time, this emergence of experiences allowed them to identify common concerns. The experiences themselves thus simultaneously shaped and were moulded by the politics of security.

Probing the actual support base of both movements is, therefore, extremely difficult. First, there are general problems of interpretation. Sociological studies are usually embedded in specific methodological assumptions that significantly influence the selection and representation of data.[29] In particular, concepts of 'class' and social stratification are so closely connected to specific cultural assumptions about politics and society that a meaningful comparison from a macro-sociological angle is not sensible. Moreover, the existing evidence is rather sketchy. Neither movement initially had an official membership. In Britain, it was not introduced until the mid-1960s to inject money into an impoverished campaign, and in West Germany it was never introduced, for fear of organizational sclerosis.[30]

Bearing these restrictions in mind, it is nevertheless possible to come to some general conclusions about movement support in both countries. The movements' social composition was quite similar. The supporters in both countries and the members of the movements were mostly middle class, better educated and younger than the average population, with the average age of supporters falling over time. Young CND activists in particular tended to be better educated than the national average and came from wealthier families, with 55 per cent receiving full-time education and 48 per cent with a grammar-school background.[31] Yet neither CND nor its West German counterparts were ever 'youth movements'.[32]

[29] Cf. Thomas Osborne and Nikolas Rose, 'Do the Social Sciences Create Phenomena? The Example of Public Opinion Research', *British Journal of Sociology*, 50 (1999), 367–96.

[30] HWR 72.86.512: Hans Werner Richter to Siegfried Bußjäger, 26 February 1960.

[31] Parkin, *Middle Class Radicalism*, 166–7. 'Young' meant between 12 and 25 years old.

[32] Philip Abrams and Alan Little, 'The Young Activist in British Politics', *British Journal of Sociology*, 16 (1965), 315–33, here 324; Robin Jenkins, 'Who are these Marchers?', *Journal of Peace Research*, 4 (1967), 46–60, here 49.

According to an informal poll at the Easter March in the Ruhr area, the bulk of activists were 'employees' (*Angestellte*, essentially 'white-collar workers'), followed by 'academics' (22 per cent); 15 per cent were self-employed, 13 per cent were civil servants (*Beamte*); 11 per cent were 'workers' and only 11 per cent classified themselves as students; 76 per cent were between 25 and 50 years of age; only 19 per cent were under 25; and only 5 per cent were over 50.[33] This low involvement of 'young people' in the West German protests was in tune with the very low-level political engagement of people under 30 in extra-parliamentary politics. Similarly, a contemporary British opinion poll showed that unilateral disarmament came to the bottom of the list of problems felt by British youth.[34] Nonetheless, CND's organizer Peggy Duff recalled in her memoirs how vibrant CND was in university cities, such as Oxford and Cambridge.[35] Despite these broad similarities in age structures, there were, however, striking differences in the patterns of age distribution. In Britain, young people up to 30 and activists over 60 were over-represented in comparison to those aged between 30 and 60.[36] In West Germany, by contrast, the age cohort of those born in the late 1920s and early 1930s—that is, those aged between 30 and 40—dominated, whereas protesters above the age of 65 made up but a tiny proportion of all activists.[37] Women made up about half of the protesters in both countries, but, with a few exceptions such as Peggy Duff in CND and Christel Beilmann in the Easter Marches in the Ruhr area, never assumed organizational roles equivalent to their social representation within the movement. Duff recalls in her memoirs that she was exposed to frequent ridicule about her brash behaviour from her male colleagues.[38] The case of female participation in the British and West German movements thus affords a unique insight into the limits to the emergence of experiences. While women did participate in the movements, they only rarely voiced their concerns *as women*. The activists' rhetoric at the time remained remarkably gender neutral (very much in opposition to the connections of 'peace' issues with particularly motherly concerns in the GDR). Specifically female experiences thus remained

---

[33] Otto, *Vom Ostermarsch zur APO*, 90.

[34] Philip Abrams and Alan Little, 'The Young Voter in British Politics', *British Journal of Sociology*, 16 (1965), 95–110, 104; Dieter Rucht and Roland Roth, 'Weder Rebellion noch Anpassung: Jugendproteste in der Bundesrepublik 1950–1994', in Rucht and Roth (eds), *Jugendkulturen, Politik und Protest: Vom Widerstand zum Kommerz?* (Opladen, 2000), 283–304, here 288.

[35] Peggy Duff, *Left, Left, Left: A Personal Account of Six Protest Campaigns* (London, 1971), 160–1.

[36] Parkin, *Middle Class Radicalism*, 140–74.

[37] Otto, *Vom Ostermarsch zur APO*, 90.

[38] Parkin, *Middle Class Radicalism*, 17, 167,171–2; Duff, *Left, Left, Left*, 146.

inaudible and frequently invisible at the time, and it was only with hind-sight that female activists constructed their subjectivity in explicitly female terms.[39]

Most activists had what one could describe as a broadly left-wing and progressive outlook: according to one survey, 78 per cent of the 1958 British marchers read the *Manchester Guardian*, 80 per cent the *Observer*, and 53 per cent the *New Statesman*.[40] Sociology students were particularly prominent among the British protesters.[41] We do not have comparable data for West Germany, but it is likely, given the involvement of many *SPD* members in the movement, that the picture was broadly similar. West German activists also tended to come from families with, politically speaking, liberal views who had been previously involved in politics.

Both the West German and British movements attracted a significant number of Christians. CND has been described as an 'amateur alliance of Christian and humanist radicals'.[42] Similarly, the West German Campaign against Atomic Death and, even more so, the Easter Marches became a form of secular–religious pilgrimages.[43] Clergymen and lay Christians played an important role in CND, perhaps a much more important one than in the Federal Republic. Canon Collins, the Revd Michael Scott, and the Methodist Donald Soper were the three most prominent. The Welsh CND in particular drew on many clergymen when advertising its activities. Kingsley Martin, Edward P. Thompson, and others came from nonconformist backgrounds, although they had secu-larized their inherited nonconformity. Ministers frequently served as chairmen or secretaries of local CND branches.[44] In West Germany, senior Protestant clergy, such as the Church President of Hesse-Nassau Martin Niemöller and the Dortmund Church President Heinrich Klop-penburg, were well represented in the Campaign against Atomic Death, but played less prominent roles in the Easter Marches.[45]

Frank Parkin's sociological research suggests that 40 per cent of former CND supporters were practising Christians, which exceeded the number of regular churchgoers. The peculiarity of CND was the strong representation

[39] Sheila Rowbotham, *Promise of a Dream: Remembering the Sixties* (Harmondsworth, 2000).

[40] Richard Taylor and Colin Pritchard, *Protest Makers: The British Nuclear Disar-mament Movement of 1958–1965, Twenty Years On* (London, 1980), 26; Driver, *The Disarmers*, 60.

[41] Parkin, *Middle Class Radicalism*, 172.

[42] Adrian Hastings, *A History of English Christianity 1920–1990* (London, 1991), 510.

[43] Gerhard Schmidtchen, *Protestanten und Katholiken: Soziologische Analyse konfessionel-ler Kultur* (Berne, 1973), 324.

[44] Hastings, *History of English Christianity*, 428–9.

[45] Otto, *Vom Ostermarsch zur APO*, 94.

of activists from 'nonconformist' backgrounds, such as Methodists, Baptists, Quakers, and Unitarians, which could all look back on involvement in pacifist associations since the late eighteenth century.[46] Although Nonconformity had lost influence in British society as a whole by the early 1950s, individual nonconformists still played a prominent role within CND. Nonconformists among British protesters outweighed Anglicans significantly: 52 per cent were Free Church members (Quakers, Methodists, Presbyterians, and Baptists), 34 per cent Anglicans, and 4 per cent Roman Catholics.[47] In a later survey, Richard Taylor and Colin Pritchard found that 43 per cent of their sample 'strongly agreed with the Christian belief system', and 41 per cent identified themselves as practising Christians during this period. On the other hand, resistance towards the Campaign was also particularly pronounced amongst nonconformists. Of the 58 per cent who called themselves 'non-believers' in the survey, 19 per cent ranked themselves as 'agnostic', 15 per cent as 'atheist', and 15 per cent as 'humanist'.[48]

Similar information is not available for West Germany. There, the relatively small number of Catholics among the activists was particularly remarkable, although Catholics made up more than half of the West German population and although they were as concerned about nuclear weapons as West German Protestants.[49] Given the Pope's reluctance to condemn nuclear weapons, the extent to which Catholics opposed nuclear weapons is surprising. The real fault line in opinions had, therefore, less to do with confessional allegiances than with attachment to the institutional Church. 'Nominal' Protestant and Catholics (77 per cent and 76 per cent respectively) were more likely to be against nuclear weapons than churchgoers (67 per cent and 62 per cent respectively).[50] This was not only a case of Christians joining the campaign because they were Christians. Rather, the archives of the West German campaign contain fascinating letters by grass-roots supporters that show how they came to identify with the campaign by trying to

[46] Michael Hughes, *Conscience and Conflict. Methodism: Peace and War in the Twentieth Century* (Peterborough, 2008), 140–79.

[47] Parkin, *Middle Class Radicalism*, 27, 74–5. This contradicts the claims of a declining influence of nonconformity, especially on the peace movement in Alan P. F. Sell and Anthony R. Cross (eds), *Protestant Nonconformity in the Twentieth Century* (Carlisle, 2003).

[48] Taylor and Pritchard, *Protest Makers*, 28 and 23; 34 and 38.

[49] BAK, B 145/4230: DIVO, 'Zum Thema "Volksbefragung und Atombewaffnung"' (Ergebnisse einer Repräsentativerhebung im Mai 1958); Daniel Gerster, 'Von Pilgerfahrten zu Protestmärschen? Zum Wandel des katholischen Friedensengagements in den USA und der Bundesrepublik Deutschland 1945–1990', *Archiv für Sozialgeschichte*, 51 (2011), 311–42, here 319–25.

[50] BAK, B 145/4230: DIVO, 'Zum Thema "Volksbefragung und Atombewaffnung"' (Ergebnisse einer Repräsentativerhebung im Mai 1958).

suture their own feelings and experiences to the emerging movements, as they did not see them represented in the organized churches or elsewhere in politics. These letters usually started by expressing the writer's 'shock' ('Erschütterung') about the 'events of recent years and decades' and were based on a vast amount of information that the writer had gleaned from reading illustrated magazines and newspapers. Fritz Haller from Aulendorf in Württemberg, a Protestant railway worker with only basic education, writing to the *KdA* head office in May 1960, thanked the 'anonymous people and friends' who were looking for solutions. He wrote that all human beings were united as 'God's children' and cited a number of Bible verses at the beginning of his letter. This issue, he claimed, thus also tied the 'whole of humanity together'. Politics was not, as some people argued, the problem—it did not spoil people's characters. Rather, Haller regarded politics as the solution, as a good character could influence politics in good and moral ways.[51]

The fact that we do not have similar sources for the British campaign might well be the result of different archival cultures. But these archival cultures reflect, at least partly, the differences in the politicization of security in the two post-war societies. British protesters could draw on a number of already existing outlets for the protests and, importantly, had an awareness of the continuities of history and campaigns that they constantly re-negotiated, but that they took for granted. In West Germany, however, supporters of the campaigns and activists had a more acute awareness for the work that was required to create social bonds, as they sought, perhaps more forcefully than their British counterparts, to write themselves into the continuity of national history, a process that was complicated further by the division of Germany. For West German activists, therefore, joining the campaign was very often also an exercise in actively expressing their democratic credentials and civility by actively producing structures of a self-consciously civilian society.[52] A letter by a Johannes Hauck from Munich to the 'most esteemed prime minister' of Bavaria from September 1958, marked 'confidential', highlights the self-awareness that campaigners had about this issue, as it drew on explicit comparisons with Britain. Instead of a party democracy, Hauck favoured a model tried out in Austria that brought all main parties together in order to achieve a true representation of popular opinion, so that Germany could make the transition from war to peace and solve 'the world-political dangers' of the time. Majority voting, by contrast, could not yet work in the Federal Republic, because,

[51] AdsD 2/PVAM000015: Fritz Haller to KdA, 17 May 1960, fos 1, 3.
[52] Till van Rahden, 'Clumsy Democrats: Moral Passions in the Federal Republic of Germany', *German History*, 29 (2011), 485–504.

in countries like Britain, where this system worked, it depended on the 'democratic and tolerant dispositions [*Gesinnung*] of its citizens'.[53]

Germans had an 'uncanny knowledge of what total annihilation was', and they knew that they could not control the violence unleashed by wars.[54] Although Britons shared in a fundamental scepticism towards their government's civil defence efforts, they were already able to form an ironic relationship with the issue, when a satirical defence advocate in the TV revue *Beyond the Fringe* in 1961, played by Peter Cook, concluded by advising viewers: 'There is nothing like a good old paper bag for protecting you.'[55]

Research on protest movements in other countries has highlighted that figures based on national reference points should be treated with care. The composition of local chapters, branches, and associations often differed markedly from the national averages. For Britain, this is particularly true for the Scottish CND, in which workers were much more strongly represented than in Britain as a whole. In particular, this was the case for the Glasgow and Clydeside areas, which had very strong working-class strongholds.[56] Although exact figures are lacking, it is likely that this is also true for certain regions within the Welsh coalfields. It is also likely that, because of the strong nonconformist traditions in Wales, religious affiliation was higher there than the national average suggests.[57] For West Germany, we do not possess survey data on local and regional campaign groups. A private and unpublished survey, carried out by Hans-Karl Rupp in 1965, suggests, however, that, on average, young people were not as well represented on the regional and local levels as national surveys suggest. Only 11 per cent classified themselves as 'students' and 'young people'.[58]

Although these figures suggest general similarities, the movements differed significantly in how they represented public opinion. While British opinion polls never registered more than 35 per cent popular support among the population for unilateral nuclear disarmament throughout

[53] AdsD: 2/PVAM000015: Johannes Hauck (Munich) (copy) to the 'esteemed Prime Minister', 22 September 1958.

[54] On this knowledge, see BAK, B145/4230: IfD, 'Die KZ Prozesse', Stimmung im Bundesgebiet, no. 357, 27 October 1958; quotation from Geyer, 'Cold War Angst', 398.

[55] *The Complete Beyond the Fringe*, ed. Roger Wilmut (London, 1982), 82. Cf. Matthew Grant, *After the Bomb: Civil Defence and Nuclear War in Britain, 1945–68* (Basingstoke, 2010), 130–6.

[56] Cf. Jane Buchan and Norman Buchan, 'The Campaign in Scotland', in John Minion and Philip Bolsover (eds), *The CND Story: The First 25 years of CND in the Words of the People Involved* (London, 1983), 52–3.

[57] BLPES, CND/1/8/8: Welsh CND pamphlet, 1960.

[58] Otto, *Vom Ostermarsch zur APO*, 90.

this period, West German pollsters returned figures above 80 per cent.[59] On a superficial level, this reflected the fact that the issues had a different salience in each political system. CND's demand for unilateral nuclear disarmament was in content much more radical than the demands of the West German movements, as Britain already possessed nuclear weapons at the time. By contrast, the West German protesters sought to forgo nuclear-capable equipment and to strive for a nuclear-weapons-free zone in central Europe. Indeed, the West German activists' demand for international disarmament was one to which even some of CND's fiercest opponents could subscribe.[60] Moreover, it was only logical that West Germans, living at the front line of the cold war in Europe, would perceive the threat from nuclear weapons in much more dramatic and immediate terms, a fact driven home by the gloomy title 'Campaign against Atomic Death'.

Differences in the ways in which different sections of society were represented highlight the complexities and ambiguities in the resonances of both campaigns. The sociological structure of the British movement reflected trends in British opinion polls much more directly than the sociological structure of the West German movement did West German ones. Polls compiled by different institutions show that Adenauer's policy of atomic armament was least rejected among those groups in the West German population as a whole most active in the movement: the younger and more educated sections of society (some 60 per cent opposed). Opposition to nuclear armaments was particularly pronounced among those who were underrepresented in the movement: workers (between 80 and 90 per cent).[61]

These different figures reflect a fundamental difference between processes of identification of the British and West German campaigns. It mattered greatly that the West German discussion was not about the stationing of Germany's own weapons and that it revolved instead around purchasing nuclear-capable equipment for the West German army that would allow it to deploy NATO weapons in collaboration with British and US

[59] Gallup, *The Gallup International Public Opinion Polls, Great Britain, 1937–1975*, i. 449, 461, 584, 668; D. E. Butler and Richard Rose, *The British General Election of 1959*, new edn (London, 1999), 71; D. E. Butler and Anthony King, *The British General Election of 1964*, new edn (London, 1999), 37, 129–31; BAK, B145/4230: Institut für Demoskopie Allensbach, 'Standorte der öffentlichen Meinung', 5 September 1958, 10; DIVO, 'Zum Thema "Volksbefragung und Atomrüstung" (Ergebnisse einer Repräsentativerhebung im Mai 1958)'.

[60] Cf., e.g., Hugh Gaitskell in the House of Commons: *Hansard*, House of Commons, 5th ser., vol. DCXVII, 776–7, 11 February 1960; and Harold Macmillan, *Pointing the Way, 1959–61* (London, 1972), 98.

[61] BAK, B145/4229, no. 291: Institut für Demoskopie Allensbach, *Die Atomrüstung*; BAK, B145/4266: EMNID-Institut für Meinungsforschung, *Die Resonanz der Bundestagsdebatte zur Außenpolitik und Atombewaffnung* (March 1958).

forces stationed in West Germany as part of the occupation regime. The feeling of helplessness in West Germany towards foreign policy was, therefore, even more pronounced than in Britain. For example, an activist called Arne H. wrote to the campaign almost immediately after its foundation in March 1958, sketching out his plans for a short play called *The Chaos*. He offered the play to the the campaign as a contribution to highlighting the 'madness of the atomic arms race', using metaphors of flooding and water to highlight the loss of control. H. evokes danger through graphic descriptions of body functions, thus replicating the language of the phantasies of annihilation similar to those developed by the *Freikorps* in the early Weimar Republic and the soldiers of the Eastern front during the National Socialist war.[62] The play unfolds in three short acts, which H. calls 'images', and it sketches the conversations between a fanatic, a rebel, a scientist, an engineer, and a dictator. The first scene (at the factory gates) shows a conversation in front of a factory guide where the rebel and the fanatic discuss the futility of protection and mention that the trade unions were unable to help as they were busy spending members' contributions. The second scene ('In a conference room'), a discussion between the scientist, the engineer, and the dictator, validates these assessments. The third scene, called 'In a barren landscape', contains graphic descriptions of death and destruction that is reminiscent of images of the empty battlefield on the Western front during the First World War: nuclear war would mean total chaos, against which the aerial bombing of the last war paled by comparison. The play warns the audience vividly that 'your swollen bodies will explode like soap bubbles', the waves will play with 'your stinking intestines'. Indeed, 'what you can see is not a stone, but the dead swollen body of a pregnant woman', and you can also see 'the severed breasts of a woman, and a children's body without arms and legs'. The play closes with a scene of complete emptiness. One can hear the constant ticking of a Geiger counter, with a grey-brown/red curtain visible at the back of the stage. A scientist babbles to the rhythm of the Geiger counter.

In its drastic depiction of nuclear 'chaos', H.'s account is not representative. But its liminality highlights especially well the core features of the identifications connected with the West German campaign.[63] Michael Geyer has identified this as the main aspect of 'Cold War *Angst*'. This angst was the expression of the fundamental fact that those Germans who

---

[62] AdsD: 2/PVAM00025: Arne H. to KdA, 27 March 1958; cf. Klaus Theweleit, *Male Phantasies*, i. *Women, Floods, Bodies, History* (Minneapolis, 1987).
[63] Cf. for a different voice Peter Fritzsche, *The Turbulent World of Franz Göll: An Ordinary Berliner Writes the Twentieth Century* (Cambridge, MA, 2011), 202–8.

disapproved of nuclear armaments saw themselves as the first future victims of a nuclear war, a fate that they thought they would be unable to control. But it also highlighted a sense of profound scepticism towards the military functions of the state: although very few of the people consulted in the opinion polls were pacifists, they cut their bonds with the state 'at a crucial sinew'.[64] The language of campaigners such as Hövel demonstrates that their rejection of the German past of militarism went hand in hand with the reproduction of its arguments and language.

SELF-OBSERVATIONS

While these sociological data reveal, in broad terms, who was most concerned about the implications of nuclear weapons for security during this time period, the structures of the polls themselves reflect the specific assumptions of those who designed them, and the parameters through which each society observed itself. The attempts by activists and observers alike to endow the movements with a clear social structure were one of the first acts of labelling and identifying the movements. They played an essential part in constituting them; so did the activists who described themselves with specific political and social attributes.

But there were important differences in how the pollsters slotted into the general political process the experiences that revealed themselves in the polls. While British pollsters regarded the experiences primarily as limited to specific sections of society, their West German counterparts treated them explicitly as tools of political power, which could be manipulated to achieve political ends. In Britain, those who compiled the polls were mainly sociologists trying to understand the society around them. In the Federal Republic, by contrast, the government, the political parties, and even the movements took a much keener interest in polling than their British counterparts. While the Adenauer government, the *SPD*, and the Christian Democratic Union (*Christlich Demokratische Union Deutschlands (CDU)*) commissioned extensive and differentiated polls (frequently classified as 'top secret') and had departments that analyzed the material, the British government and the political parties were much slower in making use of the polls, so that polling became standard practice among British political actors only from the mid-1960s onwards.[65] This reflected not

[64] Geyer, 'Cold War Angst', 386, and Biess, '"Everybody Has a Chance"'.
[65] Butler and King, *The British General Election of 1964*, 204–11; Anja Kruke, *Demoksopie in der Bundesrepublik Deutschland: Meinungsforschung, Parteien und Medien 1949–1990* (Düsseldorf, 2007), 61–86, 209–20, 392–405.

only different political structures and cultures, but also fundamentally different concepts of 'society' in both countries. West Germans had a far more homogeneous view of 'society' than their British counterparts. This was, in part, a legacy of National Socialism, but it also compensated for the loss of a united Germany.[66] Intellectuals close to the West German movement, such as Jürgen Habermas, emphasized the critical potential of 'society' understood as a 'public sphere'. Thus, 'public opinion' itself had become a contested issue in the West German politics of security, and had, by the early 1960s, became one of the most popular topics in West German intellectual discussions.[67]

Despite these different resonances, the *structures* of analysis that the polls offered were quite similar. In both societies, we can find three types of social characterization for the movements, each of which had a different importance within national political discussions: the first made assumptions about social hierarchy and was often connected to generational arguments; the second assumed a social stratification (in upper, middle, and working class) and sought to locate the movements within it; the third assumed a binary opposition between 'the people' and 'the elite' or 'the establishment'. Indeed, the term 'establishment' itself had close CND connections: it was first made famous by CND supporter A. J. P. Taylor and later popularized in an edited collection by the New Left supporter Hugh Thomas.[68] Each of these interpretations was linked to specific views about the political process and about the role of security within it. Unlike in debates about peace movements after the First World War, gender, although mentioned in the debates, did not play the role of a master frame to conceptualize the debates about nuclear weapons.[69] In West Germany, by pointing out the great scepticism of women towards Adenauer's policy of strength, only the Allensbach Institute for Demographic Research singled out 'gender' as an important determinant for attitudes towards security and nuclear weapons in its confidential polls for the government.[70]

Movement activists in both countries preferred the binary opposition between 'the people' and 'the elite'. And the West German campaigns

[66] Paul Nolte, *Die Ordnung der deutschen Gesellschaft: Selbstentwurf und Selbstbeschreibung* (Munich, 2000), 197–207.

[67] Cf. Christina von Hodenberg, *Konsens und Krise. Eine Geschichte der westdeutschen Medienöffentlichkeit 1945–1973* (Göttingen, 2006).

[68] Adam Sisman, *A. J. P. Taylor: A Biography* (London, 1994), 214.

[69] Susan Kingsley Kent, *Making Peace: The Reconstruction of Gender in Interwar Britain* (Princeton, 1993).

[70] BAK, B145/4225: Institut für Demoskopie Allensbach, 'Die Stimmung im Bundesgebiet', no. 168 (March 1958), 2.

were specifically targeted at challenging the Christian Democrats' claim that it was a *Volkspartei* (a people's party) by highlighting its nature as a *Volksbewegung* (people's movement).[71] Rudolf S., the owner of a motorcycle shop in Braunschweig, echoed this sentiment in a letter he wrote to Walter Menzel, the chairman of the Campaign against Atomic Death, in March 1958. In it, he mentioned his and the Social Democratic Party's own democratic activism in the time before 1914, and he found little to praise in the contemporary Federal Republic: 'democratic opposition in the Bonn parliament was inappropriate', he wrote, as it could be abused by the governing party, revealing the ambiguities of extra-parliamentary political involvement in the Federal Republic: scepticism towards tolerating opponents' views went hand in hand with a commitment to direct representation. 'One polemicizes humanely', Schmidt pointed out, 'one sits in committees and even contributes to a field that one used to fight against as a socialist'. This was a situation that was reminiscent of the 'madness of 39–45'. What was required instead was 'hard, but honest words and deeds', like the ones 'by Bebel, Crispien, Südekum, etc.', when 'we marched through the streets to demonstrate'.[72]

Fundamentally, this was also a struggle over who was responsible for political representation, and where that representation should take place. This was the main purpose behind the campaign to organize *Volksbefragungen* in those West German states with *SPD* governments, plebiscites that were supposed to highlight the lack of support for Adenauer policies among the West German public. The Federal Constitutional Court ruled these plebiscites unconstitutional on the technicality that foreign and defence policies were federal matters that did not fall within the remit of the German states. But an internal memorandum that a civil servant at the Federal Ministry of the Interior wrote about the planned plebiscite in the state of Hesse revealed how this dispute was fundamentally a contest over the very form of the political and the locations at which the politics of security should be carried out. The federal civil servant wrote that plebiscites were not required to gauge public opinion, since, 'in order to detect the opinion of the people, we can today draw on the methods of so-called demoscopic research . . . that private institutes have developed following the model of the north American Gallup institute. The will of the people, by contrast, is not detected and researched, but produced and voiced.' And for that purpose a democratic polity already had 'elections and other votes' that allowed individuals to take part in the 'formation of a general will'. And

---

[71] Thomas Mergel, *Propaganda nach Hitler. Eine Kulturgeschichte des Wahlkampfs in der Bundesrepublik 1949–1990* (Göttingen, 2010), 270–81.
[72] AdsD: 2/PVAM000009: Rudolf S. to Walter Menzel, 10 March 1958.

he concluded: 'One must not simply reinterpret opinion polls as elections and elections as opinion polls.'[73]

In accordance with their emphasis on representing 'the people', campaign organizers in both countries were adamant that they represented no specific political or social group and called themselves 'classless'. Instead, they stressed that they represented humankind in their campaigns against nuclear weapons, regardless of gender, class, race, or nation. CND supporters solemnly pledged themselves to 'the common cause of mankind'.[74] Parkin's survey confirms that CND's middle-class supporters had particular problems in placing themselves within a class system.[75] We can find similar evidence for the West German movement.[76] British New Left supporters remained, however, highly critical of interpretations that neglected the class character of British society.[77]

Rather than as indications for the end of social inequalities in the 'age of affluence', 'the end of ideology', or the arrival of 'postmodern' values altruistically concerned with the fate of the less well off, these statements should be interpreted as self-descriptions that served specific political purposes in the politics of security.[78] Like discussions about 'class', such arguments about the absence of social stratification have been part of the attempts of societies and social groups to invest their own social standing and the general social structure with cultural meanings. The movements' vision of being in tune with world public opinion enabled them to create a community and human fellowship that appeared to give supporters the security they so desired.[79] At the same time, this vision was a powerful political argument that created an image of a public sphere identical to that of movement; this public sphere had merely to be activated by educating the public. Yet, like the bourgeois public sphere of the eighteenth century, it was not a reality, as Jürgen Habermas has suggested, but a 'phantasy'.[80]

---

[73] BAK 116–2442: 'Stellungnahme des BMI zu Schriftsatz der Hessischen Landesregierung vom 7.6.58', 28 June 1958. AdsD: Parteivorstand minutes, Sitzung des PV am 3.9.58 in Bonn.

[74] Hull Archives Centre, John Saville papers (JS), JS-7: 'CND Charter', n.d. [*c*.1959]; Robert Bolt, 'Do you Speak Nuclear?', *New Statesman*, 24 December 1960.

[75] Parkin, *Middle Class Radicalism*, 46.

[76] Appeal from 23 April 1957, quoted in: *Blaubuch über den Widerstand gegen die atomare Aufrüstung der Bundesrepublik*, ed. Friedenskomitee der Bundesrepublik Deutschlanded (Düsseldorf, 1957), 95–6; AdsD, DGB Archives, Abt. Organisation, 24/2182: Georg Reuter to Willi Richter, 17 March 1958.

[77] Raphael Samuel, 'Dr Abrams and the End of Politics', *New Left Review*, 5 (1960), 3.

[78] Daniel Bell, *On the Exhaustion of Political Ideas in the Fifties* (New York, 1962).

[79] IISG C100, uncatalogued section: 'The H-Bomb's Thunder', Easter March song book (*c*.1960).

[80] Cf. on this general point Harold Mah, 'Phantasies of the Public Sphere: Rethinking Habermas for Historians', *Journal of Modern History*, 72 (2000), 153–82.

The activists' desire to reach out to the public, then, provided a significant degree of the momentum for the movements.

Yet, there were not only striking differences in the ways activists sought to represent the movements to the public, but also in the interpretation by those outside the movements. In Britain, observers used middle-class stereotypes to describe the protesters, characterizations that the protesters often used themselves to enhance their political and social reputation. In West Germany, by contrast, 'class' was entirely absent from social descriptions, and, if observers and movement supporters referred to social criteria at all, they highlighted the importance of 'professions'.[81] Despite Prime Minister Harold Macmillan's announcement after the 1959 general election that 'the class war [was] over' and that the Conservatives had won it, 'class' as signifier of social structure had a much greater resonance in Britain than in the Federal Republic.[82] British concepts of 'security' thus entailed specific visions of social structure. Activists and opponents alike linked the issue of 'security' to the role the 'middle classes' should play in society. They debated the question whether, in the light of the rising affluence of the 'working class', it could still serve as the enlightened and rational pillar of society that it claimed it had been since the nineteenth century.[83]

Thus, Alan Brien described the British supporters in the *Daily Mail* as 'the sort of people who would normally spend Easter listening to a Beethoven concert on the Home Service, pouring dry sherry from a decanter for the neighbours, painting Picasso designs on hardboiled eggs…'.[84] While such assessments reflect a certain dislike of the middle classes especially among Conservatives, movement supporters, by contrast, regarded the CND's middle-class character as part of its success. A report on a gathering of CND supporters in the CND *Newsletter* in January 1959, mirroring similar reports in the national press, read:

> This was not coterie stuff, this was not any gathering of eccentrics on the lunatic fringe of world affairs. This affair has long outgrown its beard-and-dufflecoat phase. The solid bourgeois multitude here could have been a share-holders meeting—and, indeed, that was what it seriously considered

---

[81] HIS, TEM 400,01: 'Aufruf zum Ostermarsch' (March 1961); Otto, *Vom Ostermarsch zur APO*, 90.

[82] Quoted from Anthony Sampson, *Macmillan: A Study in Ambiguity* (London, 1967), 165; Mike Savage, *Identities and Social Change in Britain since 1940: The Politics of Method* (Oxford, 2010).

[83] A. J. P. Taylor, quoted by David Cannadine, *Class in Britain* (Harmondsworth, 2000), 129.

[84] *Daily Mail*, 8 April 1958; *Daily Express*, 31 March 1959.

itself to be... —which does its business, or tries to, in what the brokers would call Futures.[85]

At the same time, the involvement of such 'responsible' people in extra-parliamentary politics against nuclear weapons puzzled some sociologists. The sociologist Frank Parkin coined the term 'middle-class radicals' as a catchphrase for CND supporters and as a mirror image of the 'affluent worker'.[86]

In West Germany, by contrast, interpretations about the class-bound character of the protests had a very low salience, although social structure was becoming a fashionable topic among West German sociologists at the time.[87] Despite the persistence of social inequalities, interpretations dominated West German public discourse, which assumed the end of 'class society' and the arrival of a 'levelled-out middle-class society' (*nivellierte Mittelstandsgesellschaft*), as the sociologist Helmut Schelsky called it in a highly influential contemporary definition stemming from his study on the German family.[88] 'Generation' replaced 'class' as the master frame for the interpretation of the extra-parliamentary politics of security. 'Generation' and 'youth' played the part in West Germany that 'middle-class radicalism' played in Britain.[89]

This fact was directly linked to the 'security' that generational concepts could offer in the specific situation of post-war West Germany by relating to the politics of 'normalization' and 'stabilization' after the war. Within the West German context, the term 'generation' was ideally suited to create a world of kin and community within the movement, while connecting it to a rhetoric of social and political transformation more generally. As the discussions within and outside the West German movements focused primarily on the 'young generation', the generational framework established a link between the young generation and its function in West German economic reconstruction as central to political stability. Moreover, as the concept of 'young generation' focused on the future, rather than on the past, it allowed protesters and the general

[85] *CND Newsletter*, January 1959, 1.
[86] Parkin, *Middle Class Radicalism*, 46.
[87] Cf., for example, Ralf Dahrendorf, 'Die neue Gesellschaft. Soziale Strukturwandlungen der Nachkriegszeit', in Hans Werner Richter (ed.), *Bestandsaufnahme. Eine deutsche Bilanz 1962* (Munich, 1962), 203–20.
[88] Hans Braun, 'Die gesellschaftliche Ausgangslage der Bundesrepublik als Gegenstand der zeitgenössischen soziologischen Forschung. Ein Beitrag zur Geschichte der neueren deutschen Soziologie', *Kölner Zeitschrift für Soziologie und Sozialpsychologie*, 31 (1979), 766–95.
[89] Cf. Detlef Siegfried, '"Don't trust anyone older than 30?" Voices of Conflict and Consensus between Generations in 1960s West Germany', *Journal of Contemporary History*, 40 (2005), 727–44.

public alike to distance themselves rhetorically from the troubles of Germany's most recent past.[90] By talking about 'generation' and 'youth', West German protesters, even those belonging to age cohorts born in the late 1920s and 1930s, stylized themselves as representatives of a new and democratic Germany that had remained unscathed by the problems of the past.[91] In reality, however, students and younger people were originally not the main social basis of the West German marches.[92]

For West German supporters, referring to the 'young generation' thus became a central means of moral and political criticism and an argument for a better future against alleged authoritarian thinking. Easter March founder Hans-Konrad Tempel (born 1932) took up this theme by highlighting the younger generation's role in preventing future disasters on the scale of National Socialism. While many might have rightfully claimed that they knew nothing about the crimes of the National Socialist regime, this argument did not hold true with regard to nuclear weapons.[93] The Protestant Church President of Dortmund, Heinrich Kloppenburg (born 1903), expanded on this theme by linking the involvement of a 'young generation' to West Germany's 'liberalization': 'There is, within the young generation, a turn towards thinking on one's own, which, for many, includes an active political commitment.'[94] But, rather than relying on the independence of young people, he favoured 'guidance'.[95] Although the question of youthful lifestyles was hotly debated within the movements, many sympathetic outside observers applauded the endorsement of the emerging popular culture as a democratizing element: 'No one has yet died of jazz music, a few million, however, have died by following marching tunes', a trade-union paper wrote.[96]

---

[90] Holger Nehring, '"Generation" as political argument in West European Protest Movements in the 1960s', in Stephen Lovell (ed.), *Generations in Twentieth-Century Europe* (Basingstoke, 2007), 57–78.

[91] For the general approach adopted here cf. Bernd Weisbrod, 'Generation and Generationalität in der Neueren Geschichte', *Aus Politik und Zeitgeschichte*, B8/2005 (21 February 2005), 3–9; A. Dirk Moses, 'The Forty Fivers. A Generation between Fascism and Democracy', *German Politics and Society*, 17 (1999), 94–125.

[92] Jürgen Habermas et al., *Student und Politik: Eine soziologische Untersuchung zum politischen Bewusstsein Frankfurter Studenten* (Frankfurt/Main, 1961); Boris Spix, *Abschied vom Elfenbeinturm? Politisches Verhalten Studierender 1957–1967. Berlin und Nordrhein-Westfalen im Vergleich* (Essen, 2008).

[93] HStAD: 308–84/48, 53: Report on the 1962 Easter March to the Interior Ministry of North-Rhine Westphalia.

[94] SAPMO-BArch: DY30/IV A2/10.02/301: 'Bericht über den Ostermarsch', 11 April 1963.

[95] AdsD: Präsidium, minutes, 20 February 1961.

[96] *Welt der Arbeit*, 30 May 1958; HIS, TEM 300,03 Regional Committee West, minutes, 21 February 1962; Otto, *Vom Ostermarsch zur APO*, 92.

For the West German protesters, 'generation' was not merely oriented towards the future. It also contained specific visions of the past and thus helped the protesters to redefine and reinterpret earlier political traditions, which, they argued, had been lost in West Germany's reconstruction. Easter Marchers in particular did not regard '1945' as a 'zero hour'. Rather, they commonly characterized the period between 1945 and 1948 as 'our twenties'.[97] Their central reference point was the failed hopes of Weimar. For them, the central aim was to begin afresh by remembering a period of time that was still free of the horrors of the Third Reich. In their view, the political 'restoration' of those in government who advocated nuclear armaments referred not to direct continuities with the past, but to the political elite's refusal to take the policy options of the 1920s seriously. Self-enlightenment about Germany's most recent past in which the activists themselves had participated as young children became one of the central benchmarks of their private and public activities.[98] The West German government's opinion pollsters, by contrast, identified the lack of concerns and the lack of general education and political interests with the mood of opposition against nuclear weapons. The Allensbach Institute singled out workers and women as particularly susceptible to the emerging protests and thus argued for a broad campaign of *Volkserziehung* ('people's education') to stem the tide.[99]

The West German voices more critical of the protests drew on the same assumptions and experiences of the crucial function of the 'young generation' for the stabilization and democratization of the young West German polity. But they differed substantially about what this contribution should look like. They regarded youthful lifestyles as representative of 'youth protests' and, therefore, as dangerous. For them, 'youth' and 'young generation' became metaphors of social threats, social risk, and social disintegration, in short: markers of insecurity.[100] In their view, the ideal young person was pragmatic, involved in private affairs and, in Helmut

[97] Joachim Kaiser, 'Phasenverschiebungen und Einschnitte in der kulturellen Entwicklung', in Martin Broszat (ed.), *Zäsuren nach 1945: Essays zur Periodisierung der deutschen Nachkriegsgeschichte* (Munich, 1990), 69–74, here 71.

[98] Cf. Arno Klönne and Karl Heinz Westphal, 'Generation der Anpassung?', *Solidarität*, 6 (1958), 1–2; Friedhelm Boll, 'Hitler-Jugend und "skeptische Generation": Sozialdemokratie und Jugend nach 1945', in Dieter Dowe (ed.), *Partei und soziale Bewegung: Kritische Beiträge zur Geschichte der SPD seit 1945* (Bonn, 1993), 33–57, here 39.

[99] Cf. BAK, B145/4224: 'Die Stimmung im Bundesgebiet: Die Atomrüstung', no. 191 (April 1957); BAK, B145/4230: 'Stimmung im Bundesgebiet: Volksbefragung populär', no. 354 (May 1958).

[100] BAK, ZSg. 1/262.1, 4: 'Presseanalysen zum Ostermarsch', 1961 and 1962.

Schelsky's words, 'sceptical' towards the political process, but not directly involved in it.[101]

Young protesters with their alleged emotionality challenged the precarious order of the young West German state and threatened to bring back 'Weimar conditions'. Movement references to kinship and community in particular raised conservatives' eyebrows: they feared that the movement would replace 'rational' description of the German present with utopian visions of the future, like the National Socialists in the past and the GDR in the present. Instead, they preferred models of 'private' life after the alleged politicizations of the masses during the National Socialist regime.[102]

In Britain, by contrast, generational arguments failed to gain the salience they obtained in the Federal Republic and remained confined to communist and radical–socialist circles within CND.[103] Although there existed a 'Youth CND' and a student section, and although there was a rising interest among activists, government officials, parties, and sociological circles to analyze and understand problems of 'youth',[104] the descriptions of the campaign as a youth movement came from outside and had mostly negative connotations. One reason for this difference lay in the differences in student numbers and their importance within society as a whole. By the early 1960s, there were about 118,000 students in full-time higher education (compared to 82,000 in 1954/55), and their numbers only rose after the expansion of the university system in the wake of the 1963 Robbins Report.[105] West Germany, by contrast, had around 247,000 full-time students in 1960.[106] But the relative absence of 'generational' patterns of self-observation also reflected the fact that recent British history lacked the sharp ruptures that Germany had experienced. Hence, when British observers discussed CND in generational terms,

---

[101] Cf. Robert Jenke, *Ostermarsch-Betrachtungen* (Cologne, 1964), 45–58, and Jenke, *Ostermarsch-Nachbetrachtungen* (Cologne, 1964), 34–41. On the concept, cf. Helmut Schelsky, *Die skeptische Generation: Eine Soziologie der deutschen Jugend* (Cologne and Düsseldorf, 1957), especially 488–9.

[102] Kai Herrmann, 'Erfolg und viele Kilometer', *Die Zeit*, 3 April 1964.

[103] *CND Bulletin* (January 1959), 2; Paul Rose, 'Manchester Left Club on Youth', *New Left Review*, 1 (1960), 70–1. An exception is [E. P. Thompson], *New Reasoner* (summer 1959), 1.

[104] BLPES, CND/8/2: Polls at the universities of Oxford and Cambridge (1961); for the background, cf. Lawrence Black, *The Political Culture of the Left in Affluent Britain, 1951–64: Old Labour, New Britain?* (Basingstoke, 2003), 67–76; Steven Fielding, *Labour and Cultural Change* (Manchester and New York, 2003), 168–82.

[105] David Butler and Gareth Butler (eds), *Twentieth-Century British Political Facts 1900–2000* (London, 2000), 366.

[106] Helmut Köhler, *Der relative Schul- und Hochschulbesuch in der Bundesrepublik 1952–1975: Ein Indikator für die Entwicklung des Bildungswesens* (Berlin, 1978), 168.

they denied any political connotations, but focused on the threat to morality instead or saw 'generation' as subordinate to the issue of 'class' and the effects of affluence.[107] The age cohort that defined Schelsky's 'sceptical generation' was a vague 'Generation X' in Britain.[108]

The interpretations of how the movement activists presented themselves and how they were represented endowed the movements with seemingly fixed and stable addresses within society. 'Society' as a totality, however, is, as Ernesto Laclau has pointed out, itself an 'impossible object', and imagining, creating, and producing it required significant work and political effort.[109] But these processes of identification also made this political effort possible in the first place. Identifying the protesters and the protest movement opened up the space for imagining a new world on the basis of hegemonic concepts of security. Such interpretative work was itself part of the discussions about movement politics: on the part of the sociologists, they were exercises in classifying society; for the governments and the protesters, they involved more directly a struggle for power over how the activists' experiences and expectations were and should be represented in the political process. A letter by Wilhelm Keller from a conscientious objectors' association to the chair of the West German campaign illustrates how this worked in practice in July 1959, at a time when the main campaigning effort was already over. Pleading for leaving classic social divisions aside and mentioning his own pacifist credentials, he argued that 'it [was] high time to move from an ideological and irreal pacifism towards a humanitarian, clear concept that is, given the threat of atomic war, the only alternative to self-annihilation'.[110] For Keller, as for most others who joined the movements in both countries, one utopia was beginning to give way to another.

[107] Uwe Kitzinger, writing in the *Listener*, 16 May 1963, 2; Driver, *The Disarmers*, 59, 131; Ferdynand Zweig, *The Student in the Age of Anxiety* (London, 1963), 199.
[108] Charles Hamblett and Jane Deverson, *Generation X* (London, 1964).
[109] Ernesto Laclau, *New Reflections on the Revolution of our Time* (London, 1990), 92.
[110] AdsD, 2/PVAM0000021: Wilhelm Keller to Walter Menzel, n.d. [rec. Am 15 July 1959].

3

Political Experiences and the Security of Community

The attempts at sociological identification and definition by activists and observers alike were at once struggles over the representation of the activists' political experiences. This chapter explores these diverse political experiences behind anti-nuclear-weapons activism and is concerned with delineating the social networks on which the British and West German campaigns rested. It charts the processes during which people in both Britain and Germany turned into activists, and seeks to uncover the diverse genealogies of motivations that led people towards the campaigns. This chapter's focus is on the main (and often overlapping and interconnected) groups that were involved in the protests, as most of the activists still identified themselves with other social groups and parties: intellectuals, Christians, members of the labour movements, youth movement activists, and pacifists.

Many activists were quite keen to maintain their pre-existing identifications, be they party-political or religious, and they regarded their involvement in the anti-nuclear-weapons movements as an attempt to rescue what they thought had been lost in their own life worlds. Most of them came to the campaigns because of experiences of profound dissonance within their own organizations, and they regarded their activities as both restoration and rejuvenation: just as they did not see that the threat of nuclear weapons was properly represented in the official politics of security, they also had a problem finding their own experiences, memories, hopes, and dreams represented in the various personal and organizational contexts to which they belonged. This resulted in highly ambiguous temporalities, as the momentum behind the protests derived as much from efforts at restoring something that had been lost, as from creating something new. In both countries, then, political, social, and cultural traditions, understood not as reified entities, but in terms of the manner in which knowledge about politics was passed on, were crucial in linking individual activists to the evolving campaigns.

Both countries saw 'multiple restorations' of utopian knowledges of political transformation that harked back to the 1920s and the hopes for creating a national moral community in the wake of war.[1] In Britain, this temporality found its expressions in the many forms of democratic populism that emerged from the Second World War; in West Germany we could see similar attempts to recreate a ground from which democracy and civility could be re-created and to revive an awareness of the political debates of the 1920s.[2] They linked the Depression and the outbreak of the Second World War 'in a discourse of democracy and public good'.[3] In Britain, such conceptualizations rested on the belief that wartime and the immediate post-war had created 'an existential reality to the organic conception of society in a way that had never been achieved by abstract analysis'.[4] It was the feelings that these hopes had been disappointed that allowed the anti-nuclear-weapons movements in both countries to emerge.

In both countries, the debates about nuclear weapons created, in different sections of society, very similar sentiments of a lack of representation of their experiences of the political process, in particular between their desire for security, on the one hand, and an international system and government policies that seemed to further death and destruction, on the other. J. B. Priestley expressed the feelings of many when he wrote that the MPs who had made the decision for nuclear weapons were 'surrounded by an atmosphere of power politics, intrigue, secrecy and insane invention'.[5] The activists believed that the normal political channels no longer sufficed to express their political aims. Yet the ways in which the activists framed and voiced their experiences were not entirely new departures. The activists brought with them their own cultural assumptions, which were still connected to their individual life worlds. The movements were, therefore, not merely the expressions of insecurity in the nuclear age.

---

[1] Jeffrey Herf, 'Multiple Restorations: German Political Traditions and the Interpretation of Nazism, 1945–1946', *Central European History*, 26 (1993), 21–55.

[2] Geoff Eley, 'Legacies of Antifascism: Constructing Democracy in Postwar Europe', *New German Critique*, 67 (1996), 73–100; Sean Forner, 'Für eine demokratische Erneuerung Deutschlands: Kommunikationsprozesse und Deutungsmuster engagierter Demokraten nach 1945', *Geschichte und Gesellschaft*, 33 (2007), 228–57.

[3] Geoff Eley, 'When Europe was New: Liberation and the Making of the Post-War Era', in Monica Riera and Gavin Schaffer (eds), *The Lasting War. Society and Identity in Britain, France and Germany after 1945* (Basinsgtoke, 2008), 17–43, here 39.

[4] Jose Harris, 'Political Ideas and the Debate on State Welfare, 1940–45', in Harold L. Smit (ed.), *War and Social Change: British Society in the Second World.War* (Manchester, 1986), 233–63, here 236.

[5] J. B. Priestley, 'Britain and the Nuclear Bombs', *New Statesman,* 54 (2 November 1957), 554–6, here 554.

They also offered the activists communities that created interpersonal security. While the structures of the debates in Britain and West Germany were quite similar, they differed in their meanings and the exact contents.

INTELLECTUALS

The entire CND executive until the early 1960s was a revival of the extra-parliamentary progressive movements, groupings, and 'think tanks' that had mushroomed in Britain during the 1930s.[6] Although its members rarely explicitly called themselves members of an 'elite', they were carried by the belief that their reasonableness and education would ensure that they represented disinterested values. They believed that these values would allow them to reconcile the interest claims within the British population to what they regarded as the 'general will'.[7] They now applied the civilizing mission that they had previously demanded in the context of British Empire to their home country; modes of colonial knowledge were applied to construct a vision of domestic British culture during the cold war.[8] West German intellectuals and scientists, by observing the British campaign, applied this civilizing gaze to their own campaign, and also conceived of it as a mission to civilize and democratize the young West German democracy.

The activities of some of those engaged in the first CND executive can be linked to the tradition of post-Victorian intellectuals who regarded themselves as 'public moralists' and assumed that they had to school the citizens in the necessary public and private virtues, thus pulling the nation along the road of moral progress. Affluence, shielding 'the masses' from the challenge of dealing with the nuclear threat, appeared to make this path increasingly unlikely.[9] And yet, the 'public moralists' within CND were uneasy about the appeal of their campaign. In his autobiography, the journalist and CND activist Mervyn Jones recalls watching the columns

---

[6] For the general context, see Peter Mandler and Susan Pedersen, 'Introduction: The British Intelligentsia after the Victorians', in Mandler and Pedersen (eds), *After the Victorians: Private Conscience and Public Duty in Modern Britain* (London and New York, 1994), 1–28.

[7] Jon Lawrence, 'Paternalism, Class, and the British Path to Modernity', in Simon Gunn and James Vernon (eds), *The Peculiarities of Liberal Modernity in Imperial Britain* (Berkeley and Los Angeles, 2011) 147–64, here 158.

[8] Jed Esty, *A Shrinking Island. Modernism and National Culture in England* (Princeton, 2004), 9–11.

[9] Stefan Collini, *Public Moralists: Political Thought and Intellectual Life in Britain 1850–1930* (Oxford, 1991); Collini, *Absent Minds. Intellectuals in Britain* (Oxford, 2006), 171–5 (on the 'long fifties') and 375–92 (on A. J. P. Taylor).

gather for the final day of the 1959 Aldermaston March together with the editor of the *New Statesman*, Kingsley Martin. As he stared at the thousands of people, Martin asked Jones: 'What on earth are we going to do with all these people?'[10]

A look at the biographies of the members of the first CND executive committee illustrates this interpretation. CND's first chairman, the Canon of St Paul's Cathedral in London, John Collins, had been involved in the group Christian Action, which aimed at spreading the Gospel within a society that he perceived as increasingly secular and godless. The group urged the application of the Christian principle of charity in domestic and international politics. Collins had, together with Trevor Huddleston and Michal Scott, been involved in anti-apartheid campaigns in South Africa over the course of the 1960s.[11]

The editor of the *New Statesman*, Kingsley Martin, born in 1897, was the son of a pacifist Victorian minister and had participated in earlier peace protests.[12] The Labour politician Michael Foot, born in 1913 and thus one of the youngest member of the Executive Committee, was editor of the *Tribune*, the newspaper of the Labour Left.[13] The writer J. B. Priestley, born in 1894, and his wife, the archaeologist Jacquetta Hawkes, were socially conscious intellectuals.[14] He drew extensively on the utopian strands of nineteenth-century forms of socialism, which were the product of middle-class compassion rather than proletarian resentment.[15]

CND's president Bertrand Russell, born in 1872, then in his eighties and in his position until 1960, could look back not only on its earlier involvement in anti-nuclear protests, but on a whole political life that had been characterized by a reluctance to use the traditional political machinery.[16] He had been imprisoned during the First World War for an article on peace that was deemed to be seditious, and he had advocated pacifism in the 1930s.[17] Now, in the late 1950s and early 1960s, he felt that he

---

[10] Mervyn Jones, *Chances* (London, 1987), 161.

[11] MRC, MSS 157/3/I/CS/1-78: John Collins to Victor Gollancz, 21 February 1947; Collins, *Faith under Fire*; Rob Skinner, 'The Moral Foundations of British Anti-Apartheid Activism, 1946–1960', *Journal of Southern African Studies*, 35 (2009), 399–416; Tom Buchanan, *East Wind. China and the British Left, 1925–1970* (Oxford, 2012).

[12] Cecil Hewitt Rolph, *Kingsley: The Life, Letters and Diary of Kingsley Martin* (London, 1973), 323–5.

[13] Morgan, *Labour People*, 278.

[14] J. B. Priestley, 'Making Writing Simple', in Priestley, *Delight* (London, 1949), 71.

[15] Cf. Chris Waters, 'J. B. Priestley 1894–1984: Englishness and the Politics of Nostalgia', in Pedersen and Mandler (eds), *After the Victorians*, 209–24; John Baxendale, *Priestley's England: J. B. Priestley and English Culture* (Manchester, 2007).

[16] Ronald W. Clark, *The Life of Bertrand Russell* (London 1975), 119.

[17] Cf. Ray Monk, *Bertrand Russell: The Ghost of Madness 1921–1970* (London, 2000), 163–216.

had to become involved, since 'our mood was like that of St Jerome and St Augustine watching the fall of the Roman Empire and the crumbling of a civilization which had seemed as indestructible as granite'.[18] Peggy Duff, the organizing secretary of CND, had moved from one radical cause to another, covering 'Save Europe Now', social reform, and capital punishment before becoming active in CND.[19]

Victor Gollancz, born in 1893—himself active in many other extra-parliamentary movements—agreed to become a sponsor of the Campaign.[20] He had launched the Left Book Club in 1936, had supported the 'popular front', and had been involved in the British campaign for famine relief in central Europe immediately after 1945.[21] Particularly remarkable is the example of Lord Simon of Wythenshawe (born in 1879), a Manchester industrialist and social reformer, president of Manchester CND, and for a short time treasurer of the national CND.[22] He wrote in his *Nuclear Diary:* 'I was free of executive work and decided that the nuclear problem was incomparably more serious than my favourite population problem or anything else.'[23]

Similar patterns can also be seen with other members of the first executive. Richard Acland, born in 1906, was co-opted later. The eldest son of Sir Francis Acland MP, he had, as a Liberal MP from 1935 onwards, been involved in the popular front activities of the 1930s. He held devout religious views that were the source of his political commitment and had been, together with Priestley, co-founder of the Common Wealth Party.[24] The party had been created to fill at least partially the vacuum caused by Labour's adherence to an electoral truce with the Conservatives during the Second World War: Peggy Duff had been the party's organizer, Kingsley Martin had expressed an interest, and J. B. Priestley was one of the party's co-founders.[25] CND's early executive thus almost looked like a reincarnation of the Common Wealth Party.

---

[18] Bertrand Russell, 'A Fifty-Six Year Friendship', in *Gilbert Murray: An Unfinished Autobiography* (London, 1960), 209.

[19] Duff, *Left, Left, Left.*

[20] MRC, MSS 181: Executive Committee, minutes, 27 February 1958.

[21] MRC, MSS 157/3/ND/152: Gollancz to Canon Collins, 15 September 1959; Ruth Dudley Edwards, *Victor Gollancz: A Biography* (London, 1987).

[22] Bertrand Russell, 'Campaign for Nuclear Disarmament', in Ian Hey (ed.), *80th Birthday Book for Ernest Darwin Simon: Lord Simon of Wythenshawe, b. 9th October 1879* (Stockport, 1959), 61–2, here 62.

[23] Manchester Archives and Local Studies Unit (MALSU), M 11 8/2: Nuclear Diary, 1.

[24] Richard Acland, *Only One Battle* (London, 1937), 92.

[25] J. B. Priestley, 'Hard Times', *Listener*, 23 October 1947, 711–12; 30 October 1947, 755–6; 6 November 1947, 804–5.

Donald Soper, a devout Methodist, born in 1903, formerly an active member of the Temperance Society, who had joined the Labour Party and the Peace Pledge Union (PPU) in 1937, was also co-opted to CND's executive later. Similarly, the Oxford historian A. J. P. Taylor, born in 1906, could look back on a life on the left of British politics. When active in CND, he had only recently published the *The Trouble Makers*, his Oxford Ford lectures on the tradition of radical dissent in British foreign policy. He wrote in his memoirs that, on joining CND, he 'had Bright and Cobden much in mind...I wanted to show that like them I understood the practical case for nuclear bombs as well as their advocates did, indeed better'.[26] And some reviewers of the book agreed: 'Taylor himself is a troublemaker.'[27] In the 1930s and in the 1940s, as in CND's time in the late 1950s, many of these dissenting idealists had been part of a rather uneasy coalition of short-lived organizations and campaigns, often in connection with campaigns for a 'popular front' against European fascism in the 1930s, in particular the Left Book Club,[28] of Christian groups of social reform around William Temple, or nonconformist circles.[29] Links to previous radical movements also existed on the regional and local levels. Mrs Malvin Side, from Hampstead Garden Suburb, who attended all Aldermaston Marches until the early 1970s, had started her political career at 14 as a suffragette follower of Sylvia Pankhurst.[30] Hodgess Roper, the co-chairman of the University Campaign for Nuclear Disarmament at Oxford in the 1960s, equally came from a 'radical middle class' background.[31]

The prominence of such left-wing intellectuals and groups had been boosted by Labour's election victory in 1945. Yet their members' hopes for a reordering of domestic and international society in order to prevent future wars and economic crises were soon shattered, as such visions of a socialist commonwealth, of planning, and of establishing Britain as the core of a 'third force' between the two superpowers rapidly lost credence with the apparently aggressive policies of the Soviet Union in Eastern

---

[26] A. J. P. Taylor, *A Personal History* (London, 1983), 229; A. J. P. Taylor, *The Trouble Makers: Dissent over Foreign Policy, 1792–1939* (London, 1957). On the background cf. Kathleen Burk, *Troublemaker. The Life and History of A. J. P. Taylor* (New Haven and London, 2000), 212–18.

[27] 'The Seventh Veil', *New Statesman*, 28 September 1957, 376–7.

[28] Stuart Samuels, 'The Left Book Club', *Journal of Contemporary History*, 1 (1966), 65–86; Ben Pimlott, *Labour and the Left in the 1930s* (Cambridge, 1977).

[29] E. R. Norman, *Church and Society in England, 1770–1970* (Oxford, 1976), 280–370.

[30] *The Times*, 4 April 1972, p. 2.

[31] BLPES, CND/1/3: Newsletter Oxford University CND, October 1960.

Europe.[32] When cold war tensions appeared to subside in the wake of the Geneva Conference in 1955 and when the Soviet Union started to send out signals of 'peaceful coexistence', these ideas were able to regain some of their original appeal. Processes of societal change that characterized domestic political discussions added a further dimension to the original organizers' desires to campaign for social and political change. The growing affluence in British society after the end of rationing in 1954 seemed to them to destroy the very bases on which such a reordering might rest: urgent action was, therefore, required.[33]

Although West German activists faced a profoundly different situation, given that most direct links to socialist traditions had been violently interrupted by the National dictatorship, the West German movements also relied initially on a group of academics and left-wing intellectuals who sought to educate the public. This happened in direct engagement with the framework of a civilizing mission that their British colleagues had applied. On 4 April 1957, West German scientists issued a declaration that highlighted this theme. In it, eighteen science professors from the University of Göttingen, among them Carl Friedrich von Weizsäcker, Otto Hahn, Max Born, and Friedrich von Laue, stressed their responsibility for 'possible consequences of scientific research' and rejected participation in future research for nuclear weapons for the Federal Army. They thus evoked not only their scientific responsibilities, but also their political responsibilities as citizens. The statement followed the stationing of American short-range nuclear missile batteries in April 1957 and the emergence of institutionalized nuclear research in the Federal Republic.[34] In particular, the scientists criticized Chancellor Adenauer's statement that tactical nuclear weapons were but an advanced form of artillery as 'ignorant'.[35] They thus applied the same language and arguments that the British physicist Joseph Rotblat, as well as Albert Einstein and Bertrand Russell had used in their statements on the nuclear issue:[36] their own declaration against purchasing nuclear equipment for the West German army argued by juxtaposing

[32] Jonathan Schneer, 'Hopes Deferred or Shattered: The British Labour Left and the Third Force Movement, 1945–1949', *Journal of Modern History*, 56 (1984), 199–200.

[33] On these debates, cf. Black, *The Political Culture of the Left*.

[34] For example, in his acceptance speech for the peace prize of the German booksellers' association in 1963; cf. Carl Friedrich von Weizsäcker, *Der bedrohte Frieden: Politische Aufsätze 1945–1981* (Munich, 1983), 125–37; Otto Hahn, *Mein Leben* (Munich, 1968), 231; Werner Kliefoth, 'Atomrundschau', *Atomkernenergie*, 2 (1957), 50.

[35] Text in Weizsäcker, *Der bedrohte Friede*, 29–30.

[36] Andrew Brown, *Keeper of the Nuclear Conscience: The Work and Life of Joseph Rotblat* (Oxford, 2012), 119–34. On perceptions in West Germany, see, for example, *Hannoversche Presse*, 11 July 1955.

pure scientific rationality with the dangers of political power and authority in the nuclear age. Like their British counterparts, West German scientists and intellectuals sought to universalize and make public their private moral norms. Their personal political involvement thus became an act of public philanthropy.[37] Only through a holistic application of moral norms could the dangers of nuclear weapons be avoided. Such moral knowledge could be created only through a campaign of 'education', for which the scientists would act as the intellectual leaders.[38]

The scientists who drafted the Göttingen Declaration thus shaped a new mode of political intervention in post-war West German politics, whereas Adenauer stressed the political nature of his decision and insisted on the differentiation of the political system. The scientists a mode of public commitment through rational discussion, critical decision, and the opening-up of decision-making to democratic scrutiny through the application of seemingly universal norms that Jürgen Habermas would later theorize in his book on the public sphere.[39] It appealed especially to those Protestant scientists and scholars, such as Georg Picht and Carl Friedrich von Weizsäcker, who were already open to holistic ideas through their engagement with life reform movements.[40] Only a minority of British scientists regarded science as endowed with a social function and an important role in social change.[41]

The West German scientists' statements were linked to transnational initiatives for nuclear disarmament by the scientific community, such as the manifesto by the physicist Albert Einstein and the philosopher Bertrand Russell from 1955, which urged for a peace initiative beyond the boundaries of the cold war and led to the foundation of the Pugwash Conferences in July 1957.[42] The participants in the Pugwash Conferences, founded in

---

[37] On the roots and structures of this thinking, see Bernd Weisbrod, 'Philanthropie und bürgerliche Kultur: Zur Sozialgeschichte des viktorianischen Bürgertums', in Hartmut Berghoff und Dieter Ziegler (eds), *Pionier und Nachzügler? Vergleichende Studien zur Geschichte Großbritanniens und Deutschlands im Zeitalter der Industrialisierung, Festschrift für Sidney Pollard* (Bochum, 1995), 205–20, here 209.

[38] <http://www.hdg.de/lemo/html/dokumente/JahreDesAufbausInOstUndWest_erklaerungGoettingerErklaerung/index.html> (accessed 15 April 2012).

[39] 13 April 1957, *Dokumente zur Deutschlandpolitik, III*, 3, 597–604, on 597–8; Carson, *Heisenberg in the Atomic Age*, 323, 338.

[40] Ulrich Raulff, *Kreis ohne Meister: Stefan Georges Nachleben. Eine abgründige Geschichte* (Munich, 2010), 409–27.

[41] Cf. Guy Ortolano, *The Two Cultures Controversy: Science, Literature, and Cultural Politics in Postwar Britain* (Cambridge, 2009).

[42] The text of the manifesto can be found in Morton Grodzins and Eugene Rabinowitch (eds), *The Atomic Age: Scientists in National and World Affairs. Articles from the Bulletin of the Atomic Scientists* (New York, 1963), 12. On the origins of the declaration and its reception in Britain, cf. Bertrand Russell, 'World Conference of Scientists', *Bulletin of Atomic Scientists*, 12 (1956), 41–3; Werner Kliefoth, 'Der Geist von Pugwash', *Atomkernenergie*, 3 (1958), 455–8.

the wake of the manifesto by Professor Joseph Rotblat, regarded themselves as members of an international association of scientific discussion that would lead to a thaw beyond the Iron Curtain rather than as directly related to the connections between nuclear armaments and democracy in different nations.[43] In West Germany, the manifesto found echoes in the Mainau Declaration of Nobel Prize winners of May 1955 and the declaration of the Association of German Physics Societies (*Verband deutscher physikalischer Gesellschaften*) of 26 September 1955, which contained statements against nuclear energy in general and which assumed scientists' special responsibilities with regard to sensible use of nuclear energy.[44]

The resonance that the scientists' arguments had in West Germany can be gleaned from the name the mass media gave the scientists: 'Göttingen 18'. Most of the scientists were indeed affiliated to the Göttingen Max Planck Institute, which had been among the very first research institutions to resume research on the application of nuclear energy after the Allied ban on nuclear research had been relaxed. The title alluded to the manifesto of the 'Göttingen 7' of November 1837, which had resulted in the expulsion of seven famous professors from their university posts after they had endorsed certain liberal aims that tapped traditions of German liberal democracy.[45] Like German scientists in the 1920s, and like the public intellectuals in CND, the Göttingen scientists saw themselves as educators of the public.[46] Yet, unlike in Britain, these academics were not instrumental in setting up the West German campaign, but primarily provided it with legitimacy.[47]

Yet, although they claimed to be 'apolitical', they issued a political prescriptions for West Germany's health by advocating the renunciation of nuclear weapons.[48] The 'politics of the past' played a role in their involvement as well: most of the scientists had been involved in state-sponsored research projects during the National Socialist period,

[43] Brown, *Keeper of the Nuclear Conscience*, 135–47.

[44] Text in Joseph Rotblat, *Scientists in the Quest for Peace*, 139; German discussions in AdsD, Karl Bechert papers, 21: Minutes of the Membership Association of German Physical Associations, 25 September 1955, 3–7.

[45] *Vorwärts*, 17 May 1957, 1.

[46] Cf. Hans Paul Bahrdt, 'Schamanen der modernen Gesellschaft? Das Verhältnis der Wissenschaftler zur Politik', *atomzeitalter*, 4 (1961), 75–9; Kurt Sontheimer, 'Erfordert das Atomzeitalter eine neue politische Wissenschaft?', *Zeitschrift für Politik*, NS 11 (1964), 208–23; Carl Friedrich von Weizsäcker, *Die Verantwortung der Wissenschaft im Atomzeitalter* (Göttingen, 1957).

[47] Hans Baumgarten, 'Die Taktik der Atomforscher', *Frankfurter Allgemeine Zeitung*, 15 April 1957, 1; AdsD, ASAF000177: Willy Huhn to Ansgar Skriver and Manfred Rexin, 27 November 1959.

[48] Cf., for example, Prof. Dr. Walther Gerlach, 'Die Verantwortung des Physikers', *Stimme der Gemeinde*, 10 (1958), cols 129–34.

and they felt that only international involvement and moral language could help them to become reintegrated into the international physics community.[49] In this self-interpretation, much popularized in Robert Jungk's account *Brighter than a Thousand Suns*, German scientists could appear as untainted by any involvement in the National Socialist regime: unlike scientists in other countries, they had made the moral decision to refuse working with the government to develop nuclear weapons.[50]

While the majority of West German intellectuals played not an active role, but mainly a representative one, in the foundation of the protests, an exception was the Munich Committee against Atomic Armaments (*Komitee gegen Atomrüstung*), which had been founded by the essayist and writer Hans Werner Richter and resembled CND in form and social structure. The Committee's membership file reads like a list of the Munich intelligentsia and of the educated bourgeoisie, with the politicians Hildegard Hamm-Brücher (from the liberal *Freie Demokratische Partei* (*FDP*)), Hans-Jochen Vogel (*SPD*), the left Catholic intellectual Carl Amery, and a number of Munich booksellers, publishers, and editors.[51] Moreover, Richter managed to attract a group of politically active writers whom he knew from the literary circle *Gruppe 47* (literally 'Group 47'), which he had helped to found in 1947. In many of his letters and lectures, the 'liberalization' of West German political culture and the immunization against the dangers from right-wing groupings formed the leading arguments.[52] In an odd mixture of social elitism and critical aims, they regarded themselves as intellectuals who could provide society with memory and moral guidance.[53] Yet, in terms of numbers, these public intellectuals were rather marginal in the extraparliamentary politics of security. In both countries, the vast majority of supporters joined the movements because they felt that their desires for security were not adequately represented by either the labour movements, or the churches.

---

[49] Robert Lorenz, *Protest der Physiker: Die 'Göttinger Erklärung' von 1957* (Bielefeld, 2011), 218.

[50] Robert Jungk, *Heller als Tausend Sonnen* (Frankfurt/Main, 1956) (English edn: London 1958). This has, however, been proven a myth by Mark Walker, 'Legenden um die deutsche Atombombe', *Vierteljahrshefte für Zeitgeschichte*, 38 (1990), 45–74.

[51] HWR, 72.86.512: Hans Werner Richter to Siegfried Bußjäger, 26 February 1960.

[52] Hans Werner Richter to Ernst Nolte, 10 March 1957, in Hans Werner Richter, *Briefe*, ed. Sabine Cofalla (Munich, 1997), 245; Richter to Leonhardt, 11 November 1961, in Richter, *Briefe*, 378–9.

[53] HWR, 72.86.512, 65: Press Statement of the Munich Committee against Atomic Armaments, 14 April 1958; HWR, 72.85.526, 42–63: Hans Werner Richter, 'Bilanz einer Generation' [1967].

CHRISTIANS ON THE MOVE

The experiences of a clash between personal experiences and expectations were particularly pronounced among British and West German Christians. A minority of Christians in both countries increasingly felt that institutionalized religion failed to live up to its fundamental tenets in an age of potential nuclear war.[54] The protests against nuclear weapons offered Christian activists an alternative home in which they could translate their fears into demands for security. The general context within which Christians framed their expectations was the belief, first codified by St Augustine as a norm for individual judgements of conscience, that wars fought by Christians had to be 'just', in terms of both their causes and their military practices.[55] Mass warfare, in particular the bombing of cities in the Second World War and the destructive power of nuclear weapons, put the doctrine under increasing strain. Protestant Churches in both Britain and West Germany as well as on the global ecumenical level condemned nuclear weapons in the most drastic terms.[56] As the Anglican Church was part of the fabric of the English state, and because of the traditional proximity of German Protestantism towards government as well as the close relationship between the Catholic hierarchy and the West German Adenauer government, official opposition to nuclear weapons from these groups remained rather ambivalent and subdued: this only helped accentuate many Anglicans' disappointment with their church's stance. There were, in fact, only about twelve 'unilateralist bishops and suffragans in England and Wales', out of over a hundred—namely, those from Manchester, Hulme, Birmingham, Chichester, Southwark, Llandaff, Bangor, Plymouth, and Woolwich.[57]

A minority of Christians in Britain and West Germany were increasingly dissatisfied with the ambivalent official stance of their church institutions towards what they regarded as the fundamental issue of security.

[54] On the general context in West Germany, see Christian Schmidtmann, *Katholische Studierende 1945–1973: Ein Beitrag zur Kultur- und Sozialgeschichte der Bundesrepublik Deutschland* (Paderborn, 2005), and Holger Nehring, '"The long, long night is over": The Campaign for Nuclear Disarmament, "Generation" and the Politics of Religion (1957–1964)', in Jane Garnett et al. (eds), *Redefining Christian Britain* (London, 2007), 138–47.

[55] Roger Ruston, *A Say in the End of the World: Morals and British Nuclear Weapons Policy 1941–1987* (Oxford, 1989), 17–20.

[56] British Council of Churches, *The Era of Atomic Power* (London, 1946), 7, 19; *Evanston to New Delhi 1954–1961: Report of the Central Committee to the Third Assembly of the World Council of Churches, New Delhi* (Geneva, 1961); Dianne Kirby, 'The Church of England and the Cold War Nuclear Debate', *Twentieth Century British History*, 4 (1993), 250–83.

[57] Driver, *The Disarmers*, 200; Kirby, 'Church', 281.

Canon Collins expressed the feelings of many British and West German activists when he wondered how 'a Christian or a liberal man or woman [could] stand such a denial of the basic rule that only love can expel fear?'[58] In Britain, this unease had already begun to take shape during the Second World War, when the Royal Air Force had started to bomb German civilian targets during the night, and had been galvanized into a movement against aerial bombing under the leadership of George Bell, the Bishop of Chichester, who was also a vocal advocate of unilateral nuclear disarmament.[59] In West Germany, a general scepticism towards Catholic Adenauer's foreign and defence policies added to their unease.[60] Paradoxically, both Protestant and Catholic activists in West Germany thus shared some of the same assumptions about the dangerous proximity between the Catholic Church and the Adenauer government, with *secular* critics of the '*CDU* state' among the supporters. In particular, younger Catholics in West Germany became increasingly dissatisfied with the disjuncture between Catholic moral norms, on the one hand, and, on the other, the political reality of German Catholicism, which entertained close links with the Adenauer government.[61]

But the pronouncedly Protestant activists were not only dissatisfied with the ways in which their churches addressed questions that they regarded as of supreme ethical importance. Fundamentally, their engagement in the campaigns is also an indication of the core fact that the churches had lost their ability to create a valid explanation of society and to act as an ethical guide to politics. They wanted to resurrect this claim. This shift was especially pronounced in the West German Protestant Church. In its 'formula of impotence' ('Ohnmachtsformal') that was supposed to solve the stand-off between the more conservative Lutherans and the more progressive sections within the church, it stated explicitly that it was, even within itself, unable to produce one valid explanation.[62] This

---

[58] Quoted in *Die Welt*, 19 February 1958; 'Kirche, Atom, Friede', *Junge Kirche*, 19 (1958), 159–63, here 160; George Bell, Bishop of Chichester, *Nuclear War and Peace* (= Peace Aims Pamphlet, no. 60) (London, 1955), 48–54; British Council of Churches, *The Era of Atomic Power*, 53–6, 40, 53; Methodist Church, *Declarations of Conference on Social Questions* (London, 1959), 44.

[59] Bell, *Nuclear War and Peace*.

[60] Gerhard Schmidtchen, *Protestanten und Katholiken. Soziologische Analyse konfessioneller Kultur* (Berne, 1973), 244.

[61] Walter Dirks, 'Christ und Bürger in der Bundesrepublik', *Frankfurter Hefte*, 13 (1958), 673–85, here 673. Cf. Daniel Gerster, *Friedensdialoge im Kalten Krieg: Eine Geschichte der Katholiken in der Bundesrepublik* (Frankfurt/Main, 2012), 56–76.

[62] *Berlin 1958*: *Bericht über die Tagung der zweiten Synode der EKD* (Hanover, 1959), 455–6; 'Heidelberger Thesen' [1959], printed in Günther Howe (ed.), *Atomzeitalter, Krieg und Frieden* (Witten and Berlin, 1959), 226–36. For Britain, see *The Times*, 26 August 1958, 4; *The Church and the World: The Bulletin of the British Council of Churches* (June/July 1959), 1–2.

was especially vexing for clergymen such as Martin Niemöller who regarded their own involvement as one of a constant battle for influence in society and, thus, a direct continuation of the *Kirchenkampf,* the battle against the Nazification of the Protestant Church during the Third Reich. Such a stance required a constant commitment to the practice of conscience and the reform of society as a whole. Paradoxically, it was the failure of this position to assert itself within the Protestant Church in West Germany that allowed Christians to merge political and religious meanings of activism and thus fuse political and religious languages.[63]

There was no agreement about what practical consequences should be drawn from the analysis of the nuclear arms race. The majority in the churches' hierarchy believed that, given the communist threat, nuclear deterrence might be admissible.[64] Hence, while the British Council of Churches condemned nuclear weapons as 'an offence to God and a denial of His purpose for man', it called British unilateral disarmament 'impracticable and possibly disastrous'.[65] For many Christian activists, the demonstrations and annual marches thus turned into Christian processions, a 'heyday of their personal evangelism of mankind and the victory of Christian morality', and into practices of Christian brotherhood and fellowship that they believed had been lost in society more generally.[66]

Conversely, the West German Catholic Walter Dirks expressed the feelings of many British and West German activists when he claimed that church support for nuclear armaments would lead to 'nightmare[s]' for the faithful.[67] This position was grounded in the belief that 'security' could be created only through active Christian works in the world, 'not in fine sermons, but in action'.[68] This reflected a very specific theological world view. For many activists, the Incarnation was at the very centre of the Christian belief system. The incarnate Christ had shattered the boundaries between spiritual and physical worlds. Thus, addressing humanity's

---

[63] Martin Greschat, *Protestantismus im Kalten Krieg: Kirche, Politik und Gesellschaft im geteilten Deutschland* (Paderborn, 2010), 268–90 and 317–21.

[64] T. R. Milford, *The Valley of Decision* (London, 1961), 36.

[65] British Council of Churches, *The British Nuclear Deterrent* (London, 1963), 6, 28.

[66] Quote from *Baptist Times*, 16 November 1961, 10. Cf. also *The Friend*, 21 September 1962, 1166; Walter Stein (ed.), *Nuclear Weapons and Christian Conscience* (London, 1961), 151.

[67] Walter Dirks, 'Die Gefahr der Gleichschaltung', *Frankfurter Hefte*, 13 (1958), H. 6, 379–81; Helmut Gollwitzer, *Forderungen der Freiheit: Aufsätze und Reden zur politischen Ethik* (Munich, 1957), 347.

[68] *Methodist Recorder*, 17 May 1962, 9; Martin Niemöller, 'Kirche und Gesellschaft an der Schwelle einer neuen Zeit', *Stimme der Gemeinde*, 12 (1960), cols 265–72.

physical needs and working towards preventing its destruction were spiritual acts. Christian action was, therefore, not only about religion; it related to the world as a whole: 'Beware lest you worship the Satan of Separation and not the God who came to earth to die between two thieves to save.'[69]

Official Catholic responses were strongly framed by the Pope's position on the matter, which combined a general condemnation of nuclear weapons with a tolerance towards deterrence policies and an emphasis on private faith.[70] Because of the specific conception of the Catholic Church as both a faith and a transnational organization, Catholics faced the question of disenchantment especially clearly. The key global reference point for discussions about nuclear weapons in the 1950s and early 1960s was, as for Protestants, the doctrine of 'just wars': wars could be justified, if their causes and the means with which they were waged were just. The official reading of this doctrine sought to depoliticize the issue by claiming that its anti-communist position made the Western stance in the cold war just, as it helped preserve the freedom of religion within which the Catholic Church could develop.[71]

An earlier attempt to re-create the 'Peace Federation of German Catholics' along explicitly political lines had failed in the early 1950s.[72] This had left a small group of Catholics who sought to combine political and religious commitment. They organized small-scale protests against nuclear weapons at the meetings of the Catholic laymen's association (the so-called *Katholikentage*) in 1956 and 1958, for example, by bringing a model nuclear rocket to the respective venue.[73] Moreover, through their journals *Werkhefte* and *Frankfurter Hefte*, some West German Catholics

---

[69] *Coracle*, 27 (November 1955), 15; *Coracle*, 31 (November 1957), 23; *Coracle*, 34 (March 1959), 3; *Coracle* 37 (November 1960), 31; 'Erklärung des Konvents der Kirchl. Bruderschaft im Rheinland zur atomaren Bewaffnung, Wernmelskirchen, Ostern 1957', in Gottfried Niemeier (ed.), *Evangelische Stimmen zur Atomfrage* (Hanover, 1958), 49; Ernst Wolf and Werner Schmauch, et al., *Christusbekenntnis im Atomzeitalter?* (Munich, 1959).

[70] Christmas Message 'Confirma fratres tuos', 24 December 1948, in *Acta Apostolicae Sedis*, 41 (1949), 5–15. Cf. also Christmas Message, 24 December 1944, *Acta Apostolicae Sedis*, 37 (1945), 10–23, here 18–19.

[71] Gerhard Beestermöller, 'Krieg', *Lexikon für Theologie und Kirche* (Freiburg/Breisgau, 1997), vi, cols 475–9.

[72] Daniel Gerster, 'Von Pilgerfahrten zu Protestmärschen? Zum Wandel des katholischen Friedensengagements in den USA und der Bundesrepublik Deutschland 1945–1990', *Archiv für Sozialgeschichte*, 51 (2011), 311–42, here 319–25; Friedhelm Boll, 'Die Werkhefte katholischer Laien 1947–1963. Jugendbewegung—Gesellschaftskritik—Pazifismus', in Michel Grunewald and Uwe Puschner (eds), *Le Milieu intellectuel catholique en Allemagne, sa presse et ses réseaux (1871–1963)* (Berne, 2006), 507–36.

[73] Walter Dirks, 'Die Gefahr der Gleichschaltung', *Frankfurter Hefte*, 13 (1958), 379–91.

sought to revive their plans to establish a more critical form of social Catholicism than the one represented by the CDU in West German society.[74] Some Catholics, like Christel Beilmann (1921–2005) and Arno Klönne (born 1931), both with backgrounds in Catholic youth movements, held prominent organizational positions in the Easter Marches. But most Catholics critical of the official nuclear armaments policy, especially those with functions in the state, stayed away from the demonstrations because they feared to be reprimanded by their local bishops.[75] Only John XXIII's 1963 encyclical *Pacem in terris* (1963) created the conditions for more Catholics to feel able to join the Easter Marches.[76]

From a Christian perspective, the movement became, in the words of a British activist, 'necessary not chiefly to save our skins but to save our souls.'[77] The Christian activists were thus driven not by the loss of their beliefs, but rather by the desire to generate 'security' through the re-Christianization of their societies, thus returning to their dreams of transformation of the immediate post-war years to create thoroughly non-violent and just international and domestic societies after the ravages of the Second World War.[78]

The activists' religiosity was not only conditioned by official interpretations of the revelation. It relied primarily on people's own experiences of the world. On the one hand, Christian activists emphasized their individual experiences and moral norms against the Church hierarchies and thus 'privatized' their religious beliefs. On the other hand, however, they believed that these private beliefs should be taken seriously in the politics of security and that religion should play a role in the deliberations of social justice.[79] This was not merely a transition towards 'believing without

---

[74] Eugen Kogon, 'Im heraufziehenden Schatten des Atomtodes', *Frankfurter Hefte*, 12 (1957), 301–13; Schriftleitung der Werkhefte, 'Moral und Politik der Atombombe', *Werkhefte*, 12/ 5 (1958), 116–28.

[75] Vgl. AdsD, Christel Beilmann papers, 48: Franziskus Stratmann to Christel Beilmann, 23 February 1964; ders. an Arno Klönne, 12 May 1964; ders. an Christel Beilmann, 17 January 1965 AdsD, Stankowski papers, folder 17: Martin Stankowski, 'Katholische Jugend beim Ostermarsch' [*c.*1964].

[76] 'Pacem in terris de pace omnium gentium in veritate, iustitia, caritate, libertate constituenda', *Acta Apostolicae Sedis*, 55 (1963), 257–304.

[77] *Christian World*, 27 March 1958, 8; *The Friend*, 14 September 1962, 1133; Canon John Collins, *Christian Action* (autumn 1961), 18; Walter Dirks, 'Christ und Bürger in der Bundesrepublik', *Frankfurter Hefte*, 13 (1958), 673–85, here 674.

[78] Cf. Andreas Lienkamp, 'Socialism out of Christian Responsibility: The German Experiment of Left Catholicism (1945–1949)', in Gerd-Rainer Horn and Emmanuel Gerard (eds), *Left Catholicism. Catholics and Society in Western Europe at the Point of Liberation, 1943–1955* (Leuven, 2001), 198–200.

[79] Hans W. Ohly, 'Ein "linker" Jesus', *pläne* 4–5/1965, 12–13.

belonging', or the abandonment of the Churches in an age of affluence.[80] Rather, their beliefs carried the activists into communities that did not coincide with the institutionalized churches.[81] The movements provided the spaces for activists to leave their specific milieu and to apply their politics of security to their image of society as a whole. They sought to practise a far more wide-ranging conception of Christian activities than the ones condoned by the official churches and regarded their participation in the campaigns as its realization.[82]

Although this politicization of religious experiences occurred in both British and West German protests, the process obtained a particular political resonance in West Germany. The most vocal Protestant opponents of Adenauer's nuclear policies were the Brethren (*Kirchliche Bruderschaften*), who had emerged as bodies of clergymen promoting Christian fellowship against the National Socialist regime and had already played an important role in the protests against conventional rearmaments in the first half of the 1950s.[83] They regarded the challenge posed by nuclear armaments as very similar to the one posed by the Third Reich. Confessing and bearing witness and thus transcending the material world had different implications here. Although there were discussions about the bombing war and the role of the churches in resistance movements in Britain, these issues possessed a far greater immediacy than in Germany. The memories of mass violence from the Second World War meant that many older West German Protestants involved in the campaigns still resorted to biological language when recalling their experiences of the Second World War and linking it to the expected horrors of nuclear warfare: Combatants no longer fought to protect civilians; instead they treated them as 'insects deserving extermination... For the past forty years we have been talking of total war.'[84] Nuclear weapons would force enemy states to treat each other 'in the same manner that Hitler and Stalin dealt with their domestic opposition: by wholesale slaughter'.[85]

---

[80] Grace Davie, *Religion in Britain since 1945: Believing without Belonging* (Oxford, 1994).

[81] EZA, Bestand 613, Heinrich Kloppenburg papers: 'Leiterkonferenz der Bruderschaften', 24/25 May 1961; *Peace News*, 18 April 1957, 2; *Peace News*, 11 August 1961, 8.

[82] Letter by Walter Kern, *Initiative* (June 1961), 11; Gerd Hirschauer, 'Anstelle eines Vorworts zum 14. Jahrgang 1960', *Werkhefte katholischer Laien*, 1 (1960), 1–8; Carl Amery, Die *Kapitulation oder Deutscher Katholizismus heute* (Reinbek, 1963), 40–2.

[83] Ulrich Möller, *Im Prozeß des Bekennens: Brennpunkte der kirchlichen Atomwaffendiskussion im deutschen Protestantismus 1957–1962* (Neukirchen-Vluyn, 1999), 67–8.

[84] Martin Niemöller, 'Unsere Zukunft', in Niemöller, *Reden 1958–1961* (Frankfurt/Main, 1961), 42.

[85] Helmut Gollwitzer, *Die Christen und die Atomwaffen*, 4th edn (Munich, 1958), 23–4.

By linking their activities against 'atomic death' to bearing witness for 'German guilt', West German Christians in the protests confessed their past wrongdoings, but simultaneously sought to free themselves from the web of responsibilities in which they had become entangled. This would, they believed, show 'our inhumanity', but would also offer 'atonement for the rebirth of mankind'.[86] Even for those who had been too young to have been involved in the National Socialist regime, this transcendence offered shelter from the knowledge of the most recent history. While the majority of Protestants believed that the issue had been solved with the Stuttgart Confession of Guilt (*Stuttgarter Schuldbekenntnis*) of the Protestant Church in Germany (*Evangelische Kirche in Deutschland* (*EKiD*)), those engaged with the anti-nuclear-weapons movement held that this confession was a continuous process.[87] Catholics involved in the West German movements also thought that it was necessary to atone constantly for National Socialist crimes. Their beliefs thus clashed with the official view of a Catholic *ecclesia triumphans* (triumphant Church) that had survived the National Socialist regime institutionally and morally intact.[88]

LABOUR ON THE MARCH

Such desires to create security through new forms of political engagement not only occurred in the Christian Churches. The politically most important and immediate motivations behind the British and the West German movements were linked to experiences of the social-democratic, socialist, and communist left in both countries. In a process that lasted through the 1950s, many labour movement supporters, albeit for very different reasons, came to think that the cold war and the nuclear arms race seriously hampered their social and cultural aspirations and projects.[89] In particular, they came to the realization that their parties as organizations were unable to represent their interests, experiences, hopes, and dreams. Instead, as part and parcel of programmatic reformism, the parties had

[86] Prof. D. Hans Iwand, 'Geistige Entscheidungen und die Politik', *Blätter für deutsche und internationale Politik*, 1, 20 January 1958, 56–64, here 59.
[87] For the Stuttgart Confession, cf. *Protokolle des Rates der Evangelischen Kirche in Deutschland*, ed. Carsten Nicolaisen and N. A. Schulze (4 vols, Göttingen, 1995), i. 23–103; 'Kirche, Atom, Friede', *Junge Kirche*, 19 (1958), 159–63.
[88] Walter Dirks, 'Nonkonformisten sind nicht repräsentativ', *Frankfurter Hefte*, 13 (1958), 828–9.
[89] BJL, JS-109: John Saville to Ralph [Samuel], 21 May 1958; Ulrike Meinhof and Jürgen Seifert, 'Unruhe unter den Studenten', *Blätter für deutsche und internationale Politik*, 3 (1958), 524–6; Interview with Hans-Konrad Tempel, Ahrensburg (Germany), 3 May 2002; Interview with Klaus Vack, Sensbachtal (Germany), 16 September 2002.

appeared to follow policies that clearly separated international relations and domestic reconstruction and that seemed to carry the cold war into the centre of party-political life. Over the course of the 1950s and early 1960s, the social-democratic parties in both countries came to advocate international policies that were quite similar to those suggested by the centre-right parties, while shifting their attention towards advocating moderate social reforms in the domestic political arena. These changes were epitomized by the *SPD*'s moderate Bad Godesberg Programme from 1959 and Labour leader Hugh Gaitskell's call for the abolition of clause IV of the Labour programme, which still demanded the nationalization of all industries.

What the reformists saw as a necessary step to rid the party of unnecessary traditions, the left-wing groups within the *SPD* regarded as an 'undue assimilation to existing power structures'.[90] Rather than being carried by processes of social change and the growth of affluence, they had a rather ambiguous relationship to these processes. They believed that affluence depoliticized the population and lulled them into an artificial confidence that international politics did not have an impact on their private lives. Only direct personal engagement in these issues could help prevent catastrophe.[91] Similarly, communists in Britain and West Germany derided their leadership for not taking a principled stance on nuclear weapons. At the same time, the organizational structures within the British and West German labour movements left increasingly little scope for expressing these experiences.[92] In Britain, John Osborne, a dramatist, expressed the feelings of many against the Labour leader when he wrote that he 'carried a knife in my heart for…you Gaitskell, you particularly'.[93]

While these structural developments were quite similar, the *form* of these processes in Britain and the Federal Republic differed. In Britain, only parts of the Labour Party endorsed CND, with the exception of the vote at the Scarborough conference in 1960, which was soon reversed in 1961. The historically most important and long-lasting processes of dissociation took place outside the Labour Party and within the Communist

[90] Hans Werner Richter (ed.), *Bestandsaufnahme. Eine deutsche Bilanz 1962* (Munich, 1962), 563; SAPMO-BArch, DY30-IV.A2-10.02-301: *Informationen zur Abrüstung*, 3 (September 1963).
[91] *Wir sind jung* 2/1958, 1 and 4; *Protokoll der 4. ordentlichen Jugendkonferenz der IG Metall für die Bundesrepublik Deutschland, Berlin, 8. und 9. Mai 1958* (Frankfurt/Main, 1958), 52; BJL, JS-109: Edward P. Thompson to John Saville, 31 March n.y. [1958?].
[92] AdsD, IG Metall, G1010: 'Über politische Funktion und Mentalität der Kampagne für Abrüstung', n.d. [1966]; BAK, ZSg. 1-262-1: 'Bericht über den Ostermarsch', 1963.
[93] John Osborne, 'A Letter to My Fellow Countrymen', in David Boulton (ed.), *Voices from the Crowd* (London, 1964), 154; Judith Hart in *Tribune*, 18 November 1960, 5.

Party of Great Britain (CPGB). In West Germany, by contrast, this coalition of left-wing groups enjoyed the backing of the *SPD* until the beginning of the 1960s and thus had a direct link to political decision-making. The division of Germany further complicated the issues. Because of the importance of anti-communism in West German political culture, processes of dissociation had fundamental repercussions.

Dissatisfaction with the cold war consensus in the political culture of the Labour Party and the organizational stubbornness of the CPGB executive formed, from the very beginning, the crucial context for the emergence and framing of the British movement. In the Labour Party, the polarities of the cold war had helped to produce an alliance between party leaders and the trade union right after 1945, which stabilized inner-party conflicts. CND was one of the remnants of the broader social coalition that underpinned some of Labour's policies during the 1930s and particularly during the Labour government from 1945 to 1951 and that now campaigned outside the party.[94] This alliance had been forged during the Second World War, but broke down with the first Labour government in the early 1950s. The involvement of the professional middle class in the Labour Party had been strongly linked to its ethic of service and expertise in pursuit of humanitarian ends, and in its civilizing mission at home and abroad.[95]

The Labour leadership's neglect of the links between international and domestic security and its embrace of certain features of affluent society in search for a broader voter base appeared to contradict these experiences of many grass-roots members and party intellectuals alike. They believed that, as the Labour Left's *Tribune* put it in 1959, the people needed 'to be reminded of the ideals they prized fourteen years ago'.[96]

It was the break-up of this consensus that made many Labour supporters campaign on behalf of CND.[97] The matter of nuclear weapons had already become an issue as early as 1954 when a small group of Labour MPs under Fenner Brockway's leadership formed the Hydrogen Bomb National Campaign Committee after the government's decision to acquire hydrogen bombs was made public in Britain.[98] The discussions

[94] Cf. Black, *The Political Culture of the Left*, 12–40.
[95] Cf. Gareth Stedman Jones, 'Why is the Labour Party in a Mess?', in Stedman Jones, *Languages of Class: Studies in English Working Class History, 1832–1982* (Cambridge, 1983), 239–56, especially 245–51.
[96] *Tribune*, 16 October 1959, 1.
[97] Cf. David Howell, ' "Shut your Gob!": Trade Unions and the Labour Party, 1945–64', in Alan Campbell, Nina Fishman, and John McIlroy (eds), *British Trade Unions and Industrial Politics*, i. *The Post-War Compromise, 1945–64* (Aldershot, 1999), 117–44.
[98] Fenner Brockway, *Outisde the Right* (London, 1963), ch. 13.

about a reformist party programme and about abandoning Clause IV further weakened the consensus from the mid-1950s onwards as activists felt increasingly poorly represented by the leadership.[99]

The rhetoric of cold war antagonism was no longer sufficient to guaranteeing a majority alliance between party leaders, trade unions, and ordinary members. The 1959 congress of the Transport and General Workers' Union (TGWU) carried a unilateralist resolution, and, although the vote was reversed at a subsequent congress, it indicated that the unilateralist cause of seeing domestic and international security as intimately connected might attract support from beyond the traditional left.[100] Hugh Gaitskell's antagonistic style of leadership exacerbated the tensions further. The unions previously associated with the Labour Left also moved towards unilateralism: the Amalgamated Engineering Union (AEU), the National Union of Railwaymen (NUR), and the Union of Shop, Distributive and Allied Workers (USDAW) all backed unilateralist resolutions. Accordingly, delegates rejected official defence policy proposals at the 1960 Labour Party conference in Scarborough.[101] Although the vote was reversed in 1961, unilateralist sentiment in the trade unions and among the supporters remained strong.[102]

Some constituency Labour Party activists continued to support forms of unilateralism at the national conferences, particularly against American tests, American overflights, and the stationing of US *Polaris* submarine-based missiles at Holy Loch in Scotland.[103] Unlike the West German labour movement, however, the British Labour Party was nonetheless able to reintegrate activists into its fold. Despite accusations of being communist fellow travellers, activists never had to fear a ban.[104] Especially under the leadership of the more amenable Harold Wilson from 1963 onwards, many Labour supporters from within CND rejoined the mainstream of the party.[105] Even after Wilson had betrayed his unilateral credentials after

[99] Lawrence Black, '"Still at the penny-farthing stage in a jet-propelled era": Branch Life on the 1950s Left', *Labour History Review*, 65 (2002), 202–26.
[100] Geoffrey Goodman, *The Awkward Warrior: Frank Cousins, his Life and Times* (London, 1979), ch. 20.
[101] Labour Party, *Report of the 59th Annual Conference* (Scarborough, 1960), 176–242.
[102] Keith Hindell and Philip Williams, 'Scarborough and Blackpool: An Analysis of Some Votes of the Labour Party Conferences of 1960 and 1961', *Political Quarterly*, 33 (1962), 306–20.
[103] Labour Party, *Report of 60th Annual Conference* (Blackpool, 1961), 162; *Tribune*, 2 March 1962, 1; *New Statesman*, 18 October 1963, 526.
[104] *Tribune*, 21 April 1961, 8.
[105] Raymond Fletcher in *Tribune*, 26 July 1963, 5; David Boulton in *Tribune*, 11 October 1963, 10; Michael Foot in *Tribune*, 3 April 1964, 3.

the 1964 Labour general election victory, activists remained loath to leave the party altogether.[106]

The shift towards reformism and an increasing acceptance of capitalism among the Labour mainstream also set in train processes of dissociation among socialist and Labour student groups, which came to be at the core of many grass-roots anti-nuclear-weapons protests.[107] The 1956 intervention of the conservative Eden government in Suez and the merely lukewarm protests of the Labour Party had already left many student sections dissatisfied. Conditions in the Oxford University Labour Club were particularly prone to change, as a group of students, among them also some disaffected communists, sought to create a vision of a socialist future for a Britain without nuclear weapons and a world order that went beyond the cold war.[108] Activists in the group rejected both Labour reformism and what they believed were the structural constraints of orthodox Marxism. Particularly prominent were the Canadian Rhodes scholar and Politics, Philosophy and Economics (PPE) student Charles Taylor, who had already co-founded the local Hydrogen Bomb Campaign Committee in 1954, and the Caribbean Rhodes scholar Stuart Hall, who provided connections between the local CND and the anti-colonial movement. By launching the journal *Universities and Left Review* (*ULR*), activists sought to spread their ideas. The group's basis soon extended beyond Oxford, and its focus shifted to London and the metropolitan political culture.[109] There developed a whole culture, mainly metropolitan in shape, of coffee houses and bookshops, in which students and young activists gathered and discussed the political issues of the day.[110]

Of key importance for the political debates within CND were also those activists who had become alienated from the CPGB. They had, after their protests against the Stalinist line taken by the leadership after the Soviet invasion in Hungary and after the revelation of Stalin's

[106] MRC, MSS 292-882-71-2: TUC to Barry & District Trades Union Council, 18 December 1958, on the non-proscription of CND. On reintegration into the Labour Party, cf. *New Left Review* (March–April 1961), 6; George Clark in *Tribune*, 3 March 1961, 10; *New Statesman*, 31 March 1961, 501; George Thayer, *The British Political Fringe* (London, 1965), 247–8.
[107] Perry Anderson, 'The Left in the Fifties', *New Left Review*, 29 (1965), 5–9.
[108] Raphael Samuel, 'The Lost World of British Communism, Part II', *New Left Review*, 156 (March–April 1986), 63–113, here 79. On the general background, cf. Brian Harrison, 'Oxford and the Labour Movement', *Twentieth Century British History*, 2 (1991), 226–71.
[109] David Marquand, 'The Secret People of Oxford', *New Statesman*, 13 July 1957, 43; *Isis*, 19 February 1958, 31; *Isis*, 26 February 1958, 1; *Isis*, 24 January 1962, 11; *New Statesman*, 22 March 1958, 377, on the general mood in the University.
[110] Robert Hewison, *In Anger: Culture in the Cold War 1945–60* (London, 1981), 163.

purges in the 1930s, founded the journal *Reasoner* (later renamed the *New Reasoner*) to further discussions within the CPGB. After they had left or been expelled from the CPGB, they joined forces with the group of students around the *ULR* when the journal of both groups merged to form the *New Left Review* (*NLR*) in 1960.[111]

This opened up Marxism for wider influence within the British left and ultimately led to the dissociation of many students into what they called the New Left, later one of the main support groups of CND and, in particular, the Committee of 100.[112] These movement activists were particularly influential in CND branches in the north of England and in Fife, Scotland, particularly after the *Polaris* missiles had been stationed on Holy Loch in 1962. The historians Edward P. Thompson and John Saville were the New Left's most vocal spokesmen and activists.[113]

While it is true, as Eric Hobsbawm observed, that CND had in itself 'nothing to do with the crisis in the CP', the political context in which CND emerged and the cultural traditions on which it drew cannot be explained without reference to the many activists who joined CND from the ranks of the ex-communist New Left.[114] After the tremendous shock of Krushchev's revelations about Stalin's atrocities in his 'Secret Speech' at the Twentieth Party Congress of the Soviet Union's Communist Party (CPSU) and after the violent suppression of the Hungarian uprising by Soviet forces, activists around the *Reasoner* and *New Reasoner* and, then, in the New Left campaigned for a realization of their hopes and dreams of a truly humane and socialist policy. They did this by seeking to revitalize communist politics from within by providing fora for discussions. But the CPGB clamped down on dissent within the party, so that activists were pushed out of the moral community that the party had provided them.[115] Looking back to what became the origins of the New Left, John Saville remarked that 'the idea of resigning from the Communist Party was not in our minds when we began the *Reasoner* and it was only in the following

[111] BJL, JS-112: E. P. Thompson to John Saville, n.d. [*c*.1962].

[112] Lin Chun, *The British New Left* (Edinburgh, 1993); Michael Kenny, *The First New Left: British Intellectuals after Stalin* (London, 1995).

[113] Cf. Michael Bess, 'E. P. Thompson: The Historian as Activist', *American Historical Review*, 98 (1993), 18–38; John Saville, *Memoirs from the Left* (London, 2003), 117–88; MRC, MSS 302/3/11: Fife Socialist League, Minutes Book, October 1962.

[114] Eric Hobsbawm, *Interesting Times. A Twentieth-Century Life* (London, 2002), 211; Dennis Dworkin, *Cultural Marxism in Postwar Britain: History, the New Left, and the Origins of Cultural Studies* (Durham, NC, 1997), 92.

[115] John Saville, 'The Twentieth Congress and the British Communist Party', *Socialist Register* (1976), 1–23, here 7; Doris Lessing, *The Golden Notebook* (London, 1987), 338; Michael Kenny, 'Communism and the New Left', in Geoff Andrews, Nina Fishman and Kevin Morgan (eds), *Opening the Books: Essays on the Social and Cultural History of British Communism* (London and Boulder, CO, 1995), 195–209, here 197.

months that we recognized, with great reluctance, the fundamental conservatism, not only of the leadership, but also of the rank and file'.[116]

CND provided an ideal context from which this New Left could try
to translate its ideas into practice. But the transition from identifying
themselves as 'communist' to turning to 'New Left' activism, however,
was far more complicated than is usually suggested and did not necessarily involve a complete break from previous orthodoxies. An important part of British communism consisted of a shared sense of purpose
and the feeling of mutual sacrifice by party members for the cause. This
was only heightened by the social and political isolation that many
communists experienced in cold war Britain. Coming to terms with the
exclusion from their community (which most of them had not planned)
and with the sudden collapse of the boundaries that had given their
political and social world meaning was a process that took years rather
than months.[117]

For Thompson, this project consisted of promoting a 'socialist humanism' that involved linking politics and culture in novel ways. It involved
what he saw as the reconstitution of the emancipatory aspects of the
socialist tradition, but in new moral terms. In other words, Thompson
rejected the bureaucratic form that socialism had taken in Eastern Europe
after 1945. Instead, he sought to revitalize socialism in moral terms by
stressing what one might call the libertarian elements of socialism: to
enable everyone to live freely. And he connected this to a message that
highlighted the specifically *national* importance of socialism in England.
He argued that these aspects had characterized the history of the English
labour movement from its very beginnings and was deeply entrenched in
English national identity. This evocation of tradition, also visible in
Thompson's 1963 classic *The Making of the English Working Class*, bypassed
both the anti-humanism of orthodox Communism and Trotskyism as
well as the voluntaristic renderings of contemporary liberalism.[118]

Yet, Thompson and others still presumed, like historical materialists, that
socialism was the guaranteed outcome of the historical process, a vision
towards which the younger group around the *ULR* was more sceptical.[119]

---

[116] John Saville, 'The Communist Experience: A Personal Appraisal', *Socialist Register*
(1991), 1–27, here 22.

[117] John Saville, 'The Twentieth Congress and the British Communist Party', *Socialist Register* (1976), 1–23, here 7.

[118] E. P. Thompson, 'Agency and Choice', *New Reasoner*, 5 (1958), 89–106; Bess,
'E. P. Thompson: The Historian as Activist'.

[119] Harry Hanson, 'An Open Letter to E. P. Thompson', *New Reasoner*, 2 (1957), 79–91;
Ralph Miliband, 'Socialism and the Myth of the Golden Past', *Socialist Register* (1964),
92–103.

Thompson's aim was to enable ethical moral subjects, which would not act as part of a bureaucratic or governmental machinery, or blindly follow the ideological consensus, but which would take decisions on the basis of their own conscience. Although New Left activists did not regard themselves as religious, much of their rhetoric and world views appears to have been influenced by their nonconformist background, with the emphasis on conscience and individual moral responsibilities: Christopher Hill's and Edward Thompson's families were Methodists, and Dorothy Thompson's family was of Huguenot descent. The academic and activist Ralph Milliband, the young historian Raphael Samuel, and Hyman Levy came from progressive Jewish backgrounds.[120]

Their war experiences and the hopes and dreams for socialist transformation in the immediate post-war period played a crucial role for the New Left activists, and it was the ground from which they sought to capture the lived utopias of the 1930s.[121] It was really during the war that Thompson discovered his Marxism—his father had been a missionary, then an Oxford academic, possibly of a liberal imperialist orientation, if one wants to use this term. Thompson's war service during 1942 to 1945 included stints in northern Africa, Italy, and Austria, where he fought as a tank troop leader. There, he came to see war as a stifling anonymous force and structure that worked against human agency—a trope that we can find in many other war memoirs, not only of British soldiers, and that Thompson later in the 1950s applied to the cold war. In 1947, Thompson and his mother visited Bulgaria, where his deceased brother was a hero. He spent the late summer of that year as commandant of the British Youth Brigade, volunteers engaged in the construction of a 150-mile railway across the Sava in Slovenia. He wrote about this in ways that brought his earlier war experiences together with his interpretation of socialism as practice.[122]

His socialism was, therefore, from the late 1940s onwards, already framed by an element that would, in the context of 1956, lead to his expulsion from the Communist Party: his critique of the impersonality of party and government structures, and the stress on socialist community and individual and popular agency. The campaign against the bomb nuclear weapons could, therefore, fulfil a similar function: 'The bomb must

[120] Victor Kiernan, 'Herbert Norman's Cambridge', in Roger Bowen (ed.), *E. H. Norman: His Life and Scholarship* (Toronto: University of Toronto Press, 1984), 26.

[121] Scott Hamilton, *The Crisis of Theory: EP Thompson, the New Left and Postwar British Politics* (Manchester, 2011), 49–92.

[122] E. P. Thompson, 'Omladinska Prugga', in *The Railway: An Adventure in Construction* (London, 1948), 1–32, here 32. Cf. also Saville, *Memoirs*.

be dismantled; but in dismantling it, men will summon up energies which will open the way to their inheritance. The bomb is like an image of man's whole predicament: it bears within it death and life, total destruction or human mastery over human history.'[123]

In contrast to developments in West Germany and despite its tradition in the anti-militarist campaigns of the 1930s, the CPGB itself only endorsed the protests officially in 1960 after it had become clear that CND was a success. The Party never wielded substantial influence in the campaign during the late 1950s and early 1960s. Before that, the CPGB had campaigned for 'world peace' and multilateral disarmament through the British Peace Committee and regarded the foundation of CND, with its agenda of unilateral disarmament, as a distraction from the 'battle for world peace'. In line with the Soviet Union's position of 'peaceful coexistence', the CPGB saw its main business as multilateral disarmament through international summit negotiations.[124]

In West Germany, the dissonance between the political experiences and expectations of Labour movement activists also existed before the emergence of an anti-nuclear-weapons movement and explained why activists participated. As West Germany's *SPD* organized the first phase of the protests against nuclear weapons together with prominent trade union organizations and thus contained some of these dissonances within its organizational fold, it was the protesters' activism and assertion of an independent position within the *SPD*'s campaign that turned them into identifiable political actors.

To a much greater extent than in Britain, activism in the West German protests against nuclear weapons itself created the boundaries that made it possible that the activists' experiences could be perceived as distinct and homogeneous political positions. The dissonances were particularly pronounced among student groups and activists within the *SPD*'s traditional 'front organizations', which offered social and cultural activities, such as hiking and biking in a labour-movement context. As the Communist Party had been banned in Germany in 1956, the ex-communist left was far less important for the West German campaigns than for Britain. This left the Easter Marches, the second phase of the West German movement, as the only forum through which supporters could voice their concerns in public.

[123] Thompson, 'Socialist Humanism: An Epistle to the Philistines', *New Reasoner*, 1 (1957), 143.
[124] Labour History Archive and Study Centre, Manchester (LHASC), CP/CENT/PEA/01/14: CPGB Executive Statement, 1 September 1956; CP/CENT/SPN/1/14: 'H-Bomb and Disarmament Campaign speakers' notes', 16 August 1957; Richard Taylor, *Against the Bomb*, 315–23.

Activists within the Socialist German Student Federation (*Sozialis-tischer Deutscher Studentenbund* (*SDS*)), the *SPD*'s student organization, asserted their experiences particularly especially vocally. *SDS* activists' analysis of social and international security issues, however, found less and less space within the organizational boundaries of the *SPD*, as the party came to abandon its critique against Adenauer's foreign policy and moved towards a 'policy of commonalities' from late 1959 onwards.[125] Disagreeing with the *SPD*'s official line, the student activists continued to reject the Federal Republic's social order as politically regressive and to campaign for an 'independent' position in the cold war, not least to main-tain German unity.[126] The emergence and identification of these disso-nances as a political problem was directly related to the issue of nuclear armaments. Accusations of the protesters as pro-communist, although not absent in the British context, played a much more salient role in West Germany, thus further increasing the boundaries between West German activists and the society surrounding them. With the election of Jürgen Seifert, a keen anti-nuclear-weapons campaigner and a prominent critic of the *SPD*'s reformist line, and others to the *SDS*'s executive in October 1958, the *SDS* expressed its scepticism towards a separation of individual experiences and international security policies that was gaining ground among the *SPD*'s party leadership.[127]

The first visible ruptures between *SDS* activists and the *SPD* headquar-ters had, however, already occurred half a year earlier in Berlin, the front-line city of the cold war. On 15 April 1958, the Action Committee of the Berlin Youth against Atomic Death, sponsored by, among others, the *SDS* and the *SPD*'s youth organization 'Falcons', staged a silent march under the headline 'Remember Hiroshima'. After the Berlin press attacked the march as 'pro-communist', a heavy conflict within the Berlin section of the Campaign against Atomic Death emerged. Berlin's leader of the Fed-eration of German Trade Unions (*Deutscher Gewerkschaftsbund* (*DGB*)), Ernst Scharnowski, supported by the up-and-coming Willy Brandt, announced at a meeting that American nuclear weapons had not only ended the Second World War, but also guaranteed peace in Berlin, a

---

[125] Ossip K. Flechtheim, 'Zur Frage der innerparteilichen Demokratie', *neue kritik*, spe-cial issue (October 1961), 19–22.

[126] Fritz Lamm, 'Gedanken zu einer sozialistischen Außenpolitik', *neue kritik*, special issue (October 1961), 23–7; Gerhard Ziegler, 'Sozialistische Studenten—arm, aber unge-brochen. Die XV: Delegiertenkonferenz des SDS überwand die Krise und einigte sich auf "Mittelkurs"', *Frankfurter Rundschau*, 4 October 1960, 5.

[127] Archiv APO und soziale Bewegungen, Free University Archives, Berlin (APOA): XIII o. DK., Mannheim, 22–23 October 1958: Minutes, mimeo, 2–3.

position that contradicted the very rationale of the *SPD*'s Campaign against Atomic Death.[128]

The clash between activists' own experiences and the *SPD*'s campaign organization came to a head when the autonomous Student Circles against Nuclear Armaments, which were closely linked to the *SDS*, planned, against the *SPD*'s wishes, a congress against nuclear weapons in Berlin in early 1959.[129] The congress took place on 3 January 1959 at the height of the Berlin crisis over Krushchev's ultimatum over the negotiations for the future of West Berlin. It passed a highly contentious resolution that called for immediate peace negotiations with the GDR and also adopted official GDR arguments for a German–German confederation.[130]

While it is now clear that the resolution could be passed only through gerrymandering by *SDS* members with GDR connections around the student journal *konkret*,[131] the broad support for the resolution among the participants still highlighted the increasing dissonance between the approach at the *SPD* headquarters and members' experiences.[132] Rather than a manifestation of pro-communist attitudes, this labelling was itself a product of political communications at the time. It was an assertion of what the students felt to be their vital interests and experiences, and their impression that they were not properly represented by the *SPD*'s general policies.

In the following months and years, tensions intensified.[133] October 1961, Herbert Wehner, responsible for organizational questions in the *SPD* headquarters, tabled a 27-page dossier which sought to prove that the *SDS* had become 'increasingly extremist' and suggested that simultaneous *SDS* and *SPD* membership was incompatible. The resolution was passed

---

[128] *Frankfurter Rundschau*, 26–27 April 1958, 4; Siegward Lönnendonker and Tilman Fichter (eds), *Freie Universität Berlin: 1948–1973. Hochschule im Umbruch: Auf dem Weg in den Dissens (1957–1964)* (Berlin, 1974), iii, 7–8.

[129] AdsD, 2/PVAM000024: Walter Menzel to Manfred Rexin, 14 August 1958; Notes on a Meeting between student organizations and Free University officials in Frankfurt/Main, 21 September 1958.

[130] *colloquium*, 13 (1959), 7.

[131] Klaus Rainer Röhl, *Fünf Finger sind keine Faust* (Cologne, 1974), 90–2; AdsD, ASAF000110: Club Republikanischer Publizisten, *Infodienst*, January 1959.

[132] APOA, Peter Kraft papers: 'Anti-Atomtod 1958/9'; Lönnendonker and Fichter (eds), *Hochschule im Umbruch*, 12–13; Ulrike Meinhof, 'Der Studentenkongreß gegen Atomrüstung', *Blätter für deutsche und internationale Politik*, 4 (1959), 60–1; Erich Kuby, 'Was war in Berlin wirklich los?', *Vorwärts*, 23 January 1959, 7.

[133] APOA, SDS, XIV. DK, 30 July–1 August 1959 in Göttingen: Jürgen Seifert, 'Über die Aufgaben des Sozialistischen Deutschen Studentenbundes in der gegenwärtigen Situation', mimeo, 7; Jürgen Seifert, 'Vom "58er" zum "68er". Ein biographischer Rückblick', *Vorgänge*, 32 (December 1993), 1–6.

after considerable discussions and published on 6 November 1961.[134] As the *SPD*'s organization served as marker for acceptable left-wing politics in the Federal Republic during this time period, this pushed *SDS* activists, against their will, outside the parameters of respectable politics. They now became, even more than they had been already, distinct and identifiable political actors. The Easter Marches were now the only forum in which *SDS* supporters could voice their concerns and practise their ideas, so that the marches increasingly became a reservoir for *SDS* protesters' political activism.[135]

Contrary to contemporary perceptions and many historical interpretations, experiences of dissonance within the communist left mattered far less in the Federal Republic than in Britain.[136] As in the other groups, changing perceptions of the cold war and domestic politics combined in increasing the differences of experience between the communists and their milieu. Communist involvement in the West German protests against nuclear weapons is a hotly debated issue to the present day, and it is worthy to be explored in some detail. The German Communist Party had been banned since 1956, and communist agitation took place clandestinely in so-called 'camouflage organizations' (*Tarnorganisationen*), such as the *Fränkischer Kreis* (Franconian Circle) around the Würzburg Professor of Linguistics Franz Schneider, the *Deutscher Club 1954* around Wolfgang Harder, a professor of history at the Wuppertal Institute of Education, and, from 1960, the *Deutsche Friedens-Union*, a party set up under the leadership of Renate Riemeck, a professor at the Wuppertal Institute of Education, to gain support for the 'peace' policies of the GDR among the West German middle class.[137]

Yet, as the GDR's policy increasingly moved away from revolutionary aims and from actively pursuing policies of German unification in the West, and as the nature of clandestine work put more and more pressure on West German communists, the majority of West German communists abandoned active politics, dissatisfied with the dissonances between

---

[134] AdsD: Parteivorstand, minutes, 16 October 1961, 5; Parteivorstand, minutes, 6 November 1961, 2–29. Cf. also *Vorwärts*, 18 June 1960, 1.
[135] Archiv Aktiv: Minutes of the Easter March central committee, 25 February 1962, Kassel; SAPMO-BArch DY30/IV.2/10.02/225, 4: 'Kundgebung der IdK in Essen', 6 December 1959; Jürgen Seifert, 'Innerparteiliche Opposition', *Frankfurter Hefte*, 15 (1960), 765–72.
[136] Cf. Hubertus Knabe, *Die unterwanderte Republik: Stasi im Westen* (Berlin, 1999), 182–7.
[137] BAK, B106/16053: 'Bericht des Bundesamtes für Verfassungsschutz, betr.: Besprechung mit Dr. med. Fritz Katz, Iserlohn, 25 June 1958'; BAK, B136/3788: 'Die kommunistischen Hilfsorganisationen', 1 March 1959; BAK, B 136/3787: Dr. Barth to Chancellor Adenauer, 11 January 1963; *Der Spiegel*, 23 August 1961.

hyperbolic rhetoric from the East German regime and the lack of active policies.[138] Those who joined the West German movements were, therefore, far from 'unwitting assets' of the GDR. The vast majority of communists joined the marches independently as they searched for a forum in which they could express their experiences. Conversely, non-communist activists remarked positively that the old divisions between the two strands of the labour movement had been overcome and that a pragmatic alliance could take place in the light of the cold war perils.[139]

The organizers who participated under instructions from GDR authorities were, therefore, increasingly dissatisfied with the coherence of communist activism.[140] Thus, viewed from a movement perspective, the participation of communists was an exercise in integration: the perceived boundaries between society and 'movement' came to be stronger than their identification as 'communist'. This is also demonstrated by the ways in which the government and the *SPD* labelled the marches. While the secret intelligence reports knew of the participation of individual communists, the official government statements suggested that communists and the Easter Marches were identical. It thus helped to sharpen the contours of the movement in the domestic political debate further and drew the small minority of communists and the majority of non-communists within the Easter Marches more closely together.[141]

Crucially, during this process of integration, communists further adapted their experiences and expectations and demilitarized their political language and insignia. Calls for 'human fellowship' now replaced the demands for a 'fight for peace', and violent behaviour in Communist theory and action, still widespread in the immediate post-war years, had disappeared almost completely. Unlike communist and socialist 'peace' activists in the Weimar Republic, communists now rejected military

---

[138] 'Sie sind einsam oder züchten Rosen: Was aus den Hamburger KP-Funktionären geworden ist', *Die Zeit*, 30 April 1959, 5; Till Kössler, *Abschied von der Revolution: Kommunisten und Gesellschaft in Westdeutschland 1945–1968* (Düsseldorf, 2005), 406–17.

[139] Hamburger Institut für Sozialforschung (HIS), WOL2, folder 'Ostermarsch 1962': Report on the 1962 Easter March, 23 April 1962, 3; BAK, ZSg. 1-262,1: 'Ostermarsch 1961', 'Ostermarsch 1962'.

[140] SAPMO-BArch, DY30/IV.2-10.02/120, 121: 'SPD-Führung und Volksbewegung gegen Atomrüstung', 20 August 1958; SAPMO-BArch, DY30/IV.2/10.02/224, 304–5: 'Bericht über die Ostermärsche der Atomwaffengegner 1962 in Westdeutschland, 2 May 1962; SAPMO-BArch, BY1-2407: Minutes, Politburo, KPD (Ost), 25/26 July 1958; SAPMO-BArch, DY30/IV.2-2.028/67, 25: Albert Norden to Heinz Willmann, 21 January 1960; SAPMO-BArch, DY30/IV.2-2.028/68, 150: Willmann to Büro Norden, 9 June 1961; SAPMO-BArch BY1/569: 'Bericht Kreis Essen, Zur Arbeit mit den Neuaufgenommenen', n.d. [1963].

[141] HStAD, NW 374/75: Report 'Der Infiltrant', n.d. [1959], 3.

forms of organization by juxtaposing pictures of civil and civilian life with images of marching soldiers.[142]

The small socialist and highly localized groups of activists that sought to revive German socialist traditions through networks and journals over the course of the 1950s mattered more in West Germany than party politics, however. The importance of such journals lay in the fact that they provided forums for reviving within a small network positions that wished to create a 'third force' between communism and capitalism in world politics at a time when such positions were still outside the parameters of activism. Together, they provided the space from which a West German 'New Left' could emerge.[143] The most important of these journals were *Funken* ('Sparks', published 1949–59), published in Stuttgart by the former exile Fritz Lamm, *Die Andere Zeitung* ('The Alternative Paper'), and *Sozialistische Politik* ('Socialist Politics', 1954–66), edited by Peter von Oertzen and Theo Pirker from Bovenden near Göttingen in northwest Germany. For some activists, their involvement with the journals created the conditions from which they could think about challenging the very structure and form of the political in the Federal Republic.[144]

YOUTH MOVEMENT ACTIVISTS

While political and religious experiences of dissonance between experiences and expectations were the most important processes that contributed to the strength and composition of the British and West German movements, their particular shape was influenced by experiences within small socialist and religious life-reform groups, as they connected cultural activities with political engagement. Next to the socialist journals, they form a neglected strand within the genealogies of the West German New Left that found a political space in the West German protests against nuclear weapons. Such experiences were much weaker in Britain than in West Germany. Although they had a considerable impact on the history of the British Committee of 100, where traditions of life-reform

[142] SAPMO-BArch, BY1/312: Picture, *Kronprinz-Echo*, n.d. [1953]; SAPMO-BArch, BY1/308: KPD-Essen, leaflet, 'Brüder in eins nun die Hände!', n.d. (probably 1957).

[143] Gregor Kritidis, *Linkssozialistische Opposition in der Ära Adenauer. Ein Beitrag zur Frühgeschichte der Bundesrepublik Deutschland* (Hanover, 2008).

[144] Peter von Oertzen, 'Behelfsbrücken. Linkssozialistische Zeitschriften in der Ära der "Restauration" 1950–1962', in Michael Buckmiller and Joachim Perels (eds), *Opposition als Triebkraft der Demokratie:Bilanz und Perspektiven der zweiten Republik* (Hanover, 1998), 87–100.

movements, radical pacifism, and anarchism were revived, they were comparatively less important for CND. In the Federal Republic, by contrast, the experiences of activists coming from the front organizations of the *SPD* mattered greatly for the ways in which the marches came to be identified as seemingly homogeneous political actors. Their experiences had a far greater, albeit usually neglected, influence on the shape of the West German movements in the late 1950s and early 1960s than student activists. They were particularly strong in the Ruhr area and in the southern parts of Hesse.[145]

By continuing to campaign against nuclear weapons even after the *SPD* headquarters and the trade unions started to abandon the campaign, activists from the Falcons (*Sozialistische Jugend. Die Falken*) and the Friends of Nature Youth (*Naturfreundejugend*) organizations expressed not only their deep concerns about nuclear armaments, but also their misgivings that they could no longer express these worries within their own organizations more generally. While they had formed an essential part of social-democratic and socialist lives in the 1920s, organizations such as the Falcons and the Friends of Nature had, after the reconstruction of the *SPD* after 1945, come to be on the sidelines of social-democratic politics as the party sought to appeal to a broader audience.[146]

In West Germany in particular, many of the West German organizers and activists could look back on an involvement in (frequently male-dominated) youth movements or party youth organizations, often with Christian overtones.[147] Arno Klönne (born 1931), student of the political scientist Wolfgang Abendroth and later press secretary of the Easter Marches, had been involved in a *bündisch* Catholic youth group throughout the National Socialist years. After 1945, he was the head of a local group of the Catholic pupils' association *Neudeutschland*, which was independent of the official Federation of German Catholic Youth (*Bund der deutschen Katholischen Jugend*).[148] Christel Beilmann, Easter March

[145] Stefan Goch, '"Wie immer zu spät"—Sozialdemokratische Vorfeldorganisationen im Ruhrgebiet zwischen Wirtschaftskrise und "Restauration"', in Matthias Frese and Michael Prinz (eds), *Politische Zäsuren und gesellschaftlicher Wandel im 20. Jahrhundert: Regionale und vergleichende Perspektiven* (Paderborn, 1996), 689–731, here 715–16.
[146] AdsD: Präsidium, minutes, 23 January 1961; 'IG-Druck Jugend begrüßt Ostermarsch', *Saar-Woche*, 21 December 1963, 5; Jochen Zimmer, 'Das Abseits als vermiedener Irrweg: Die Naturfreundejugend in der westdeutschen Friedens- und Ökologiebewegung bis zum Ende der APO', in Heinz Hoffmann and Jochen Zimmer (eds), *Wir sind die grüne Garde: Geschichte der Naturfreundejugend* (Essen, 1986), 93–170, here 131.
[147] On the background, cf. Arno Klönne, *Blaue Blumen in Trümmerlandschaften: Bümdische Jugendgruppen in den Jahren nach 1945* (Witzenhausen, 1990).
[148] Interview with Arno Klönne, Paderborn, 20 August 2002; interview with Erdmann Linde, Dortmund, 26 August 2002.

organizer in the Ruhr area, had been a Catholic girls' movement leader during the Second World War.[149]

These activists were in constant osmosis with other groups that tried to revive the community spirit of the associations of the 1920s and 1930s. Thus, Theodor Ebert, later a theorist of non-violent direct action and involved in conscientious objectors' organizations, and Klaus Vack, later full-time organizer of the Easter Marches, could look back on an active involvement in the social-democratic Friends of Nature youth organizations. Andreas Buro, also in the Easter March executive, worked as a youth adviser (*Jugendpfleger*) in Kassel city council at the beginning of the 1960s.[150]

Particularly remarkable for the Easter Marches was its relation to the group *d.j.1.11*, originally founded by Eberhard Köbel 'Tusk' under right-wing auspices in the mid-1920s. Köbel had joined the Communist Party in 1932 and became a member of the socialist resistance group Red Chapel (*Rote Kapelle*) around Harro Schulze-Boysen. During the 1940s, he left Germany for Sweden and Britain, where he established contacts to the fellow-travelling Free German Youth (*Freie Deutsche Jugend (FDJ)*) and became its chief propagandist in the Eastern zone of occupation in 1948 before being sacked in disgrace by the new GDR regime in 1951.[151] The Easter Marches had shed the often aggressive and militarist style of the original *d.j.1.11* group and the Free German Youth. But Klönne revived ideas of male community and life-reform by republishing the *d.j.1.11* journal *pläne* in 1956–57 as a student paper at the University of Münster in order to bring politics and youth groups together. At the end of the 1950s, members of working-class youth associations joined the magazine's editorial board. Among them were Herbert Faller, the head of the Friends of Nature youth association and later head of the Easter Marches in Hesse, Fred Gebhardt, an organizer for the Falcons, a socialist youth movement, and the Dortmund pupil and Falcon member

[149] Cf. the autobiographical sources in Christel Beilmann, *Eine katholische Jugend in Gottes und dem Dritten Reich: Briefe, Berichte, Gedrucktes 1930–1945. Kommentare 1988/89* (Wuppertal, 1989), 134–56.
[150] Andreas Buro, *Gewaltlos gegen den Krieg: Lebenserinnerungen eines Pazifisten* (Frankfurt/Main, 2011); Klaus Vack, *Das andere Deutschland nach 1945: Als Pazifist, Sozialist und radikaler Demokrat in der Bundesrepublik Deutschland. Politisch-biographische Skizzen und Beiträge* (Cologne, 2005).
[151] *pläne* 6–7 (1963); Kay Tjaden, *rebellion der jungen: die geschichte von tusk und von dj. 1.11* (Frankfurt/Main, 1958); Fritz Schmidt (ed.), *tusk: Versuche über Eberhard Köbel* (n.p. [Witzenhausen], 1994).

Frank Werkmeister, both involved in the Easter Marches in the Ruhr area.[152]

pläne became the main Easter March journal in West Germany from 1961 onwards, and issued a record with Easter March songs in 1962–63. It played a particularly important role in keeping traditions of political song and folk music alive in West Germany, when they came under increasing suspicion of pro-communist leanings in the anti-communist climate of the Federal Republic.[153] This strand of traditions was especially prominent in the Ruhr area. Activists from the pacifist Catholic groups, Friends of Nature, the trade-union youth groups, and the Falcons retained their strong identification with these groups, while they were being slowly integrated into mainstream confessional and party cultures elsewhere in the Federal Republic.[154] There were important continuities between involvement in *FDJ* activities in the early 1950s and the Easter Marches in the early 1960s.[155]

PACIFISTS

Only a minority of Easter March supporters came from the German Peace Society (*Deutsche Friedensgesellschaft (DFG)*), which had been licensed in the British zone of occupation as early as November 1945 and managed to achieve an overall membership of about 30,000, comparable to that during the Weimar Republic.[156] The *DFG* moved closer and closer to fellow-travelling organizations, such as the *Deutsche Friedens-Union* in the early 1960s, so that the organization lost credibility for most middle-class pacifists. Cold war political culture therefore had a direct impact on

[152] Heiner Halberstadt, 'Protest gegen Remilitarisierung, "Kampagne Kampf dem Atomod" und Ostermarschbewegung in Westdeutschland', in Ulrich Herrmann (ed.), *Protestierende Jugend: Jugendopposition und politischer Protest in der deutschen Nachkriegsgeschichte* (Weinheim and Munich, 2002), 313–27; Roland Gröschel, *Zwischen Tradition und Neubeginn: Sozialistische Jugend im Nachkriegsdeutschland. Entstehung und historische Wurzeln der Sozialistischen Jugend Deutschlands—Die Falken* (Hamburg, 1986), 153.

[153] Robert von Zahn, 'pläne und der Aufstand gegen die Republik', in Zahn (ed.), *Folk und Liedermacher an Rhein und Ruhr* (Münster, 2002), 77–127, here 85.

[154] Arno Klönne, 'Kampagnen im Ruhrgebiet gegen die Rüstungspolitik: Erinnerungen und Reflexionen eines Zeitzeugen', in Jan-Pieter Barbian and Ludger Heid (eds), *Die Entdeckung des Ruhrgebiets: Das Ruhrgebiet in Nordrhein-Westfalen 1946–1996* (Essen, 1997), 107–12.

[155] 'Noch einmal: Meißnertag 1963', *Neue Politik*, 8 (1963), 12–13; Arno Klönne, 'Die Jugend vom Hohen Meißner', *Wir sind jung*, 16 (1963), 8–11.

[156] *DFG Informationsdienst*, no. 8/1963, 7. For the participation in the Easter Marches, cf. AdsD, 2/PVAM000042: Dietlind Hohage to Alexander von Cube, 15 February 1961.

motivating pacifists to search for new forms of political activism that
went beyond traditional middle-class pressure groups.[157] Although
small in numbers, many non-violent pacifists played a vital role in the
local and regional organization of the activities of the West German
Campaign against Atomic Death and the Easter Marches. Often closely
connected with religious and social-democratic politics, pacifists not
only rejected nuclear weapons, but they also sought non-violent means
of conflict solution in society and politics. This group was, despite
strong traditions in Britain, much more influential in the West German movement.

The organizer of the first German Easter March, the Hamburg teacher
Hans-Konrad Tempel, a Quaker, epitomized this background. He argued
from a position of strict non-violence in politics in general and international affairs in particular, and argued that this could be achieved only if
social relations in everyday life created security through non-violence.[158]
Tempel belonged to the strictly anti-communist Association of Conscientious Objectors (*Verband der Kriegsdienstverweigerer* (*VK*)). Ten thousand
members strong, the *VK* had been founded by left-wing trade unionists,
SPD members, and former supporters of the now defunct neutralist *Gesamtdeutsche Volkspartei* around Helene Wessel and Gustav Heinemann as a
conscientious objectors' union in 1958.[159] Many of the original Easter
March activists knew each other through the Hamburg Action Group for
Non-Violence around Tempel, through which regular workshops on the
revitalization of citizenship through non-violent direct action had been
held since the early 1950s, and were in close contact with their British
colleagues.[160]

This group, dissatisfied with an approach that focused on military service only, had already organized the first West German vigil against
nuclear weapons in April 1958, following a meeting of the Hamburg
Campaign against Atomic Death. In December 1959, it organized a vigil
against French nuclear weapons tests at the French Consulate General in

[157] Appelius, *Pazifismus in Westdeutschland*, ii. 490, 497, 512.
[158] Archiv Aktiv, Hamburg, folder 14, VK: 'Vorschlag für die Tagesordnung für die
Bundeskonferenz', 15–16 November 1958, Cologne.
[159] Cf. the remiscences of Hans-Konrad Tempel and Helga Tempel, 'Ostermärsche
gegen den Atomtod', in Christoph Butterwegge et al. (eds), *30 Jahre Ostermarsch. Ein
Beitrag zur politischen Kultur der Bundesrepublik Deutschland und ein Stück Bremer Stadthge-
schichte* (Bremen, 1990), 11–14; Guido Grünewald, *Zwischen Kriegsdienstverweigerergewerkschaft und politischer Friedensorganisation: Der Verband der Kriegsdienstverweigerer
1958–1966* (Hamburg, 1977).
[160] Archiv Aktiv, Hamburg, folder 'Aktionskreis für Gewaltfreiheit': List of members
(*c*.1957).

Hamburg. After the press reports on 6 December 1959 about the stationing of British Honest-John missiles in Bergen-Hohne, the group decided
to organize a march to the area.[161] The planning for the Easter March was
taken over by a committee for the Easter March to the rocket test site
Bergen-Hohne, with Tempel as spokesman and coordinator.[162] The *VK*'s
federal executive endorsed the 'enterprise "Easter March"' at the end of
January 1960 and underwrote the venture with 300 Marks. Initially, the
Hessian section of the social-democratic 'Friends of Nature' youth organization also expressed an interest in taking part, but eventually cancelled
over fears of a lack of participation.[163]

Equally important for local and regional activities of the Campaign
against Atomic Death and the Easter Marches were the supporters around
the other main conscientious objectors' association, the 7,000-strong
Internationale der Kriegsdienstgegner (*IdK*), the official West German
branch of the War Resisters' International. The *IdK* followed the traditions
of the middle-class socialist Federation of War Resisters (*Bund der Kriegsdienstgegner*), which had been founded around the feminist Helene Stöcker
in 1919. While non-violence played an important role here as well, the
activists' emphasis on active grass-roots citizenship with the aim of thoroughly reforming all social relationships played a much stronger role than
in the *VK*.[164] Important for the networks were a conference centre in the
north German town of Bückeburg and discussion circles around the non-
violent pacifist Nikolaus Koch. Nikolaus Koch was the head of the Catholic Academy in Harzburg, but also had close connections to a Buddhist life
reform group around Paul Debes and Helmut Hecker in Hamburg.[165]
Conscientious objectors played a far less important role within CND, as
National Service was to be phased out by 1960, paradoxically as the result
of Britain's shift to a strategy of nuclear deterrence.[166] Activists joining
CND from associations like the PPU played an even less important role

---

[161] Wolfgang Kraushaar (ed.), *Die Protest-Chronik 1949–1959: Eine illustrierte Geschichte von Bewegung, Widerstand und Utopie* (4 vols; Hamburg, 1996), iii. 1245–6.
[162] HIS, TEM 400,01: 'Pressemitteilung', 16 January 1960.
[163] HIS, TEM 400,01: Klaus Vack to Hans-Konrad Tempel, 13 March 1960.
[164] Guido Grünewald, *Die Internationale der Kriegsdienstgegner (IdK): Ihre Geschichte
1945–1968* (Cologne, 1982), 7–12.
[165] Cf. 'Bericht von der Versöhnungsbund-Jahrestagung', *Friedensrundschau*, 6 (1955),
5–22; Archiv Aktiv, folder 'Freundschaftsheim b. Bückeburg': Nikolaus Koch, 'Aktiver
Widerstand mit Mitteln Gandhis gegen die Politik des Verderbens', Hagen/Westfalia n.d.
[*c*.1952]; Michael Scott, 'Gewaltloser Widerstand', *Stimme der Gemeinde*, 10/19 (1958),
cols 693–700; Joan Mary Fry, *Zwischen zwei Weltkriegen in Deutschland: Erinnerungen einer
Quäkerin* (Bad Pyrmont, 1947).
[166] TNA CAB 129/86: Sandys's revised draft of his Defence White Paper, 26 March 1957;
TNA DEFE 4/95: 'Long-Term Defence Policy', attached to Chiefs of Staff Committee
conclusions, 4 February 1957.

than pacifists in the West German campaign, although the PPU's paper *Peace News* initially served as the movement's main form of media communication.[167]

FELLOWSHIP AND COMMUNITY

The debates about nuclear weapons, therefore, highlighted the ways in which the cold war nuclear arms race worked to create community. To some extent, the debates within the various groups, especially within the Labour and socialist parties and the churches, were also debates about ideas and practices of forging social bonds and thus involved different concepts of socialization. For the activists, 'community' and 'society' were not opposed forms of social organization. Instead, the language of 'community' and 'fellowship' was both a precondition for and a result of the social interactions between protesters from very different backgrounds. As the terms 'community' and 'fellowship' were able to speak to very different political and social groups—from Christians over pacifists to humanists—they helped create a common identification. Moreover, once the movements had emerged, the concepts 'community' and 'fellowship' helped the activists find interpersonal security and, to outside observers, endowed the movements with a seeming homogeneity. While the relevance and the contents of these processes differed, the processes themselves during which such a 'fellowship' and 'community' emerged were remarkably similar.

While the British and West German activists' political experiences and expectations were very diverse, they nonetheless converged: they expressed dissonances between their hopes and projects and their experiences of the world around them in terms of their opposition to nuclear weapons. Christians could load the concept with meanings about Christian fellowship; pacifists and humanists with their hopes for a peaceful and rational world; for activists coming from the labour movement, it meant the realization of hopes for a socialist fellowship. It thus gave the protesters back the sense of belonging that they had lost in their own life worlds. On an international level, the concept of 'fellowship' also helped to create the impression of synchronicity between movements in different countries among observers and thus to make them appear as part of one global movement against nuclear weapons.[168]

---

[167] Ceadel, *Semi-Detached Idealists,* 426; Taylor and Pritchard, *Protest Makers,* 23–4.
[168] Interview with Arno Klönne, Paderborn, 20 August 2002; interview with Klaus Vack, Sensbachtal, 17 September 2002.

Paradoxically, the ideas for such a community were quite similar to the ideas and realities of military male comradeship and thus possessed highly gendered connotations.[169] 'Human fellowship' focused on the duties of its practitioners towards each other to treat each other equally, respectfully, and fairly. In contrast to military notions of comradeship, however, the movement's concept of fellowship did not centre around fighting, but defined endurance in emphatically non-violent ways. Moreover, the concept of 'universal fellowship' differed from military ideas of comradeship by creating a feeling of belonging without excluding specific groups a priori. Rather, its very strength lay in the overlap of exclusive and inclusive elements: it created a feeling of exclusivity among the protesters, while still maintaining a universal appeal.[170]

Fellowship was not just a theoretical concept, but it was also practised on the marches, by activists eating in communal kitchens, sleeping together in tents, and singing together, or merely by marching together. Particularly West German Easter March activists appropriated youth-movement traditions while marching, using specific forms of dress and the characteristic banners (see Figure 2). The ordering of this community was leisurely, yet orderly, and was, despite accusations of communist subversion, in marked contrast to the military style of communist comradeship in the earlier 1950s.

Within the fellowship, women activists rarely made direct claims for specific female interests: neither in Britain nor in West Germany did the presence of women campaigners lead to salient female arguments about 'peace' and 'security'. In both movements, arguments that defined women as mothers and claimed their specific responsibilities for future generations were confined to the debates about nuclear weapons tests, rather than nuclear disarmament generally. Although social policies in both countries aimed to reconstruct families around motherhood, explicit mention of a politics of motherhood sat oddly with the dominant anti-totalitarian cold war consensus.[171] In the Federal Republic in particular, arguments of motherhood conjured up memories of National Socialist

---

[169] Rolf Schroers, 'Maschinist und Partisan', *Frankfurter Hefte*, 16/3 (1961), 149–56, 149–50. On the background, cf. Thomas Kühne, *Kameradschaft: Die Soldaten des nationalsozialistischen Krieges und das 20. Jahrhundert* (Göttingen, 2006), 71, 85.

[170] Cf., for example, Theodor Michaltscheff, *Gewissen vor dem Prüfungsausschuß* (Hamburg, 1962); Interview with Arno Klönne, Paderborn, 20 August 2002.

[171] Robert G. Moeller, *Protecting Motherhood: Women and the Family in the Politics of Postwar West Germany* (Berkeley and Los Angeles, 1993); Pat Thane, 'Familiy Life and "Normality" in Postwar British Culture', in Richard Bessel and Dirk Schumann (eds), *Life after Death: Approaches to a Cultural and Social History of Europe during the 1940s and 1950s* (Cambridge, 2003), 193–210.

Figure 2. Easter March North 'From Bergen-Hohne to Hamburg', Hans-Konrad Tempel, centre, 1961. (Image courtesy of HIS, TEM 200, B01)

policies; since 1945, they had also come to be associated with communist arguments. In the cold war context, therefore, most female campaigners preferred to use seemingly gender-neutral arguments about peace and security, and were content with campaigning under the auspices of (an essentially male) 'fellowship'.[172]

The predominant idea of a gender-neutral 'fellowship' meant, therefore, that *explicitly* female contributions to the campaigns against nuclear

---

[172] Jill Liddington, *The Long Road to Greenham: Feminism and Anti-Militarism in Britain since 1820* (London, 1989), 172–94; Irene Stoehr, 'Frieden als Frauenaufgabe? Diskurse über Frieden und Geschlecht in der bundesdeutschen Friedensbewegung der 1950er Jahre', in Jennifer A. Davy, Karen Hagemann and Ute Kätzel (eds), *Frieden—Gewalt—Geschlecht: Friedens und Konfliktforschung als Geschlechterforschung* (Essen, 2005), 184–204, here 199–202.

weapons and towards security remained invisible and were pushed to the margins of the campaign.[173] The ambiguities of the gendered politics of security come into even sharper relief, if they are seen against the background of governmental discourses about the position of men, women, and the family in politics. Both the British and the West German government specifically targeted women in their capacities as 'housewives and mothers' through their social policies. It seems that even women at the time regarded female activism outside the boundaries of 'hearth and home' only as legitimate if it coexisted with a denial of their womanhood. In the highly gendered environment of the campaigns, women were only rarely allowed to assert themselves as political activists—frequently, they were assigned household chores. John Saville's wife, for example, was allowed to stay with Eric Hobsbawm in London for the Easter March weekend under the condition that she prepared meals for him.[174] And, if women did participate in the general movement debates, they were frequently ridiculed or ignored.[175] Nonetheless, specifically women in their late forties and early fifties, often with backgrounds in the moderate suffrage movement (among them Peggy Duff, Vera Brittain, Diana Collins, Jacquetta Hawkes, the Labour politician Edith Summerskill, and the biologist Antoinette Pirie), played important roles as campaign organizers both on the national and at local levels. While the trend was less pronounced in West Germany, women still participated in the movements as citizens concerned about nuclear weapons, yet not as acting subjects. The Hampstead branch of the Women's Cooperative Guild had played a key role in the organizational formation of one of the first-single issue campaigns against nuclear weapons, the National Committee for the Abolition of Nuclear Weapons Tests (NCANWT).[176] In Britain, CND's Women's Group ceased to function as a separate body by 1960, and its successor, the Liaison Committee for Women's Peace Groups, never managed to define the parameters of the discussion.[177] In the West German movement, such sections had never existed. While groups that advanced maternalist arguments, such as WOMAN (World Organization of Mothers of All Nations), participated in the campaigns, they never played a decisive role for the movement rhetoric and discourses.[178] These

[173] Cf. by contrast, Lawrence Wittner, 'Gender Roles and Nuclear Disarmament Activism, 1954–1965', *Gender & History*, 12 (2000), 197–222.

[174] Interview with John Saville, Hull, 23 July 2003.

[175] Interview with Hans-Konrad and Helga Tempel, Ahrensburg, 23 August 2003.

[176] Parkin, *Middle Class Radicalism*, 150.

[177] BLPES, CND/7/18: 'Women and Nuclear Weapons', pamphlet, n.d. (*c*.1960).

[178] IfZ, ED 702/7: Various press statements by the Munich Easter March committee, 1961–4.

findings, nonetheless, sit rather awkwardly with approaches that highlight the 'remasculinization' of British and West German societies during this period.[179] While the discourse might have been gender neutral, women still voiced their experiences and thus constituted themselves as active campaigners.

The historical specificity of the fellowship and community the movements created lay in the fact that the language and practice of community managed to bring together the very activists without forcing them to give up previous identities and identifications. The activists thus engaged in the politics of security in a double sense: first, and explicitly, by offering alternative visions of the cold war order; and, second, by providing a variety of activists with individual security by giving them a community and endowing their political views with new meanings.

---

[179] Robert G. Moeller, 'The "Remasculinization" of Germany in the 1950s: Introduction', *Signs*, 24 (1998), 101–6, here 106.

4

Organizing the Extra-Parliamentary Politics of Security

Concepts of 'fellowship' and 'community' were crucial for generating a feeling of belonging within the movements and for re-creating a synchrony between experiences and life worlds within the movements. As political actors, however, the movements also required organizations in order to regulate the multitude of communications about security and to turn them into political aims. Activists' political experiences and the form of social organization were, therefore, intimately related. Movement organizations aided the activists in discussing their aims and in communicating their visions of 'security' to the wider public by providing them with rules and procedures that enabled them to translate their manifold experiences into political aims. But the movements' organizational structures not only facilitated communications; they were themselves products of communicative processes.

Organizational structures endowed the protests with a political label. They gave activists and the general public a specific address—a name—on which they could call and thus helped establish networks of activists and aided political identification.[1] Thus, organizations made it possible that both activists and the general public could conceive of their protests not merely as events, but as part of a general and sustained political campaign. They helped create a seemingly stable political location that could be addressed by political actors and thus facilitated identification.[2] At the same time, however, the organizational structures of the campaigns created their own dissatisfactions: once the extra-parliamentary politics of

---

[1] Cf. Roland Roth, 'Kommunikationsstrukturen und Vernetzungen in neuen sozialen Bewegungen', in Roth and Dieter Rucht (eds), *Neue Soziale Bewegungen in der Bundesrepublik Deutschland* (Frankfurt and New York, 1987), 68–88.

[2] Elisabeth S. Clemens, 'Organizational Form as Frame: Collective Identity and Political Strategy in the American Labor Movement, 1880–1920', in Doug McAdam, John D. McCarthy, and Mayer N. Zald (eds), *Comparative Perspectives on Social Movements: Political Opportunities, Mobilizing Structures, and Cultural Framings* (Cambridge, 1996), 205–26.

security had been organized, some activists came to feel that the official routines and procedures hampered the fulfilment of their personal political goals. This gave rise to novel organizational dynamics that moved the politics of security on. Especially in West Germany, the link of the Campaign against Atomic Death to the *Sozialdemokratische Partei Deutschlands* (*SPD*) and the trade unions provided much cause for dissatisfaction and disillusionment.

By focusing on the main movement organizations, this chapter assesses how the movement organizers met these multiple challenges. It examines the constantly evolving organizational structures of the British and West German campaigns, the media they used to communicate with the public, and the attempts to establish transnational organizational structures. In particular, it demonstrates how the 'repertoires of collective action' available to the British and West German activists were reflected in the movement organizations.[3] Throughout, it is important to bear in mind that the organization of the politics of security in both countries was a highly gendered process.[4] Women were, because of gender, often channelled away from formal leadership positions and remained confined to informal leadership level.

The main organizational structures of the British and West German movements against nuclear weapons were quite similar. Both were coalitions of groups and individuals of, broadly speaking, left-wing political persuasion. While women occasionally played a role as organizers, the organizational structures were dominated by men. Neither campaigns introduced fundamentally new features into domestic politics. Rather, as the previous chapter has demonstrated, the characteristic feature of both movements was that they rested on pre-existing social and political networks and that they creatively reappropriated older organizational and protest traditions in their campaigns for more security. It was this ambiguity that made them so attractive to significant sections of the British and West German population.

The organizational development of both campaigns ran counter to the classic expositions of organizational theory, which assumes an increasing bureaucratization, a growing absence of accountability, and an increase in consensual strategies.[5] Both campaigns became increasingly differentiated functionally, but not to the detriment of grass-roots involvement. In both

[3] Charles Tilly, *From Mobilization to Revolution* (Reading, MA, 1978), 1.

[4] Belinda Robnett, 'African-American Women in the Civil Rights Movement, 1954–1965: Gender, Leadership, and Micromobilization', *American Journal of Sociology*, 101 (1996), 1661–93, here 1667.

[5] John D. May, 'Democracy, Organization, Michels', *American Political Science Review*, 59 (1965), 417–29.

countries, this process was driven by conditions that were specific to the protest groups. The forms of this organizational change differed, however. In Britain, the late 1950s and early 1960s saw the split of the campaign in different organizations, CND and the Committee of 100. In West Germany, one campaign, the Campaign against Atomic Death, structured along elite lines, dissolved, and a new movement emerged with the 'Easter Marches of Nuclear Weapons Opponents', which united all groups engaged in protests against nuclear weapons. Here, the foundation itself of a campaign outside the boundaries of a political party was contentious.

Yet the forms and historical developments of these organizations differed significantly. While most West German activists joined the anti-nuclear-weapons protests as members of other organizations, the organization of the British movement itself was much stronger and more centralist. This made the West German movement far more flexible in constantly adapting to new challenges, while the more firmly structured British movement had problems containing different views about 'security' within it.

CND: 'SOCIETY' OR 'CAMPAIGN'?

In terms of organization, the British protests centred around CND. CND's typical feature was that it rested on the self-organization by individuals who came together to campaign for the general aim of nuclear disarmament. CND was, initially, no more than a think tank-cum-pressure group whose members did not dream of taking their cause to the street. CND's organizational history was thus framed by the clash between the founders' limited ideas about grass-roots involvement, on the one hand, and the growth of popular support for CND, on the other. CND's founders were quite unprepared for the mass support their campaign generated and had problems adjusting their organization accordingly.[6]

Almost from its foundation, there was, therefore, considerable disagreement within CND about whether it should act as a political 'campaign' or a rather traditional 'society'.[7] It was mainly this debate that framed CND's organizational development. While the British campaigners agreed on their main goal—unilateral British disarmament to achieve more security—there existed no consensus on how to communicate this

---

[6] *Peace News*, 17 November 1961, 5; *Peace News*, 20 September 1963, 1.
[7] MALSU, M11 8/9A: 'What Next?', *Bulletin of the North-West CND* (November 1959), 1.

aim to the wider public. The main group in CND's executive sought to enlist the support of well-known individuals and influence Labour Party and parliamentary opinion through lobbying. The Direct Action Committee (DAC) and, later, the Committee of 100, by contrast, favoured demonstrations that might involve nominal violations of the law. Rather than rely on 'educational methods', the DAC and the C100 sought to break through 'the barrier of silence' through civil disobedience that offered unique potential 'by virtue of its news value'.[8]

Ironically, CND's problems in dealing with mass support stemmed from the strength of Britain's associational culture and the genealogies of political, social, and moral reform movements, which had, for at least a century, had their centre in middle-class London boroughs as well as in semi-metropolitan cities, such as Manchester and Edinburgh.[9] A closer look at CND's organizational origins demonstrates this. CND's immediate predecessor was the National Committee for the Abolition of Nuclear Weapons Tests (NCANWT), whose history had begun in the mid-1950s as a much more small-scale enterprise. It was linked to the rich traditions of middle-class metropolitan culture as well as to a section of the urban-based women's movement that stood at the centre of three overlapping spheres: cooperatives, feminism, and the labour movement. The NCANWT emerged from the Golders Green and Suburb Women's Cooperative Guild. The Guild had, under the leadership of the retired civil servant and former suffragette Miss Gertrude Fishwick, organized protests against nuclear weapons tests since July 1955 in the Hampstead area. It enjoyed strong links with the Society of Friends (Quakers), the local trade-union branches and Labour Party wards, the Fellowship of Reconciliation, and the Cooperative Women's Guilds. Arthur Goss, proprietor of the *Hampstead and Highgate Express* and an active Quaker pacifist, became the group's new chairman, while Fishwick remained responsible for the Golders Green area. The NCANWT was set up at a meeting in Alliance Hall, Palmer Street, London, in late November 1956 with the help of the National Peace Council, an umbrella organization for various non-communist peace movements. As the personal networks, grown through personal acquaintances and joint campaign in the past, compensated for the lack of formal organizations, there was no need to think about formal decision-making and communication structures. Within the first four months after its foundation, seventy-five local

---

[8] Bertrand Russell writing in *Encounter*, 16 (1961), 93.
[9] Cf. Brian Harrison, 'A Genealogy of Reform in Modern Britain', in Christine Bolt and Seymour Drescher (eds), *Anti-Slavery, Religion, and Reform: Essays in Memory of Roger Anstey* (Folkestone and Hamden, CT, 1980), 119–48.

NCANWT groups had been established after publications of advertisements in the *News Chronicle* and *Manchester Guardian*, the paper of the liberally oriented middle class.[10] The rise in public support required the campaign to employ a full-time secretary, Peggy Duff, who had known some of the NCANWT organizers through her involvement as the organizing secretary of the Common Wealth Party.[11]

Throughout, three interrelated issues influenced the NCANWT's organizational developments, and they were to characterize CND's organizational debates as well. First, the NCANWT was an essentially liberal body. It believed in reasoned argument and persuasion and accepted the British political and party system as a basis from which to achieve change. It focused on elite opinion rather than obtaining mass support.

This implied, second, that the NCANWT rejected DAC's direct action campaigns. The DAC had been founded in spring 1957 to support pacifist Harold Steele's attempt to sail into the Pacific in protest against British H-bomb tests. While the DAC and some local branches promoted direct action, picketing at weapons factories and missile bases, and organized protests against French tests in the Sahara,[12] the NCANWT's National Council focused on applying political pressure on parties, especially the Labour Party, and on organizing legal demonstrations of protests to mobilize public opinion.[13] Third, the NCANWT's general policy meant that it refused to adopt a thoroughly pacifist stance; it was intent on keeping its focus on the single issue of unilateral renunciation of nuclear weapons tests and, from November 1957, on unilateral nuclear disarmament, and did not seek to widen its campaigns to weapons and armaments in general, as advocated by the Fellowship of Reconciliation, the Society of Friends (Quakers), and the Peace Pledge Union (PPU).[14] The question of anti-communism did not greatly influence the organizational debates and developments of the NCANWT. Although most of the NCANWT's leading members were firmly anti-communist, the issue did not arise initially, as the Communist Party followed a firmly multilateralist line until 1959.[15]

---

[10] Driver, *The Disarmers*, 31; Richard Taylor, *Against the Bomb*, 7–9.

[11] Duff, *Left, Left, Left*, 3–9.

[12] Richard Taylor, *Against the Bomb*, 156–67.

[13] *Manchester Guardian*, 12 April 1957; MRC, MSS 181: Executive Committee, minutes, 25 September 1958; Frank Allaun to *Peace News*, 9 January 1959, 2; *Peace News*, 18 April 1959, 1.

[14] Richard Taylor, *Against the Bomb*, 12–14.

[15] John Callaghan, *Cold War, Crisis and Conflict: The CPGB 1951–68* (London, 2003), 141–51.

These organizational, social, and ideological characteristics formed the basis for CND's organization and underlay its problems in creating an efficient politics of communication. Its foundation was closely linked to the social networks around the NCANWT and, like CND, was initially founded as a small pressure group of (mostly male) metropolitan intellectuals around the *New Statesman* journalist Kingsley Martin.[16] Peggy Duff became CND's full-time organizer and secretary. When CND was founded, the NCANWT handed over its assets and contacts as well as its premises in 146 Fleet Street, London, to the new campaign. Eric Baker, the general secretary of the National Peace Council, gave the premises rent-free to CND.[17]

CND's executive committee continued to show a remarkable cultural homogeneity from the late 1950s into the early 1960s. Throughout 1958, nineteen people were, at one time or another, members of the executive committee. Thirteen of them were listed in the current *Who's Who*, four were journalists, at least twelve were authors, and almost all of them had, at one time, written for the national press. Most were associated with the Labour Party or at least firmly sympathetic towards it. Canon Collins and Peggy Duff became key figures in policy-making and strategy, while the importance of J. B. Priestley and Kingsley Martin declined. Michael Foot and A. J. P. Taylor played particularly forceful roles. Similar founding processes played themselves out on the local level in England, Scotland, and Wales.[18]

The result was that, from hindsight, CND's executive at its foundation was closer to the associational world of Edwardian Britain than to the forms of organizations that dominated the student protests of the later 1960s. Unlike in these Edwardian associations, however, no formal campaign membership existed. CND organizers sought to remain an essentially elite organization that lobbied parliament and parties, rather than built up a mass membership. Moreover, had CND constituted itself as a membership organization, it would, in all likelihood, have been proscribed by the Labour Party. This formed an important precondition for future growth to a social movement.[19]

After CND's first public meeting in mid-February 1958, local CND chapters sprang up across the country. By the end of 1958, there were 200 groups across Britain. This made some organizational adjustments necessary,

[16] Canon John L. Collins, *Faith under Fire* (London, 1966), 303.
[17] MRC, MSS 181: Executive Committee, minutes, 21 January 1958; Richard Taylor, *Against the Bomb*, 16–20; Driver, *The Disarmers*, 43.
[18] Richard Taylor, *Against the Bomb*, 23–5.
[19] MRC, MSS 181: National Executive, minutes, 28 January 1958.

as there was increasing conflict between the executive's structure and the manifold interests at the local level. Yet even once CND had gone public, the intellectuals in the executive committee did not systematically address the question of how to harness the broad popular support for the movement for its aims, without destroying its diversity. Although Peggy Duff organized the campaigns efficiently, the great support had taken the executive by surprise, and the intellectuals assembled in it did not see the need for a more thorough engagement with the question of movement communication.[20]

This led to a growing disjuncture in the ways in which executive and grass-roots supporters sought to address the problem of 'security'. The executive responded by replicating the organizational structure of the early Labour Party. In order to solve the problems of coordination with the rank and file, the executive set up a coordinating committee in autumn 1958. The purpose of this committee was to establish links with the constituent bodies of the movement. It was to serve primarily as a body for discussion, through which information could travel in both directions. The introduction of annual conferences was another means of improving intra-movement communications. Over the course of 1958 and 1959, the executive encouraged the establishment of regional councils to coordinate the work of the local groups. Yet decision-making continued to lie with the (unelected) executive, whose social composition was maintained by co-optation rather than election.[21] More specifically, the problems reflected the efforts of a group of 'public moralists' both to maintain their intellectual status in the debates about security and to enlighten and guide the British population towards what they regarded as sensible political aims.[22]

Hence, tensions within CND's organization increased as the executive struggled to cope with the *Eigen-Sinn* of its supporters. This situation resulted in frequent complaints from the rank and file who, in the words of one 1958 conference delegate, 'were not prepared to be general hewers of wood and drawers of water without some representation on the executive committee'.[23] The main theme of these discussions was how CND should campaign: through education and gentle pressure alone, or also through public demonstrations? This theme had been visible as early as March 1958. Only after intensive discussions and perceived pressure from

---

[20] MRC, MSS 181: National Executive, minutes, 2 January 1959.
[21] MRC, MSS 181: National Executive, minutes, 25 May 1959, 11–12 April 1959.
[22] Stefan Collini, *Public Moralists: Political Thought and Intellectual Life in Britain 1850–1930* (Oxford, 1991).
[23] BLPES, CND/1/1: Jim Roche (Leeds), 'Annual Conference, 1958', report.

the grass roots did the CND executive agree to join the DAC on a march from London to the governmental nuclear weapons research establishment in Aldermaston, Berkshire.[24]

Thus, there emerged two campaigns in one: the grass-roots popular movement, which remained virtually unrepresented in the executive; and the executive itself, which showed disdain for 'the masses'. Looking back, A. J. P. Taylor bemoaned that CND 'had become too democratic'.[25] And Diana Collins showed outright disgust at social-movement politics when she wrote to Jacquetta Hawkes in February 1958 that 'the thought of spending a social evening organised by our long-haired bearded friends instead of an evening with you and Jack [Hawkes's partner, J. B. Priestley] fills me with such despondency and gloom that I can hardly bear to contemplate it'.[26]

The executive and activists responded to these challenges of intra-movement communications by founding bodies that represented special interests and advanced their very own ideas of the politics of security. Thus, an organization emerged over time that split CND into different social and professional groups that lobbied for their specific aims. There was, for example, a CND scientists' organization, a Youth CND, a Universities' CND, and a Women's CND. There also existed a Labour advisory committee, which was made up of Labour politicians sympathetic towards CND.[27] From 1961, Christian presence within the Campaign was institutionalized in an own subgroup: Christian CND (CCND), run by Pamela Frankau, Francis Jude, and Diana Collins,[28] with its own journal *Rushlight*. CCND never grew very large: only fourteen people were actively involved in 1962, and the mailing list of its journal *Rushlight* contained only 750 names.[29] This pattern reflected the specific features of British political life. British society was divided into a multitude of distinct, but often overlapping, groups and associations that all dealt with specific problems. In terms of social organization, there were many societies, but no concept of 'society' as a whole.[30]

[24] MRC, MSS 181: National Executive, minutes, 17 November 1958; Richard Taylor, *Against The Bomb*, 28–9.
[25] A. J. P. Taylor in conversation with Richard Taylor, quoted in Richard Taylor, *Against the Bomb*, 60.
[26] Letter to Jacquetta Hawkes, 16 February 1958, quoted in Richard Taylor, *Against the Bomb*, 47.
[27] MRC, MSS 181: National Executive, minutes, 5 October 1958.
[28] 'Christians Confer on the Bomb', *Sanity* (November 1961), 1; MRC, MSS 181: National Executive, minutes, 30 June 1961.
[29] BLPES, CND/7/17/8: Mailing list for *Rushlight*, n.d. (*c.*1962).
[30] Cf. Ross McKibbin, *Classes and Cultures: England 1918–1951* (Oxford, 1998), 528–36.

The functional differentiation of CND's organization was ultimately not able to prevent internal tensions from coming to a head. Open discussions started in spring 1959 when Bertrand Russell proposed at the annual conference that the executive be elected and a membership scheme be introduced. The proposal was rejected. Instead, the conference voted to increase the members of the executive committee, so that local groups could be represented through delegates from the regional councils.[31]

Labour's defeat at the 1959 general elections appeared to expose the weaknesses of CND's Labour-centric strategy even further. By contrast, the success of the 1960 Aldermaston March, whose final rally attracted between 60,000 and 100,000 people, lent more credence for those who argued for a strategy based on direct action. For many grass-roots activists, developments in the international arena further accentuated the need for new forms of action. The crisis of a U2 spy plane in Soviet airspace, the shooting-down over the USSR of an American RB47 reconnaissance plane, and the collapse of the Paris disarmament summit in June 1960 appeared to require some more dramatic forms of action that were 'in keeping with the needs of the situation'.[32]

The foundation of the Committee of 100 (C100) was a direct result of these organizational problems.[33] But it did not really reflect grass-roots concerns either. Through its advocacy of illegal ways of campaigning, such as the invasion of army barracks and air force bases, the C100 soon came under constant police and secret service surveillance. From 1962 onwards, more of its activists were in jail than demonstrating on the streets.[34] Following the anarchist tradition of 'propaganda by the deed' became increasingly difficult.

While the C100 continued to campaign for human fellowship, its communicative practices came to resemble the initiation rites of male secret societies in order to protect itself from intrusion by secret service agents. This increased the C100's coherence as a movement, but it weakened its overall appeal. Together with an influx from a younger and more active group of members, the pressures of constant police and secret service surveillance led to the break-up of the C100 from a relatively compact structure with a leading group of people into an amorphous collection of almost autonomous units with no authoritative leadership.[35] Instead of

---

[31] BLPES, CND/1/2: Annual Conference, Report, 1959.

[32] Ralph Schoenman, 'Preface', in Schoenman (ed.), *Bertrand Russell: Philosopher of the Century* (New York, 1967), 1; Nicolas Walter, 'Non-Violent Resistance: Men against War', *Non Violence*, 63 (1963), 31.

[33] This modifies the views in Collins, *Faith under Fire*, 318.

[34] 'Letters to the Editor', *Daily Telegraph*, 23 June 1962, 8; John Morris, 'Civil Disobedience: 1962', *Peace News*, 7 September 1962, 4.

[35] IISG, C100 papers: Minutes, 27 May 1961 (comment by John Morris).

one C100, there existed thirteen regional Committees of 100 from 1962 onwards, which lacked a powerful executive body.[36]

In the wake of the C100's foundation CND sought to address the issue of intra-movement communication by reforming the constitutional set-up and making it more systematic.[37] The executive's plan for a new constitution carried the day at CND's annual conference in 1961. It entailed the establishment of a pyramidal organization, with local groups at the base and the executive at the apex. CND policy was to be decided by annual conference. Members of the annual conference were delegates from each local group and each specialist section. The national coordinating committee was abolished and replaced by a national council, which, in the period between conferences, determined overall policy and strategy.[38] The elections resulted in a national council and an executive that was not strikingly different from its predecessors: Canon Collins remained chairman and Ritchie Calder vice-chairman.[39] In late April 1961, putting the personal issues between Russell and Collins aside, the CND executive also established a liaison committee with the DAC and the C100.[40]

Yet conflicts continued over the question of whether to campaign with CND candidates at by-elections. This strategy was favoured by a group around Nigel Young and CND treasurer Laurie Kershaw from the London CND, who founded an Independent Nuclear Disarmament Election Committee in 1962 after unilateralist motions had been rejected at the Labour Party conference.[41]

Faced with these persistent problems of intra-movement communications, the CND's executive committee agreed to a major overhaul of its structure and practice at the beginning of 1963. A new management sub-committee was established in order to supervise CND's day-to-day business, consisting of the officers, three members of the executive, and the national council.[42] The reorganization strengthened CND's centralized structure and pushed the public figures who had initiated CND further to the sidelines. Canon Collins resigned in 1964 and Peggy Duff in 1966–7. In 1966, CND became a membership organization, thus leaving its past as a political *movement* behind.[43]

[36] IISG, C100 papers: Peter Cadogan, 'Memo on the Problem of Initiative' circular, 13 December 1962; East Anglia C100, *Newsletter*, 2 (June 1962), 3.

[37] Duff, *Left, Left, Left*, 155.

[38] BLPES, CND/1/3: National Executive, minutes, 30 April 1961.

[39] BLPES CND/1/4: 'Annual Report, 1960–61'.

[40] BLPES CND/1/3: National Executive, minutes, 30 April 1961.

[41] Richard Taylor, *Against the Bomb*, 85; Labour Party, *Proceedings of the 59th Annual Conference* (Scarborough, 1960), 76–242.

[42] MRC, MSS 181: National Council, minutes, 28 May 1961.

[43] Duff, *Left, Left, Left*, 225.

THE WEST GERMAN MOVEMENTS: FROM ORGANIZING SOCIETIES TO MOBILIZING SOCIETY

As in CND, the organizational communications within the West German movements were characterized by differences between the activists' *Eigen-Sinn* (sense of one's own agency) and the policies of the executive. Yet the coding of these communications differed. It mainly revolved around the distinction of communism/anti-communism rather than legitimacy. The cold war conflict had a more immediate impact on the West German movement in structuring the organizational cultures themselves and in transforming existing forms of organizations into a political movement. It was mainly this framing of the discussion that allowed the West German movement to make a transition from the *SPD* campaign that sought to mobilize its members in order to reach 'the public' into a movement that sought to mobilize West German 'society' as a whole.

Organizations played a more significant role for channelling people into the movements in West Germany than in Britain throughout the period, although they lost in importance as the movements became established. This is why intra-movement communications and the adaptations to new demands happened more smoothly in West Germany than in Britain. While problems of intra-movement organization led to the split of the British movement into CND and the more radical C100, the West German movement was characterized by a chronological split that divided it into two distinct political phases. While the first phase was directly linked to the politics of the Social Democratic Party and the trade unions, the second phase led to the foundation of a grass-roots movement independent of party-political influences. These differences reflected different political and social contexts. After the destruction of working- and middle-class associations during the Nazi regime,[44] associational culture in the young Federal Republic was not yet fully developed, so that the organizations of the Labour movement played a large role for mobilizing activists.

More importantly, the impact of cold war political culture on the movement was more significant in the Federal Republic. Particularly during the second phase of the West German Marches, the protests faced a generally antagonistic climate and a massive government campaign against them. There were widespread accusations of fellow-travelling, and the organizers had to overcome serious practical obstacles when applying

---

[44] Cf. Peter Fritzsche, *Rehearsals for Fascism: Populism and Political Mobilization in Weimar Germany* (Oxford, 1990).

for permissions to march on the Easter weekend. The Easter Marches, therefore, developed more into the direction of the British C100, yet without becoming a secret society with initiation rites. Instead, the rhetoric of fellowship and community remained as open as it had been intended by the organizers. Both these factors enabled the organizers to devise a much more sophisticated and efficient intra-movement communication that made constant self-observations and, thus, adjustments of strategy possible. From the beginning of the campaign in 1958, the *SPD* brought its campaign strategies to bear on the Campaign against Atomic Death and focused on organizing communications, rather than organizing people. The Campaign was a part of the *SPD*'s party machinery. Like the British Campaign, it was set up 'to enlighten the public', but it did so much more emphatically.[45]

Unlike in the movements against conventional rearmament in the early and mid-1950s, the *SPD* now became directly involved in the protests and used methods tested out in election campaigns for internal and external campaign communications.[46] The Campaign was clearly set up in order to sway 'public opinion' beyond the traditional working-class voter base in the upcoming elections in the important state of North Rhine Westphalia, after the general elections in autumn 1957 had resulted in an absolute majority for the *CDU*.[47] It constantly used polls to gauge public opinion and determine whether the campaign was successful.[48] There was a systematic collection of press cuttings, which were fed into the decision-making process. The Campaign organizers used the *SPD*'s papers to propagate the message of the 'Fight against Atomic Death', and prominent journalists were contacted to write in favour of the Campaign in the other main papers.[49]

Although the organizers used means (such as posters, newspaper adverts, and even films) similar to ones the party had already used in election campaigns in the Weimar Republic, they no longer relied on direct

[45] AdsD: Parteivorstand, minutes, 20 November 1957.
[46] Cf. the interpretation by Jost Dülffer, 'The Movement against Rearmament 1951–55 and the Movement against Nuclear Armament 1957/59 in the Federal Republic: A Comparison', in Maurice Vaïsse (ed.), *Le Pacifisme en Europe des années 1920 aux années 1950* (Brussels, 1993), 417–34, here 434.
[47] AdsD, 2/PVAJ000305: Werbe- und Propaganda-Ausschuß, minutes, 1957–1958, 10 January 1958; Detlef Lehnert, *Sozialdemokratie zwischen Protestbewegung und Regierungspartei 1848–1983* (Frankfurt/Main, 1983), 186.
[48] On the connection to electoral considerations within the SPD, cf. AdsD, Bruno Gleitze papers: 'Werbe-Ausschuss, Meinungsforschung,—, 1954–1957'.
[49] AdsD, 2/PVAM000013: Axel Eggebrecht to Alexander Maaß, 22 November 1960; *EMNID-Informationen* (February 1961), 6; AdsD, 2/PVAM000030: Alexander von Cube to Alexander Maaß, 24 June 1960.

communication with its members alone. The focus extended beyond the immediate *SPD* and trade-union membership to (West) German society as a whole. Unlike the CND executive, the Campaign headquarters never addressed the government and specific sections of society or interests groups only. It addressed (West) German 'society', rather than its societies. The name of the campaign in some regions was *Volksbewegung gegen den Atomtod* (People's Movement against Atomic Death).[50]

This reflected the desire not just to campaign for a specific cause, but also to mobilize 'the people' and the 'public sphere' as a whole. The title also echoed calls for a progressively defined 'Volksgemeinschaft', which had become prominent in the *SPD* during the First World War, but was also attractive for all those who had identified with the National Socialist 'Volksgemeinschaft'.[51] In addition, the cold war helped to create coherence of 'society' in the eyes of the *SPD* organizers. The key binary opposition communism/anti-communism facilitated communications about movement aims and organizations both within the Campaign and between the Campaign and 'the public'. Within, it created an initial basic consensus about campaign strategy and practice.[52] Outside, the main goal was to shield the Campaign against accusations that it was a communist fellow-travelling organization and that it represented the 'real interests of the German people'.[53]

After its launch, the Campaign spread across the Federal Republic as regional and local committees were set up. This often followed local and independent initiatives, but the local campaigns were soon integrated into the top-down organization and run, by and large, under the auspices of the *SPD* and the Federation of German Trade Unions (*Deutscher Gewerkschaftsbund* (*DGB*). Thus, the links between party, trade unions, and the Campaign's organization were replicated on the local level. The regional and local committees acted merely as executive organs of the central committee, and their role was to assist in the regional and local distribution of the campaign material that had been compiled centrally, rather than to

---

[50] AdsD, *DGB* Archives, Abt. Organisation, 24/2194: 'Volksbewegung Kampf dem Atomtod, Arbeitsausschuß Hessen', circular, 19 December 1958.

[51] Cf. Paul Nolte, *Die Ordnung der deutschen Gesellschaft: Selbstentwurf und Selbstbeschreibung* (Munich, 2000), 197–207.

[52] AdsD, 2/PVAM000031: DGB Bundesvorstand (Georg Reuter) to Heinrich Ihrig, 25 June 1958; AdsD, IG Metall archives, G1010: Walter Menzel to Willi Richter, 5 October 1961.

[53] AdsD 2/PVAM000031: North Rhine Westphalian Regional Committee of Campaign against Atomic Death, minutes, 8 May 1958. On the counter-campaign by the CDU in the context of the CDU's general communication policies, cf. Frank Bösch, *Die Adenauer-CDU: Gründung, Aufstieg und Krise einer Erfolgspartei (1945–1969)* (Stuttgart, 2001), 237–67.

participate in policymaking. It is, therefore, not surprising that the campaign was strongest where the *SPD* did particularly well in local, regional, and state elections, such as in the *SPD* district of South Hesse.[54]

Unlike in Britain, the main question that framed the discussions about intra-movement communications in West Germany did not explicitly address campaign strategy. Although there was considerable discussion about plans put forward by some Social Democrats and trade unionists to launch a general strike in protest against the government plans, the main debate focused on the question of how to maintain an anti-communist stance, while launching protests outside the conventional political channels of parliament, party, and interest group.[55] Because of the common heritage of radicalism, all Labour movement campaigns came to be exposed to accusations of communist bodies sponsored by the GDR after the banning of the German Communist Party in 1956. These bodies operated in the Federal Republic under similar names, such as the 'Action Committees for Atomic Disarmaments'.[56]

Anti-communism permeated the West German intra-movement communications so much that there was a constant interchange with civil servants in the Foreign Office and the Ministry of Defence who felt sympathetic towards the *SPD* and leaked classified information to the Campaign. This often involved the *SPD*'s office in East Berlin, which entertained close connections to the West German government and probably also had informers among West Berlin students.[57] Moreover, the Campaign offices appeared to be under observation from the Federal Constitutional Protection Agency (*Bundesamt für Verfassungsschutz*), at least until spring 1958.[58] The Campaign's executive wrote to its members increasingly frequently advising them against associating themselves with

---

[54] AdsD, Menzel papers: circular by the SPD's *Kommunalpolitische Zentralstelle*, 17 March 1958; AdsD, 2/PVAM00008: Alexander von Cube (*Vorwärts*) to Maaß, 23 December 1958; AdsD, Parteivorstand, minutes, 25 April 1958; Minutes of the meeting of the *DGB*'s executive committee, 4 March 1958, in Klaus Schönhoven and Hermann Weber (eds), *Quellen zur Geschichte der deutschen Gewerkschaftsbewegung im 20. Jahrhundert* (13 vols, Bonn, 2005), xii. 263–5.

[55] Cf., for example, the minutes of the *DGB* executive committee meetings, 28 March 1958 and 1 April 1958, in Schönhoven and Weber (eds), *Quellen*, 273 and 280–5.

[56] Heinrich Hannover, *Politische Diffamierung der Opposition im freiheitlich-demokratischen Rechtsstaat* (Dortmund-Barop, 1962), 121–3; Werner Hofmann, *Stalinismus und Antikommunismus: Zur Soziologie des Ost-West-Konflikts* (Frankfurt/Main, 1967), 152–4.

[57] AdsD, 2/PVAM000024: Manfred Rexin to Alexander Maaß, 7 April 1959. On the background, cf. Wolfgang Buschfort, *Das Ostbüro der SPD: Von der Gründung bis zur Berlin-Krise* (Munich, 1991).

[58] HWR, 1.43.507: 'Seminar in Feldafing', 6–9 November 1958, 17. On the background, cf. Wolfgang Buschfort, *Geheime Hüter der Verfassung: Von der Düsseldorfer Informationsstelle zum ersten Verfassungsschutz der Bundesrepublik (1947–1961)* (Paderborn, 2004).

these groups—decisions that the supporters, lacking the intelligence information, often found exaggerated, or did not understand.[59] The Campaign's supporters thus found themselves in an almost impossible position. On the one hand, they had to defend themselves against accusations even by Social Democrats to be Moscow's 'fifth column'. On the other hand, if they reacted by weakening their message towards general humanitarian appeals, their critics might accuse them of being the willing tools of the *SPD*'s public-relations machine.[60]

Subsequent developments of intra-organizational communications were, therefore, driven by the top-down nature in which the executive dealt with the clash between the activists' *Eigen-Sinn* and the *SPD*'s attempts to strengthen its central organization at its Stuttgart conference in May 1958, which was part of a longer-term effort to 'modernize' the party.[61] The *SPD* and the trade unions supported the Campaign against Atomic Death's communication aims as long as their observation of social reality appeared to pay off. Initially, opinion polls suggested that the Campaign had indeed increased the opposition party's standing in the population. Yet, when opinion polls and, finally, the devastating election results in North Rhine Westphalia in summer 1958 suggested otherwise, discussions began in the *SPD* to stop the campaign.[62] The Federal Constitutional Court's ruling on 30 July 1958 against plebiscites on a *Land* level against nuclear weapons, and the Campaign's main protests in the summer, provided the Campaign's opponents with the necessary arguments.[63]

Likewise, the *DGB* tried to strengthen its central organization. It had also come under increased strain, as its Christian trade-union affiliates had become increasingly dissatisfied with the executive's open support for a campaign against the Adenauer government and as overtures by the East German Trade Union Federation (*Freier Deutscher Gewerkschaftsbund* (*FDGB*)) increased the risk that campaigns might be 'hijacked' by the *SED* regime.[64] Although the Campaign continued to exist on paper, its

---

[59] AdsD: Präsidium, minutes, 20 February 1961.

[60] HWR, 72.86.512: Hans Werner Richter to John Collins, 24 April 1960.

[61] Cf. Kurt Klotzbach, *Der Weg zur Staatspartei: Programmatik, praktische Politik und Organisation der deutschen Sozialdemokratie 1945–1965* (Bonn, 1996), 570–8.

[62] AdsD, 3/BEAB000557: SPD Berlin, minutes, 13 October 1958.

[63] *Parlamentarisch-Politischer Pressedienst*, 1 August 1958; *Bulletin des Presse- und Informationsamtes der Bundesregierung*, 106 (14 June 1958), 1065–6, 1068; BAK, B106/2437: 'Zur Frage der Verfassungsmäßigkeit von Volksbefragungen. Rechtsgutachten der Verfassungsabteilungen des BMI und BMJ' [n.d., *c.* May 1958].

[64] Cf. *Protokoll 5. Ordentlicher Bundeskongress, Stuttgart, 7.–12. September 1959*, ed. Bundesvorstand des Deutschen Gewerkschaftsbundes (Düsseldorf, n.d.), 707–10; minutes of the 8th meeting of the *DGB* federal executive, in Schönhoven and Weber (eds), *Quellen*, 4 February 1959, 431–5, here 432.

main activities were now limited to calls for nuclear disarmament on Labour Day (1 May), which continued until 1963.[65] The Hessian and North Rhine Westphalian regional committees had already ceased their activities in autumn 1958.[66]

From spring 1958, the organizational strengthening of the Campaign began to clash with several grass-roots initiatives on the local level. This was particularly the case in Berlin, where, because of the permeable border with the GDR, independent extra-parliamentary campaigns could easily be portrayed as communist-inspired. In April 1958, the foundation of the Campaign's Berlin regional committee had been marred by earlier accusations of communist subversion, since it had supported a protest demonstration by the Falcons, a social-democratic youth organization, in Neukölln.[67]

Similar discussions surrounded the student congress against nuclear weapons, which was held in Berlin in January 1959. The initiative had come from the Berlin Student Committee around the moderates Manfred Rexin and Ansgar Skriver. Yet, from the beginning, the Campaign's national executive had been sceptical of such a congress for fear of communist subversion, a fear that was heightened by Krushchev's Berlin ultimatum on 27 November 1958. While there is some evidence for communist activities at the congress, what was noteworthy was that even non-communist and moderate students used their opposition to the *SPD*'s anti-communism as an organizational and communicative resource.[68] Although cloaked in the language of anti-communism, this was essentially a debate about the role of grass-roots involvement within *SPD* politics.[69]

Activists were, in the end, left without a campaign organization. While they maintained their original policy goals, their activities became dispersed across several existing pacifist, youth, and labour movement associations as well as independent local activities. Yet, their general concern

---

[65] AdsD: Präsidium, minutes, 23 January 1961, 3; AdsD: *DGB* Archives, Abt. Organisation, 24/9006: 'Pressemitteilung der SPD, betr.: Ostermarsch-Bewegung', 7 November 1963; AdsD, 2/PVAM000033: Maaß to Ollenhauer, 22 March 1962; AdsD, IG Metall Archives, G1285: Maaß to Brand, 25 January 1962.

[66] AdsD: Präsidum, minutes, 20 February 1961, 1–2; AdsD, *DGB*, Abt. Organisation, 24–2215: 'Information für den BV des DGB über die Vorbereitung zum "Ostermarsch 1963"', 31 January 1963.

[67] *Die Welt*, 14 April 1958, 5; *Berliner Tagesspiegel*, 15 April 1958, 3; *Frankfurter Rundschau*, 26–27 April 1958, 3; AdsD, ASAF000177: Circular by the 'Studentenausschuß gegen Atomrüstung', Berlin, 2 July 1958.

[68] Röhl, *Fünf Finger sind keine Faust*, 90–2.

[69] AdsD: Parteivorstand, minutes, 9–10 January 1961, 8–9; Präsidium, minutes, 20 February 1961, 837–8.

for the issue of nuclear weapons and their previous involvement in extra-parliamentary politics provided them with the political and social resources to found and join a new campaign. While the Campaign against Atomic Death had depended entirely on pre-existing organizational structures, the 'Easter Marches of Nuclear Weapons Opponents' gradually emerged from the bottom up. While there was still some organizational cohesion and a central office, 'grass-roots' involvement and 'movement' became the concepts that began to frame intra-organizational communications.

The Easter Marches' organization developed out of discussions about how to organize an opposition outside parliament within what some supporters called 'democratic totalitarianism'. Even activists outside the remit of the socialist left in the Federal Republic, such as Hans-Konrad Tempel, subscribed to such interpretations as they feared that existing social organizations such as parties and trade unions had been brought into line with the Adenauer government and offered little scope for alternative politics. Protests therefore had to focus on 'social self-organization from below' and on 'direct action' in order to realize their aims.[70] The communist/anti-communist coding continued to influence discussions about how to organize 'security'. But it was primarily important for describing the movement from the outside and created cohesion in an environment in which actions left of the parameters of the *SPD* came with almost automatic supervision by the secret services and, possibly, practical consequences.[71]

The organizers continued to maintain the *SPD* Campaign's emphasis on communicating with 'the people'. But they developed methods of organizational self-observation further, as they realized that it was primarily through appearances in the mass media—rather than merely the Campaign's name—that the different protest events appeared as a sustained political movement. While the *SPD* campaign had mainly focused on rationalizing internal communications, internal and external movement communications had become inextricably connected in the Easter Marches. By aiming to reach individual members of 'the public', rather than sections of it, the organization remained in constant movement.[72] This approach had been conditioned by the dominance of the communist/

---

[70] HIS, TEM200,03: 'Wie soll es weitergehen?', Central Committee, minutes, 6/7 May 1961.

[71] AdsD, 2/PVAM000033: Alexander Maass to Walter Menzel (KdA), 22 March 1962; Siegward Lönnendonker (ed.), *Linksintellektueller Aufbruch zwischen 'Kulturrevolution' und 'kultureller Zerstörung': Der Sozialistische Deutsche Studentenbund (SDS) in der Nachkriegsgeschichte (1946–1969). Dokumentation eines Symposiums* (Opladen, 1998), 80–1.

[72] HIS, TEM 200,03: Central Committee, minutes, 6/7 May 1961.

anti communist coding: 'Because of the danger of the appearance of "Eastern friends of peace"...under an associational banner, we would like to stress in our letters and flyers as well as on posters that only individuals and not organizations are allowed to take part.'[73]

Most importantly, through its very organization and the communication about it, the movement became linked to West Germany's political system. In view of the Easter Marchers, it not only organized West German security, but also West German democracy.[74] But reaching the public remained a 'phantasy'.[75] The movement was part of West German society, but remained outside it. Widespread accusations in the West German press about the non-, if not anti-democratic, nature of the campaign and its allegedly communist clientele maintained the border.[76]

Despite the lack of an elaborate organizational structure and communication regime, the Easter March organizers were keen to translate their own views about campaigning into movement politics. In leaflets entitled 'Suggestions for Participants', the organizers asked the marchers to follow the organizers' orders 'swiftly and visibly', 'especially when the reason for the decision is not immediately obvious'.[77] Karl A. Otto has described this organizational regime as 'authoritarian' and thus implicitly linked these policies to specifically German traditions of political culture. Unlike CND and the later West German 'extra-parliamentary opposition', he argues, the Easter Marches lacked an 'emancipatory' potential.[78] But, in comparative perspective, CND as an organization had far more problems with grass-roots politics than the West German Easter Marches. The West German Easter Marches had much more in common with the loose structure of the C100 and the British New Left.

The Easter Marches did not have a federal executive, but merely a 'Central Committee' (*Zentraler Ausschuß*), which had been set up provisionally at a meeting in Bergen in early November 1960 and formally

[73] HIS, TEM 200,03: Tempel to the conscientious objectors' groups in Braunschweig, Bremen, and Hanover, n. d. [*c.*14 or 15 January 1960]. On the background, cf. Rolf Seeliger, *Die außerparlamentarische Opposition* (Munich, 1968), 125.
[74] HIS, TEM 200,03: Central Committee, minutes, 6–7 May 1961.
[75] Cf., for this wording, Harold Mah, 'Phantasies of the Public Sphere: Rethinking Habermas for Historians', *Journal of Modern History*, 72 (2000), 153–82.
[76] HIS, TEM 400,01: circular regarding libel cases against claims of communist subversion, 27 November 1961.
[77] HIS, TEM 100, 04: 'Ratschläge für Teilnehmer' [n.d., *c.*1961]; Central Committee, minutes, 3 July 1960; Horst Bethge, '"Die Bombe ist böse": Wie der Ostermarsch in Hamburg entstand', in Jörg Berlin (ed.), *Das andere Hamburg: Freiheitliche Bestrebungen in der Hansestadt seit dem Spätmittelalter* (Cologne, 1981), 357–68.
[78] Otto, *Vom Ostermarsch zur APO*, 73–4.

constituted itself in late January 1961.[79] The Central Committee (CC) brought together the various regional sections of the campaign and its supporters and discussed the 'political thrust of the campaign', particularly with regard to speeches, slogans, and leaflets; it set the guidelines for organizational planning, represented the campaign on a federal level, and administered the everyday business.[80] The CC's decisions were definitive and did not require the consent of other campaign bodies, but local and regional committees could make suggestions for their slogans.[81]

The main purpose of this organization was not, as in Britain's CND and in the *SPD*'s Campaign, primarily to control and to restrict information flows. Its aim was in this, 'a loose unit of action of citizens with similar ideas', to allow such information flows to occur in the first place, thus making it possible for the activists to regard themselves as supporters of a sustained movement, rather than of isolated protest events.[82] In line with the growth of the Campaign after the huge success of the 1962 Marches, the CC set up an executive office in September 1962. The executive office's responsibility was the financial and organizational running of the campaign as well as public relations.[83] From May 1963 onwards, the executive office published a campaign newsletter in order to maintain an interest in the campaign while no demonstrations took place: the *Informationen zur Abrüstung* (Disarmament Information), primarily directed at march participants rather than the general public, appeared in ten to twelve issues per year and contained 'factual knowledge'.[84] After much discussion, the CC also decided to launch a 'press service' (*Pressedienst*), compiled by the Bochum activist Christel Beilmann, who had close links to the Catholic *Werkhefte* group. The 'press service' was to be sent to West German newspapers, journals, and the local and regional committees. More than CND, the Easter Marches made use of a systematic analysis of opinion poll data and of the press reports in order to determine how to focus its campaign about security.[85]

[79] HIS, TEM 100,04: Central Committee, minutes, 5–6 November 1960; 21–22 January 1961.
[80] HIS, TEM 200,03: 'Grundsätze des Ostermarschs der Atomwaff engegner', 14–15 October 1961.
[81] HIS, WOL: Regional Committee West, minutes, 21 March 1963; AT: Central Committee, directive, March 1963; Central Committee, minutes, 2–3 March 1963.
[82] HIS, TEM 200,03: 'Grundsätze'; Dr Schulze and Dieter Simon to the local members of these associations, 5 December 1960; IfZ, ED702/53: ICDP circular (*c.*1963).
[83] HIS, TEM 200,03: Buro to Central Committee, 28 July 1963; Otto, *Vom Ostermarsch zur APO*, 210.
[84] HIS, TEM 300,06: Central Committee, minutes, 22/23 September 1963.
[85] HIS, TEM 200,03: Buro to Tempel, 5 March 1962.

Yet, despite the importance of the federal organization for the campaign as a whole, the local and regional committees were responsible for the practical aspects of the organization. Unlike in Britain, there was no single national protest event in the Federal Republic. The regional and local committees emerged out of the interaction of the original coordinating committee's attempts to spread the march across the Federal Republic after the relative success of the first march in 1960. In autumn 1960, the initial Easter March coordinating committee wrote to potential allies, mostly through pacifist networks, and asked for cooperation.[86] These groups then contacted potential participants in the regions and in the localities and encouraged the foundation of local committees.[87] There were initially four regional committees: north (for Hamburg and surroundings), west (for the Ruhr area), south-west (for Baden-Württemberg), and south (for Bavaria). In 1963, a 'central' regional committee (for the Frankfurt/Offenbach region) was set up.[88]

To a much greater extent than in CND, discussions—often endless—became the trademark of the West German Easter Marches. Indeed, while they had initially been a measure to prevent the split of the campaign,[89] 'talking about' and 'discussing' issues soon became deeply entrenched in the habits of the organizers and the participants. Indeed, 'discussion' was soon used to advertise the marches as a truly democratic venture and became a hallmark of West German extra-parliamentary culture.[90] The different shape of the committee minutes underlines the importance of discussions. While CND and C100 minutes merely showed the results of meetings, Easter March committee minutes documented the debates extensively.

Paradoxically, therefore, anti-communism helped bolster, rather than weaken, the chances for extra-parliamentary protests. The dominance of the East–West conflict in West German politics thus prevented the infighting we could see in the British case. It explains both why the SPD so easily rid itself from the Campaign and why its supporters continued the grass-roots work in other movements.

---

[86] HIS, TEM 100,04: Tempel to Stubenrauch, Head of the Wuppertal VK group, November 1960.
[87] HIS, TEM 200,03: Regional Committee West, minutes, 30 March 1962.
[88] HIS, TEM 200,03: Stubenrauch circular, 28 January 1961; 'Arbeitsordnung', Regional Committee West, 26 October 1962; Otto, *Vom Ostermarsch zur APO*, 87, 211–12.
[89] HIS, TEM 200,03: Vack to Tempel, 13 June 1961.
[90] Nina Verheyen, *Diskussionslust: Eine Kulturgeschichte des "besseren Arguments" in Westdeutschland* (Göttingen, 2010).

BEYOND BORDERS: TRANSNATIONAL
MOVEMENT ORGANIZATIONS

The British and West German movements claimed that they represented global interests. But the differences in organizational cultures seriously hampered the organization of communications about 'security' across national borders.[91] The communications between the two movements were fraught with problems. These problems of establishing and sustaining transnational bodies reflect the difficulties of a politics of communication between two movements that operated in two very different political contexts in the cold war and that had to appeal to very different audiences.

There were very few direct connections between CND and its West German counterparts, the Campaign against Atomic Death and the Easter March Committee, apart from the regular exchanges of a few marchers. During the first phase of the protests between 1958 and 1960, the transnationalization of the protests was hampered by the different positions of the *SPD* and the British Labour Party towards the protests. This meant that the traditionally strong bonds between German and British Labour and the organizational structure of the Socialist International could not be used to support the protests.[92] Although the British and West German parties' executives agreed on the importance of multilateral efforts for disarmament, this meant different things in each national context. In Britain, the Labour executive's emphasis on *multilateral* disarmament was diametrically opposed to CND's agenda of *unilateral* nuclear disarmament. In the Federal Republic, the *SPD*'s opposition to the arming of the *Bundeswehr*, the West German army, with nuclear-capable equipment implied a general opposition to Adenauer's 'policy of strength' and conditioned its launch of the 'Campaign against Atomic Death'.[93] The contacts between the British and West German movement were, apart from the rare exchanges of speakers, rather thin.

The West German campaign headquarters did not even seem to have been aware of the existence of a counterpart in Britain until the summer

[91] These findings contradict the arguments by Akira Iriye, *Global Community: The Role of International Organizations in the Making of the Contemporary World* (Berkeley and Los Angeles, 2002), 6.

[92] AdsD, 2/PVAM000020: Menzel to Albert Carthy (Socialist International, London), 25 November 1959.

[93] AdsD: Parteivorstand, minutes, 24 January 1958; for Britain: Archives of the British Labour Party, Series One: National Executive Committee Minutes, part 5: 1956–9 inclusive: 'Summary Report of the meeting between the International Committees of the Labour Party NEC and the TUC General Council held in Transport House at 10.30 a.m. on Thursday', 6 March 1958.

of 1958, almost half a year after both campaigns had been founded. Thus, when the *SPD*-run Campaign received a letter from CND asking for some information about it, the West German campaign office tried to secure information about its counterpart's credentials by writing to the International Department of the Labour Party. The Labour Party, in turn, was not keen to help, since CND was regarded by Transport House, the Labour headquarters, as a divisive force. As a result, the party warned the *SPD* to avoid cooperation. The *SPD*, in turn, misunderstood Labour's political language, and classified CND as Communist.[94]

The first contacts between CND and parts of the West German movements were not established between the *SPD*-run Campaign and CND, but by the Munich Committee against Nuclear Armaments, run by the German writer and intellectual Hans Werner Richter and very similar to CND in organizational structure and social composition.[95] The contact was facilitated by the BBC journalist Christopher Holme, whom Richter knew from one of the *Gruppe 47* conferences. Richter had written to him and asked him to be put in touch with Bertrand Russell and Canon Collins in order to establish a more 'international' form of protest.[96]

Even these contacts between two organizations with very similar outlooks proved very cumbersome. Richter initiated the European Federation against Nuclear Weapons (EF), which was founded in London and Frankfurt in early 1959. The EF aimed to prevent nuclear proliferation and to achieve general nuclear disarmament and it sought to campaign for the civilian use of atomic energy. The EF's London headquarters, in CND's offices, was supposed to coordinate joint campaigns in the future.[97] In striking contrast to its rhetoric of a 'world community', however, participants at EF meetings insisted that the Federation should not undermine the national positions of the individual movements and be sensitive of different national issues.[98] The EF's successor organization, the International Confederation for Disarmament and Peace (ICDP), was not very successful in creating an international community of protesters either. It was founded at a conference in Oxford in January 1963 with the goal of

---

[94] AdsD, 2/PVAM000007: folder 'Tarnorganisationen'; PolArchAA, B31/247: German Embassy London to Foreign Office, Bonn, 'Betr.: Labour Partei und SPD', 30 April 1963; BLPES, CND/7/24: Duff to Menzel, 17 May 1958; CND/1/45: Report on the Moscow Conference, 1962.

[95] HWR, 72.86.511: 'Mitgliederliste', 'Verfassung', n.d. [*c*.1958].

[96] HWR, 72.86.512, fo. 55: Christopher Holme to Hans Werner Richter, 2 April 1958.

[97] HWR, 72.86.512, 20: Statutes of the European Federation against Nuclear Arms, n.d. [*c*.1959].

[98] HWR 72.86.512, 158: Report about the European Congress against Nuclear Armaments, 6 February 1959.

creating a non-aligned equivalent to the communist World Peace Council. Again, the aims were high: 'to demand and foster a fundamentally new way of thinking and to use new forces and means to counter the arms race in order to build an international community of values.'[99] But the ICDP's programme pointed out that the 'different views and sovereignty [*sic*!] of the member organizations should not be infringed'.[100]

The problems of coordination has already started before the conference. Hans Werner Richter, who had always supported a strong non-aligned nuclear weapons movement, was against the participation of members of the World Peace Council as observers.[101] Canon Collins had invited the delegates anyway—with the result that the group around Hans Werner Richter did not attend the conference. Discussions about the prudence of inviting communist delegates also took place among British activists and greatly hampered the reputation of the newly founded ICDP.[102]

Established institutions, by contrast, offered a better environment for direct transnational communications. Hence, the War Resisters' International (WRI) turned into the key transnational organization for the British and West German anti-nuclear-weapons protests. The WRI had been founded by radical—that is, non-bourgeois—pacifists in the early 1920s. It was through this organization and its journals that the first group of protesters in northern Germany established contact with its British counterparts and, indeed, with pacifists from all over the world who thought along similar lines. In the 1920s and 1930s, the WRI had been primarily concerned with assisting conscientious objectors. In the 1950s and 1960s, however, it was instrumental in spreading the ideas linked to non-violent civil disobedience and non-violent direct action. The WRI's headquarters at the time was in Enfield (Essex), near London. The headquarters was dominated by the British peace movement around the PPU with its journal *Peace News* and had strong links with the C100. Tony Smythe, the WRI's director in the early 1960s, was also a prominent C100 activist.

Through its West German branches (the *Internationale der Kriegsdienstgegner—Deutscher Zweig* (*IdK*) and, from the early 1960s, the *Verband der Kriegsdienstverweigerer* (*VK*)), the WRI was able to distribute information,

[99] IfZ, ED702/52: ICDP, Constitution, n.d. [*c.* January 1963].
[100] IfZ, ED702/52: 'Statement of the Aims of the ICDP', n.d. [*c.* January 1963].
[101] HWR, 72.86.512: Christian Mayer-Amery to Hans Werner Richter, 15 July 1959; Hans Werner Richter to Siegfried Bußjäger, 17 April 1960.
[102] Diana Collins to *Peace News*, 29 March 1963, 5; Judith Cook to *Peace News*, 1 March 1963, 3; Behörde des Bundesbeauftragten für die Unterlagen des Staatssicherheitsdienstes der ehemaligen Deutschen Demokratischen Republik (BStU) MfS-Hauptverwaltung Aufklärung, no. 193, 000162–000168: 'Einzelinformation über die Tätigkeit der Europäischen Föderation gegen Atomrüstung und die "Internationale Konferenz für allgemeine Abrüstung und das Verbot aller Atomwaffen"', n.d.

much more efficiently than the EF and the ICDP. The publications carried reports from conferences, advice on reading, and registration forms for conferences in a form that was accessible to all supporters. The WRI's West German journal, the *Friedensrundschau*, published a 'Letter from England' in every issue, informing West German readers of the most recent developments in Britain. The journal frequently carried articles that discussed different forms of protest, most importantly non-violent civil disobedience. In particular, the German WRI branch and the *VK* publications could tap the particular West German and British conditions by relying on local authors, who translated the message into the local political and protest traditions.[103]

The ideas for Easter Marches outside Britain first emerged in WRI networks. The links between the later organizers of the Easter March, Hans-Konrad Tempel, and his fiancée, Helga Stolle, started in the early 1950s. It was at the WRI's eighth Triennial Conference, which took place in July 1954 in Paris, that Tempel became acquainted with activists from the British peace movement such as April Carter, Stuart Morris, and Fenner Brockway.[104] The conferences not only contributed to the formation of a transnational network of protesters, but were also instrumental in bringing together the dispersed activities of the West German movement. At the 1954 conference, Tempel met Ingeborg Küster, the later organizer of the Munich Easter Marches.[105] The circles around the WRI and its West German branches were also important in linking the Hamburg group around Tempel, which organized the first Easter Marches, to a wider circle around Andreas Buro, then an official in the youth department at Kassel city council, later one of the main organizers of the Easter Marches.[106] Through his job, Buro was in touch with representatives of various groups around the emerging New Left in West Germany, such as Klaus Vack of the youth organization of the 'Friends of Nature' and Herbert Faller of the socialist youth organization the 'Falcons', who were both to become important organizers for the national and Hessian regional campaigns.[107]

At the WRI conferences, activists from the US civil rights movements acquainted West Europeans with the practice of Gandhian-type civil disobedience, thus reinvigorating the theoretical discussions about these forms of protest, a debate whose origins can be traced back to the 1920s.

---

[103] Cf., for example, Hilda von Klenze, 'Brief aus England', *Friedensrundschau*, 14 (1960), 15; Klenze, 'Brief aus England', *Friedensrundschau*, 17 (1963), 15–16.

[104] IISG, WRI-7: Reports from the 8th Triennial Conference, Paris 1954.

[105] IISG, WRI-7: List of conference participants at the WRI's 8th Triennial Conference, Paris, 1954.

[106] IISG, WRI-226: Andreas Buro to Tony Smythe, 3 September 1960.

[107] On these traditions, cf. Zimmer, 'Das Abseits als vermiedener Irrweg'.

The WRI's 1957 conference in London was attended by Bayard Rustin, later the organizer of Martin Luther King's civil disobedience campaigns in the United States, and by Christopher Farley, later a C100 activist, who was among the first to transfer sit-downs and the occupation of military bases and government buildings systematically to a West European setting.[108]

The conferences were mostly elite and middle-class affairs. The costs of travelling at the time were still significant and at least a rudimentary knowledge of foreign languages was required. Although meetings mainly took place in the summer months, it is probable that they primarily appealed to full-time activists, students, academics, and others who could afford the time and the money.[109] One could, therefore, argue that these contacts did not really matter as they concerned the networks of a particular minority. However, it is important to see that the participants in the WRI conferences acted as multipliers of information in their local war resisters', Easter March, or student movement groups, wrote articles in the relevant journals, and thus helped to spread information. Through their contacts with British protesters and through the news reports, they showed other protesters what forms of protests were possible. The exchange of marchers, often through local affiliates, was important in this context.[110]

MASS MEDIA AND ORGANIZATIONAL COMMUNICATIONS

In both countries, the media played an important role in framing the movement organizations. The media functioned as intermediaries. Reports in the media allowed the movements to reach beyond different and separate public spheres. Thus, the media provided notional links between activists across the country, and they connected the internal movement organization, on the one hand, and 'the public', on the other. It was primarily through media reports that national protest *events* came to be connected to a national and even international *movement* against nuclear weapons.[111]

---

[108] IISG, WRI-7: Complete lists of those attending the 1957 conference, London.

[109] IISG, WRI-63: Details for the WRI Study Conference at Blaricum near Amsterdam, 12–19 August 1961.

[110] IISG, C100-2: George Clark, 'Convenor's Notes', 27 March 1962; IISG, WRI-226: Andreas Buro to Tony Smythe, 2 November 1960.

[111] Karl Christian Führer, Knut Hickethier, and Axel Schildt, 'Öffentlichkeit—Medien—Geschichte: Konzepte der modernen Öffentlichkeit und Zugänge zu ihrer Erforschung', *Archiv für Sozialgeschichte*, 41 (2001), 1–38, here 6.

For the movement organizers, 'media' meant primarily printed sources. The radio was important, but, because of the absence of images, could not directly convey the marchers' commitment. Television, albeit of rising importance in both countries, carried almost no reports on the marches, even though both CND and the Easter Marches produced films showing the marching experience.[112]

In order to facilitate communications among activists, the British and West German movements set up their own papers. Rather than address a wider audience, they mainly served to structure movement discussions, inform the readers of events, and provide them with information about the political background to the campaign as well as about the scientific and ethical questions related to nuclear weapons. The national and regional CND executives published a monthly *Bulletin*, which informed supporters about the events of the campaign. *Peace News*, the PPU's paper, also came to function as CND's journal: it provided a mix of information and reports, book and music reviews, as well as a calendar of events. In January 1961, CND replaced its monthly *Bulletin* with the more ambitious journal *Sanity*.[113] By September 1961, *Sanity* had a print run of around 15,000; by May 1962, it fluctuated 'about the 30,000 mark'. By 1963, sales of *Sanity* were at about 40,000.[114]

The *SPD* and the *DGB* primarily used their own papers, such as *Vorwärts* and *Welt der Arbeit*, as well as several regional newspapers run under *SPD* auspices for this purpose. They also set up a journal called *atomzeitalter* (atomic age), which was to foster 'rational and enlightened debate' about atomic energy. Unlike CND with *Sanity* and the pre-existing *Peace News*, the Easter March committee did not launch its own journal. It relied substantially on journals of the Christian and labour movement groups that participated in the movement. The committee also resorted to producing a monthly ten-page newsletter to supplement its pamphlets and flyers, which contained more factual information and much less essayistic material than the British counterpart.[115] This material was focused on 'objective' and primarily textual reporting in order to provide its supporters with arguments for the cause. Some sympathetic student papers, such as *pläne* (plans) and *konkret*, also featured reports on the Easter Marches. Information on the print runs of these journals is not

---

[112] Cf. Knut Hickethier, 'Medien', in Christoph Führ and and Carl-Ludwig Furck (eds), *Handbuch der deutschen Bildungsgeschichte* (6 vols, Munich, 1998), vi. 1, 602–10; Martin Harrison, 'Television and Radio', in Butler and King (eds), *The British General Election of 1964*, 156–84.
[113] Richard Taylor, *Against the Bomb*, 73.
[114] BLPES, CND/1/4: CND annual reports 1961–2 and 1962–3.
[115] HIS, TEM 200,03: Central Committee, minutes, 14–15 October 1961.

available, but they were likely to have been substantially lower than *Sanity's*. However, the broad spread of reports on the Easter Marches in journals of interested social groups provided the West German campaigns with a far more substantial audience in the long run.

Media reports were not only important to provide activists with information about the campaign. They also made it possible that activists who attended a meeting in one geographical area could feel themselves as part of a movement that embraced the whole country, if not the globe. As the audiences at public meetings and demonstrations were rather limited, the British and the West German movement organizations relied on reports about these in the press, the radio, and on television in order to make themselves heard. In Britain, organizers faced fewer obstacles. The centralized character of the campaign and the location of the final rallies in London from 1959 onwards ensured a modicum of press interest. The emergence of an increasingly nationalized press market in the late 1950s and early 1960s bolstered this further.[116]

The situation in the Federal Republic was initially more problematic, particularly after the *SPD* had withdrawn its support network of party and regional newspapers, but it resulted in an eventually far more elaborate organization of movement-media relations. The West German press landscape was more regionalized and thus made federal-wide reporting more unlikely, particularly when the protests took place in smaller towns in the countryside. Apart from some regional, and often communist-leaning newspapers, there were initially few reports of the early Easter Marches in the German national press. Ironically, some press reports stated dryly that there was nothing to report.[117]

These problems, in conjunction with the constant stream of accusations of communist subversion, made West German activists much keener than their British counterparts to find out what the press and 'the public' thought about them. The West German activist Hans Magnus Enzensberger even called for the 'most cool-blooded and fantasy-driven exploitation of all psychological opportunities' in order to advertise the campaign.[118] While both movements sought to make use of opinion polls to show that 'the public' was on their side,[119] the Easter March organizers

[116] A. J. Beith, 'The Press', in Butler and King (eds), *The British General Election of 1964*, 185–203.

[117] 'Ostermärsche wurden kaum beachtet', *Der Tagesspiegel*, 5 April 1961.

[118] Hans Magnus Enzensberger, 'Einige Vorschläge zur Methode des Kampfes gegen die atomare Aufrüstung', *Blätter für deutsche und internationale Politik*, 4 (1958), 410–14.

[119] BLPES, CND/1/56: 'Public opinion', draft, *c*.1960; Driver, *The Disarmers*, 99; AdsD, Parteivorstand, minutes, 23 October 1958; BAK, ZSg. 1/E-70: 'Informationen für die Presse, April 1963'.

went further and placed increased importance on the ways in which they were seen in the media: they sent out briefing material to the press and analyzed press reports far more systematically than their British counter-parts. From the beginning, the Easter March organizers analyzed press reporting systematically. In 1960, they identified around 134 reports on the Easter March with 17 photos, though this was disappointing, given that there were around 1,500 newspapers in West Germany at the time. In 1961, the observers counted 956 press reports with 170 pictures. In 1962, the Easter March observers counted 1,163 press reports, while reporting was restricted to March and April. In 1963, the period of re-porting started in January and carried on until June, indicating the expan-sion of interest in 'the movement', rather than in protest events.[120] From the mid-1960s, 'advertisement' became even more important for the West German campaign, while it was never as professionally organized by the British one.[121] CND's attempt to mobilize 'public opinion' remained rather rudimentary. Its 'Tell Britain' campaign did not lead to any signifi-cant results, as no detailed reports were sent back to CND's head office. And its attempt to use sociology students living in caravans to poll the residents of Welwyn Garden City in order to determine the Campaign's social support base remained rather haphazard.[122] The British and West German governments sought to counter the campaigns with their own public-relations campaigns, and thus helped to confirm the boundary be-tween movements and their environment.[123]

In Britain, by contrast, very few CND protesters were as cynical about employing the media to spread the cause as Mabel Murgatroyd in P. G. Wodehouse's short story 'Bingo bans the Bomb'. Mabel, daughter of an aristocrat, persuades her old school friend Bingo Little to stage an impromptu protest on Trafalgar Square and argues: 'The papers feature it next morning, and that helps the cause. Ah, here comes the rozzer now, just when we need him.'[124] Such a media-conscious attitude was more charac-teristic of the C100 than of CND. The supporters of civil disobedience

---

[120] Otto, *Vom Ostermarsch zur APO*, 140–2.
[121] HIS, Ostermarsch Nord, folder 1: Leaflet, Regional Committee South, 26 August 1965.
[122] BLPES, CND/1/24: 'Campaign Caravan', leaflet, *c*.1962, and CND/1/65: 'Tell Britain', pamphlet *c*.1961.
[123] TNA PREM 11/2778: Macmillan to the Chancellor of the Duchy of Lancaster, 24 March 1958; Detlef Bald, 'Die Atombewaffnung der Bundeswehr in den fünfziger Jahren: Öffentlichkeit und die Kontrolle der Militärpolitik', in Jost Düllfer (ed.), *Parlamentarische und öffentliche Kontrolle von Rüstung in Deutschland 1700–1970* (Düsseldorf, 1992), 203–17, here 210–11.
[124] P. G. Wodehouse, 'Bingo Bans the Bomb', in Wodehouse, *Plum Pie* (London, 1966), 119–36, here 122.

used the media as an argument for their form of protest. Bertrand Russell himself mentions the importance of the media for this kind of protest in his *Autobiography*:

so long as constitutional methods were employed, it was very difficult—and often impossible—to cause the most important facts to be known. All great newspapers are against us. Television and radio gave us only grudging and brief opportunities for stating our case... It was very largely the difficulty of making our case known that drove some of us to the adoption of illegal methods. Our illegal actions, because they had sensational news value, were reported, and here and there, a newspaper would allow us to say why we did what.[125]

Russell's observations after a sit-down in front of the British Ministry of Defence was true for the West German movement as well: 'Our movement depends for its success on an immense public opinion and we cannot create that unless we raise the authorities to more action than they took yesterday...'.[126] Even in CND, internal movement organization and 'public opinion' remained directly connected. Once this connection was severed, the movement would lose its momentum, and would reveal to the outside world the many discordant voices within it.[127]

The dynamic nature of these processes of organizing people with many different experiences highlights that it makes little sense to fault political movements like CND for their lack of organizational strength.[128] The problem was rather that CND's existing organization did not manage to mediate between activists and the general public, as it remained focused on face-to-face contacts and political meetings, rather than addressing 'the public' as a whole.[129] Because of the fluid nature of these discussions about organization, 'organizational structure' was never a 'collective identity'. Organization was crucial for turning the various protest events into identifiable political movements and seemingly homogeneous political entities. But the presence of activists' experiences meant that the extraparliamentary politics of security was never stable or static and always remained on the move.

---

[125] Speech to a Youth CND conference in Birmingham, 15 April 1961, quoted in Bertrand Russell, *The Autobiography of Bertrand Russell* (3 vols, London, 1978), iii. 139.

[126] Quoted in Brian Masters, *The Swinging Sixties* (London, 1985), 206.

[127] Frank Allaun, 'In with a Bang, Out...', in John Minnion and Philip Bolsover (eds), *The CND Story: The First 25 years of CND in the Words of the People Involved* (London, 1983), 56–7.

[128] This is the argument in Chun, *The British New Left*, xvi; in Richard Taylor, *Against the Bomb, passim*, and in Otto, *Vom Ostermarsch zur APO, passim*.

[129] Cf. the criticism by Stuart Hall, 'Peace Politics', *Sanity* (May 1963), 5.

5

'Peace', the Nation, and International Relations

Their organizations gave CND and the West German movements a clear address within their political systems and provided them with channels of communication that were able to translate the 'noises' of the manifold experiences of movement activists into clear messages. Yet their momentum came from framing the issue of 'security' in specific ways. It was this framing that gave the movements not only a social coherence, but also a discursive one. While the nuances were contested within the movements, there was a basic consensus. Both movements were 'against nuclear weapons'.

Behind the movements' clear agendas lurked a more complicated set of policy proposals that were deeply ingrained in nationally specific experiences and in specific ways of framing the role of their respective nation in world affairs. While the British and West German activists brought with them a multiplicity of views about international relations, we can nevertheless see nationally specific ways of framing the issue of nuclear armaments. At the core of this convergence around nationally specific issues were the activists' severe misgivings about a real and substantial defence policy problem that arose from the nuclearization of the strategies of the NATO countries since the mid-1950s. For the protesters, then, the issue of nuclear armaments was much less about utopian ideals of 'peace'. Instead, they were primarily concerned about preserving 'security' and 'order' at a time when the arms race between the superpowers had become a 'functional substitute for war' and when subsequent crises in international relations—first over Berlin in 1958–59, then over the shooting of an American spy plane by the Soviet Union, again over Berlin in 1961 and in Cuba, in autumn 1962—appeared to illustrate this analysis.[1]

Events in international relations, the framing of 'security' and the movements' dynamics were thus intimately related. They reflected the

---

[1] Andreas Wenger, *Living with Peril: Eisenhower, Kennedy, and Nuclear Weapons* (Lanham, MD, 1997), 248.

fundamental changes in the international landscape after the 1955 Bandung Conference of non-aligned nations and after the crises connected
with Krushchev's Secret Speech at the CPSU's Twentieth Party Convention, the Soviet suppression of the Hungarian reform movement, and the
Suez crisis in 1956. These developments brought a general softening of
the ideological entrenchment of the late 1940s and early 1950s and thus
created the space for ideas to emerge that could not be slotted neatly into
a bipolar cold war mindset: socialist aims now percolated beyond the
labour and communist movements into the extra-parliamentary arena
and were often combined with appeals to nationhood and national self-
determination. While many of the progressive hopes of the mid-1940s
had been put on shelf almost immediately after the Second World War,
they were now being revived under new auspices.[2]

   This chapter analyses the interpretations and expectations that emerged
from developments in domestic and international politics and links these
to the protesters' conceptions of the role of their nation in international
affairs. While the basic parameters of the debates about these issues were
remarkably similar in both Britain and the Federal Republic, the form
and content of the arguments differed. Both movements propagated ideas
of a political morality framed in the context of the nation.

HUMANITARIAN FRAMES

The foundation from which activists were able to achieve this and recognize themselves as part and parcel of the same movement was a 'global
imaginary of integration' that was based on a humanitarian interpretation
of the activists' responsibility.[3] This global imaginary opposed the politics
of containment that operated according to the binary code of a divided
world by imagining the world as a family united by its common humanity. This project was, at times, framed as a commitment to human rights,
as an imagined global brotherhood of mankind, or as a common humanity forged by the overwhelming global relevance of the question of life
and death in the nuclear age.[4] This meant that interpersonal sympathy

---

   [2] Cf. O. Arne Westad, *The Global Cold War* (Cambridge, 2005); Jason Parker, 'Cold
War II: The Eisenhower Administration, the Bandung Conference, and the Reperiodiza-
tion of the Postwar Era', *Diplomatic History*, 30 (2006), 867–92.
   [3] Christina Klein, *Cold War Orientalism: Asia in the Middlebrow Imagination,
1945–1961* (Berkeley and Los Angeles, 2003), 23. See the argument by Ziemann, 'A
Quantum of Solace?', 372–3.
   [4] Andrew Oppenheimer, 'West German Pacifism and the Ambivalence of Human Solidarity, 1945–1968', *Peace & Change*, 29 (2004), 353–89.

rather than law was, for activists, the fundamental moral capacity: talking about 'humanity' meant that everyone was part of this 'circle of the we', as the circle of people to whom we ascribe rights and whom we feel obliged to treat decently.[5]

Thus, those who marched on the annual Aldermaston Marches felt that they enacted a theme similar to the one of the 'Family of Man' photographic exhibition that had toured the United States and Europe during the mid-1950s as part of the American government's effort to highlight the advantages of Western civilization over Eastern despotism, thus appropriating government rhetoric as part of their experiences.[6]

> I belong to a family, the biggest on earth
> A thousand every day are coming to birth.
> Our surname isn't Hasted or Dallas or Jones
> It's a name every man should be proud he owns.
> It's the family of man keeps growing,
> The family of man keeps sowing
> The seeds of a new life every day.

Differences of belonging are submerged under a 'universalist scope of identification'[7]: the metaphor 'family' suggested an intimate relationship of activists, although they lived far away from each other. In Britain, this conceptualization of humanity as a family also had resonances with wartime propaganda that had portrayed Britain as one big family, a highly inclusive metaphor and constellation, where the members of the family are known primarily through their internal functions, but also by their professions.[8]

In both countries, the Protestant missionary Albert Schweitzer was a symbol for these global connections within one humanitarian framework. He had called nuclear armaments a 'disaster [Unglück] for humanity'.[9] Schweitzer as a symbol for this global connectedness thus also functioned as a 'symbolic guardian of European colonial continuity after 1945'. This had a particular meaning in Germany, a country that did not have any formal colonial possessions outside Europe after 1918: Schweitzer's moral

---

[5] David Hollinger, 'How Wide is the Circle of the We? American Intellectuals and the Problem of Ethnos since World War II', *American Historical Review*, 98 (1993), 317–37.
[6] *The Family of Man: The Greatest Photographic Exhibition of All Time*, created by Edward Steichen for the Museum of Modern Art (New York, 1955). The following extract (text and music by Fred 'Karl' Dallas) is from IISG, C100 uncatalogued collection: CND songbook.
[7] Oppenheimer, 'West German Pacifism', 372.
[8] Geoffrey G. Field, *Blood, Sweat and Toil: Remaking the British Working Class* (Oxford, 2012), 183–216.
[9] Appeal from 23 April 1957, quoted in Friedenskomitee der Bundesrepublik Deutschland (ed.), *Blaubuch über den Widerstand gegen die atomare Aufrüstung der Bundesrepublik* (Düsseldorf, 1957), 95–6.

example could highlight the moral rejuvenation of West Germany after the Second World War and thus underwrite an exculpation of Germans.[10]

THE EMPTY PEACE

Another transnational frame of reference came to connect the British and West German movements. Viewed from the outside, CND and its West German counterparts were peace movements, their supporters 'peaceniks'. Some observers at the time even claimed that the activists severely weakened Western defence: 'While...supported by the high-minded through the doctrine of example', the leader of the British Labour Party Hugh Gaitskell argued in 1960, just after the Scarborough Party conference had adopted resolutions that argued for Britain's uni-lateral nuclear disarmament, '[peace] is popular with others for purely escapist or beatnik reasons, and with others, again, because they are fellow-travellers, if not avowed Communists'.[11] Yet, neither CND nor the West German movements framed the issue of nuclear armaments in their country primarily as one of 'peace'. While the traditional peace organizations, such as the British Peace Pledge Union (PPU) and the German Peace Society (*Deutsche Friedensgesellschaft*) were still active and while a small minority of activists understood themselves as paci-fists, the movements defined themselves much more precisely as 'for nuclear disarmament' or 'as against nuclear weapons'. Given the in-volvement of a number of pacifists in prominent positions in both the British and West German movements, this is surprising. Although the main British movement journal was called *Peace News*, 'peace' mattered very little in the programmatic statements and the activists' personal reminiscences. Although they often discussed 'world peace', the vast majority of CND and West German activists would not have consid-ered themselves as supporters of a peace movement, nor as pacifists: 'Let's admit it frankly,' a West German activist remarked in 1963, 'the words peace, peace society, peace council, peace party have, through all kinds of conceptual confusions, entirely lost their meanings and have

---

[10] Nina Berman, *Impossible Missions? German Economic, Military and Humanitatian Efforts in Africa* (Lincoln, NE, 2004), 96–7.
[11] Hugh Gaitskell at the Labour conference in Scarborough, October 1960, quoted in Philip Williams, *Hugh Gaitskell* (Oxford, 1982), 579. Replicating these prejudices: Paul Mercer, *'Peace' of the Dead: The Truth Behind the Nuclear Disarmers* (London, 1986).

been discredited so much, that they can merely provoke a sorry smile...'.[12]

'Peace' had, despite its progressive origins, lost much of its legitimacy in post-Second World War Western Europe. Beginning with the 'World Congress of Intellectuals for Peace' in Wrocław in 1948 and culminating in the Stockholm Peace Appeal in March 1950, Communist Parties across Western and Eastern Europe had launched an international peace movement under the auspices of the World Peace Council in order to campaign against 'Western imperialism'. While the Soviet Union and its allies were havens of peace, the West was denounced as 'totalitarian' and war prone. Conversely, the West portrayed itself as the camp of 'freedom', where 'peace' was a given, and accused the Soviet Union of totalitarian tendencies.[13] The majority of activists in Britain and West Germany at the time were clearly concerned about appearing too close to the communist movement. Yet their hesitation to use the word 'peace' to frame the issue of nuclear weapons policies went beyond fears of political recrimination, or considerations of how best to advertise the movement.[14]

The reluctance to use the word 'peace' also reflected, both in Britain and in the Federal Republic, direct or appropriated experiences of mass death and military and civilian suffering. Vera Brittain observed during the Blitz that 'our island is no longer a detached unscarred participant, sharing in the conflict only through the adventures of masculine youth'.[15] After the Second World War, therefore, 'peace' as a utopian vision was no longer an option to endow activists with sufficient momentum to sustain the movement: 'Pacifism', John Middleton Murry wrote in June 1945, 'assumes an irreducible minimum of human decency...which no longer exists'.[16] Momentum for the campaigns in the late 1950s and early 1960s came not from 'peace', but from the far more specific focus on 'nuclear disarmament'. The focus was no longer an abstract notion whose contents

[12] Hermann Speelmann to Dr. Gerhard Schmidt, 12 October 1963, quoted in Appelius, *Pazifismus in* Westdeutschland, ii. 513; interviews with Hans-Konrad Tempel, 19 August 2002, and Arno Klönne, 22 August 2002; SAPMO-BArch, DY30-IV.2.-2.028: 'Bericht über den Ostermarsch West 1963', 2 May 1963; *Peace News*, 29 November 1963, 2.

[13] SAPMO-BArch, DY30-IV 2-10.02-120, 145–7: 'Der Kampf für eine atomwaffenfreie Zone in Eurppa unter Einschluß der beiden deutschen Staaten—Hauptaufgabe der gegenwärtigen Epoche [1958]'.

[14] *Peace News*, 2 January 1959, 2; *Peace News*, 11 August 1961, 3; HIS, TEM 100,04: 'Aufruf zum Ostermarsch 1960'; Tempel to Andreas Buro, 2 April 1962; SAPMO-BArch, DY30 J IV 2/2/643: 'Außerordentliche Sitzung des PB der SED am 23 April 1959'.

[15] Vera Brittain, *England's Hour* (London, 1941), xiii.

[16] *Herald of Peace*, 22 June 1945, 2. Cf. also Mass Observation, *Peace and the Public*; Ceadel, *Semi-Detached Idealists*, ch. 11.

pointed to the future. Instead, the activists' emphasis developed utopias in and through their everyday interactions.[17]

This emphasis on a pragmatic concept of security rather than a utopian vision of peace becomes particularly obvious if one examines one context more closely, in which 'peace' did play an important role in movement debates about international relations: in the discussions about the Soviet Union's proposals for 'peaceful coexistence'. Nikita Krushchev had proposed such a policy in September 1954 to signal a change of emphasis in foreign policy after his election as First Secretary of the Central Committee of the Communist Party of the Soviet Union, and it became an important buzzword in discussions about foreign-policy issues. While movement activists used the term, few picked up on its history and connotations, although communists in Britain and West Germany did not deny the concept's lineage when propagating their cause.[18]

Krushchev's concept referred back to Soviet foreign policy immediately after the First World War. At that time, Chicherin, the Soviet delegate to the International Economic Conference in Genoa, argued that immediate 'world revolution' was not possible in the present situation, and therefore proposed a Soviet foreign policy that would accept that the 'old social order' and the 'new order coming into being' existed in parallel, while adhering to 'Communist principles'.[19] This meant, in practice, maintaining the general antagonism between 'the West' and the Soviet Union, but transferring the battles from the military to the ideological and economic levels.

When British and, more rarely, West German protesters picked up the concept, they used it with quite different connotations. While the Soviet concept of 'peaceful coexistence' was essentially dynamic and still oriented towards rapid socio-economic change that would ultimately lead to socialism and communism around the world, most protesters entirely ignored this dynamic element when framing the international situation. Instead, they defined 'coexistence' as an end to the superpower competition, which, in turn, would lead to an end of the arms race. They used 'peaceful coexistence' as a synonym for the creation of a nuclear-weapons-

<hr/>

[17] *Peace News*, 18 August 1961, 8; *Peace News*, 25 August 1961, 1; AdsD, DGB, Abt. Organisation 24–9005: Brochure for the public platform of the DGB regional committee Lower Saxony, Den nächsten Krieg gewinnt der Tod. August 1914: Erster Weltkrieg, September 1939: 'Zweiter Weltkrieg', 30 August 1964.
[18] Andrew Rothstein, *Peaceful Co-Existence* (Harmondsworth, 1955); LHASC, CP/CENT/SPN/1/14: 'H-Bomb and Disarmament Campaign', speaker's notes, 16 August 1957; Till Kössler, *Abschied von der Revolution: Kommunisten und Gesellschaft in Westdeutschland 1945–1968* (Düsseldorf, 2005), 369–85.
[19] Quoted from Rothstein, *Peaceful Co-Existence*, 35.

free zone in Europe, as the Polish Prime Minister Rapacki and, at various stages, the British politicians Anthony Eden and Hugh Gaitskell had recommended.[20] Yet others used 'peaceful coexistence' as a theme to develop the concept of a 'non-nuclear club' of great powers around the world, which would, in turn, inspire others to disarm as well.[21] In Britain, therefore, most protesters emphasized that the maintenance of the status quo in the international system should be maintained, while only some argued for socio-economic changes at home.

British activists thus framed the issue of nuclear weapons for Britain in a pragmatic fashion. They campaigned for the country's unilateral disarmament and for the withdrawal of American bases from British soil in order to dissociate Britain from the arms race and not make it the possible target for an attack. They realized only gradually that this would have implications for Britain's NATO membership. From 1960 onwards, particularly during and immediately after the Cuban missile crisis in autumn 1962, there were calls from within the movement that Britain leave NATO.[22] From the beginning of 1958, there had also been voices in Britain that called for the ending of patrols by US Strategic Air Command bombers above the British Isles.[23]

West German Easter Marchers used the term 'peaceful coexistence' similarly, most famously in their slogan 'Either Coexistence, or No Existence', which filtered through to Britain as well.[24] Like British activists, they had shed ambitions for an all-encompassing 'peace' that would rest on a new socialist socio-economic order and favoured incremental reforms instead.[25] By the early 1960s, the West German activists had not only lost the original concept's connotation of socio-economic change. They had also lost the one element that had given the West German activists' framing of international relations their specificity and momentum: the link between nuclear weapons policies and German unity. Willy Brandt, keeping his distance from the nuclear weapons movement in the late 1950s and early 1960s, had this in mind when he coined the slogan about 'No Existence' at a speech at the Berlin *SPD*'s state party convention in

[20] *Peace News*, 21 November 1958, 4; *Peace News*, 20 March 1959, 4.
[21] Wayland Young, *Strategy for Survival: First Steps in Nuclear Disarmament* (Harmondsworth, 1959); *Peace News*, 27 November 1959, 1.
[22] MRC, MSS 181/4: Stuart Hall, *Steps towards Peace*, CND pamphlet (London, 1962).
[23] *Peace News*, 18 July 1958, 1.
[24] HIS, TEM 200,03: 'Slogans zum Ostermarsch 1961', March 1961; Heinz Kraschutzki, 'Koexistenz oder No-Existenz', *Friedensrundschau*, 12 (1958), 3–5; *Peace News*, 10 March 1961, 10.
[25] HIS, TEM 200,03: Vack to Tempel, 20 August 1962; 'Aufruf zum Ostermarsch 1960'.

May 1955. He criticized notions of 'peaceful coexistence' as being too status quo oriented. Such an understanding, he argued, meant that 'coexistence was no-existence for the whole German people', since 'the line that cuts Germany into half is for us not just a line on the map, but a cut through millions of German families…'.[26]

The Campaign against Atomic Death, following social-democratic foreign-policy concepts since the foundation of the Federal Republic, had still emphasized this element. It had pointed out that the acquisition of nuclear-capable equipment for the German army would drive an even deeper wedge between East and West Germany: 'Preventing atomic armaments and reunification are linked like rain and corn: preventing atomic armament is the first step, the only step possible at this time on the path towards reunification!'[27] The SPD's 'Plan for Germany' (*Deutschlandplan*) of 18 March 1959 had reiterated these demands by demanding military disengagement in central Europe.[28] Yet, on 30 June 1960, shortly after the failed Paris Conference on solving the crisis over German division, Herbert Wehner, one of the main drafters of the plan, declared that the plan was now 'a thing of the past' and offered the *CDU* a foreign policy of cooperation.[29] The Easter Marches, by contrast, only rarely mentioned German reunification explicitly and instead campaigned for nuclear disarmament around the world, as the circumstances had changed significantly: the first batteries of nuclear-capable rocket launchers for the West German army had started to arrive and, in August 1961, the Wall had gone up in Berlin.[30]

From the early 1960s onwards, after the decision to arm the *Bundeswehr* with nuclear-capable equipment had been passed in the West German parliament by the Christian Democratic majority, the West German movement became increasingly concerned with worldwide disarmament. From the late 1950s to the early 1960s, CND and the West German movements constantly framed and reframed their expectations of the international order. Their conceptions of the international situation were not entirely new, however. Rather, they appropriated concepts for an international order that had circulated since at least the late 1940s,

---

[26] Willy Brandt, 'Rede des Präsidenten des Berliner Abgeordnetenhauses von Berlin, Brandt, auf dem Landesparteitag der Berliner SPD, 22 Mai 1955', in Siegfried Heimann (ed.), *Willy Brandt. Berlin bleibt frei: Politik in und für Berlin 1947–1966* (Bonn, 2004), 186–94.

[27] BAK, ZSg. 1-E/70: 'Kampf dem Atomtod' (April 1958), 15; Claus Rainer Röhl, 'Zwei Volksbewegungen', *konkret*, 14 (1958), 1; Hans Werner Richter to Ernst Nolte, 10 March 1957, in Richter, *Briefe*, 245–7.

[28] *Europa Archiv*, 14 (1959), 187–91.

[29] *Deutscher Bundestag, Stenographische Berichte*, 3. *Wahlperiode*, 46, 30 June 1960, cols 7055–6; Herbert Wehner, 'Redliche Bestandsaufnahme', *Vorwärts*, 3 June 1960, 1.

[30] AdsD, 2/PVAM000005: 'Kampf dem Atomod', pamphlet, 23 March 1958, 6.

but had gradually lost currency among parties and governments. This created constant movement, as the activists sought to push their societies 'back to the future'. Only a minority of activists from the New Left went beyond this status quo oriented framework. They argued that security could be maintained only through rapid socio-economic change across the world. This meant the decline of the anti-nuclear-weapons movements, but the emergence of new movements in both countries, which framed the issue of 'security' altogether differently.

DEBATING NATIONHOOD AS SECURITY STRATEGY

While the protesters constantly redefined their goals to respond to a rapidly changing international landscape, one element in their analyses remained seemingly fixed: the role they assigned to their nation in international politics. British protesters, although they sometimes differentiated their use of words, normally used 'English' as synonymous with 'British' national identity. Through framing the issue of nuclear armaments in this way, the activists sought to represent their own aims as directly connected to their nations' interests and thus facilitate communications with their societies at large. The dynamic of appealing to concepts of 'nationhood' in the political process lay in the fact that they could be filled with different meanings, yet at the same time offered the movements a clear location in the political debates. Particularly for British activists, appeals to the nation's greatness provided them with a coherent theme and thus seeming coherence over time, while they constantly adapted to the changing international and domestic situations. Interestingly, Scottish nationalism did not matter in these framings, even after the *Polaris* missile basis had opened at Holy Loch: activists regarded the base as detrimental for Britain's national security, rather than as an infringement for Scottish rights.[31]

Defining and debating their nation's role in world affairs thus served the protesters as a security strategy; it was through redefining nationhood that the activists expressed their desires for a safer world and for a safer home. Paradoxically, the debates among activists about how their own nations should be defined frequently took place through mutual observations of the other movement. The protesters' analyses of their own and the other country's history played a crucial role in these observations. British activists regarded themselves as the representatives of the lead nation:

[31] *Peace News*, 1 November 1963, 7; *Peace News*, 20 September 1963, 1.

'Britain's conscience cannot be saved by waiting for other nations... Unilateral renunciation of nuclear weapons is both a moral duty in itself and the greatest contribution that Britain can make to... hastening a multilateral agreement'; 'to subordinate armed force in the service of national sovereignty to a world code of law'.[32]

Movement activists at the time would have rejected an interpretation that highlighted their concepts of national belonging and would have pointed out that they were concerned about the 'fate of the world' and in solidarity with nations across the globe. West German protesters, in particular, would have had difficulties identifying what they thought of the German nation. Because of the division of the country, Germany existed only in the form of a question, something that had been lost after war and National Socialism.[33] Contemporary commentators and historians have followed this interpretation and assumed that a German national identity had been lost after 1945. Ute Frevert has even gone so far as to suggest that national identity after 1945 'was not felt from the inside, but attributed from the outside'.[34] In Britain, despite CND's explicit appeals to nationhood, the situation was remarkably similar, and historians have only started to uncover these constructions since the early 1980s.[35] Perspectives that assume that national identity was not a relevant parameter in post-1945 Britain and West Germany overlook, however, that the definition of national citizens as members of a world community was itself part of the resources that endowed national specificities with symbolic power, as it allowed the activists to create resonance for their claims in their respective societies.[36]

These processes reveal a complex dialectic between innovation and existing cultural norms. Activists accepted what Lauren Berlant has called the 'national symbolic': 'the order of discursive practices whose reign within a national space produces, and also refers to, the "law" in which the accident of birth within a geographic/political boundary transforms individuals

---

[32] BLPES, CND/1/2/, Policy statement, 1962–3.
[33] Martin Wengeler, 'Die Deutschen Fragen: Leitvokabeln der Deutschlandpolitik', in Karin Böke, Frank Liedtke, and Wengeler, *Politische Leitvokabeln in der Adenauer-Ära* (Berlin and New York, 1996), 325–77, here 355.
[34] Ute Frevert, 'Die Sprache des Volkes und die Rhetorik der Nation: Identitätssplitter in der deutschen Nachkriegszeit', in Arnd Bauerkämper, Martin Sabrow, and Bernd Stöver (eds), *Doppelte Zeitgeschichte: Deutsch-deutsche Beziehungen 1945–1990* (Bonn, 1998), 18–31, here 21.
[35] Jodi Burkett, 'Re-Defining British Morality: "Britishness" and the Campaign for Nuclear Disarmament 1958–1968', *Twentieth Century British History*, 21 (June 2010), 184–205.
[36] Cf. the arguments in Krishan Kumar, 'Nation and Empire: English and British National Identity in Comparative Perspective', *Theory and Society*, 29 (2000), 575–608.

into subjects of a collectively held history.'[37] Traditionally, nationalism had provided societies with a 'discourse of sacrificial inscription' into the nation through the willingness to die for the nation.[38] British and West German activists, by contrast, reversed this relationship by using ideas of nationhood to express their sacrifice to *prevent* a war that would mean that they would die for their nation as civilians. But most of the activists were not pacifists. They still drew on concepts of national ordering and discipline, and did not generally reject the use of violence for political purposes.

It is striking to what extent the constitution of both movements as seemingly coherent political actors depended on defining them as linked to their respective nation. For the Labour defence expert Denis Healey, CND was nothing less than 'jingoism with an inferiority complex',[39] and David Marquand, then a member of the Young Fabians within the Labour Party, pointed out in 1960 that

CND is to the left what the Suez expedition was to the right: the last brave hope of British nationalism... Even more than the right, members of CND cannot imagine a world in which British moral gestures would in fact count for very little; and if told that is the world they live in, they refuse to believe you.[40]

Likewise, West German activists considered defining the meaning of Germany after 1945 as an 'oppositional topic'.[41]

In both movements, activists came to combine concepts of a concern for humanity as a whole with ideas about a specifically *national* morality. In doing so, they did not 'invent' the nation from scratch, but they reformulated expectations of the immediate post-war years, or even the 1920s, which they had either directly experienced, or to which they became acquainted through discussions with their colleagues.

While the government emphasized the role of nuclear weapons for maintaining Britain's leadership in world affairs, the protesters saw the

---

[37] Lauren Berlant, *Anatomy of a National Fantasy: Hawthorne, Utopia, and Everyday Life* (Chicago, 1991), 20.

[38] Geoff Eley, 'Making a Place in the Nation: Meanings of "Citizenshipo" in Wilhelmine Germany', in Geoff Eley and James Retallack (eds), *Wilhelminism and its Legacies: German Modernities, Imperialism, and the Meanings of Reform, 1890–1930* (New York, 2003), 16–33, here 17.

[39] Denis Healey, 'The Pattern of Western Unity', *New Leader*, 22 January 1962, 22.

[40] David Marquand, 'England, the Bomb, the Marchers', *Commentary*, 29 (May 1960), 384; Hinton, *Protests and Visions*, viii–ix.

[41] Hans Magnus Enzensberger's acceptance speech for the 1963 Büchner Prize: 'Darmstadt, am 19 Oktober 1963', in Enzensberger, *Deutschland, Deutschland unter anderm: Äußerungen zur Politik* (Frankfurt/Main, 1967), 14–26 as well as Hans Werner Richter to Georg Ramseger, 4 December 1961, in Richter, *Briefe*, 385–6.

unilateral renunciation of nuclear weapons as the only way to preserve Britain's status as a great power. It would be an act of moral leadership that would confirm Britain's place in the world as a civilized country and a 'peaceable kingdom'.[42] Accordingly, CND's 1962 Manifesto pointed out that 'a Britain that publicly told the world, still aware of her resounding history, that she was siding at least with the forces of sense, and reason, and right, would rally behind her thousands of people from the non-communist world'. By linking CND so firmly to specific visions of British nationhood, CND became 'part of the nation's future'.[43]

At a time when British intellectuals and politicians debated the sources and nature of Britain's decline as a world and imperial power, J. B. Priestley found much solace in CND: 'We British no longer have any bright image of ourselves. And perhaps, among other things, we [in CND] went campaigning for that image.'[44] Priestley was not an isolated voice. In 1958, a group of campaign supporters met the tired protesters when they walked onto the field in front of the Aldermaston nuclear weapons research site and proclaimed with a loudspeaker: 'Lift up your hands and be proud. The lead has been given to the English people. Britain must take up that lead in the world. "England, arise, the long, long night is over."'[45] York CND's banner on the 1958 Aldermaston March expressed this sentiment by proclaiming: 'Let Britain lead', a slogan that was reminiscent of propaganda from the Royal Navy at the beginning of the twentieth century: 'Britain's unilateral action ended the slave trade: let Britain lead again.'[46]

The appeal to Britain's moral core was intimately bound up with the protesters' visions for a different Britain. Often tapping Christian rhetoric, activists regarded the Bomb as the symbol for the break-up of community into alienated human beings who had come to support violent assertions of British greatness such as the 1956 Suez invasion.[47] They believed that CND would help to refound that community and serve as an example to the world. In a 'Memo to our Next Prime Minister' on 'our

---

[42] BLPES, CND/10/1: 'Let Britain Lead', CND pamphlet, n.d. [1962], 10; Jon Lawrence, 'Forging a Peaceable Kingdom: War, Violence and the Fear of Brutalization in Post-First World War Britain', *Journal of Modern History*, 75 (2003), 557–89.

[43] BLPES, CND/1/2/1: CND Policy statement for 1962/3; *Sanity*, March 1962, 1.

[44] *New Statesman*, 19 May 1961, 786. On the debate about 'decline', cf. Anthony Sampson, *Anatomy of Britain* (London, 1962), 327. On the background, cf. Richard English and Michael Kenny (eds), *Rethinking British Decline* (Basingstoke, 2000).

[45] *Peace News*, 11 April 1958, 8. Cf. also: *Peace News*, 26 September 1958, 1; *Sanity* (December 1961), 2; 'CND Manifesto (1962)', *Sanity* (March 1962), 1; *Sanity* (January 1963), 4; *New Reasoner*, 4 (1958), 37; MRC, MSS 181/4: K. Zilliacus, *Arms and Labour*, pamphlet, n.d., 58.

[46] *Peace News*, 11 April 1958, 8; Lorna Lloyd and Nicholas A. Sims, *British Writing on Disarmament 1914–1978: A Bibliography* (London and New York, 1979), 12.

[47] *Sanity* (August 1963), 10.

role in the modern world', CND Vice-Chairman Ritchie Calder reiterated these claims: 'Do me a personal favour, Prime Minister, give me back my ride in my own country. Let me push out my chest, and say, "I am British."'[48] Such moral (rather than military-heroic) renderings of nationhood occurred at a time when, in plays like *Oh! What a Lovely War!*, non-heroic narratives of warfare were beginning to emerge in British popular culture that emphasized the moral, rather than the military, function of soldiers.[49]

West German protesters were, initially, less emphatic in highlighting their nation's role in the world and focused instead on German division alone. Increasingly, however, West German activists came to advance ideas of Germany's special role in the world as a peacekeeper that were strikingly similar to the ones voiced by British protesters. The problems in finding and defining boundaries in an age of insecurity, spurned by decolonization and the debate about economic decline in Britain and the division of the country in Germany, appeared to result in the use of very similar symbolic resources, which endowed the activists with meaning.

Focusing on the implications of nuclear armaments for German reunification, activists involved in the Campaign against Atomic Death emphasized that Chancellor Adenauer's policies were 'anti-German'.[50] Yet, another theme that was already present in earlier discussions came to overlap this topic, particularly after the building of the Berlin Wall had made the country's immediate reunification even less likely. In striking similarity to British protesters, West German activists carved out a new role for the Federal Republic: 'the service that we could [give] to America and the world as harbingers of reconciliation.'[51]

For the West German activists, the division of Germany and the experiences of being on the front line in the cold war thus became assets in international relations. Unlike British protesters, however, West German protesters used, in line with general public discourses, the very absence of any concepts of nationhood as the main symbolic resource for developing a view on the West German nation's role.[52] It became West Germany's national mission to shed all allegiance

[48] *Sanity* (October 1962), 2; Stephen King-Hall, *Defence in the Nuclear Age* (London, 1958), 221–2.
[49] Michael Paris, *Warrior Nation: Images of War in British Popular Culture, 1850–2000* (London, 2000), 227.
[50] AdsD, IG-Metall, G1010: Prof. Dr. Karl Bechert, 'Deutsche Politik im Schatten der Atomdrohung' [1958], 23; Fritz Erler's speech in the Bundestag, 23 January 1958, in *Deutscher Bundestag, Stenographische Berichte, 3. Wahlperiode*, 44 (1958), 23 January 1958, cols 368–75, here col. 375C.
[51] BAK, Zsg. 1-E/70: 'Kampf dem Atomtod' (April 1958), 23, 24.
[52] *Jahrbuch der öffentlichen Meinung 1947–1955*, ed. Elisabeth Noelle and E. Peter Neumann, 2nd edn (Allensbach, 1956), 126 (July 1952).

to national politics. Accordingly, activists came to argue in favour of a
policy that 'did not serve the interests of the one or the other side in one
country, but that served a new, world-wide security policy'.[53] National
power thus came, along with redefinitions of notions of masculinity at the
time, to lie in morals rather than in might.[54] This tuned-down rhetoric
was in marked contrast to the GDR's hyperbolic, emotional, and aggressive propagation of a 'national mobilization of all Germans in the fight for
peace and national unity' among groups of the West German far left and
far right.[55]

In accordance with their primarily moral definition of their nations,
the British and West German protesters believed that their definitions of
nationhood could do without boundaries towards outsiders and enemies.
Everyone was potentially included, and it was precisely the absence of
such explicit boundary mechanisms that endowed the campaigns with
the momentum to attract people with different experiences. It was through
transcending the dominant boundary mechanisms of nationhood at the
time that the movements gained their own distinctive character.

Movement activists in both countries tended to believe that the Soviet
Union was less aggressive and more trustworthy than the British and West
German governments portrayed it. This is why they assumed that nuclear
weapons were not necessary for deterrence in the first place, and this is
why they thought that conversations across the Iron Curtain would lead
to a lessening of tensions.[56] Yet, only very few protesters actively endorsed
Soviet policies, mostly marvelling at the alleged success of 'planning' in
the Soviet Union. The majority within CND remembered the Moscow
Trials, the Hitler–Stalin Pact, Russia's 'winter war' against Finland, and

---

[53] Senator a. D. Ernst Plate, 'Hamburg und Rostock', *Blätter für deutsche und internationale Politik*, 3 (1959), 765–6, here 765; BAK, ZSg. 1-262/3: *Informationen zur Abrüstung*, no. 3 (September 1963), 6; BAK, Zsg. 1-214/1, 4: 'Scheidung der Geister und
Wege', Hamburg n.d. [*c.*1962]; HIS, Sbe540, folder 'Friedensbewegung 50er und 60er
Jahre'.

[54] Appeal from 23 April 1957, quoted in Friedenskomitee der Bundesrepublik Deutschland, *Blaubuch über den Widerstand* 95–6; Stefan Andres, 'Nicht ein drittes Mal!', *Blätter
für deutsche und internationale Politik*, 3 (1958), 299–304, here 304.

[55] 'Informationsmaterial zur Lage im DGB und zu den Aufgaben der Kommunisten in
den Gewerkschaften', in Manfred Wilke and Hans-Peter Müller (eds), *SED-Politik gegen
die Realität: Verlauf und Funktion der Diskussion über die westdeutschen Gewerkschaften von
SED und KPD/DKP 1961 bis 1972* (Cologne, 1990), document VII, 440, 451.

[56] HWR, 72.86.512, 310: Hans Werner Richter to Christel Küpper, 6 November 1961;
HWR, 72.86.511, 110: 'Grüße des Komitees gegen Atomrüstung', Munich, 1958; BAK,
ZSg. 1-214/1: 'Scheidung der Geister und Wege', Hamburg, n.d., Internationale der
Kriegsdienstgegner; Lyng [Peter Rühmkorf], 'Zum 8. Mai', *Studenten-Kurier*, 1 (1955), 4;
'Wendemarke Berlin', *konkret*, 1 (1959), 1–2; Ulrike Meinhof, 'Deutschland ohne
Kennedy', *konkret*, 12 (1963), 6.

Krushchev's 'Secret Speech', which had exposed the purges for the first time.[57]

British protesters were, in general, more outspoken in their criticism of the United States' foreign policy than their West German colleagues. Yet only few protesters subscribed to a deeply ingrained ideological anti-Americanism that defined the United States in essentialist terms as the natural enemy of the respective nation. Instead, in accordance with their affirmation of British greatness, they focused on British sovereignty and rejected what they saw as American hegemony in the post-Second World War world. They campaigned to prove that their country was 'not just an appendage of the United States':[58] 'For the first time since 1945 Britain would have an independent voice. For the first time she would be free to engage in the politics of peace, externally struggling to export disarmament and internally building the new society which disarmament would make possible.'[59] This element became particularly clear in the protests against US bases and overflights.[60] Yet, most CND activists heavily criticized Bertrand Russell when, during the Cuban missile crisis, he described President Kennedy and his advisers as 'American madmen', while being much milder towards the Soviet leader, Nikita Khrushchev.[61]

Protesters in both countries not only defined their respective nation by referring to the present, but also endowed their campaigns with specific momentum by drawing on the past as a symbolic resource. British protesters tried to recapture something that had been lost in post-Second World War developments, while West German protesters tried to uncover their past in order to be able to untie themselves from the net of German history.[62] Events like the desecration of the Cologne Synagogue on Christmas Day 1959 and the trials of high-ranking National Socialists gave Germany's most recent National Socialist past a particularly high salience.[63]

---

[57] Darren G. Lilleker, *Against the Cold War: The History and Political Traditions of Pro-Sovietism in the British Labour Party 1945–89* (London, 2004).

[58] Alan Shuttleworth, 'Tests: The Case for Unilateral Action', *Sanity* (April 1963), 7.

[59] 'Target Britain', *Sanity* (July 1963), 5.

[60] *Peace News*, 27 December 1957, 1; *Peace News*, 28 July 1961, 3; *Sanity* (July 1961), 1; *Sanity* (December 1961), 2; 'Back to Christmas Island', *Sanity* (January 1962), 1; *Sanity* (March 1962), 4.

[61] Bertrand Russell, *Unarmed Victory* (London, 1963), 36, 39.

[62] Cf. Susanna Schrafstetter, 'The Long Shadow of the Past: History, Memory and the Debate over West Germany's Nuclear Status, 1954–69', *History & Memory*, 16 (2004), 118–45.

[63] Cf. 'Die Menschen Israels zur Zeit des Eichmann-Prozesses', *Gewerkschaftliche Monatshefte*, 6 (June 1961), 353–5; 'Eichmann und die Jugend', *Rheinischer Merkur*, 4 August 1961, 1.

For most British protesters, the Second World War formed the central positive reference point. Mentions of the wartime spirit abounded in CND's publications and speeches. *Tribune*, the paper of the Labour Left, compared the first Easter March to 'the turn of the tide' at Dunkirk.[64] In a similar vein, a CND pamphlet pointed out that the movement was 'an upsurge of the spirit of the British people on a scale that recalls "our finest hour" in 1940...Now we seize another chance to win through the pressing dangers to a better future for ourselves and mankind.'[65]

The success of the Anti-Corn Law League in the 1846 and Irish independence in 1921 were other frequent points of historical reference.[66] At the 1962 Aldermaston March, CND's banners pointed to Britain's leadership in ridding the world of the slave trade.[67] Speaking at Manchester's Free Trade Hall, A. J. P. Taylor proudly presented CND as the successor to the free traders John Bright and Richard Cobden.[68] At the 1963 Aldermaston March, there were plans for a gathering near Windsor Castle to sign a new version of the *Magna Carta*. Protesters were to gather 'in the fields of Runnymede' in order to ask the Queen to support the cause of unilateral disarmament.[69]

Looking across the Channel to Germany, therefore, CND activists regarded the plans to provide the German army with nuclear-capable equipment with great dismay. They feared that it would prevent a more permanent settlement of the German question and increase the likelihood of nuclear war in Europe.[70] Many CND protesters had already rejected the conventional armament of the Federal Republic in the early 1950s, primarily because they feared a resurgent Germany. Many who were now in CND had been anti-appeasers during the 1930s. Some agreed with the views of Sir Robert Vansittart that there was a deep-seated flaw within the German national character.[71] Accordingly, supplying nuclear-capable equipment to the West German government was, for them, a novel form of appeasement.[72] For Kingsley Martin, the West German

---

[64] 'All out for the March!', *Tribune*, 4 April 1958, 1.
[65] BLPES, CND/10/1: 'Flowing Tide', CND pamphlet (1960), 1.
[66] BLPES, CND/1/4: 'Is it any use?', n.d.
[67] 'Marchers' Diary', *Sanity* (Easter Sat. 1962), 4; (Easter Sun 1962), 4.
[68] A. J. P. Taylor, *A Personal History*, 229.
[69] *Sanity* (February 1962), 7; 'Save the Queen Anthem', *Peace News*, 4 April 1958, 3.
[70] Richard Crossman, 'Berlin Edge of the Pit', *New Statesman*, 28 August 1962, 222.
[71] Politisches Archiv des Auswärtigen Amtes, Berlin (PolArchAA), B31/247: Letter by the German Embassy London, 30 April 1963; *Peace News*, 21 November 1958, 4; *Peace News*, 10 April 1959, 1; 'Exhibition: National Socialism in Frankfurt', *Peace News*, 12 August 1960, 3; *Sanity* (March 1962), 2. For the background, cf. Donald Cameron Watt, *Britain Looks to Germany: British Opinion and Policy towards Germany since 1945* (London, 1965).
[72] Richard Gott, '25 Years After', *Sanity* (September 1964), 1.

Defence Minister Franz Josef Strauß was the 'most dangerous man in Europe' and, thus, a new Hitler.[73] Accordingly, many CND supporters regarded the division of Germany almost as a blessing and the GDR as a legitimate state, an attitude that was to lead to frequent conflicts between West German and the British movement activists, as many West German activists had not fully accepted German division.[74]

Yet, in general, CND activists differentiated between the West German government and the protesters: while the government was in continuity with National Socialist policies of national grandeur, the protesters were signs of a growing mood among the real and better Germany.[75] The German Democratic Republic sought to encourage these feelings against the German government among the British protesters, especially by asking Hilda Forman, a British Communist Party (CPGB) member, to form a 'circle of friends' for the GDR, particularly among CND youth groups.[76]

West German activists used the past not as an example, but as a motivation to march away from it. While British activists sought to establish a new kind of nation in the present, West German protesters regarded their campaign as an act of redemption from Germany's most recent past.[77] This theme ran through the history of both the Campaign against Atomic Death and the Easter Marches and provided the activists with constant momentum, even once new issues, such as the Vietnam War and the planned Emergency Legislation, had crowded out their interest in nuclear weapons.[78] The main parliamentary debate on nuclear armaments and the public launch of the Campaign against Atomic Death took place on

---

[73] HWR, 1.43.408: Kingsley Martin, 'Es gibt keinen Krieg für die Freiheit', in *'Europa ruft', Europäisches Komitee gegen Atomrüstung*, London, 17/18 January 1959, 33; HWR, 72.86.512, 143: *Trierischer Volksfreund*, 20 January 1959, 3; 'Gibt es "den" Deutschen?', *Westfälische Rundschau*, 27 January 1959.

[74] Working Class Movement Library, Salford (WCML), Allaun papers: Frank Allaun, letter to *The Guardian*, 17 October 1963.

[75] MRC, MSS 181/4: K. Zilliacus, *Arms and Labour*, CND pamphlet, n.d., 9, 31; 'Germany reaches for the Bomb', *Sanity* (September 1964), 1; PolArchAA, B31-152: Report by the German Embassy, London, on Gaitskell's speech in the House of Commons, 1 March 1958.

[76] SAPMO-Barch, DY30/IV 2/20/243, 218: 'Reisebericht der Kollegin I. Lessing' [mid-December 1957]; SAPMO-Barch DY30/IV 2/20/243, 233: Gerhard Waschewski to SED Central Committee, Dept. of Foreign policy (Comrade Liebig), 24 February 1958; PolArchAA, Referat 304 [Bestand 31], vol. 188: 'Die Aktivität der SBZ in Großbritannien', 21 May 1960.

[77] HStAD, RW 115 203, 171: 'Martin Niemöller: Das Ende der Demokratie'; RW 115 268, 118–19: Max Stierwaldt to Schmidt, 18 November 1960.

[78] Belinda Davis, 'Violence and Memory of the Nazi past in 1960s–70s West German Protest', in Phillip Gassert and Alan Steinweis (eds), *Coming to Terms with the Past in West Germany: The 1960s* (New York, 2006), 245–86.

23 March 1958, the twenty-fifth anniversary of Hitler's Enabling Act.[79] Exploiting the symbolic date in a somewhat hyperbolic fashion, Helmut Schmidt argued for the parliamentary opposition: 'We say to the German people... that the decision to equip both parts of our fatherland with nuclear weapons directed against each other will be seen by history as a decision as important and ominous as the Enabling Act was previously for Hitler.'[80]

Increasingly, explicit mention of *national* factors withered away, and activists came to define their specific national task, not as citizens of a nation, but as 'constitutional patriots'.[81] Protesting became, in Hans-Konrad Tempel's words, a duty that flowed directly out of Germany's history:

The German people have already once been accused of holding their tongues, where brave words and deeds would have been necessary. Millions of people lost their lives in concentration camps like Bergen-Belsen. Yet all of mankind is threatened with destruction from the continuation of test explosions and atomic armament. It is essential to counter this danger through an unmistakeable [and] total rejection of all preparations for atomic war in East and West.[82]

It seems to be no coincidence that the West German protesters used references to camps when making their point. It was through the pictures of the camps that the Allies had confronted the West Germans with their responsibilities for National Socialist crimes.[83] The protesters thus revived and redefined a prominent leitmotif of the discussions about 'democratic renewal' immediately after the end of the war. They echoed the existentialist philosopher Karl Jaspers, who had, in his 1946 book *The Question of German Guilt*, called for the transfiguration of the German nation state into a stateless nation and of German citizens into 'pariahs' who would assume the burden of moral responsibility after collapse of the German nation state.[84]

---

[79] AdsD, 2/PVAM000005: 'Das Leben retten—den Frieden sichern: Der Frankfurter Kongreß ruft alle zum Kampf gegen den Atomtod', 23 March 1958, 4.

[80] *Verhandlungen des Deutschen Bundestages, Stenographische Berichte*, 3. Wahlperiode, 20 March 1958, cols 1040–45; see col. 880; for Fritz Erler's remarks on the critical reactions to this speech, cf. Fritz René Allemann, 'Wie sag's ich meinem Volke?', *Die Zeit*, 27 March 1958, 7.

[81] IfZ, ED 702–5: Circular by Hans-Konrad Tempel, 16 March 1961; BAK, ZSg. 1 262/1: Report on the 1963 Easter March, 3; *Informationen zur Abrüstung*, nos 7–8 (February 1964), 3; HStAD, NW 308–84, 48–53: Report on the 1962 Easter Marches to the Interior Minister of Nordrhein-Westfalen, April 1962; SAPMO-BArch, DY30/IV 2/10.02/120, 321: 'Auszüge aus den Reden auf den Ostermarsch-Kundgebungen 1962'.

[82] Reprinted in Karl A. Otto (ed.), *APO. Die außerparlamentarische Opposition in Quellen und Dokumenten, 1960–1970* (Cologne, 1989), 53.

[83] Habbo Knoch, *Die Tat als Bild: Fotografien in der deutschen Erinnerungskultur* (Hamburg, 2001).

[84] A. Dirk Moses, *German Intellectuals and the Nazi Past* (Cambridge, 2007).

Both movements, therefore, had diametrically opposed positions in their political systems. While CND activists affirmed Britain's national past and criticized the government for squandering it, West German activists sought to reappropriate democratic traditions in German history so that the history of their present would not yet again turn into a 'history of false orders and tragic subordination'.[85] Nevertheless, both movements framed their national identity in ways that gave their own nation a mission in international affairs.

ALLIANCES

Over time, British and West German activists came to shift their views away from an emphasis on nuclear weapons alone and began to highlight what they regarded as the underlying problem of nuclear armaments: the impact that NATO, the Western defence alliance, had on *national* security. Instead of envisioning an entirely new international order, most activists framed their responses to nuclear armaments by reformulating and reviving experiences that pointed to 'the nation' as the centre for the international system. They revived, in various shapes and guises, proposals from the periods immediately after the Second World War and after the 1955 Geneva Conference, which called for a neutralization of central Europe. Initially, in their transnational discussions about this issue, which engaged creatively with ideas from Eastern European politicians, the majority of protesters regarded such proposals as primarily foreign-political devices. Only with the increased influence of the New Left from around 1962 onwards did discussions of a neutral, yet socialist 'third force' in world affairs gain prominence.[86] Kwame Nkrumah's Ghana in particular served as an example for the power of what activists called an 'active' or 'positive' neutralism visible among African and Asian nations since the 1955

[85] HWR, 72.86.511, 108: 'Grüße des Komitees gegen Atomrüstung', Munich, March 1958; 'Unser Marsch ist eine gute Sache' [1963], quoted in Baier, 'Ruhrgebiet', 132; HWR, 72.86.511, 65: Speech by Hans Werner Richter at the Circus Krone, Munich, for the Committee against Atomic Armaments, 18 April 1958.

[86] Lyng [Peter Rühmkorf], 'Zum 8. Mai', *Studenten-Kurier*, 1 (1955), 4; Kurt Hiller, 'Zur Mathematik der Wiedervereinigung', *Studenten-Kurier*, 3 (1956) (suppl.); 'Wendemarke Berlin', *konkret*, 1 (1959), 1–2; Ulrike Meinhof, 'Deutschland ohne Kennedy', *konkret*, 12 (1963), 6; AdsD, ASAF000177: 'Bericht über das Treffen von Vertretern der studentischen Atomausschüsse aus Hamburg, Berlin, Heidelberg, München und anderen Universitätsstädten', 16–18 May 1959; IfZ, ED702-2: Ostermarsch-Zentraler Ausschuß, 'Einige Argumente für's Bonner Lobby' (n.d.).

Bandung Conference and, especially, the 1962 anti-nuclear-weapons summit in Accra (Ghana).[87]

British and West German protesters assumed that both the Eastern and Western power blocs had lost the coherence of the early 1950s, primarily because of social developments in the Eastern bloc, but also because of the falling-out among Western allies in the wake of Britain's and France's Suez intervention in 1956.[88] The Soviet Union's calls for 'peaceful coexistence' seemed to suggest some movement in the East, to which the Western governments had insufficiently responded. In the words of a British observer, the world was 'in a state of tension and anarchy and tend[ed] towards war rather than peace. Unresolved disputes [dotted] the landscape like sleeping volcanoes.'[89]

Initially, British protesters did not discuss the United Kingdom's role within NATO. Most of the evidence points, however, to a tacit acceptance of NATO's role. Many British protesters even warned of the dangers that Britain's dissociation from the Western Alliance might have for international stability.[90] During this early period, the protesters took up the various disengagement proposals that British and East European politicians had developed since the Geneva Conference: the Eden Plan, the Macmillan Plan, the Gaitskell Plan, and the Rapacki Plan were all quoted in order to highlight the importance of reducing conflicts over central Europe and keeping the arms race under control.[91] This stance gave CND a unique degree of support, even among members of the defence establishment who supported NATO unquestioningly, but doubted that Britain would profit from possessing its own stock of nuclear weapons.[92]

While CND's basic consensus was solely concerned with matters of foreign policy, two increasingly vocal groups within CND regarded foreign policy as an element of social policy: the Labour Left and the New Left. They sought to create momentum for the campaign by reviving

[87] E. P. Thompson, 'N.A.T.O., Neutralism and Survival', *Universities & Left Review*, 4 (1958), 49–51; Hans Werner Richter to Georg Ramseger, 4 December 1961, in Richter, *Briefe*, 385–6; C. L. R. James, *Nkrumah and the Ghana Revolution* (London, 1962).

[88] HIS, TEM 100,04: 'Aufruf zum Ostermarsch 1960'; *Peace News*, 5 July 1958, 1.

[89] MRC, MSS 181/4: Mervyn Jones, 'Freed from Fear: A Policy for Britain without H-bombs', n.d. [c.1961].

[90] *Peace News*, 1 August 1958, 6; *Peace News*, 25 September 1959, 1; *Peace News*, 27 November 1959, 1; *Peace News*, 16 August 1963, 3.

[91] Cf. Young, *Strategy for Survival*; Martin Ceadel, 'Supranationalism in the British Peace Movement during the Early Twentieth Century', in Andrea Bosco (ed.), *The Federal Idea: The History of Federalism from Enlightenment to 1945* (2 vols, London and New York, 1991), i. 169–91.

[92] *Peace News*, 11 November 1959, 1.

conceptions of international order that were closely connected to domestic political and socio-economic change. A possible third group was the British Communists, who were still largely opposed to CND in 1958–59, as they believed that unilateral disarmament might discredit the Soviet Union's disarmament initiatives within the UN framework. From 1960 onwards, despite the Party's attempts to convert CND into a 'peace movement', they formed but a small minority of supporters within CND.[93]

Those activists who regarded themselves as part of the Labour Left regarded the international situation of the late 1950s as the verification of their arguments of the late 1940s. Without mentioning NATO, but with major implications for Britain's role within it, they thus revitalized third-force proposals from the period immediately after the Second World War. They argued for a 'third force', led by Britain, between the superpowers that would act as a moderating influence in international relations and that would combine the best elements of 'capitalism' and 'socialist planning'.[94] Part of CND's foreign-policy agenda was, therefore, the last glimmer of the ideas of the traditional Labour Left, developed during the Second World War and most prominently discussed in 1946–47 under different international circumstances. Its short triumph was the success of a unilateralist motion at the 1960 Labour Party conference. This group's opponents were those Atlanticist Labour politicians with close links to the United States, who were active in the Bilderberg group and around the journal *Encounter*.[95]

As in the late 1940s, Labour Left politicians warned of American hegemony and the implications for British sovereignty. The apparent dependence of British foreign and defence policy and strategy on American technology and general guidance confirmed their fears about the dangers flowing from an Atlanticist foreign policy. Members of this group not only resented the hegemony of the capitalist United States in the West; they also feared a resurgent (West) Germany, possibly equipped with nuclear weapons, within a NATO framework.[96]

Positively, they envisioned Britain as a 'third force' in world politics, a crucial mediator between the Eastern and Western bloc. Grouped around it would be the former colonies, ideologically united within a socialist

[93] Cf. Callaghan, *Cold War, Crisis and Conflict*, 145–9.

[94] Jonathan Schneer, 'Hopes Deferred or Shattered: The British Labour Left and the Third Force Movement, 1945–49', *Journal of Modern History*, 56 (1984), 197–226.

[95] Lawrence Black, ' "The Bitterest Enemies of Communism": Labour Revisionists, Atlanticism and the Cold War', *Contemporary British History*, 15 (2001), 26–62.

[96] WCML, Allaun papers: 'The Arms Race and Economic Development', c.1961; *Peace News*, 10 August 1960, 8.

Commonwealth that would avoid the Soviet Union's sins, but could, at the same time, benefit from the advantages of planning for a fair and just society. Rather than through nuclear weapons, Britain would maintain its 'greatness' through its ideological mission. The activists' support for the disengagement proposals, even if they came from beyond the Iron Curtain, was the practical side of the coin.[97]

The other group of activists within the British movement that regarded foreign and social policies as inextricably linked was the New Left.[98] With its growing influence within the Campaign from the early 1960s, New Left activists revived the dynamic connotations of the term 'peaceful coexistence'.[99] Superficially, the New Left's ideas resembled those of the Labour Left. But the New Left's emphasis on grass-roots politics and its sceptical attitudes towards socialist planning within the Eastern bloc gave their arguments a different character. Rather than advocating a 'third force', therefore, New Left activists saw Britain as the spearhead for 'active neutrality' or 'positive neutralism'.[100] In contrast to what they regarded as the 'passive' neutrality of Sweden and Switzerland, this kind of active neutrality was to be the 'reverse of isolationism'. It was to entail an active and 'indeed aggressive' foreign policy that was aimed at relaxing East–West tensions, dismantling the military blocs, and resuming 'economic, political and cultural intercourse between the Communist and non-communist world'. It was to lead to the 'elaboration of details of a possible diplomatic détente and the affirmation of a community of human aspiration at levels deeper than diplomacy', which flowed from socialist premises.[101]

For the British New Left, the existence of NATO was the expression of the division of the world into two camps, a situation that contained 'within [it] the threat to man's peaceful advance, indeed to man's future existence'.[102] Underlying this analysis was the belief that fighting against

[97] J. B. Priestley, 'Britain and the Nuclear Bombs', *New Statesman*, 54, (2 November 1957), 554–6. On the background, cf. Stefan Berger and Darren Lilleker, 'The British Labour Party and the German Democratic Republic during the Era of Non-Recognition, 1949–1973', *Historical Journal*, 45 (2002), 433–58.

[98] Edward P. Thompson, 'Revolution', *New Left Review*, 3 (1960), 3–9; Edward P. Thompson, 'Why not?', *New Left Review*, 2 (1960), 1.

[99] BJL, uncatalogued collection: E. P. Thompson to John Saville, n.d. (*c.* October 1956).

[100] For an elaboration of this policy with special regard to colonial issues, cf. Michael Barratt Brown, 'Third World or Third Force?', *New Left Review*, 20 (1963), 32–6; Keith Buchanan, 'Bingo or UNO? Further Comments on the Affluent and Proletarian Nations', *New Left Review*, 21 (1963), 21–9.

[101] BJL, JS-109: Edward P. Thompson, 'Active Neutrality' [MS, n.d., *c.*1959]; MRC, MSS 181/4: *CND April Notes* (1965), 2.

[102] BJL, JS-112: 'The New Left: General Statement Adopted by a Joint Meeting of the Editorial Boards of the *New Reasoner* and the Universities and *Left Review on Sunday*', 26 April 1959.

nuclear weapons and nuclear strategies was not enough. Rather, the New Left assumed that it was the strategy of nuclear preparedness and the cold war itself rather than Britain's own bomb that was the ultimate danger. It was, therefore, wrong for Britain to be part of an alliance that insisted on manufacturing and deploying bombs. Thus, Stuart Hall argued in a CND pamphlet that Britain had given up any flexibility in framing its foreign policy. Once Britain had accepted the Alliance's premises, it was obliged to follow 'every other dangerous twist in the weapons race'. NATO's failure to seriously consider the Rapacki and Macmillan plans for disengagement had illustrated how little could be done to move towards peace 'from a position well within an alliance which is committed to the strategies of war'.[103] For Hall, as for many New Left activists, the case against the bomb became a case against all nuclear alliances and strategies.

Conversely, many New Left activists argued that the United States and the Soviet Union be brought to talk to each other only if the ground was cut away beneath the feet of the two camps. First precedents had been set at the 1955 Bandung Conference as well as with Yugoslavia's peculiar position in world politics and Poland's suggestions for disengagement. New Left members believed that such measures would have an extraordinary effect on the structure of international relations. If one NATO member contracted out of the two camps, they predicted, the summit deadlock would collapse. This would free socialist movements across Europe and sound the death knell to the Stalinism within the British, French, and other Communist Parties across Europe.[104] They pointed out that only Britain had, through its traditional ties to the Commonwealth and the strength of the labour movement there, the strength to pursue such a policy.[105]

Underlying these ideas was the assumption that communism was not inherently authoritarian but had merely become so during the 1930s. Proponents of this view claimed that 'the Cold War reinforce[d] and sustain[ed] these features, which sooner or later [were] likely to crumble under internal pressures in a period of international relaxation'. At the same time, only such a period of relaxation would allow Western societies like Britain to advance on their way towards truly democratic socialism, which would not suppress but encourage the voicing of people's individual experiences.[106] Labour movements in Britain, France, and Italy, New

[103] MRC, MSS 181/4: Stuart Hall, 'N.A.T.O. and the Alliances', CND pamphlet, [n.d., c.1961, 5.
[104] BJL, JS-109: Edward Thompson to John Saville, 9 November 1957.
[105] *Peace News*, 11 April 1958, 8; Edward P. Thompson, 'Outside the Whale', in Edward P. Thompson (ed.), *Out of Apathy* (London, 1960), 141–94, here 178, 186; MRC, MSS 181/4: Stuart Hall, 'Steps towards Peace', CND pamphlet, 1962.
[106] *Peace News*, 25 August 1961, 1; *Peace News*, 22 March 1959, 4.

Left supporters argued, could thus regain their unity and follow similar policies at home. The same situation would allow a movement towards unification in Germany to begin.[107] This would solve the 'cramp' of Europe that George F. Kennan had diagnosed in his BBC Reith lectures.[108] If the cold war continued, by contrast, 'the half-frozen antagonists' would become 'more sluggish in their reactions, more stupid in their thoughts', merely amassing destructive power for the maintenance of power blocs and bases. The ensuing inertia would make it difficult to adequately address the many problems of the time. Thompson even mused that 'some new Bismarck' might well emerge in Bonn, or, referring to President de Gaulle's policy of giving France a nuclear *force de frappe*, that 'some shabby Corsican in France' might possess the atom bomb.[109]

New Leftist activists only rarely used foreign-political and strategic arguments in isolation against Britain's NATO membership. For the New Left's supporters within CND, NATO was not so much a military alliance, but the expression of a specific political, social, and economic ideology that emphasized apathy and consumption rather than active participation in public life. The Western Alliance was the symbol of 'Natopolitan ideology', the post-Second World War liberal consensus in the West.[110] Significantly, however, although the New Left activists played a prominent role in framing international security, CND as a whole lost popular support when it followed New Left arguments and argued for Britain's exit from NATO. Most activists' experiences did not lead them to develop such long-term visions of socio-economic change; they remained satisfied with the more limited proposals that focused on an end to nuclear weapons testing.

While West German protesters also voiced experiences that emphasized what they regarded as national interests vis-à-vis alliance policies, the vast majority of West German activists lacked a utopian vision similar to the one propagated by the British New Left. Instead, they focused on incremental changes, while emphasizing the overarching aim of international stability. Contemporary rhetoric emanating from the Adenauer government suggests that the Easter Marches campaigned outside the

[107] BJL, JS-109: Edward P. Thompson, 'Active Neutrality' [MS, n.d., *c.*1959]; John Rex and Peter Worsley, 'Campaign for a Foreign Policy', *New Left Review*, 4 (1960), 49–62.
[108] BJL, JS-109: Edward P. Thompson, 'Active Neutrality' [MS, n.d., *c.*1959].
[109] Peter Worsley, 'Imperial Retreat', in Edward P. Thompson (ed.), *Out of Apathy*, 101–40; MRC, MSS 181/4: John Gittings and Richard Gott, 'Nato's Final Decade', CND pamphlet (1964), 25–6; Mervyn Jones, 'Freed from Fear: A Policy for Britain without H-bombs', n.d. [*c.*1961]. 1–2.
[110] BJL, JS-109: Edward P. Thompson to John Saville, n.d. [*c.* spring 1958]; for a critical reading, cf. Raphael Samuel, 'Born-Again Socialism', in Oxford University Socialist Discussion Group (ed.), *Out of Apathy: Voices of the New Left* (London, 1989), 39–57.

parameters of the Western Alliance.[111] The GDR's propaganda machine did indeed play no small role in publicizing disengagement plans in West Germany and thus provided the West German protesters with arguments. Yet, from the activists' perspective, these proposals were not forms of indoctrination, but merely *expressed* their experiences and expectations.[112]

Unlike in the British movement, there were only very few in the West German Easter Marches who saw a link between foreign and social policy that was close to Communist ideology.[113] Such a link had been a characteristic feature of the *SPD* and Communist Party programmes in the late 1940s and early 1950s, but had, since Erich Ollenhauer's election as party leader and the banning of the *Kommunistische Partei Deutschlands* (Communist Party of Germany (*KPD*)) in 1956, disappeared from the party-political discourse.[114] Not even national–neutralist sentiments made it into the many Easter March leaflets and pamphlets, and they remained confined to either far-right or far-left publications.[115]

While the British New Left activists emphasized the ideological components of NATO, the overwhelming majority of West German anti-nuclear-weapons protesters both within the Campaign against Atomic Death and within the Easter Marches primarily questioned the *military* component of the alliance. Some sections in the West German movement questioned the reliability of American protection, given that the Soviet Union now appeared to be able to hit the United States with intercontinental missiles. Like the West German government, they feared that the United States would not risk Washington or New York City for Berlin. Because of the restrictions on 'acceptable' political expression that the cold war imposed on the Federal Republic's political culture, even these, in comparison with the British New Left's more moderate suggestions, aroused suspicions within the main political parties and the government.[116]

---

[111] For the perception in the SPD, cf. AdsD: Parteivorstand, minutes, 17 February 1961.

[112] BAK, B106/16053: Sicherungsgruppe des BKA (Dr. Brücker) to Innenminister, Dept. VI A 3, 24 April 1958.

[113] IfZ, ED702-2: Dr. Andreas Buro, 'Zielsetzung des Ostermarsches [Kurzfassung des Referats am 30. Juni/1. Juli 1962]'.

[114] Cf. the arguments in Arnold Sywottek, 'Die Opposition der SPD und der KPD gegen die westdeutsche Aufrüstung in der Tradition sozialdemokratischer und kommunistischer Friedenspolitik seit dem Ersten Weltkrieg', in Wolfgang Huber and Johannes Schwerdtfeger (eds), *Frieden, Gewalt, Sozialismus: Studien zur Geschichte der sozialistischen Arbeiterbewegung* (Stuttgart, 1976), 496–610.

[115] Alexander Gallus, *Die Neutralisten: Verfechter eines vereinten Deutschland zwischen Ost und West 1945–1990* (Düsseldorf, 2001), ch. 6.

[116] BAK, B106/16053: Sicherungsgruppe des BKA (Dr. Brücker) to Innenminister, Dept. VI A 3, 3 May 1958.

Although the majority of protesters expressed their desires for a security policy that was determined nationally, they did not argue for a foreign policy that was entirely independent of Alliance considerations. Rather, they disagreed with Alliance policies in the specific area of nuclear weapons policies. While the *SPD* had still highlighted the adverse impact that nuclear armament would have for the prospects of German unification, Easter March activists already focused their policies on the Federal Republic only.[117] The majority of West German activists expressed expectations of a rather static international system. Although the Easter Marches had been organized against the wishes of the *SPD* executive, the activists merely continued to advocate disengagement and a nuclear-free zone in central Europe after the *SPD* had abandoned such plans. While the party had already moved, under Brandt's leadership, towards a more dynamic conception of international politics, the momentum that drove the Easter Marches remained the desire to create security through a relatively static *national* security policy and regarded this as an imperative that flowed from Germany's experience of violence in the Second World War.[118] The majority of the German population, by contrast, lived a life of 'perpetual holidays, with the Germans in the middle, as calm as the Swiss in the remotest mountains', and ignored the dangers of the current international system.[119]

Rather than fundamentally question Adenauer's policy of political integration into the West, most West German protesters sought to establish different priorities. Instead of arguing for a strengthened military alliance, as the Adenauer government had (for example by establishing a multilateral force), they advocated rather static plans for military disengagement, whose origins harked back to the immediate period after the Second World War. George F. Kennan's proposals for a neutralization of central Europe, which he had first voiced in the BBC's Reith Lectures in late 1957 and which were published in Germany in 1958, were especially popular. They revived his proposals from the late 1940s and were founded on the emphasis of psychological and ideological defences.[120] *SPD* politicians, including Helmut Schmidt, also drew heavily on the Gaitskell Plan.[121] These

---

[117] Cf. Gallus, *Neutralisten*, 237–64.

[118] Rolf Elker et al. (eds), *Beiträge zur Geschichte des SDS* (Berlin, 1987), 45.

[119] Eugen Kogon, 'Die Insel der Friedfertigkeit', *Frankfurter Hefte*, 13/8 (1958), 525–30, here 525.

[120] Kennan, *Russia, the Atom, and the West*. For the reception in the Federal Republic, cf. 'Kennan gegen Atomwaffen für den Kontinent', *Frankfurter Allgemeine Zeitung*, 3 December 1957.

[121] Cf. Hartmut Soell, *Helmut Schmidt: Vernunft und Leidenschaft* (Munich, 2003), 311–58; 'Das Selbstverständnis von Friedenskämpfern', *neue kritik* (January 1961), 22; 'Gegen Atomwaffen in Ost und West', *neue kritik* (May 1961), 31–2.

proposals implied, in striking similarity to American, British, and Soviet governmental plans of the late 1950s and early 1960s, freezing the geostrategic map of Europe and plans for internationally controlled disarmament.[122]

Rather than regarding NATO and the other nations as the fundamental problem, most West German protesters, like their British counterparts, blamed the lack of progress towards a multilateral détente on their own government. While NATO had been founded to roll back communism, the West German activist Arno Klönne argued, this goal had already lost currency in Washington by 1955; it had remained 'the lie on which Adenauer had built the Federal Republic's integration into NATO' in 1955. Everyone, apart from West German politicians, Klönne argued, agreed with proposals to lessen tension in central Europe, but Bonn's security policies had hit a dead end.[123]

The fundamental reason why the Easter Marches generated such concerns within the *SPD* and within the West German government was, therefore, not that they advocated new and radical policies, but rather that they advocated programmes that expressed the experiences of the Second World War and thus contradicted the policies of normalization and the 'politics of the past' of the West German government.[124] Significantly, Helmut Schmidt, a former *Wehrmacht* major, was initially a staunch supporter of the Campaign against Atomic Death, as it appeared to reflect his war experiences. Unlike those who remained attached to the movement, however, he redefined his war experiences in the light of subsequent international developments. As the two crises over the future of Berlin in 1958–59 and 1961 and the crisis over Cuba in 1962 did not result in wars, he came to argue that deterrence worked. The likelihood that nuclear weapons would be used remained close to zero. Living with the atomic bomb had become possible.[125] By contrast, the Easter Marchers who had experienced the Second World War either as children or as adult civilians continued to believe that the use of nuclear weapons remained likely and that defending West Germany with nuclear weapons would destroy the country.[126]

[122] AdsD, 2/PVAM000036: Minutes of the meeting of the European Federation against Nuclear Arms, Bonn, 23–24 September 1961.
[123] BAK, ZSg. 1-262/3: Arno Klönne, 'Zur Situation der Europa- und Deutschlandpolitik', *Informationen zur Abrüstung*, 38–39 (September–October 1966), 5.
[124] Norbert Frei, *Adenauer's Germany and the Nazi Past: The Politics of Amnesty and Integration* (New York, 2002).
[125] Helmut Schmidt, *Defense or Retaliation: A German Contribution to the Consideration of NATO's Strategic Problem* (London, 1962); Soell, *Schmidt*, 333–62, 473–85.
[126] BAK, ZSg. 1/262-1: Helmut Gollwitzer, 'Ostermarschrede '64'; 'Politik der Sicherheit durch Abrüstung in Mitteleuropa: Ein Sofortprogramm für die Bundesrepublik Deutschland, vorgelegt von der Kampagne für Abrüstung—Ostermarsch der Atomwaffengegner' [n.l., n.d. *c*.1966].

FOREIGN LANDS: THE COLONIAL QUESTION

From the mid-1950s onwards, the challenge to the Western alliances posed by the ever-present threat of nuclear confrontation between the super-powers was joined by what contemporaries perceived as an equally danger-ous and dynamic element in international affairs: the emergence of a vigorous, broad-based, and assertive nationalism throughout the develop-ing world. These nationalist stirrings not only posed a major challenge to the world order of cold war. They also promised to exacerbate the already existing tensions between Washington and Moscow, as the two superpow-ers competed for the loyalty and resources of the newly emerging areas and introduced a further element of instability into the international system. Nowhere had the connection between the two elements become clearer than during the crises of Suez and Hungary in autumn and early winter 1956.[127] From the perspective of Western activists, the cold war was rap-idly becoming a global conflict: 'The last button may be pressed precisely because the hungry two-thirds are not going to stand it much longer.'[128]

Thus, from the early 1960s onwards, British and West German protesters increasingly incorporated assessments of the situation in the decolonizing world into their experiences of international insecurity; but more dynamic conceptions of the politics of security defined as solidarity with decoloniz-ing movements around the world took some time to take hold. In both movements, there existed a broad consensus among different groups of ac-tivists that national self-determination was of crucial importance and that the colonies should be 'liberated' as quickly as possible. It was this theme, more than any other, that provided the British and West German protesters with the links between their protests against nuclear weapons and against colonialism; as the developing countries had a right to national independ-ence, so the protesters asserted that right for their own countries. Paradoxi-cally, however, this theme generated much more momentum for the movement in West Germany, which lacked an immediate colonial past, than for CND, which campaigned in the midst of decolonization.

In Britain, the New Left, in particular, voiced concerns about the role of nuclear weapons for the 'developing world'. But they did so in ways that did not transcend dominant interpretations of decolonization and

---

[127] Peter Worsley, 'The Anatomy of Mau Mau', *New Reasoner* (Summer 1957), 13–25, here 25; Stuart Hall and Norm Fruchter, 'Notes on the Cuban Dilemma', *New Left Review*, 9 (1961), 2–11, here 2; Keith Buchanan, 'The Third World: Its Emergence and Contours', *New Left Review*, 18 (1963), 5–23.

[128] BLPES, CND/1/71/44: *Focus*, 34, Labour Party Conference, Thursday, 3 October 1963, 10.

thus expressed expectations of the majority of CND activists. For most
CND activists imperial questions merely formed a canvas on which they
projected their particular views of Britain or, mostly, England. They did
not directly identify with the cause of national liberation.[129] They came to
regard the campaigns against nuclear weapons and in favour of rapid
decolonization as two sides of the same coin:

It is not just that hunger, misery and despair are the most likely cause of the out-
breaks of revolt that can become the occasion of nuclear war—we need only to
note that place where the bomb was nearly used, Korea, Viet Nam and Laos, the
Congo, Cuba—but the bomb above all demands that the peoples of the rich and
poor lands find a framework for joint action.[130]

In the Federal Republic, by contrast, a small number of activists came, as
part of their arguments against French intervention in Algeria, to identify
much more emphatically with the cause of 'national liberation': 'Algeria is
everywhere; it is here, too, like Auschwitz, Hiroshima and Budapest.'[131]
Initially, the majority of West German activists had not perceived the
imperial dimension as important. However, through engagement in various transnational socialist networks and through reporting in periodicals,
a small minority of West German activists began to emphasize the importance of decolonization, in particular with regard to Algeria.[132] Even once
West German activists had discovered the importance of Third World
nationalism for international politics from around 1961 onwards, they
interpreted it primarily as an inspiring realization of true neutrality
between the Soviet Union and the United States. Like the majority of
their British counterparts, they also marvelled at the opportunities for
economic development in the former colonies, such as the new port of
Tema and the Volta Dam project in Ghana. Unlike British activists,
however, West German protesters never regarded it as their mission to
lead the camp, or to implement similar policies in central Europe.[133]

[129] *Sanity* (Good Fri./Sat. 1963), 1; E. P. Thompson, 'N.A.T.O., Neutralism and Survival', *Universities & Left Review*, 4 (1958), 49–51; 49–51; E. P. Thompson, Peculiarities of
the English', *Socialist Register*, 2 (1965), 339–42.
[130] Michael Barratt Brown, 'Third World or Third Force?', *New Left Review*, 20 (1963),
35; Peter Worsley, 'Imperial Retreat', in Edward P. Thompson (ed.), *Out of Apathy*, 113.
[131] Hans Magnus Enzensberger at the opening of the Algeria exhibit in Frankfurt,
June 1961, quoted from Claus Leggewie, *Die Kofferträger: Das Algerien-Projekt der Linken
im Adenauer-Deutschland* (Berlin, 1985), 76.
[132] But see Ulrich Lohmar, 'Um die Zukunft Afrikas und Asiens', *Unser Standpunkt*,
6 (June 1953), 8; APOA, SDS/DK 1958: K. Pöhle, 'Die Auslandsarbeit des SDS', mimeo-
graphed report for the delegates' conference 1958.
[133] Heinz Kloppenburg, 'Accra und Genf. Beratungen über den Frieden', *Junge Kirche*,
23 (1962), 387–91; *Das Argument. Blätter der Westberliner Studentengruppe gegen Atomrüstung*, 10, 12 November 1959, 2.

Only after the question of German unification had lost its salience in the wake of the building of the Berlin Wall in August 1961 did a minority of West German activists from circles around the Socialist German Student Federation take the situation in the developing world more seriously. In close engagement with ideas from the American and the British New Left, activists from the Socialist German Student Federation (*Sozialistischer Deutscher Studentenbund* (*SDS*)) within the Easter Marches now argued for a dynamic movement 'from below' that would give neglected groups in colonial societies a voice.[134] As the West German activists conceived of German nationhood as an empty space that could be realized only by reaching out to humanity as a whole, they connected developments at the centre and the periphery much more directly than their British colleagues. Many within the *SDS* now argued that the Federal Republic would be increasingly affected by events in Europe and the world: 'we need to overcome the geographical boundaries of the nation, even of Europe and the West—in a world divided in three we have to orient ourselves as One World in order to win the future and overcome the barriers of the past.'[135] The suppression of colonial peoples was thus essentially the same as the suppression of dissent at home: 'If we are silent,' Hans Magnus Enzensberger argued, 'we cannot hope to be immune towards totalitarianism from left and right' at home.[136] Combining this theme with the trope of German unification, Hans Magnus Enzensberger argued with regard to Algeria that the war was 'also waged in our name, [and Algeria] is as close to us as national self-determination of the GDR'.[137] West German activists regarded support for 'national liberation' elsewhere as an act of self-defence (*Notwehr*): 'Not only peace and freedom are indivisible, but also torture, hunger and war. Either we abolish them or they abolish us.'[138]

For many West German activists, especially those coming from the *SDS*, looking closely at the Third World revealed what remained hidden in the West: the suppression of national independence movements

---

[134] Thomas von der Vring, 'Neue Linke, Partei, Staat', *neue kritik*, 9 (January 1962), 2; Jürgen Schaltenbrand, 'Einige Anmerkungen zum Begriff der Neuen Linken', *neue kritik*, 9 (January 1962), 3; Michael Vester, 'Die Linke in den USA', *neue kritik*, 17 (July 1963), 2.

[135] Ossip K. Flechtheim, 'Die Neue Linke in der Neuen Welt', *Frankfurter Hefte*, 18 (1963), 148–50; Ekkehart Krippendorff, 'Amerikanische Politik in Asien', *Frankfurter Hefte*, 18 (1963), 229–42.

[136] *Das Argument*, 15 (1960), 162; *Standpunkt*, nos 3–4 (May 1958), 2.

[137] *Das Argument*, 15 (1960), 141–2.

[138] Hans Magnus Enzensberger at the opening of the Algeria exhibition in Frankfurt, June 1961, quoted in Leggewie, *Koffertträger*, 76.

through the United States and the capitalist world system.[139] For *SDS*
activists, this 'fight against militarism and war' could be waged only 'as a
struggle for fundamental structural reforms of economy and society'.[140]
By the mid-1960s, when nuclear weapons had lost their salience in West
German debates, the war had come home to the West German activists.
Many had experienced the war only as children, but they believed that
what they saw in the television and news media showed the violence that
'the system' could generate. Violence was real in the colonies, but it
remained 'structural' in the Western world, inhibiting the growth of
individuals.[141] Unlike the majority of British activists, West German activists thus began to switch the coding of the debate from one that focused on 'security' to one that focused on 'violence' and 'non-violence'.
'Peace' as a utopia of human fulfilment re-emerged in movement discussions from the mid-1960s onwards. Through their constant reframing of
the issue of nuclear weapons, *SDS* activists had moved away from defining 'security' pragmatically as 'order' and 'stability'. Instead, they argued
that lasting security could be achieved only through fundamental *changes*
both to the structure of international relations and to socio-economic
structures at home.[142]

In Britain, such arguments had a much smaller resonance within CND,
as the rather critical reaction of many British activists towards Perry
Anderson's similar interpretation of imperialism shows.[143] Whereas British anti-nuclear-weapons protesters were confronted with the very real
problems of decolonization, for West German activists the Third World
had, in the words of Oskar Negt, an abstract, albeit much closer, presence
in the metropoles.[144] Foreign observers picked up these crucial differences
between the British and West German attitudes, as well. African representatives at a European–African conference at Castle Burg (on the river
Wupper) in Germany criticized the lack of 'politicization' of the British

[139] Hans-Jürgen Krahl, 'Angaben zur Person', in Krahl, *Konstitution und Klassenkampf*
(Frankfurt/Main, 1971), 19; SDS Delegates' Conference, quoted in Jürgen Briem, *Der
SDS: Die Geschichte des bedeutendsten Studentenverbandes der BRD seit 1945* (Frankfurt/
Main, 1976), 272.
[140] Ossip K. Flechtheim, 'Die Neue Linke in der Neuen Welt', *Frankfurter Hefte*, 18
(1963), 148–50; Ekkehart Krippendorff, 'Amerikanische Politik in Asien', *Frankfurter
Hefte*, 18 (1963), 229–42.
[141] Johan Galtung, 'Violence, Peace and Peace Research', *Journal of Peace Research*, 6
(1969), 167–91.
[142] Jürgen Seifert, 'Die Neue Linke. Abgrenzung und Selbstanalyse', *Frankfurter Hefte*,
18/1 (1963), 30–40, especially 33–4.
[143] Norman Birnbaum, 'Die Briten. Ideologie und Wirklichkeit in England', *Frankfurter Hefte*, 16/7 (1961), 439–51, especially 445; *alternative*, 22 (February 1962), 2.
[144] Leggewie, *Kofferträger*, 68.

delegation.[145] Only few British activists at the time commented critically on race violence in Britain and on the violent oppression of colonial uprisings by the British government.[146] The anthropologist Peter Worsley was one of the very few New Left activists who feared that the 'culture of violence' among British forces abroad would, in the medium term, introduce violence into society in the mother country and thus 'dehumanize' it.[147] Likewise, only a small minority of British activists disputed the writings of the French anti-colonial activist Frantz Fanon, who highlighted violence as a feature of colonialism and argued that large differentials in wealth between Britain and the majority of developing countries made 'class solidarity' impossible and would lead only to neo-colonialism.[148] From this perspective, Britain's moral leadership in unilateralism was merely a continuation of colonialism by other means.[149] The majority of British activists disagreed with such framings, however.

An important root for the activists' inability to reinvent the movement lay in the positive definition of Britain's foreign policy. They thought that not weapons and force, but Britain's moral lead, should be the backbone of its foreign and defence policies.[150] The protesters' image of themselves as citizens (or even subjects!) of a 'peaceable kingdom', together with a fundamental trust, grown through history, that Britain would not turn 'fascist', made these views plausible and prevented the switching of codes towards one of violence/non-violence. Quoting the nineteenth-century liberal John Stuart Mill, Edward P. Thompson and John Saville argued for a foreign policy that would 'redeem the character of our country.'[151] The activists' central claim chimed well with 'liberal views of the Empire', in which empire was not a source of military pride and greatness, but

[145] Siegward Lönnendonker, Bernd Rabehl, and Jochen Staadt, *Die Antiautoritäre Revolte. Der Sozialistische Deutsche Studentenbund nach der Trennung von der SPD* (Opladen, 2002), 196.
[146] For later statements by former activists, cf. the structural argument by Stuart Hall et al., *Policing the Crisis* (London, 1978); Birmingham Centre for Contemporary Cultural Studies, *The Empire Strikes Back* (London, 1982), and the ideological one by John Rex and Sally Tomlinson, *Colonial Immigrants in a British City* (London, 1979), 37. On the general context of these debates, cf. Chris Waters, ' "Dark Strangers" in Our Midst: Discourses of Race and Nation in Britain, 1947–1963', *Journal of British Studies*, 36 (1997), 207–38.
[147] Peter Worsley, 'Imperial Retreat', in Edward P. Thompson (ed.), *Out of Apathy*, 135.
[148] Stressed by Keith Buchanan, 'The Third World: Its Emergence and Contours', *New Left Review*, 18 (1963), 5–23; Buchanan, 'Bingo or UNO? Further Comments on the Affluent and Proletarian Nations', *New Left Review*, 21 (1963), 21–9.
[149] Hamza Alavi, 'Imperialism Old and New', *Socialist Register*, 1 (1964), 104–26.
[150] Driver, *The Disarmers*, 27.
[151] John Saville and E. P. Thompson, 'John Stuart Mill and E.O.K.A.', *New Reasoner*, 7 (1958–9), 1–11, here 11. On the similarity to mainstream discussions in Britain, cf. Wendy Webster, *Englishness and Empire 1939–1965* (Oxford, 2005), 136, 140–1.

evidence of Britain's civilizing mission and moral leadership.[152] For British protesters, British global power was the bringer of freedom. Thus, the activists revived and adapted ideas of a 'people's empire' that had become popularized during the Second World War.[153] Some activists even displayed an 'enlightened paternalism':[154] 'There are still some colonies in the world...which are too small for full independence, or whose people need further guidance and education before they can govern themselves.'[155]

As much as the British Prime Minister Harold Macmillan and CND protesters differed on the issue of nuclear weapons, they agreed on the basic functions of British diplomacy. Revisionists in the Labour Party at the time criticized this attitude as an 'unholy alliance of Commonwealth fanatics on the right and nuclear disarmers on the Left'.[156] Rather than attacking imperialism as such, they criticized the specific form decolonization took: 'Britain is in a unique position in all this. What India has achieved would be nothing compared to the immense pressure Britain could generate, in alliance with India, Ghana, Yugoslavia and backed by the uncommitted countries, for world peace and active neutrality.' It would bring Britain 'into association with that enormous Afro-Asian world whose giant figures so rightly dominate the pygmy Whites in the cartoons of Abu'.[157]

Through Britain's unilateral disarmament, therefore, this grouping of states would ultimately lead to the emergence of a neutral group of nations in international affairs, a development that British actions could bring about and that would ultimately lead to radical social change at home.[158] Pointing to the emergence of an African group of states that distanced itself from both the United States and the Soviet Union, the New Left activist John Rex demanded that 'the Voice of the African Congress...be heard at the polls in Britain, because ultimately the Congress

[152] P. J. Marshall, 'Imperial Britain', *Journal of Imperial and Commonwealth History*, 23 (1995), 379–94, especially 386. Stephen Howe, *Anticolonialism in British Politics: The Left and the End of Empire, 1918–1964* (Oxford, 1993), 37.
[153] Webster, *Englishness and Empire*, 36, 53; S. R. Mehrotra, 'On the Use of the Term "Commonwealth"', *Journal of Commonwealth Political Studies*, 2 (1963), 1–16.
[154] John Darwin, *Britain and Decolonisation: The Retreat from Empire in the Post-War World* (Basingstoke, 1988), 63.
[155] MRC, MSS 181/4: Mervyn Jones, 'Freed from Fear: A Policy for Britain without H-bombs', n.d. [*c*.1961], 12; A. J. P. Taylor, in *Encounter* (February 1963), 65; A. J. P. Taylor, *A Personal History*, 291; Michael Foot writing in *Tribune*, 11 October 1957, 2.
[156] Anthony Crosland, 'On the Left Again: Some Last Words on the Labour Controversy', *Encounter*, 10 (1960), 3–12, here 3.
[157] Peter Worsley, 'Imperial Retreat', in Edward P. Thompson (ed.), *Out of Apathy*, 136–7.
[158] Edward P. Thompson, 'Outside the Whale', in Edward P. Thompson (ed.), *Out of Apathy* (London, 1960), 181.

and the Labour Party are part of the same movement'.[159] This would, New Left activists believed, help us 'recapture something of their vision of what Socialism is about'.[160]

Despite these differences between the British and the West German movements, which emerged from around 1963 onwards, they shared an important characteristic that distinguished them from many earlier peace movements and from the protests of the later 1960s. Neither British nor West German activists framed 'nuclear disarmament' as part of a whole-sale programme of change in domestic and international society. Only a minority rediscovered conceptions of a positively defined 'peace'. Instead, the activists' focus came to lie on proposals to deal with what they regarded as the dangerous present.

[159] John Rex, 'Labour's Task in Central Africa', *Universities & Left Review*, 6 (1959), 7–12, here 12; Paul Hogarth, 'In Styrdom's South Africa', *New Reasoner* (Autumn 1957), 46–55, here 55; John Rex, 'Africa's National Congress and the British Left', *New Reasoner* (Autumn 1957), 56–64; Harry Hanson, 'Britain and the Arabs', *New Reasoner*, 6 (1958), 2–14.

[160] MRC, MSS 181/4: Mervyn Jones, 'Freed from Fear: A Policy for Britain without H-bombs', n.d. [*c*.1961]. 5; John Rex, 'Africa's National Congress and the British Left', *New Reasoner* (Autumn 1957), 64.

6

Demonstrating Security

I am just a lonely pilgrim,
Plodding through this world of sin.
But I want to build a city,
Where all people can march in.

.   .   .   .   .

I am just a weary traveller,
Travelling through this world of woe,
But I'm working for that morning,
When there'll be peace down here below.[1]

It was primarily on the protest marches themselves that the activists embodied the movements and the definitions of 'peace', national identity, and international relations they stood for, and that they expressed their desire for security against the threat of nuclear war. They were a key part of what Wini Breines has called 'prefigurative politics': the marchers' performance symbolized the world the marchers wanted to construct.[2] On the marches, the boundary between the activists and the society surrounding them became visible. At the same time, the marches themselves symbolized the journey which the activists intended their society as a whole to take.[3] It was by marching and protesting that British and West German protesters came to experience fellowship and belonging: they came to feel as a band of 'lonely pilgrims', 'travelling through this world of woe'.[4] The marches were

---

[1] IISG, C100, unsorted collection: 'When the Saints go marching in', Easter March Song booklet, n.d. [c.1961].
[2] Wini Breines, *Community and Organization in the New Left, 1962–1968: The Great Refusal* (New Brunswick, NJ, 1982), 6.
[3] Doug McAdam, Sidney Tarrow, and Charles Tilly, *Dynamics of Contention* (Cambridge, 2001), 55–6, 322.
[4] *Sanity* (October 1961), 2; Rechtsanwalt Dr. Hamann, 'Dürfen Deutsche denken? Das Recht auf Opposition in der Bundesrepublik', *konkret* (February 1962), 5; HIS, TEM 300,03: Circular Herbert Stubenrauch, 28 January 1961; Jens Daniel [i.e. Rudolf Augstein], 'Die Stunde der Opposition', *Friedensrundschau*, 15 (1961), 2–3.

experiences of conversion and signified progress towards what activists dreamt of as a more civilized world: 'On the road from Aldermaston we shall be marching from the tyranny of destruction to the beginnings of creative democracy.'[5]

For many activists, 'belonging' to something posed a dilemma, either because, like the former communists in Britain or the left-wing Social Democrats and pacifists in the Federal Republic, they had not yet overcome their previous senses of belonging; or because they had never felt that they belonged to a specific political or social group. Yet, at the same time, taking part in protests gave them a clear label, as Sheila Rowbotham observes: 'Back in Leeds, I wore my CND badge...with pride. I had turned into a kind of collective outsider now; people fell away from me in W. H. Smith. We had touched on a twitchy nerve of state security and were now denounced as hoodlums in the newspapers.'[6]

West German protesters encountered similar reactions.[7] But in a political system that was on the front line of the cold war they had different implications. While police reactions were not generally more heavy-handed or authoritarian than in Britain and public reactions were not more adversarial per se, the establishment of a movement beyond the labour movement and the peace associations was itself a highly controversial and contested political act.

The emotions of marching, singing, and protesting together as well as encountering often inimical reactions from observers forged the protesters together into a community, increasing the political distance between them and their observers or opponents. For many activists, the experience of marching together on the Easter weekends in the company of individuals they would normally avoid or ignore broke many of the social codes with which they had structured their lives. The marches were, therefore, life-changing experiences. They not only allowed protesters to express their experiences and expectations, but also made the protesters part of a new community.[8]

Yet the marches were also part of the movements' communication efforts. They advertised the cause, not only through the speeches held, but also

---

[5] *Peace News*, 6 April 1959, 4.

[6] Rowbotham, *Promise of a Dream*, 68, 72.

[7] Klaus Beer, *Auf den Feldern von Ulm: In den wechselnden Winden von Adenauer bis Brandt* (Blaubeuren, 2008), 70–2; Vack, *Das andere Deutschland nach 1945*, 68–72.

[8] CND song, 'Don't you Hear the H-Bomb's Thunder?', printed in David Widgery (ed.), *The Left in Britain, 1958–1968* (Harmondsworth, 1976), 99; BLPES, CND/1/4: 'Is it any use?', n.d.; 'Unser Marsch ist eine gute Sache', quoted in Frank Baier, 'Ruhrgebiet—Leben, Kämpfen, Solidarisieren', in Zahn (ed.), *Folk und Liedermacher an Rhein und Ruhr*, 129–93, here 132.

through the marching order, the route, and the timing.[9] Most of the interaction between protesters and the society surrounding them was, however,
no longer merely through face-to-face encounters. It was frequently mediated through reports in newspapers and, to a lesser degree, on the radio and
on TV.[10] Although there were many strands and developments within each
campaign, they constituted, from hindsight at least, one coherent movement. This coherence was achieved through the unity of themes to which
the speakers and rallies referred and through the ways in which the media
reported on them. The movements observed the societies around them and
tried to appeal to them. At the same time, they were observed by the media.
This chapter examines the processes through which the protest marches and
other forms of demonstration came to constitute the 'movements' and the
forms of activism and citizenship connected with them. In particular, it
analyses how the two movements were connected, and how similar ideas
had specific resonances within the two national contexts. It also discusses
the ideas of activism connected with the movements.

SECULAR PROCESSIONS

While the demonstrations organized by the Campaign against Atomic
Death had still resembled the model of public assemblies championed by the
nineteenth-century labour movement, the British Aldermaston and West
German Easter Marches transcended this model. They no longer showed
parallel lines of bodies and the integration of individuals into a mass of people striving for a common goal.[11] Instead, the marchers strove to show their
individuality. It was the differences among the marchers, their vivid, yet solemn character and the lack of cohesion, that struck observers when looking
at pictures taken at the Easter Marches. On photographs, we can see women
and men with prams, often wearing duffle coats. Children accompanied the
march, and many activists carried musical instruments (see Figure 3).[12]

---

⁹ Oscar Strobel, Michael Schumann, and Hans Schreiner, 'Der Marsch zum Römerberg—Die Zornigen und die Zahmen—Marschieren oder Diskutieren. Interviews mit den
Teilnehmern des Anti-Atom-Schweigemarsches 20. Mai 1958', *Diskus—Frankfurter Studentenzeitung*, 8 (June 1958), F2/F3; *Sanity* (October 1961), 2.
¹⁰ Bernd Weisbrod, 'Medien als symbolische Form der Massengesellschaft: Die medi-
alen Bedingungen von Öffentlichkeit im 20. Jahrhundert', *Historische Anthropologie*,
9 (2001), 270–83, especially 280–1.
¹¹ Beatrix W. Bouvier, 'Es wird kommen der Mai … Zur Ikonographie des Arbeitermai
im Kaiserreich', *Archiv für Sozialgeschichte*, 33 (1993), 570–85, here 579; Dieter Rucht,
'"Heraus zum 1. Mai!": Ein Protestritual im Wandel', in Rucht (ed.), *Protest in der
Bundesrepublik: Strukturen und Entwicklungen* (Frankfurt/Main and New York, 2001),
143–72.
¹² *pläne* (special Easter March issue, 1962), no pagination.

Figure 3. Aldermaston March, Easter 1958. (Photograph courtesy of CND)

More than the one-day gatherings of the Campaign against Atomic Death, the Aldermaston Marches and the West German Easter Marches thus created an own order of time and space that was highly symbolic. The term 'movement' expresses a notion of temporal change as a spatial path.[13] The very act of marching over Easter thus became an expression of movement towards more security and symbolized the conquest of an own regime of time and space. At the same time, the marches visibly separated the activists from the society around them and thus made the movement distinctly visible.

---

[13] Reinhart Koselleck, '"Progress" and "Decline": An Appendix to the History of Two Concepts', in Koselleck, *The Practice of Conceptual History: Timing History, Spacing Concepts* (Stanford, CA, 2002), 218–35, here 220.

The Easter weekend was particularly apt for such connotations, as it carried Christian notions of new beginnings and the resurrection. Through the marches, the protesters endowed Easter with their own meanings. Instead of going to church and for the traditional Easter walk (*Osterspaziergang*) with their families, the protesters went on the march, thus redefining the Christian message of Easter in explicitly political terms, transcending the norms of privacy at the time and yet expressing their own private moral economies. It was this language of pacifist brotherhood and not the political rationality of socialism that was at the root of British and West German extra-parliamentary protests in the 1960s when they argued for 'a new, world-wide security policy'.[14] Not many activists were quite as exuberant about the Easter message as student leader Rudi Dutschke, who noted in his diary on 14 April 1963: 'Jesus has risen, joy and gratitude accompany this day; the revolution, the decisive revolution of world history has happened, the revolution of the world through all-transcendent love.'[15]

Such a rhetoric of the discovery of human fellowship and love could also be found in Britain and has its roots in specific Protestant traditions.[16] But there were subtle differences to West German interpretations. CND supporters asserted after the marches: 'The brotherhood of man is no longer a notion, it's here.'[17] In West Germany, by contrast, protesters were less certain about whether this kind of brotherhood already existed. At the end of the Easter Marches in the Rhineland, they sang, to the tune of a famous children's lullaby and thereby conceptualized the marches themselves as the origins for the dynamic creation of a community of activists. Like the *sýmbolon* that helped Christians in the Roman Empire recognize each other, the emotions that they had gathered on the marches would serve as a sign for the progress of their campaign:

Now go home, preserve the dream/which we have all had

.   .   .   .   .

Peace is not a shadow.
Only don't fear the darkness that will surround us.
Even if the night falls black and tight/a small star light will have risen.[18]

---

[14] BAK, ZSg. 1 262/1: 'Ostermarsch 63', 10; BAK, ZSg. 1–262/3: *Informationen zur Abrüstung*, 3 (September 1963), 6; BAK, Zsg. 1–214/1: 'Scheidung der Geister und Wege', Hamburg n.d., 4; HIS, TEM 200,03: 'Grundsätze des Ostermarschs der Atomwaffengegner', n.d. [*c.*1961].

[15] Rudi Dutschke, *Jeder hat sein Leben ganz zu leben. Die Tagebücher 1963–1979*, ed. Gretchen Dutschke (Cologne, 2003), 17.

[16] Cf. Veldman, *Fantasy, the Bomb and the Greening of Britain*, 156–79.

[17] Robert Bolt, 'Do you Speak Nuclear?', *New Statesman*, 24 December 1960; BJL, JS-7: CND Charter, n.d [*c.*1959].

[18] Gerd Sommer, 'Abendlied zu Ostern', *Liederkorb*, 5 (Mainz, 2001), 1.

For some British protesters, the marches were annual calls for repentance and renewal, both a physical act of atonement and a spiritual revival. The thousands of marchers who strolled through the countryside evoked such national myths as Chaucer's *Canterbury Tales*. One CND supporter described the march as 'a civilising mission, a march away from fear towards normality, towards human standards, towards the real people in the nursery rhyme whose houses are over the hill but not so far away that we will not get there by candlelight, whose hands are set to the plough and the making of things'.[19] British activists' aim was to bridge the gap between their own civility, composure, and earnestness and what they regarded as their uncivil surroundings. The marches were, therefore, also educational experiences. British marchers also regarded their activism as a means that helped them both discover the dangers that nuclear weapons posed and make these threats visible, first to themselves and then to society: 'Many must have been surprised by the immensity of the enclosed area [of the Atomic Weapons Establishment at Aldermaston] and struck by the brutal contrast between the dark, dense forest of rich pine through which we had just marched and the planned waste land of man-made structures with which we were suddenly confronted. It all had a nightmarish quality.'[20]

'Peace' and 'security' thus became something that happened in the direct experiences between people, in the family, whereas 'war' was an anonymous and institutional force.[21] Throughout, the British and West German organizers emphasized 'self-discipline', not least to counter accusations by the public, by the police, and by the media that they disturbed the public peace.[22] A briefing paper for the first Aldermaston March, calling it a 'procession', requested that participants 'march in single file along the lanes, it is not necessary to keep 15 yards apart as in London. Our line of approach is that we are only expecting to behave as a party of hikers, except that we are hikers who have not come to admire the countryside but to present a point of view.'[23]

[19] Denis Knight, secretary of CND's film and television committee, quoted by Christopher Driver, *The Disarmers*, 58; Editorial, *Peace News*, 6 March 1959, 4; Stuart Hall, 'Peace Politics', *Sanity* (May 1963), 5.

[20] Martin Grainger, 'Marching against Britain's Death Factory', *CND Newsletter*, 12 April 1958, 2–6.

[21] Cf., for example, G. Nitsch, 'Gewaltloser aktiver Widerstand', *Das Argument: Blätter der Westberliner Studiengruppen gegen Atomrüstung*, 11, 12 November 1959, 5.

[22] HStAD, NW308–87, 89: 'Ratschläge für die Teilnehmer des Ostermarschs der Atomwaffengegner', n.d. [c.1961]; Gottfried Wandersleb, 'Polizeiverordnungen gegen Grundgesetz?', *Deutsche Volks Zeitung*, 1 October 1962.

[23] Hugh Brock papers, J. B. Priestley Library, Commonweal Collection, University of Bradford, Bay D, box 2, folder 'Operation Gandhi. Briefing for main procession', n.d. (c. January 1958).

In practice, however, the march organizers were not always successful in achieving this aim. There were reports of activists camping at illicit sites, or leaving the main column of the march.[24] Moreover, the finely scripted procession did not, in practice, always work out in fostering social bonds within. Martin Grainger, a CND activist on the first march, wrote with disappointment about everyone just leaving after the final appeal had been read out at Aldermaston on Easter Monday 1958: 'The appeal was not very successful,' he remarked. 'People persisted in drifting away. They had heard it all so many times before.'[25]

Throughout, the organizers tried to tap a code of respectability and disapproved of any spontaneous disruptions of the orderly structure of the march. On the 1959 March, the CND Annual Conference agreed that 'to preserve the dignity and unity of the March...and to prevent invidious distinction or misunderstanding, it should be conducted without shouting of slogans and with periods of silence'.[26]

ALDERMASTON

The first British demonstration was a three-day 'walk' over Easter from Trafalgar Square to the village of Aldermaston, around fifty miles away, just outside Slough in Berkshire and the site of the nuclear weapons research establishment. The journalist and CND organizer Mervyn Jones later recalled that the weather was atrocious, 'with bitter cold and incessant rain', which turned to snow. While the crowd on Trafalgar Square had been a good one, it was in danger of falling apart later on.[27] The marchers carried banners with black and white 'Ban the Bomb' slogans. Some held boards with the CND symbol, later more generally associated with peace movements around the world, others wore CND buttons. On Easter Sunday 1958, services were held on fields nearby.[28]

When the direction of the march was reversed from 1959 onwards, the services were replaced by speeches of notables, often practising clergy, such as Canon Collins or the Methodist Donald Soper.[29] On the march

---

[24] *Peace News*, 18 April 1958, 5; *Peace News*, 17 April 1959, 3; *Peace News*, 14 April 1961, 5; MRC, MSS 181: Executive Committee, minutes, 28 January 1958; Rowbotham, *Promise of a Dream*, 67–8.

[25] *CND Newsletter*, 12 April 1958, 6.

[26] *CND Newsletter* (March 1960), 3.

[27] Mervyn Jones, 'Aldermaston 1958', in John Minnion and Philip Bolsover (eds), *The CND Story: The First Twenty-Five Years of CND in the Words of the People Involved* (London, 1983), 44–5.

[28] Cf. *Peace News* (special issue, Easter 1958), 3.

[29] Cf. the special editions of *Peace News* on Easter 1959, 1960, and 1961.

and when they entered towns, the protesters sang songs. Over the years, a whole repertoire of songs developed, such as 'Don't you Hear the H-Bomb's Thunder', usually to old trade-union or labour-movement tunes. From 1959 onwards, jazz bands and skiffle groups accompanied the march. On one march, even a Calypso band with Rastafarians played songs from the Caribbean.[30] The press often highlighted beards and duffle coats, often to the distaste of some CND organizers, as the main characteristics of CND activists. At the same time, some marchers tried to maintain standards: one could still see sombre, older men in long grey macs, with carefully polished shoes.[31]

Many blues and skiffle musicians had close links to the movement. Especially at CND meetings in university towns, music was played and poetry was read and discussed.[32] And, while music was never as controversial on British marches, it raised some problems: 'The Englishman, unlike the American, doesn't sing edifying songs, and unlike the Irishman hasn't any songs of recent currency known to middle-class marchers which symbolise "damn the Government", like the Peeler and the Goat, or the Sean Bhean Bhocht, even when only whistled.'[33]

Like the music and banners, the elaborately planned structure of the march was supposed to convey the image of both order and variety. There were usually different sections in the march. The famous members of the executive walked ahead to endow the march with credibility. Different regional and local groups followed, together with CND's professional suborganizations, catering for students, Christians, or scientists. In another section of the march, foreign guests walked with banners stating their country of origin.[34] Although there were Scottish campaigns against the *Polaris* submarine depot at Holy Loch from the early 1960s onwards, these campaigns were, because of their direct-action character, never perceived as an integral part of CND.[35] Scottish and Welsh CND supporters travelled to southern England and London to participate in the marches.[36]

---

[30] Cf. Bill Schwarz, '"Claudia Jones and the *West Indian Gazette*": Reflections on the Emergence of Post-Colonial Britain', *Twentieth Century British History*, 14 (2003), 264–85, here 272–3.

[31] Jones, *Chances*, 161.

[32] Rowbotham, *Promise of a Dream*, 71.

[33] *Peace News*, 16 May 1958, 3.

[34] Cf. *Peace News*, 6 March 1959, 4; *Peace News*, 7 March 1958, 2; *Peace News*, 7 April 1961, 1.

[35] Minnion and Bolsover (eds), *CND Story*, 52–5.

[36] Cf. *Peace News*, 6 March 1959, 4.

The organizers changed the direction of the route in subsequent years, ending with a rally on Trafalgar Square rather than on a field in the Berkshire countryside. This indicates the increasing importance that the organizers gave to political demonstrations at the centre of power, Westminster and Whitehall, rather than the remote country-side, where there was a lack of reporting and attention for the cause. Moreover, the change of route attracted more people and underlined the London-centric character of the British campaign. It attracted 20,000 people in 1959. For 1960, the estimates for the final rally on Trafalgar Square vary between 60,000 and 100,000 participants. In 1961, about 45,000 people participated, making the rallies the largest demonstrations London had seen since VE Day. From 1962 onwards, participation declined, and no full marches took place from 1964 onwards.[37]

THE WEST GERMAN 'EASTER MARCHES'

The British marches themselves served as a 'model' for the West German Easter Marches when a group of Hamburg Quakers around Hans-Konrad Tempel revived the flagging Campaign against Atomic Death by staging an Aldermaston-style march in northern Germany. This emergence of the two campaigns within the framework of the British 'model' and West German 'imitation' is itself interesting, as it neglects the fact that Gandhi's non-violence resistance in India had been a mutual reference point for British and West German pacifists in the late 1940s and early 1950s. It had been their engagement with Gandhi's methods that had opened up this new space for political involvement. The story of this translation process was also the story of a transition from discussion towards production of new forms of politics, from latency to realization.[38]

For British and West German pacifists in the mid- to late 1940s Gandhi was primarily an icon, whom they slotted into primarily Christian narratives of suffering.[39] While the Peace Pledge Union (PPU) formed a Non-Violence Commission in 1949 that met regularly from January 1950 in Dick Shepard's house and while West German activists were aware of this,

---

[37] Jo Richardson, 'Tea for 20,000', in Minnion and Bolsover (eds), *CND Story*, 45–7; Richard Taylor, *Against the Bomb*, 42, 57, 77, n. 6.

[38] My argument here is indebted to Sean Scalmer, *Gandhi in the West: The Mahatma and the Rise of Radical Protest* (Cambridge, 2011), 9–72, who consulted and analyzed some of the same source material.

[39] Andrew Oppenheimer, 'Air Wars and Empire: Gandhi and the Search for a Usable Past in Postwar Germany', *Central European History*, 45 (2012), 669–96.

the PPU had not yet officially endorsed non-violent direct action as a campaign strategy. The focus was 'study' and 'self-training'. Information was exchanged through a 'travelling file'.[40] It is only on the basis of dissatisfaction with these discussions that some British pacifists demanded moving towards action. In January 1951, Ethel A. Lewis wrote to Kathleen Rawlins: 'I really feel that it is rather useless to merely meet pleasantly at intervals, to talk—waiting vaguely for the day when it might be useful to lay [*sic*] down in the road to demonstrate agst. "something or other".'[41] A campaign called 'Operation Gandhi' was founded by the pacifist Hugh Brock in December 1951 as an experiment in practising direct action in order to awaken Britons' conscience.[42] They staged a number of protests at nuclear and chemical warfare installations across the country, and also took part in a transnational campaign against apartheid in South Africa.[43] In late 1957, activists from 'Operation Gandhi' met to discuss new forms of direct action, such as larger-scale protest marches. Alex Comfort, a PPU activist (later the author of *The Joy of Sex*), gave the reasons for choosing the Aldermaston atomic weapons research establishment as the site for annual marches: 'It covers an area of nearly two square miles and is some tow [*sic*] or three miles from Aldermaston railway station. Something like 50 squatters would be required to make an effective demonstration at the main gate...but a squat would be of great rallying value to the pacifist movement and should be of news value.'[44] The establishment of these annual marches meant that, although both West German and British pacifists shared an awareness of the links to Gandhi, the transnational origins of the British marches disappeared from public discussions, and the British marches themselves became a model for protests.[45]

The West German marches remained much more localized than the British ones, and their observers emphasized the solemn character of the march. The first Easter March started in Hamburg on Good Friday and

---

[40] *Peace News*, 11 November 1949, 3; *Peace News*, 18 August 1950, 6.

[41] J. B. Priestley Library, University of Bradford, Hugh Brock Papers, Folder 'Pre-Occupation Gandhi': Ethel A. Lewis to Kathleen Rawlins, n.d., stamped 29 January 1951.

[42] J. B. Priestley Library, University of Bradford, Direct Action Committee and Committee of 100 papers (April Carter), Bay F, folder 'PPU Non Violence Commission': Non-Violence Commission of the PPU, minutes, 12 December 1951; J. B. Priestley Library, University of Bradford, Hugh Brock Papers, Folder 'Pre-Occupation Gandhi': Kathleen Rawlins to Hugh Brock, 19. December 1951.

[43] *Peace News*, 21 March 1952, 8; 1 October 1953, 1; 5 March 1954, 3, 4 July 1952, 5; 24 April 1953, 1; 17 February 1956, 1–2; 24 February 1956, 6.

[44] J. B. Priestley Library, University of Bradford, untitled leaflet, PPU, London, Operation Gandhi Newsletter, no. 1, n.d., 1.

[45] Scalmer, *Gandhi*, 206–38.

was to reach the rocket site Bergen-Hohne, around eighty miles away, on Easter Monday. Some 120 protesters marched in twosomes or three-somes on pavements or on the verges, as the use of public road space had been prohibited by the police. Behind a banner stating 'Easter March Hamburg—Bergen-Hohne' walked protesters in mackintoshes with more banners and posters, all in yellow and black, followed by two to three cars, mostly for carrying the baggage (see Figure 2, p. 124). Small groups from Bremen, Braunschweig, Hanover, and Göttingen joined the Hamburg contingent. They were mostly part of the pacifist networks around the German Peace Society (*Deutsche Friedensgesells-chaft*), the conscientious objectors' organization *Verband der Kriegsdien-stverweigerer*, and other groups.[46] In 1961, the direction of the marches was turned around. Activists now marched from what they called 'death centres' into larger cities.[47] From 1963, the marches became shorter, and the direction of the marches was reversed to lead into the bigger cities rather than to military bases, the so-called death centres, in the countryside. This was due to the emphasis on more explicitly political aims that the later organizers had.[48]

The West German marches were not only regional in their general scope, but there were different marches in each region, which converged on one central place, usually a regional military installation, such as Bergen-Hohne or, later, Dortmund. This *Sternmarsch*, the march in the form of a star, showed a very specific understanding of the spatialization of time on demonstration marches, as the separate demonstration routes occupied one temporal location. Some activists also pointed out that it symbolized radiation.[49] Unlike in Britain, there was no strict marching order with banners denoting professional, local, regional, or national affiliations. Moreover, the slogans had to be approved by the march organizers, and marshals monitored that the agreed slogans were not altered or replaced.[50] Silence on the marches was not only an expression of solemnity, but also a form of self-policing against 'communist subversion'. Yet, a skiffle group had joined the first march from Hamburg to Bergen-Hohne, and played when the marchers entered the towns, where activists

[46] Bethge, '"Die Bombe ist böse"', 359–60.
[47] Interview with Hans-Konrad Tempel, Ahrensburg (Germany), 18 August 2002.
[48] Bethge, '"Die Bombe ist böse"', 367.
[49] BA–MA, BW2/20203: 'Ostermärsche in der Bundesrepublik, 1961, Dokumentation und Photos', n.d. [*c*.1961]; 'Aufruf zum Ostermarsch', 1960; Thomas Ballistier, *Straßenpro-test. Formen oppositioneller Politik in der Bundesrepublik Deutschland* (Münster, 1996), pp. 41–2.
[50] HIS, TEM 100,04: 'Kernsätze für die Redner des Ostermarsches der Atomwaffengeg-ner' [n.d., *c*. autumn 1960].

were served sandwiches and drinks. Subsequently, some activists urged for more fantasy and colour in a world of cold war apathy and in order to attract more people.[51]

These regulations concerning the marching order and the slogans were as much a result of self-policing as of police restrictions: on several marches, the police confiscated slogans on suspicion of communist subversion. Occasionally, during the following years, the police prohibited certain routes and confiscated banners, only some of which had been prohibited in advance.[52] On one of the marches in the Ruhr area, the police also prohibited the singing of certain songs, as the authorities regarded them as too polemical for an Easter weekend. Yet the marchers continued by whistling them.[53] While British political culture was characterized by a similarly high degree of anti-communism, it rarely entailed any practical consequences, a fact of which West German commentators were acutely aware.[54]

West German activists also sought to convey an image of almost forced leisureliness in order to distance themselves from the military tradition of marching.[55] Indeed, British cartoons even made fun of this marching tradition by showing two CND activists kicked in their backs by a tall, blond, goose-stepping activist behind them: 'Our foreign friends are wonderfully committed, but I wish I did not march in front of the German contingent.'[56]

The marchers slept in barns, public gymnasia, and youth centres on the way. As in Britain, the group held meetings in all larger towns and distributed leaflets with details about the impact of nuclear-bomb explosions along the route. Very few people turned up to these meetings and gatherings, and there were, as in Britain, frequent accusations from bystanders of communist subversion, acts that the Easter March organizers described

---

[51] Hans Konrad and Helga Tempel, 'Berührungsängste und ihre Auswirkungen beim ersten Ostermarsch 1960', in Komitee für Grundrechte und Demokratie e.V. (ed.), *Geschichten aus der Friedensbewegung: Persönliches und Politisches*, collected by Andreas Buro (Cologne, 2005), 5–12; Cf. also the debates in *Wir sind jung*, 17 (September 1964), 24–5; *pläne*, 11 (1962), no pagination; IfZ, ED702/7: Minutes of the committee meeting of the regional council south of the Easter Marches, 4 February 1963.

[52] HStAD, NW 308–84, 48: Regierungspräsident Arnsberg (Westfalia) to Interior Minister of North Rhine Westphalia, 2 May 1962.

[53] HIS, WOL2, Folder 'Ostermarsch 1962, Kreis Mettmann': Report by Gertrud Wolfers about the Easter March 1962, 23 April 1962.

[54] Hilda von Klenze, 'Brief aus England', *Friedensrundschau*, 17 (1963), 26; Sebastian Haffner, 'Die Deutschen und ihre Kommunisten', *Friedensrundschau*, 17 (1963), 10–11, here 10.

[55] HIS, WOL2, folder 'Ostermarsch 1963, Kreis Mettmann': 'Ein Schritt genügt heute: Aufruf zum Ostermarsch 1963'.

[56] Reprinted in 'Gegen die Bombe zu Feld gezogen', *Die Kultur* (May–June 1961), 1.

as 'defamation', a concept whose implications were well known to Germans who had lived during National Socialism.[57] At times, the marchers found barns or restaurants closed although accommodation or meals had been promised. There was usually a makeshift Easter service on the way on Easter Sunday.[58] Marching through rainy and cold weather over Easter served as a symbol for the marchers' commitment and turned the marches almost into secular pilgrimages for a reawakening.[59] Often, astonishment dominated immediate reactions to the marches, as 'a phantasmagorical train of people, reminiscent of a medieval procession of flagellants against the plague in a Bergman film', walked past them.[60] In rare instances, West German protesters faced counter-demonstrations that ended violently. An earlier protest of the Campaign against Atomic Death in Dortmund in June 1958 ended with a knife attack by a CDU member on the driver of the speaker van and with criminal damage to the van's tyres.[61]

On the final rally of the first march in Bergen-Hohne, on Easter Monday, around 800 people gathered. Here, close to the site of the former concentration camp Bergen-Belsen, the organizers made several speeches linking a potential future nuclear and the previous Holocaust.[62] The emotions on the first march ran so high that many marchers had tears in their eyes when they arrived in Bergen-Hohne.[63] In subsequent years, the Easter Marches also ended on Easter Monday with final rallies, often, from 1961 onwards, with guest speakers from abroad. Especially the German Trade Union Federation (*Deutscher Gewerkschaftsbund* (*DGB*)) was concerned about the date. Its organizers feared that trade unionists' involvement in Easter rallies would have a negative impact on turnout during May Day rallies, a problem that, they believed, did not exist in Britain, as there were no May Day celebrations there.[64]

---

[57] Cf. Erich Kuby, 'Aggressive Illusionen', *pläne*, 6–7 (July 1962), 6–8.

[58] HIS, TEM 200,03: Central Committee, minutes, 6–7 May 1961.

[59] Hans-Konrad and Helga Tempel, '... *das man da wohnen möge': Vision und Erfahrung eines gemeinsamen Lebens* (Bad Pyrmont, 1986), 11.

[60] Kai Hermann, 'Erfolg und viele Kilometer', *Die Zeit*, 3 April 1964, 1.

[61] AdsD, DGB, Abt. Organisation, 24/2193: 'Telefonat zwiscxhen der CDU-Geschäftsstelle Dortmund und der Polizei-Pressestelle', 26 June 1958.

[62] HIS, TEM 100,04: Leaflet for the 1960 Easter March.

[63] Andreas Buro, 'Damals in Bergen-Hohne flossen Tränen', in Komitee für Grundrechte und Demokratie e.V. (ed.), *Geschichten aus der Friedensbewegung: Persönliches und Politisches*, 15–20; AdsD, IG Metall Archives, G1010: 'Arbeitspapier für den Ausschuß "Kampf dem Atomtod" über die politische Funktion und Methodik der Arbeit der Kampagne für Abrüstung', n.d. [*c*.1964].

[64] AdsD, IG Metall, G1010: Federation of German Trade Unions circular to all members of the Federal Executive, the executives of the member unions and the district and local committees, 20 June 1961.

From 1961 onwards, there were marches across West Germany, in the north, in the west, in the south-west, and in the south-east. While they now usually ended in larger cities, such as Hamburg, Munich, or Dortmund, they kept their decentralized character. This not only had to do with West German federalism, but it also reflected the fact that there was, in the late 1950s and early 1960s, still no accepted central place of protest in West Germany, such as Westminster, Whitehall, and Hyde Park in London, or the Mall in Washington. Many still regarded only Bonn as the provisional capital. Conditions in Berlin were not conducive to protests either. Because of fears of communist subversion, rules were particularly strict there.[65]

The marches also appealed to regional political traditions and sites of memory. The Bavarian march, for example, went past the Dachau concentration camp and frequently carried the distinctive Bavarian flag with the white and blue diamonds. The marches in the Ruhr area were influenced much more by the labour-movement traditions than the marches in the south and north. Here, as in Hesse, groups such as the 'Socialist Youth: Falcons', or the youth organizations of the Friends of Nature played an important role in the public presentation of the marches. Music was very prominent, especially jazz, skiffle, and folk. From the mid-1960s, the Easter Marches often became sights for political cabaret festivals.[66]

While the first rally was attended by only a few hundred people, in 1961 about 23,000 people participated in the final Easter March rallies across the Federal Republic. In 1962, a report to the East German government identified 'marching columns' as long as three kilometres in the Western marches. By 1964, more than 100,000 in the whole of Germany took part.[67] Possible police reactions and the legal implications constrained the marches in both countries: Britain was no less restrictive than West Germany. Activists in both countries were under strict instructions to follow the demands of the police and the stewards immediately and unquestioningly. Stewards were required by law.[68] In West Germany, organizers drew special attention to the 'rules of assembly', which set great store by the formal correctness of the marches and, in particular, demanded that music on the marches be declared in advance.[69]

---

[65] Cf. Andreas W. Daum, *Kennedy in Berlin* (Paderborn, 2003), 159–60.

[66] HIS, WOL2, Folder 'Ostermarsch 1962, Kreis Mettmann': Report by Gertrud Wolfers about the Easter March 1962 [23 April 1962].

[67] Rupp, *Außerparlamentarische Opposition*, 130–43; SAPMO-BArch DY30/IV 2/10.02/224, fo. 286: 'Bericht', 2 May 1962.

[68] HIS, TEM 100,04: 'Organisationsplan', [n.d., *c.*1961], 4; HStAD NW 308–87, 90: 'Ratschläge für die Teilnehmer des Ostermarschs der Atomwaffengegner', n.d. [*c.*1961]; *Isis*, 23 January 1963, 3; *Sanity*, April 1963, 5.

[69] HIS, TEM 200,03: Central Committee, minutes, 2/3 June 1961, 3.

At times, local and regional West German police authorities prohibited slogans calling politicians 'murderers'. But activists reacted by mocking the police's decision and covering the original slogans with the words 'This slogan has been banned.' Joking about the police was, in general, quite widespread.[70] Very popular was chanting 'The police is always with us' to the tune of a nursery rhyme.[71] At times, local and regional police authorities refused to grant permission to march alongside federal roads and past barracks.[72] A 1961 report by the police authorities in North Rhine Westphalia complained of the disruptions of the Easter holiday caused by 'demonstrating people chanting and singing' and regretted that the march

did not make a good impression on ordinary citizens. The participants, who walked partly barefoot and had young children and toddlers in prams full of luggage with them, gave a very undisciplined picture. Participating dogs, carrying blankets with the rune of death, and the participants' behaviour during breaks—they slept on the ground—completed a picture which was in contrast to the solemnity of the Easter holidays.[73]

The surveillance and policing of the British marches were quite similar to those of the West German authorities. Permission to stage public marches in London was not granted by the Metropolitan Police Authority, but by the Ministry of Works. In 1958, Whitehall barred the Aldermaston marchers from holding an orderly rally on government-controlled land.[74] Like their West German counterparts, CND activists were occasionally fined for 'obstructing traffic'.[75] This was a key site of debate about identifying the marches as political actors: it symbolized the struggle for power between the marchers' chronology of the Easter weekend and that of the public authorities. In both countries, the police or the secret services occasionally photographed the marchers, actions that the German *Spiegel* likened to snipers (*in Heckenschützenmanier*) as it appeared constantly to fix the protesters' identities.[76]

[70] HIS, TEM 200,03: Central Committee, minutes, 2/3 June 1962, 5.
[71] Kai Hermann, 'Erfolg und viele Kilometer', *Die Zeit*, 3 April 1964, 1.
[72] HIS, TEM 200,03: Central Committee, 2/3 June 1962, 5.
[73] HStAD, NW 308–84, 49: Regierungspräsident Arnsberg (Westfalia) to Interior Minister of North Rhine Westphalia, 2 May 1962.
[74] TNA: WORK 16/2067: 'Campaign for Nuclear Disarmament: Assemblies, Demonstrations etc. in Parks' (12 June 1961).
[75] Robert Bolt, *A Matter of Life* (London, 1963), 46.
[76] 'Regen im April', *Der Spiegel*, 5 May 1965, 6–7, here 7; *Peace News*, 1 August 1958, 1.

Most of the British government's regulatory activity was, however, directed against the Committee of 100 (C100) rather than CND.[77] In September 1961, for example, the British government denied the Committee the use of Trafalgar Square. When C100 activists staged a sit-down nonetheless, almost a thousand people, including Bertrand Russell, were arrested under the Defence of the Realm Act.[78] After the 1963 campaign, organized by some activists of the C100, which exposed the top-secret Regional Seats of Government, a *Peace News* issue reporting on the incident was censored, and the activists were charged under the Official Secrets Act.[79]

The pictures of the marches in the national press displayed images that showed respect for state power until the end of the 1950s. Protests thus appeared limited to certain points of the year and to certain localities. Only at the beginning of the 1960s did confrontational pictures return to the West German media with regard to the Easter Marches and other protests: the police was shown carrying protesters away.[80] The West German media interpreted these pictures with a cultural code similar to the one they had used to describe the riots of mostly working-class youth (*Halbstarke*). In Britain, the conflicts of state authorities with 'Mods' and 'Rockers' formed the reference point.[81]

Significantly, despite the mass media attention they received, the radical activists remained a fringe group in Britain. Significantly, the Committee's anti-statist rhetoric, which singled out the violence of the British state, did not sound plausible in the British context. The observation of the C100's activities in West Germany, by contrast, often via conferences organized by the War Resisters' International, helped West German activists to rediscover their own national protest traditions.[82]

---

[77] TNA: CAB 21/6027: 'Security Significance of Membership of the Campaign for Nuclear Disarmament (CND) and other Unilateralist Organisations' (March 1960); TNA: PREM 11/4284: Activities of the Committee of 100 (May 1962); TNA HO 325/163: material on the C100 Marham RAF base, May 1963.

[78] *The Guardian*, 18 September 1961, 3; Driver, *The Disarmers*, 164.

[79] TNA: DPP 2/3432, DPP 2/3678, and PCOM 9/2208: Material on Michael Randle, Peter Moule, and Helen Allegranza. On the court cases, cf. Driver, *The Disarmers*, 164–70.

[80] Cf. 'Böse Ahnungen', *Der Spiegel*, 24 April 1963, 33–4, and the article on the British 'Spies for Peace' campaign, *Der Spiegel*, 24 April 1963, 70.

[81] For Britain, cf. Stanley Cohen, *Folk Devils and Moral Panics* (St Albans, 1972). For West Germany, cf. Axel Schildt, *Moderne Zeiten: Freizeit, Massenmedien und 'Zeitgeist' in der Bundesrepublik der 50er Jahre* (Hamburg, 1995), 177.

[82] Richard Taylor, *Against the Bomb*, 190–269. On the transnational circulation of these ideas, see Holger Nehring, 'National Internationalists: Transnational Relations and the British and West German Protests against Nuclear Weapons, 1957–1964', *Contemporary European History*, 14 (2005), 559–82.

PROTEST EVENTS

Throughout the first phase of the West German movement, the Campaign against Atomic Death, the polarization between marchers and public had been far less pronounced. The dominant form of protest was the mass rally and meeting, rather than the march, and, through the links to the *SPD* and trade unions, the protesters remained directly connected to institutionalized politics.[83] The geographical distribution of the Campaign's protests thus reflected the strength of local labour-movement traditions, with peaks of activity in the area around Frankfurt, Hamburg, Munich, and the Ruhr area as well as the southern areas of North-Rhine Westphalia. These forms of protests required far less commitment and could be much more tightly regulated and controlled by the organizers. The duration of the protests was rather short, the structure had clearly been outlined by the organizers, and, unlike in the Easter Marchers, the supporters mostly acclaimed announcements.[84]

This was in tune with the *SPD*'s traditions, but also sought to appeal to a distinctly middle-class audience. At the opening ceremony of the Campaign against Atomic Death in the Frankfurt Congress Centre, the Frankfurt Youth Symphony Orchestra and a Frankfurt choral society played classical music. The speeches also sought to convey an image of solemnity and humanitarian pathos.[85] The whole ceremony was reminiscent of the Paulskirche movement against German rearmament from the mid-1950s in which the *SPD* had taken part less visibly.[86]

After the launch of the Campaign, local rallies, usually endorsed by the *SPD* and the trade unions, took place. Particularly noteworthy were several demonstrations at factories in Bielefeld, a short strike by Hamburg dock workers (probably organized by communists), and a silent march through Hamburg's city centre.[87] In Berlin, the Falcon group staged what was probably the first sit-down in the history of the Federal Republic by blocking the tramways in the city centre.[88] Several thousand workers also went on strike in the Wolfsburg and Braunschweig *Volkswagen* factories.[89]

[83] AdsD, 2/PVAM00007: Draft for a circular, 27 October 1959.
[84] Cf. the map in Kraushaar, *Die Protest-Chronik,* iv. 2514.
[85] AdsD, 2/PVAM00005: Programme of the meeting (March 1958) and the collection of speeches.
[86] For a picture of the solemn character of the opening ceremony, cf. the picture taken of the Frankfurt KdA rally on 3 June 1958; cf. Wolfgang Kraushaar (ed.), *Frankfurter Schule und Studentenbewegung. Von der Flaschenpost zum Molotowcocktail 1946–1995,* 2nd edn (3 vols, Hamburg, 1998), i. 134.
[87] *Die Welt*, 28 March 1958, 3.
[88] Kraushaar, *Die Protest-Chronik*, iii. 1846–7.
[89] *Frankfurter Allgemeine Zeitung*, 29 March 1958, 2.

The threat of 'communist subversion' and the desire to keep the upper hand in the local protests led to discussions between the trade unions and the *SPD* whether to advocate a general strike against nuclear armaments.[90] While Menzel and the *SPD* headquarters continued to push for at least a short symbolic strike action in the run-up to NATO's conference in Copenhagen in May 1958, the *DGB* was loath to commit itself formally to a strike: it feared a break-up of its Christian-orientated trade union branches which officially supported Adenauer's policies.[91]

Apart from the marches and demonstrations, activists in both countries staged other more limited protests in order to maintain the campaigns' momentum. They were mostly concerned with occupying specific dates for public commemorations. Prominent examples included Hiroshima Day on 6 August and Anti-War Day on 1 September, the latter also held in the GDR. These usually took the form of vigils, and often copied official ceremonies, such as wreath-laying at war memorials in Britain, or processions with torches through the city centres in West Germany.[92] Many German anti-war-day protests were gatherings at concentration-camp sites, such as Dachau and Bergen-Belsen.[93] At times, these vigils also entailed carrying black wooden crosses.[94] In Britain, activists did not stage wreath-layings on 1 September, but they reappropriated Remembrance Sunday for their anti-war protests. They staged wreath-layings at the local cenotaphs, interpreting the memory of war as an anti-war message.[95]

1 September was quite contentious as a day of memory in the Federal Republic. The majority of the population still remembered, in line with Nazi propaganda, 3 September 1939—the day when Britain declared war on Germany—as the outbreak of war, and not 1 September—the day when Germany invaded Poland. Moreover, the communist World Peace Council had proclaimed 1 September as 'World Peace Day' in the early 1950s, which discredited the date further in West German public debates. Yet trade union youth associations introduced the anti-war day into the Easter Marches' reservoir of protest from around 1961 onwards, starting in the area around Frankfurt/Main and Offenbach. In 1962, a report to

---

[90] *Die Andere Zeitung*, 10 April 1958, 6.
[91] *Frankfurter Allgemeine Zeitung*, 31 March 1958, 2; *Die Welt*, 1 April 1958, 6; AdsD, DGB, Abt. Organisation, 24–2216: Extract from the minutes of the federal executive, 5 December 1967.
[92] *Sanity* (August 1963), 9; *Frankfurter Rundschau*, 7 August 1962, 3; 'Kriegsgegner protestieren mit Fackeln', *Mannheimer Morgen*, 3 September 1965.
[93] *Gewerkschaftspost*, 10 (October 1963), 21.
[94] HIS TEM 200,03: Central Committee, minutes, 6–7 May 1961.
[95] *Sanity* (December 1962), 3; *Sanity* (December 1963), 4.

the *DGB* counted 5,962 participants at events in 282 *DGB* districts.[96] In order to control and steer the events, the *DGB* actively endorsed the events from 1964 onwards.[97] It aimed at in-door events in trade-union buildings that had an educational character and involved discussion with experts, the showing of films, such as *The Bridge* (*Die Brücke*, by Bernhard Wicki) and *All Quiet on the Western Front*, as well as readings from anti-war literature.[98]

While experiences of marching were often very individual, many of the protests came to have a transnational dimension as well. 'Transfer' or 'diffusion' of specific concepts mattered less in this respect than common emotions and belonging. The observation among the activists that they were not alone and that they were united by a common cause when marching together was fundamentally important. Activists imposed their own timing on the Easter weekend across Western Europe, and the exchange of marchers between Britain, West Germany, and other countries demonstrated this.[99] The moral rhetoric of a world community and human brotherhood was the expression of this feeling. Internationalized marches 'gave a powerful impression of solidarity and unity without much conscious liaison having been attempted'.[100] Activists thus performed the world community they strove to create.[101] As one of the speakers at a War Resisters' International (WRI) conference elaborated: 'Co-operation works best on the basis of action rather than that of the exchange of ideas or on the day-to-day work.'[102] Although there were isolated instances of peace marches beyond borders, they never attracted any major press coverage and resonance.[103]

---

[96] AdsD, DGB, Abt. Organisation, 24/5801: 'Betr. 1. September' [n.d., *c.*1962].

[97] AdsD, DGB, Abt. Org. 24/9005: 'Vorlage für den geschäftsführenden Bundesvorstand', 19 July 1962; 'Beschluß des DGB-Bundesausschusses', 24 July 1962.

[98] AdsD, DGB, Abt. Organisation, 24/9005: 'Vorschläge für Veranstaltungen zum 1. September', *c.*1962.

[99] IfZ, ED 702–52: ICDP, Report of Inaugural Congress held at Tyringe, Sweden, 9–13 January 1964, Volume One: Working Sessions, 42–5.

[100] IISG, WRI-11: Tony Smythe, 'W.R.I. and the International Peace Movement', WRI 11th Triennial Conference, Stavanger (Norway), Document 5, p. 4.

[101] For examples of such performative acts in a different campaign, cf. Michael S. Foley, *Confronting the War Machine: Draft Resistance during the Vietnam War* (Chapel Hill, NC, and London, 2003).

[102] IISG, WRI-11: Comments by Theodor Michaltscheff on a paper by Pierre Martin, WRI 11th Triennial Conference, Stavanger (Norway), 27–9 July 1963.

[103] Cf., for example, Günter Wernecke and Lawrence S. Wittner, 'Lifting the Iron Curtain: The Peace March to Moscow of 1960–1961', *International History Review*, 21 (1999), 900–17.

Figure 4. CND symbol

SIGNS OF BELONGING

Activists expressed solidarity not only through their actions, but also through the symbols they used. It was through the exchange of delegations and marchers as well as through the journals of the national peace movements that the universally recognized symbol found its way into peace campaigns around the world and turned the experience of community and fellowship into something that could be easily identified. It was used by the protesters to assure themselves of a common cause in a world that they perceived as antagonistic. The sign (see Figure 4), developed by the artist Gerhard Holtom, showed the semaphoric N and D (for Nuclear Disarmament), surrounded by a circle.

The sign replaced the white dove on a blue background that had been used by the communist-sponsored peace movements since the late 1940s as the main symbol of peace activism in the late 1950s and early 1960s. With its straightforward and highly abstract character, it was supposed to convey the message of rationality and objectivity. Even the material out of which badges were manufactured was chosen accordingly.[104] The symbol was, at times, made out of 'natural material' such as clay, to symbolize the campaign's holistic character. The more radical C100 used badges and banners which showed a white CND symbol on a red background, thus demonstrating C100's belief in revolutionary social change.[105] The West German Easter Marches produced a badge that resembled the tags that soldiers carried.

Movement activists interpreted the symbol alternatively as an 'unborn child', as a bent cross symbolizing the 'death of man', or even as a 'rune

---

[104] Cf. Duff, *Left, Left, Left*, 115–16; *Peace News*, 26 June 1959, 2.
[105] George Thayer, *The British Political Fringe: A Profile* (London, 1965), 174.

Figure 5. Poster, Campaign against Atomic Death, June 1958: 'Think about yourself and yours. Therefore: No to Atomic Death. Three times no!' (Courtesy of AdsD, 6/PLKA006493, poster by Ernst Jupp)

of death', an interpretation preferred by many Germans.[106] The CND symbol could be found on West German Easter Marches from 1961 onwards. It found its way onto flyers and pamphlets from about 1962 or 1963 onwards.[107] Similarly, the demonstrators in both countries would carry posters that were kept entirely in black and white to show the seriousness of the situation.[108] One activist criticized the choice of symbols. While he

---

[106] BJL, JS-6: *CND Newsletter*, 8, 19 June 1958; IISG, WRI-235: 'Was bedeutet dieses Zeichen?', *Der Kriegsdienstgegner: Mitteilungsblatt der WRI Deutscher Zweig* (October 1963); 4 (1963), 10.

[107] IISG, WRI-252: Klaus Vack to the WRI, 28 September 1962; HIS, TEM 200,03: Circular no. 1, Ostermarsch der Atomwaffengegner, 11 November 1961.

[108] Kraushaar, *Die Protest-Chronik*, iii. 1838; Kurt Vogel, 'Ostermarsch der Atomwaffengegner', *Wir sind jung*, 2 (June 1961), 5–7.

drew attention to the importance of 'propaganda techniques' in order to win over 'the most primitive people', he regretted that 'our symbol is more about death than about life', while Hitler had chosen the 'positive sun wheel' to advertise his message.[109] The *SPD*-run campaign, concentrating primarily on mass meetings, had not developed its own symbol, but adopted Albert Schweitzer's head instead (see Fig. 5).[110] It is striking, however, that the British and the West German campaign used primarily abstract images or the power of personalities who were regarded as leaders in morality to convey their message. The leaflets that both campaigns distributed, and the posters they had designed, used the traditional modernist form of political campaigning, as Benjamin Ziemann has highlighted: they listed facts and figures, often contrasting the 'wrong' view of their respective government with their own 'right views' and using scientific information and statistics to underline the rationality of their claims.[111]

SECURITY AS 'NORMALITY'

Much of the power of protest marches lies in the display of strength through the assembly of a large number of bodies. In protest marches, the physical body also becomes a symbolic representation of the social body, and concerns about social order become translated into concerns about bodily control. Rather than entirely transcending dominant connections between gender and emotions, they still replicated elements of the dominant gender regime. They did not show their strength as the male 'virility' of soldiers. Instead, male and female protesters displayed tuned-down emotions that tapped discourses of rational (male) citizenship.

Theirs was an emotionally restrained body politic on the move. While political and social scientists until the late 1960s regarded emotions as a key to understanding all political actions, the British and West German activists themselves denied their emotions. Instead, they claimed the rationality of their cause, an aspect that both governments were quite concerned about, as it made their task for excluding the movements from respectable politics more difficult.[112] Mervyn Jones pointed out: 'This is a

---

[109] IfZ, ED 702/7: Heinrich Frieling, 'Fragen der Werbung' 9 (n.d., *c*.1964).
[110] Kraushaar, *Die Protest-Chronik*, iii. 1834; on the political relevance of this image, see Benjamin Ziemann, 'The Code of Protest: Images of Peace in the West German Peace Movements, 1945–1990', *Contemporary European History*, 17 (2008), 237–61, here 247.
[111] Benjamin Ziemann, 'The Code of Protest, 247–8.
[112] TNA PREM 11/2778: Macmillan to the Chancellor of the Duchy of Lancaster, 24 March 1958; PolArchAA B31/116: London Embassy to German Foreign Office, 11 March 1958; *Konrad Adenauer: Reden 1917–1967*, ed. Hans-Peter Schwarz (Stuttgart, 1987), 357.

campaign that urges people to reflect, not to destroy; to march a silent mile, not to shout; to dissent, not to obey; to be themselves, not to take sides; to love, not to hate; to live and let others live, not to kill or die.'[113]

Although women took part in the demonstrations and thus shared in this demonstration of citizenship, internal documents highlight how male activists did not treat women as equally legitimate rational citizens: women were confined to duties that were connoted female, such as typing leaflets, cooking, and nuts-and-bolts organizing, but most women were not allowed to *voice* their claims to citizenship by participating in discussions or giving speeches on the marches.[114]

By framing their emotions in this way, the protesters tapped and replicated two discourses. First, they sought to counter accusations that they undermined the very security they wished to create by taking their cause to the streets, as the cold war consensus connoted street politics primarily with 'communist agitation'.[115] Second, they sought to contradict possible accusations, familiar after the First World War, that their 'female' emotions endangered national security.[116] For the majority of protesters, 'security' was the re-creation of order on the marches. Restraint and control were the key words in both countries. While the governments accused the protesters of overly emotional and unreasonable behaviour, the activists highlighted their rationality and reason against the government's atomic 'madness'.[117] 'One can', wrote the Protestant priest Heinrich Vogel, 'if one is a citizen of a divided fatherland, take the map and say once again: 'atomic armament of German forces—I speak candidly –: crime, madness.'[118] They also pointed to the 'nervous character' of the age and demanded a 'relaxation' (*Entspannung*) of tensions.[119] Conversely, activists frequently compared nuclear

[113] Mervyn Jones, 'The Time is Short', in Norman MacKenzie (ed.), *Conviction* (London,1958), 199.

[114] Duff, *Left, Left, Left*, 231.

[115] Paul Betts and David Crowley, 'Introduction', *Journal of Contemporary History*, 40 (2005), 213–36; Claire Langhamer, 'The Meanings of Home in Postwar Britain', *Journal of Contemporary History*, 40 (2005), 341–62.

[116] Cf., for example, Hermann Speelmann to Dr. Gerhard Schmidt, 12 October 1963, quoted in Appelius, *Pazifismus in Westdeutschland*, 513.

[117] BAK, ZSg. 1–262/3: 'Informationen zur Abrüstung', 3 (Sept. 1963); 'Angst—ein schlechter Ratgeber', *Westfälische Rundschau*, 18 November 1957, 2; 'Atomwaffen und Atomangst', *Industriekurier*, 28 March 1958; BAK B145/4224: IfD, Stimmung no. 291, 'Die Atomrüstung' (April 1957), 5. For Britain MRC, MSS.181/4: Benn W. Levy, *Britain and the Bomb. The Fallacy of Nuclear Defence*, CND pamphlet [n.d.], 3; *Peace News*, 20 February 1959, 5; *Peace News*, 22 May 1959, 6.

[118] Heinrich Vogel on the East-Berlin Synod, April 1958, quoted in *Berlin 1958*, 51.

[119] BAK, ZSg. 1-E/70: Helene Wessel, 'Das Leben in Gefahr', in *Kampf dem Atomtod* (Bonn, 1958), 13; J. B. Priestley, quoted in Minion and Bolsover (eds), *The CND Story*, 15.

armaments to unthinking and essentially irrational 'child's play'.[120] Instead of transcending the British and West German governments' emphasis on 'normality', the activists merely turned the logic around and claimed that their governments were fearful and irrational. The CND highlighted the emphasis on rationality by naming its journal *Sanity*.[121]

Most activists in both countries demonstrated their own individual emotional control, whereas they discussed the nuclear arms race under the rubric of 'atomic madness', 'insanity', and other concepts that signified the loss of rational control.[122] Even those protesters who favoured non-violent direct action stressed their self-control and their endurance to withstand constant recriminations and the use of violence by the police. As Pat Arrowsmith pointed out: 'I must not provoke violence. Violence must be seen to be done to me.'[123]

The protesters not only tried to show their emotional restraint in words. The vigils that the protesters held demonstrated this restraint: they showed a small number of activists holding posters or banners, and carrying candles or, in West Germany, torches. During these vigils, both British and West German activists demonstrated against the acceleration of time that they saw during the series of international crises in the late 1950s and early 1960s: over Berlin in winter 1958–59, again in August 1961, and over Cuba in autumn 1962.[124] Interestingly, there were no significant differences between arguments that the British and West German movements used to describe these crises, and the fundamental message conveyed did not change over time. Nor were there significant differences in which events they designated to be 'critical'.

The symbolic meanings of their reactions to crises were rather paradoxical; the protesters framed the events as 'crisis' and thus accelerated the feeling of time, yet they simultaneously employed vigils as symbolized attempts to slow down time. This mechanism was unique in creating a community among protesters, as the call for community, rationality, and

---

[120] AdsD, 2/PVAM000044: Circular by the *Naturfreundejugend*, 27 September 1959, 2; Bertrand Russell, *Has Man a Future* (Harmondsworth, 1961), 121; John Brunner, *The Brink* (London, 1959).

[121] MRC, MSS 181/4: Benn Levy, *Britain and the Bomb*, CND pamphlet *c.*1961; *Sanity or Suicide?* (*c.*1960).

[122] BAK, ZSg. 1-E/70: Stefan Andres, 'Dem Atomwahnsinn in den Arm fallen', in *Kampf dem Atomtod* (Bonn, 1958), 25.

[123] Anthony Carew, 'Woman with a Bomb on her Mind', *Daily Herald*, 30 November 1961.

[124] On the concept of 'crisis' and its relationship to Christian and humanist thinking cf. Reinhart Koselleck, 'Some Questions Regarding the Conceptual History of "Crisis"', in idem, *The Practice of Conceptual History. Timing History, Spacing Concepts* (Stanford, 2002), 236–47.

calm addressed Christian and humanist voices alike.[125] Vigils thus both symbolized the need for security through stabilization and served as a strategy for the activists themselves to control their emotions.

In both countries, the emotional economies during times of crisis had three directly connected elements. First, protesters in both countries framed these crises, through a constant seam of leafleting and through reporting in the movement press, not as events but as processes that could either run out of hand and result in nuclear warfare, or be contained and controlled. Second, by staging vigils across their countries (rather than in the capital only), they gave these crises a concrete geographical location in the middle of the community in which they protested. Even West German protesters staged very few vigils in Berlin, the centre of two international crises during this time period, as police restrictions on demonstrations were particularly harsh there.[126] Third, the protesters used the vigil to slow down the fast-paced historical processes and symbolize the need for calm and rationality in an age of accelerated time. Conversely, the activists accused politicians of looking for 'quick solutions' and 'being out of control'.[127]

There were, however, differences in the forms the activists used to convey the message of a calm and controlled emotional economy. The Campaign against Atomic Death used prominent politicians and theologians to demonstrate for calm and rational decisions in Germany's capital Bonn as well as in regional capitals; they held torches, thus tapping the code of the memory of war.[128] Many local groups of the Campaign against Atomic Death and of the Easter Marches, by contrast, sought to convey the message of calm in a more casual setting, while they still maintained sobriety and absolute silence as a symbol for self-control and rationality. Pacifists around Tempel had become acquainted with the more casual form of vigil during their visits to Britain.[129]

Only a small minority of protesters in Britain, mostly from within the C100 and the DAC, sought to transcend these restrained emotional

---

[125] 'A round-up of international action against the Bomb', *Peace News*, 6 March 1959, 6; AdsD 2/PVAM00024: Handout, Berliner Studentenkongreß, n.d. [January 1959]; *Peace News*, 4 August 1961, 1, on Berlin; *Informationen zur Abrüstung*, 3 (1963), 3–8; Hilary Bourne, 'In Fleet Street', *Sanity*, October 1962, 3.
[126] HWR, 72.86.519, 240 and 242–6: Kloppenburg to Wilhelm Keller, copied to Hans Werner Richter 'with sincere wishes', 11 December 1961; HIS, TEM 700,02: 'Entwurf zu einem Gründungsmanifest: Komitee der 100'.
[127] *Sanity*, December 1962, 7; HIS, TEM 300,02: 'Anregungen für's Bonner Lobby' (October 1962).
[128] BAK, image 183-57383-0001.
[129] Interview with Hans-Konrad Tempel, 20 August 2002; Kraushaar, *Die Protest-Chronik*, iii. 1850.

economies by accelerating time and by urging for a rapid decision in favour of 'peace'. Instead of holding vigils, they staged sit-downs in front of embassies, most famously in front of the Soviet and American embassies in London during the Cuban missile crisis. For them, security was no longer connected to an urge to achieve stability. Instead, they highlighted the need for socio-economic changes and movement in order to achieve a long-lasting 'peace' and stability. This is illustrated by the symbolic action of two radical pacifists during the Cuban missile crisis. Pat Arrowsmith and Wendy Butlin staged a 'flight to Ireland' in order to survive nuclear war on the Irish west coast.[130] Here, the strategy to achieve personal security from nuclear attack converged with the desire to maintain movement.

Marches and other forms of protest thus became symbols of the wish for the normalization and pacification of each society after the war, in which the natural order of things was restored.[131] The media, by contrast, sought to find what they regarded as moral degeneration on the marches. Trying to prove rumours of sexual laxity, one British tabloid sent a shabbily dressed female student to the 1963 march in the hope that she would be importuned—an attempt that remained entirely unsuccessful.[132] In West Germany, we can find many of the same themes in the reporting on the Easter Marches, but they were usually brought together under the coding 'communist subversion'. Thus, illicit sex became not only a danger to morality, but also an important factor in weakening the West German body politic vis-à-vis the East. Beard-wearing youngsters were thus deemed dangers to public order, which, in turn, would lead to communist subversion.[133]

From a social-historical perspective, the appeals to rationality reflected the specific emotional economy of the middle classes and not least the strong nonconformist presence on the marches.[134] Moreover, by displaying self-control, restraint, and rationality, the protesters redefined military

---

[130] Letter to *The Guardian*, 31 October 1962, 8.

[131] BAK, ZSg. 1–214/1: 'Scheidung der Geister und Wege', Hamburg, n.d. [*c.*1960], 5; *Sanity* (January 1963), 4.

[132] Brian Masters, *The Swinging Sixties* (London, 1985), 204; BLPES, CND/1/4: CND annual reports 1961–2 and 1962–3; 'Young CND', *Sanity* (Easter March special 1963), 1; HIS, TEM 200,03: Central Committee, minutes, 14/15 October 1961, 4.

[133] 'Ostermärsche wurden kaum beachtet', *Der Tagesspiegel*, 5 April 1961, 3; Hans Magnus Enzensberger, 'Einige Vorschläge zur Methode des Kampfes gegen die atomare Aufrüstung', *Blätter für deutsche und internationale Politik*, 4 (1958), 410–14, here 414; IfZ, ED 702/7: Dr Heinrich Frieling, 'Fragen der Werbung', n.d. [*c.*1964].

[134] Kai Arne Linnemann, 'Die Sammlung der Mitte und die Wandlung des Bürgers', in Manfred Hettling and Bernd Ulrich (eds), *Bürgertum nach 1945* (Hamburg, 2005), 185–220, here 206.

notions of masculinity by showing non-violent restraint, peaceful comradeship, and domesticated fatherhood.[135]

Although the protesters in both countries displayed the same themes of an emotionally controlled body politic on the move, these emotional economies had very specific national resonances and functions. In Britain, the emotional economies of restraint met accusations, most famously by Aneurin Bevan at the 1957 Labour Party conference, that nuclear disarmament was the expression of 'an emotional spasm'.[136] The protesters' emotional economies coincided with the image of austerity that was common in British political culture in response to the war years. Rationality and emotional control played an important role in debates within the British labour movement, on the left and on the right.[137] Restraint on the marches also reflected an emphasis on moral seriousness, earnestness, and rationality as key characteristics of masculinity embodied by liberal Christian gentlemen.[138]

Most importantly, however, the emotional economies of restraint in Britain tapped the specific version of British national identity that had emerged in response to the violence of the First World War and that interpreted British society as a 'peaceable kingdom'. Since the 1920s, the civility of extra-parliamentary protests in Britain had become a central argument for their legitimacy. According to this view, public opinion was understood as sober, unassertive, and domestic. It found its expression in the 1936 Public Order Act, still valid in the late 1950s and early 1960s, which allowed a police officer to demand the name of anyone judged to be disrupting a meeting. The Act standardized the law relating to threatening and insulting behaviour likely to cause the breach of peace.[139] Acting in accordance with these views guaranteed a high degree of support across British society. For example, when the police ordered Oxford student Richard Wallace to stop selling *Peace News* in Oxford, he was

---

[135] Irene Stoehr, 'Phalanx der Frauen? Wiederaufrüstung und Weiblichkeit in Westdeutschland 1950–1957', in Christiane Eifler and Ruth Seifert (eds), *Soziale Konstruktionen— Militär und Geschlechterverhältnisse* (Münster, 1998), 187–204; Thomas Kühne, ' "Aus diesem Krieg werden nicht nur harte Männer heimkehren": Kriegskameradschaft und Männlichkeit im 20. Jahrhundert', in Kühne (ed.), *Männergeschichte—Geschlechtergeschichte: Männlichkeit im Wandel der Moderne* (Frankfurt/Main and New York, 1996), 174–92, here 188–9.

[136] Mervyn Jones, *Chances: An Autobiography* (London, 1987), 133, 145.

[137] Martin Francis, 'The Labour Party: Modernisation and the Politics of Restraint', in Becky Conekin, Frank Mort, and Chris Waters (eds), *Moments of Modernity: Reconstructing Britain 1945–1964* (London, 1999), 152–70, here 153–4.

[138] Susan Kingsley Kent, *Gender and Power in Britain, 1640–1990* (London, 1999), 202–28.

[139] Lawrence, 'Forging a Peaceable Kingdom; Charles Townshend, *Making the Peace: Public Order and Public Security in Modern Britain* (Oxford, 1993), 132–7.

defended in court by the young Tory politician Jonathan Aitken, who emphasized the importance of freedom of expression.[140]

While some of these sources were present among West German protesters as well, the emphasis on 'rationality' tapped an at once narrower and broader strand of public discourse. It went to the core of West Germany's 'anti-totalitarian' consensus. In the Federal Republic, extra-parliamentary politics could easily be represented as a revival of National Socialist marches or as results of communist subversion. Indeed, despite the restrained emotional economies, some remnants of these traditions were still visible. The protesters' vocabulary continued to draw on military terms such as *Einsatzgruppen* and *Trupps* to refer to specific sections. And West German activists did not use the term 'steward' or 'Ordner' but the military term 'Ordonnanz' (for ordinance officer).[141]

Their emphasis on rationality helped the activists to distance themselves from both National Socialism and Communism as well as the street politics of the Weimar Republic. Both within general public discourse and among movement supporters, emotions remained connected to communist or foreign 'guest workers'. 'Jazz music' in particular, used as a synonym for all kinds of musical styles beyond the mainstream repertoire, appeared to suggest an uncontrolled sexuality. Sexual licentiousness and exuberance were, during the 1950s and early 1960s, also associated with National Socialism.[142]

The protesters of the first Easter Marches in northern Germany tried to achieve normalization through 'silent discipline' on the marches. On the early marches, protesters emphasized their 'correct' and 'normal' clothing.[143] Such emphasis on 'objectivity' (*Sachlichkeit*) also served as a crucial way of distancing the protesters from the Nazi past.[144] Indeed, many

[140] Rowbotham, *Promise of a Dream*, 70.

[141] HIS, Archives of the Easter March Regional Committee North, folder 1: Lübeck Easter March committee, minutes, 30 April 1965.

[142] Heinz Abosch, 'Politik in der Tradition eines Wahnes', *Stimme der Gemeinde*, 17 (1965), cols 525–30; 'Tradition oder neue formen', *Wir sind jung*, 3 (1958), 8–11, here 11; a photo showing guestworkers and 'Afro-Asian students' in *pläne*, 4–5 (1961), no pagination; HIS, TEM 100 B01: Circular, Hans-Konrad Tempel to Easter March activists, 4 April 1960, 2; circular no. 1, Tempel to local groups, 11 February 1961; Fritz Vilmar, 'Ostermarsch', *neue kritik*, 3 (1962), 14–15, here 15.

[143] HIS, TEM 300,04: Central Committee, minutes, 2–3 June 1962, 3; 'Wir legen Wert auf gute Rasur', *Der Spiegel*, 14 April 1965, 68–71; Günter Hammer, 'Mit Bärten und Gitarren', *Westfälische Rundschau*, 26 March 1967.

[144] AdsD, DGB, Abt. Organisation, 24/2193: Ernst Scharnowski, speech in Berlin, 24 April 1958. On the semantics of the term, cf. Willibald Steinmetz, 'Anbetung und Dämonisierung des "Sachzwangs": Zur Archäologie einer deutschen Redefigur', in Michael Jeismann (ed.), *Obsessionen: Beherrschende Gedanken im wissenschaftlichen Zeitalter* (Frankfurt/Main, 1995), 293–333.

pictures taken from the Campaign against Atomic Death and Easter March rallies show activists in jacket and ties.[145] Some protest marches had also carried banners with the slogan 'No experiments!', thus using Adenauer's 1957 election slogan against his government's policies.[146] The campaigns' posters often used black and white, or black and orange colours, in order to convey the message soberly. From 1963–64, however, the cultural code started to change. There now emerged a very peculiar mixture of information, and more dramatic forms, such as political cabaret or humorous stunts.[147] The Munich-based German section of the Situationist International mocked this emphasis on rationality and calmness in its leaflet on 'Calmness of Nerves! No Experiments!'[148]

Particularly in the Ruhr area, the marches became increasingly colourful, with folk music and skiffle groups taking part.[149] The British occupation forces had introduced folk and skiffle in the Ruhr area, both as part of their democratization efforts and as part of the soldiers' lifestyles.[150] Some Easter March activists had become involved in the local folk scene, which produced its own artists, such as Fasia Jansen and Dieter Süverkrüpp, and which later began to attract singers from outside the Federal Republic, such as Joan Baez and Pete Seeger.[151] As in the United States and Britain, folk music offered the activists a particularly good opportunity to establish links with 'the people' and present themselves as home-grown movements.[152] Some West German activists also wanted to reconsider the length of the marches: they claimed that four days were too demanding and discouraged potential participants.[153] Others did not want the marches to be manifestations of sombre mourning, but instead to show, particularly through music, signs of life.[154] Others complained, however, that music would ridicule the 'earnest' character of the march and wished to maintain

---

[145] Cf. the picture taken of the Frankfurt rally on 3 June 1958, printed in Wolfgang Kraushaar (ed.), *Frankfurter Schule und Studentenbewegung: Von der Flaschenpost zum Molotowcocktail 1946–1995*, 2nd edn (3 vols, Hamburg, 1998), i. 131.

[146] Cf. the picture in Kraushaar (ed.), *Die Protest-Chronik 1949–1959*, iii. 1853.

[147] Cf., for example, 'Die neue Agitation: Zu den Veranstaltungen des Ostermarsches', *Frankfurter Rundschau*, 30 March 1967, 3.

[148] Printed in Kraushaar (ed.), *Frankfurter Schule*, i. 132.

[149] HIS, TEM 300,04: Central Committee, minutes, 2/3 June 1962, Kassel, 2; IfZ ED702/7: Regional Committee South, minutes, 4 February 1963. For a West German perception of the British marches, cf. Kraushaar, *Die Protest-Chronik*, iii. 1840.

[150] Bernhard Hanneken, 'Folk in Nordrhein-Westfalen', in Robert von Zahn (ed.), *Folk und Liedermacher an Rhein und Ruhr* (Münster, 2002), 11–75.

[151] AdsD, DGB, Abt. Organisation, 24/9007: 'Protest—Folksong—Jazz', Easter March leaflet, 28 March 1966; Joan Baez: Porträt einer Folklore-Sängerin' (1964).

[152] A. L. Lloyd, *Folk Song in England* (St Albans, 1975), 372.

[153] SAPMO-BArch, DY30/IV2/10.02/224, 286: 'Bericht', 2 May 1962.

[154] Helmut Gollwitzer, 'Osterrede 64', *pläne* (April 1964), no pagination; BAK, ZSg. 1–262/1, 3: 'Ostermarsch 63: Bericht über die Kampagne für Abrüstung', 9.

the endurance need to march for four or five days over the Easter weekend as a crucial indication of the marches' integrity.[155]

PRACTISING CITIZENSHIP

By marching on the Easter weekend, the protesters cast themselves both as possible future victims of governmental policies that would lead to death and destruction and as enlightened pilgrims who sacrificed their Easter weekend for the cause of democracy and humanity. Their own fate, that of democracy, and that of humanity became inextricably linked in a moment of hope, collective rebirth, and transformation. For the activists, the movements themselves thus became instruments for creating moral subjects who transcended the dominant mode of contemporary citizenship, which acted mainly through parliaments, parties, and elections.[156] Activists in both countries often regarded their protests as a 'duty'. Britons thereby echoed Victorian ideals of character, duty, and service in the context of their campaign.[157] West Germans, in part, had translated such ideals into the context of their own campaigns when engaging with British campaign literature. But these could also tap notions of liberal citizenship that held that individual rights derived from social membership and were directly related to service to a common good.

While both movements were quite similar in their endeavours to re-define citizenship, their notions of civic responsibility had very different implications in each national context. The marchers' concepts of citizenship combined political status with a set of social practices and thus turned the marches into 'a site of intense struggle' about civic activism.[158]

The ideal of citizenship on British marches harked back to ideals first expressed by New Liberalism at the beginning of the twentieth century and then again in the Second World War that had created a 'characteriological narrative of war' where civic commitment was demonstrated

[155] HIS, TEM 200,03: Circular no. 1, Easter March Central Committee, 11 February 1961; BAK, ZSg. 1 262/1, 2: 'Ostermarsch 63'; 'Jazz', *Wir sind jung*, 3 (1958), 9; HIS, WOL2, folder 'Ostermarsch 1962, Kreis Mettmann': 'Bericht von Gertrud Wolfers über den Ostermarsch 1962', 23 April 1962.

[156] HWR, 1.43.408: J. B. Priestley, 'Die totalitäre Macht der Atomwaffen', *Europa ruft*, 17/18 (January 1959), 28.

[157] Emrys Hughes, 'Wir taten nur unsere Bürgerpflicht', *Friedensrundschau*, 15 (1961), 10–11; HWR, 72.86.512, 373: 'Bitte, kein salto morale' [*c.*1961]; *Peace News*, 13 December 1957,12; *Peace News*, 4 April 1958, 1; 'Demonstrating the English Way', *Peace News*, 30 November 1962, 1.

[158] BLPES: CND 4/2/14: Executive Committee Report on Easter Demonstrations, 13 September 1962; Arthur Greenwood, 'Why do we go on Marching?', *Tribune*, 29 March 1963, 5.

through the good character of enduring hardship. Here, citizenship was both a brave and quiet heroism and a sacrifice of private and personal interests for a global public collective good in times of general political apathy.[159]

While the West German activists highlighted the same themes, they linked them less to a possible national regeneration and more to the enactment of democracy and thus to Germany's most recent history. This democracy had, they claimed, become stale under the dominant anti-communist consensus and was in danger of reverting to a totalitarian mode. More than their British counterparts, they emphasized the importance of individual resistance against 'the state'. This scepticism towards state authority revealed profound feelings of injury after the experience of the last war, when they bemoaned the dominance of 'military norms of security' in German public life.[160] Marching over Easter thus became an enactment of both security and West German democracy. This kind of thinking found expression in the slogan 'Our "No!" to the Bomb, is a "Yes!" to Democracy'.[161]

Exercising one's civic duty through marching could itself change the course of history, expressed in the German slogan 'better active than radio-active': protesters empowered themselves with agency by calling themselves 'active' and thus creating a new form of subjectivity.[162] One of the main CND songs, also sung on German marches, elaborated how such an involvement might matter by asking:

> Shall we lay the world in ruin?
> Only you can make the choice.
> Stop and think of what you're doing.
> Join the march and raise your voice.[163]

---

[159] Geoffrey G. Field, *Blood, Sweat and Toil: Remaking the British Working Class* (Oxford, 2012), 382; Richard Gott, '25 Years After', *Sanity* (September 1964), 3; *Candis* (February 1961), 1; *Peace News*, 31 May 1957, 6; Jürgen Habermas, 'Unruhe erste Bürgerpflicht', *Diskus—Frankfurter Studentenzeitung*, 8/5 (June 1958), 2.

[160] Eugen Kogon, 'wer pariert wird prämiert', *pläne*, 4–5 (1965), 21–2.

[161] HIS, Sbe540, Folder Ostermarsch 1963 and Folder Friedensbewegung 50er und 60er Jahre: 'Aufruf zum Ostermarsch 1963 (Auszug)' and 'Aufruf zum Ostermarsch 1964 (Kurzfassung)'; IfZ, ED702-2: Dr Andreas Buro, 'Zielsetzung des Ostermarches' [30 June/1 July 1962], 5; 'Strategiediskussion 1961: "Wie soll es weitergehen?"', in Karl A. Otto (ed.), *APO: Die außerparlamentarische Opposition in Quellen und Dokumenten, 1960–1970* (Cologne, 1988), 68–9; Christel Beilmann, 'Ostermarch-Überlegungen (1964), in Otto (ed.), *APO*, 97–9.

[162] *pläne*, 9/19 (1962), no pagination; 'Briefwechsel zwischen Erich Kuby und dem Präsidenten des Deutschen Bundestages', *Frankfurter Hefte*, 13 (1958), 453–7, here 455; *Sanity* (October 1963), 7.

[163] Printed in Widgery (ed.), *The Left in Britain*, 99.

A CND leaflet elaborated on this activist message: 'There are some things you have to do whether you are likely to succeed or not...It is the millions who say: "It is no use, nothing to do with me", who are responsible for the fact that there are still nuclear weapons in the world.'[164] In the Federal Republic, such claims resonated with experiences of West Germany's most recent past. Through civic activism, the protesters hoped to urge German society to end its 'holiday from history'. They evoked at once Germany's most recent past and expressed the wish to overcome it through civic activism.[165]

The small minority of activists in Britain and in the Federal Republic who favoured non-violent direct action radicalized this voluntaristic conception of citizenship and thus sought to collapse the boundary between protesters and observers.[166] They invaded RAF rocket sites in East Anglia in early 1961 and staged a sit-down in front of the Ministry of Defence in February and on Trafalgar Square in April 1961.[167] On the 1963 Aldermaston March, C100 activists tried to occupy the top-secret regional seats of government in their 'Spies for Peace' campaign, releasing maps with the precise locations and phone numbers of these underground bunkers that were to serve as government locations in case of nuclear war.[168] West German protesters replicated military notions of masculinity in non-violent ways by founding a 'non-violent civic army' (composed mainly of men) in the Stuttgart area to express their opposition to conscription and nuclear weapons: 'ruthless fighting' until the very end had now been replaced by the *konsequent*, the consequential, forceful, and consistent 'deployment' (*Einsatz*) for non-violence.[169]

---

[164] BLPES, CND/1/4: 'Is it any use?', n.d.; IfZ, ED702/5: European Easter Manifesto, 1961; Edward P. Thompson, 'Agency and Choice', *New Reasoner*, 5 (1958), 89–106; Alasdair McIntyre, 'Notes from the Moral Wilderness—1', *New Reasoner*, 7 (1958–59), 90–100; McIntyre, 'Notes from the Moral Wilderness—2', *New Reasoner*, no. 8 (1959), pp. 89–98;

[165] Prof. D. Hans Iwand, 'Geistige Entscheidungen und die Politik', *Blätter für deutsche und internationale Politik*, 1, 20 January 1958, 56–64, here 57; Arno Klönne, 'Die Jugend meint es ernst', *Blätter für deutsche und internationale Politik*, 3 (March 1958), 351–2; *Diskus—Frankfurter Studentenzeitung*, 8 (June 1958), F2; Edgar Weick, 'Ostermarsch und Politik', *neue kritik*, 5 (1964), 3–4.

[166] *Peace News*, 16 May 1958, 1; *Peace News*, 18 December 1959, 3; IISG, C100–1: Minutes of the National Committee of 100, Friends Institute, Birmingham, 6–7 April 1963; Nikolaus Koch, *Was ist Friedensdienst?* (Witten-Bommern, 1955); G. Nitsch, 'Gewaltloser Aktiver Widerstand', *Das Argument: Blätter der Westberliner Studentengruppe gegen Atomrüstung*, 10, 12 November 1959), 5; Theodor Ebert in *Peace News*, 6 September 1963, 6–7.

[167] Adam Roberts, 'The Police at Midnight', *New Statesman*, 22 September 1961; Peter Cadogan, 'From Civil Disobedience to Confrontation', in Robert Benwick and Trevor Smith (eds), *Direct Action and Democratic Politics* (London, 1972), 169–70.

[168] Stuart Hall, 'The Secret Society of War', *Sanity* (May 1963), 6.

[169] Cf. Theodor Ebert, 'Auf der Suche nach einer gewaltfreien Alternative zur Bundeswehr—Erfahrungsbericht eines Friedensforschers', Vortrag im Rahmen der Friedenswoche im Evangelischen Gemeindezentrum Eckstein in Nürnberg, 2 November 2005 <http://www.lebenshaus-alb.de/mt/archives/003350.html> (accessed 2 June 2012).

By using their bodies to claim civic rights, they implied that, in the absence of transcendental and national bonds, only the body remained as the last security. Consequently, the citizenship injured through nuclear weapons policies could be healed only through a thorough reform of life in small communities, at the military bases as well as in small communes. For many activists, citizenship, life reform, and nuclear weapons thus became intimately connected.[170]

Explicitly female claims to citizenship were rare in both the British and West German campaigns. Most of the activists' conceptions of citizenship remained concerned with the abstract individual.[171] Only at the beginning of the protests in 1958 and 1959 could we find claims that rooted female activism directly in the 'biological ground of sexual relations and a mother's existential care for the next generation'.[172] Throughout, women in Britain staged campaigns more visibly than their West German counterparts. Peggy Duff recalls that one Aldermaston coach was even nicknamed 'the brothel', in virtue of its female passengers. Crucially, however, like the majority of (particularly older) women who called themselves 'feminist' at the time, CND's women did not feel much sympathy with radical feminism.[173]

One of CND's first demonstrations featured 2,000 women marching in black from London's Hyde Park to Trafalgar Square.[174] The women's group within CND continued to arrange conferences that stressed the 'the genetic dangers which are of such special concern to women'. In autumn 1961, four women with prams led several hundred marchers to the Soviet Embassy in London to protest against the resumption of weapons tests: 'we can't just go on cooking food for our families when we know it is being contaminated with radioactive poisons.'[175] In 1961, Joan Littlewood

---

[170] BLPES, CND/9/24/21: 'Our Candidate—Humanity', C100 leaflet, n.d; *Peace News*, 1 February 1963, 7; *Peace News*, 13 September 1963, 5; *Peace News*, 8 May 1964, 11; *Resistance*, 7 May 1965, 16; MRC, MSS 181/4: Campaign Caravan Workshops: The Welwyn Workshop, Brochure, Summer 1963; Rowbotham, *Promise of a Dream*, 68.

[171] Cf. the critique of this model by Carole Pateman, *The Disorder of Women: Democracy, Feminist and Political Theory* (Cambridge, 1989).

[172] AdsD, 2/PVAM000005: 'Das Leben retten—den Frieden sichern: Der Frankfurter Kongreß ruft alle zum Kampf gegen den Atomtod', 23 March 1958, 4; from a socialist angle: HIS, Archiv des Regionalausschuß Nord des Ostermarsches der Atomwaffengegner bis 1965, Folder 1: Appendix to the letter Karl Jacob to Hans-Jürgen Willenberg, 4 April 1965, Poem 'bitte der mütter an mars'; BAK, B145/4230: Institut für Demoskopie, 'Die Stimmung im Bundesgebiet: Standorte der öffentlichen Meinung', 354, 5 September 1958.

[173] Duff, *Left, Left, Left*, 132, 153.

[174] Parkin, *Middle Class Radicalism*, 150.

[175] *Daily Mail*, 6 November 1961, 4. MRC, MSS 181/4: *Tomorrow's children* [n.d., *c*.1961], 5–6; BLPES, CND/7/18: Circulars from 1962–4.

put on a CND rally in the London Albert Hall with jazz and political speeches and anti-*Polaris* folk songs, including 'The misguided Missiles and the Misguided Miss'.[176] Interestingly, however, often such gendered versions of citizenship were propagated by both female and male activists, revealing the emergence of specifically domestic versions of masculinity at the time.[177]

THE FORCES OF CONSCIENCE

By campaigning for a morally pure version of citizenship, both male and female activists not only displayed, but also reconstructed, moral subjects after the ravages of the Second World War.[178] Marching over the Easter weekend thus became an important source of the self in two societies in which recent memories of war and expectations of possible nuclear annihilation merged. In order to justify their involvement, the protesters invoked their 'conscience' as their authority. The pacifist Hans-Konrad Tempel argued that conscience 'forced upon' him a 'real democratic consciousness'.[179] 'Conscience' is the classical institution of individual self-observation, 'the inner court' in Immanuel Kant's words. It focuses the decision on the individual rather than on the authority of institutions. It guides individual choice by providing certain interpretations of reality and is an instance of self-observation and self-control. Moreover, according to most Western codes of law, it is only conscience that allows people, in extreme circumstances, to break the law.[180] By emphasizing their subjectivity that could be generalized into public moral norms, the protesters also cast themselves as victims of government policies and thus merged, as survivors, with the past victims of the bombing wars in central Europe

---

[176] *The Guardian*, 22 November 1961, 3.

[177] Diana Collins, 'Women of the World Unite for Nuclear Disarmament', *Sanity* (January 1962), 3; Kraushaar, *Die Protest-Chronik*, iii. 1851, 1853; *pläne*, no. 4–5 (1961), no pagination.

[178] HWR, 1.43.408: J. B. Priestley, 'Die totalitäre Macht der Atomwaffen', Europa ruft, 17–18 January 1959, 28; AdsD, 2/PVAM0000018: Gerhard Niemz to Committee against Atomic Death, 8 August 1960; AdsD, 2/PVAM000020: Ernst Stracke to Alexander Maaß, 4 December 1959. Cf. Kathleen Canning and Sonya O. Rose, 'Gender, Citizenship and Subjectivity: Some Historical and Theoretical Considerations', *Gender & History*, 13 (2001), 427–43, here 432.

[179] IfZ, ED 702/5: Circular by Hans-Konrad Tempel, 16 March 1961; Julius R. Kaim, 'Proteste des Gewissens', *Frankfurter Rundschau*, 28 February 1958.

[180] Jacob Grimm and Wilhelm Grimm, *Deutsches Wörterbuch*, iv (Leipzig, 1911), s.v. 'Gewissen'; Heinz Dieter Kittsteiner, *Die Entstehung des modernen Gewissens* (Frankfurt/Main, 1995), especially 13–14.

and Japan.[181] While the pattern of staging the politics of conscience was quite similar, its political implications differed substantially.

Both movements drew on the example of the 'conscience' of the Hiroshima reconnaissance pilot Major Claude Eatherly and his interview with the philosopher Günther Anders. Anders remarked that it was a promising sign that Eatherly could not come to terms with what had happened: it meant that he was 'able to keep [his] conscience alive, although [he was] switched on to a technical apparatus as part of a machine ...'.[182] In the same vein, after describing radiation injuries, A. J. P. Taylor asked at CND's inaugural meeting: 'Is there anyone here who would want to do this to another human being?'[183] West German protesters staged their protests even more emphatically as a 'crusade of conscience', showed a slideshow entitled 'conscience at the crossroads', and argued that conscience had to be 'woken up'.[184]

The moral economy of conscience also revealed an ethical sensibility that emphasized the composure of the individual.[185] It went to the heart of traditional definitions of *Bürgerlichkeit* or bourgeois values in Germany and Britain: the middle class could claim, with its particular ideas, interests, and universal moral values, to represent humanity as a whole and its general principles. Similarly, such discourse of moral authority and an 'aristocracy of the common weal' cut across the cold war liberal assumptions about the end of class society and of ideology.[186] In Britain,

---

[181] HStAD, NW 308–84/48–53: Report on the 1962 Easter Marches to the Interior Minister of North Rhine Westphalia; Editorial, *Peace News*, 6 March 1959, 6; Driver, *The Disarmers*, 58.

[182] *Off limits für das Gewissen: Der Briefwechsel Claude Eatherly, Günther Anders*, ed. Robert Jungk (Reinbek, 1961), 19; English edn: *Burning Conscience* (London, 1961).

[183] Mervyn Jones, *Michael Foot* (London, 1994), 227; Masters, *The Swinging Sixties*, 200–1; *Die Welt*, 19 February 1958, 3; 'Kirche, Atom, Friede', *Junge Kirche*, 19 (1958), 159–63.

[184] BAK, ZSg.1-E/70: 'Das Nein zum nuklearen Selbstmord', ed. Kampf dem Atomtoid [n.d.]; AdsD, 2/PVAM000018: Naturfreundejugend, LV Rheinland to Campaign against Atomic Death, 28 February 1959; Fritz Katz at the Easter March rally 1962, *pläne*, 9 (1962), no pagination; Gerd Burkhardt, 'Die Veränderung der Welt durch die Atomwaffen (II)', *Frankfurter Hefte*, 14/10 (1959), 707–24, here 724.

[185] Hannelies Schulte, *Stimme der Gemeinde*, 6 (1961), 190; HIS, TEM 200,03: 'Wie soll es weitergehen?', Central Committee, minutes, 6–7 May 1961.

[186] 'Der Marsch zum Römerberg—Die Zornigen und die Zahmen—Marschieren oder Diskutieren. Interviews mit den Teilnehmern des Anti-Atom-Schweigemarsches 20. Mai 1958', *Diskus—Frankfurter Studentenzeitung*, 8 (June 1958), F2; SAPMO-BArch, DY30/IV.2/10.02/225, 4: 'Kundgebung der IdK in Essen', 6 December 1959. Background: Robert G. Moeller, 'Germans as Victims? Thoughts on a Post-Cold War History of World War II's Legacies', *History and Memory*, 17 (2005), 147–94, here 162.

such arguments found parallels in earlier condemnations of the bombing of German cities.[187]

The Marches on Easter weekends thus turned into events that helped placate at once the respective national conscience and the bonds of humanity. British critics of CND and its rhetoric of conscience feared a Germanization of British political culture. The German idea of conscience, following Kantian interpretations, interpreted it as an a priori fact of reason and during the nineteenth century had come to emphasize the pathos of decision.[188] British political thought, by contrast, had emphasized its social character, stemming from interaction with people within society:

> it is clear… that the Christian conscience does require us to be ready to surrender the political purposes of our nation if the only alternative is intolerable devastation for humanity… The opportunity for personal martyrdom will remain under whatever political system we live—there is always an opportunity to be 'dead' for Christ. But to bring down the world by way of political protest smacks more of *Götterdämmerung* than of Christian witness.[189]

In West Germany, such arguments of conscience and moral witness had very specific meanings, which revealed the specific characteristics of the German conscience. These meanings were never monolithic, as activists constantly debated the shape and form the politics of conscience should take. Yet what made the West German discussion special was that 'bearing witness' and revealing 'conscience' equated past and possible future German victimhood in quasi-religious terms, a trope that also played an important role in the debates about *Wiedergutmachung* in the early to mid-1950s and memories of German bomb warfare.[190]

Protesters thus came to connect their own activism against nuclear weapons to West Germany's violent past and its future as a democracy.[191] At times, elements of the 'Nazi conscience'[192] shone through—for example, when one protester argued that the 'enemies of the people' (*Volksfeinde*) had to be revealed and 'their trade' had to be stopped.[193] Others

---

[187] 'This is our Campaign—and these are its aims' *Sanity*, October 1962, 4–5.

[188] Heinz Dieter Kittsteiner, 'Das deutsche Gewissen im 20. Jahrhundert', in Richard Faber (ed.), *Politische Religion—Religiöse Politik* (Würzburg, 1997), 227–42.

[189] Alan Booth, *Christians and Power Politics* (London, 1961), 73–8; Booth, 'Christian Theology and Modern Warfare', *Brasseys Annual* (1962), 155.

[190] Cf., for example, Klaus Vack, 'Anmerkungen zum Antikriegstag', *Wir sind jung*, 4 (1962), 4–6, here 4.

[191] Christel Beilmann, 'Ostermarsch-Überlegungen (1964)', repr. in Otto (ed.), *Vom Ostermarsch zur APO*. 97–9.

[192] Claudia Koonz, *The Nazi Conscience* (Cambridge, MA, and London, 2003).

[193] AdsD, 2/PVAM000019: Wolfgang Otto to Walter Menzel, 15 May 1959.

turned the history of the *Volksgemeinschaft* against Adenauer's government: 'But it's always the same: whoever warns, is expelled from the community!'[194] Thus, the West German protesters implicitly evoked deeply
buried, but present, layers of memory of the bombing war and personal
injuries, and they brought them into the public sphere.

Importantly, West German activists, much more than their British
counterparts, assumed that conscience was intricately related to guilt
and responsibility. West German activists adopted the same language
used to describe the German resistance against Hitler.[195] Conversely,
protesters believed, like Alexander and Margarete Mitscherlich in
their book about 'the inability to mourn', that individual conscience
has lost critical function during the Third Reich because of general
obedience to Hitler.[196] They thus turned themselves *ex post* into
resisters who redeemed German guilt, yet constituted themselves as
victims, this time not of National Socialism and allied bombing, but
of their own government. The idea was that the protesters could
detach themselves, like the resisters, from German guilt through a
subjective act.[197]

While conscience had remained confined to the private sphere in the
immediate post-war years, West German activists now used it as a public
argument and thus contradicted especially those who believed that only
public silence could provide the environment for penance.[198] They claimed
the identity of human personality and citizen. Thus, protesters explicitly
contradicted one of the central elements on which modern statehood
depended: the Hobbesian ideas that conscience was nothing but a subjective, private opinion and that personality and citizenship were two distinct phenomena.[199]

---

[194] HIS, Archiv des Regionalausschuß Nord des Ostermarsches der Atomwaffengegner
bis 1965, Folder 1: Poem 'Die Henker werden noch umjubelt!'; Letter to Willenburg,
16 November 1964.

[195] Cf. Annedore Leber (in collaboration with Willy Brandt and Karl Dietrich Bracher),
Das Gewissen steht auf. 64 Lebensbilder aus dem deutschen Widerstand (Berlin and Frankfurt/
Main, 1954).

[196] Alexander Mitscherlich and Margarete Mitscherlich, *Die Unfähigkeit zu trauern:
Grundlagen kollektiven Verhaltens* [1967] (1967, Munich and Zurich, 1991).

[197] For this interpretation, cf. Benjamin Ziemann, ' "Vergesellschaftung der Gewalt" als
Thema der Kriegsgeschichte seit 1914: Perspektiven und Desiderate eines Konzeptes', in
Bruno Thoß and Hans-Erich Volkmann (eds), *Erster Weltkrieg—Zweiter Weltkrieg: Ein Ver-
gleich* (Paderborn, 2002), 757.

[198] Walter Künneth, 'Die evangelisch-lutherische Theologie und das Widerstandsrecht',
in *Vollmacht des Gewissens* (Frankfurt/Main and Berlin, 1960), i. 160–70.

[199] Reinhart Koselleck, *Kritik und Krise: Eine Studie zur Pathogenese der bürgerlichen Welt*
(1959; Frankfurt/Main, 1973), 21, 29–31.

Those Germans who had not been able to bear their conscience and to deal with defeat in 1945 had committed suicide. West German activists, in particular, connected their appeals to conscience with images of 'mass suicide', yet they did not explore the implications in more detail. It is no coincidence that West German protesters were especially keen to refer to nuclear armaments as leading to collective 'suicide'.[200]

Accordingly, the Protestant clergyman Heinrich Grüber, a supporter of the West German campaign, reported the impressions of a doctor who had survived Auschwitz and now worked in Albert Schweitzer's mission in Lambarene: 'Germans will, with the same perfection with which they have prepared and used the final solution for the Jews, prepare, execute, or permit the final solution of its own people.' As during the Third Reich, 'a group of knowing people now prepare things, while others watch; if Germans don't turn round, they will follow the men whom they once so adored and thus show the way from mass murder to mass suicide.'[201] Activists also drew on the memory of such acts when talking about 'nuclear suicide' and linked it to overcoming the cold war mindset: The 'romantic motto... "better dead than red" [in the original: "besser tot als Sklav"]', they argued, replicated Hitler's policies, as 'he had drawn innumerable people into the spell of his desperate mentality'.[202]

British protesters also alluded to the theme of 'nuclear suicide', but they linked it much more directly to specific political issues and their distrust in political leaders. For example, CND criticized Prime Minister Sir Alec Douglas-Home's statement that Britain was prepared to be blown to dust over Berlin by wondering: 'What right does Sir Alec have to decide that we should all turn into atomic dust with him?'[203] In general, British activists used abstract arguments rather rarely and restricted themselves to critiques of affluent society. Typical of the latter interpretation is Doris Lessing's despair at the 'blind forces of modern civilisation': 'Exhausted with the pressure of living, each of us might say "Oh for God's sake, press the button, turn down the switch, we've all had enough."'[204]

---

[200] BAK, ZSg. 1-E/70: 'Das Nein zum nuklearen Selbstmord', ed. Kampf dem Atomtod [n.d.]; Peter Nellen, 'Mit der Atombombe leben?', *Gewerkschaftliche Monatshefte*, 11 (February 1960), 65–74, here p. 72.

[201] Heinrich Grüber, 'Von Auschwitz nach Lambarene', *Stimme der Gemeinde*, 17 (1965), cols 67–8; Helmut Gollwitzer, 'Die Atombombe und der Friedenspreis' *Junge Kirche*, 20 (1959), 287–92, here 289; Martin Niemöller, 'Dulce et decorum est pro patria mori', *Stimme der Gemeinde*, 11 (1959), cols 385–92, here col. 390.

[202] Helmut Gollwitzer, 'Die Christen und die Atomwaffen', *Stimme der Gemeinde*, 10 (1958), cols 5–14, here cols 12–13.

[203] 'This is the man who holds Britain's future in his hands' *Sanity*, November 1963, 1.

[204] Doris Lessing, *A Small Personal Voice: Essays, Reviews, Interviews*, ed. Paul Schleuter (New York, 1974), 7.

Critics of CND, even nonconformists, argued, by contrast, that, when religious values themselves were at stake, it was a Christian duty to defend them: 'it would be better for nations to be wiped out than that they should submit to be morally murdered by the poison of Communist totalitarianism.'[205] Tapping CND's rhetoric of suicide, but comparing CND to the PPU's support for appeasement in the 1930s, the Bishop of Willesden claimed that 'nuclear war might lead to the destruction of humanity and destroy us all, and therefore it is virtual suicide. That is the risk, a terrible risk, and we have to face it. We also have to face what…is equally suicide and that is exposing the world to the most diabolical thing the world has ever seen.'[206]

TRANSCENDENCE

Through its absolute and transcendental character, the moral symbolism of the marches had a unique capacity to bring the various strands of the protest movements together. It helped the movements to reduce the complexity of the issues at stake, to relate their claims to their wider visions of society, to legitimate their aims, and, not least, to motivate their supporters. It was also unique in being able to reduce the fundamental insecurities that the protesters feared. By staging the marches as amalgams of victimhood and sacrifice (both expressed by the German word *Opfer*), they connected their own aims to the established patterns for dealing with fears of death, related their cause to 'humankind' and 'sacralized' their community. In that sense, the protests had the equivalent, but politically opposite, function of war memorials.[207]

They empathized with both the Jewish victims of Nazi persecution and the victims of the bombing in Hiroshima and Nagasaki. When they drew on a language of the war crimes tribunals and the metaphors of a universal 'Christian cosmos', Auschwitz and Hiroshima appeared as small steps towards global nuclear annihilation. From this perspective, in the words of the Protestant clergyman Heinrich Vogel, 'Hiroshima [was] more than a gas chamber, it [was] Hell!'[208] This equalization of Hiroshima and

---

[205] *Christian World*, 13 March 1958, 1.
[206] *Prism* (September 1958), 1.
[207] Sabine Behrenbeck, *Der Kult um die toten Helden: Nationalsozialistische Mythen, Riten und Symbole 1923 bis 1945* (Vierow, 1996).
[208] *Deutsche Friedensgesellschaft-Informationsdienst*, 10 (1958), 9; Martin Niemöller, *Martin Niemöller zu atomaren Rüstung. Zwei Reden* (Darmstadt, 1959), 28; Heinrich Vogel, 'Der Ruf von Hiroshima', *Stimme der Gemeinde*, 11, no. 14 (1959), col. 417–26, here col. 420–2.

Auschwitz could be found in the British context as well, and indeed across the world.[209] Rather than being only part of the West German memory landscape, such arguments were part of movement dynamics, as they provided a universal language of victimhood. As such, they were directly connected to the ways in which the activists tried to constitute themselves as political actors. This had a particular meaning in West Germany, however: here, it was effectively an attempt to write themselves into Jewish stories of suffering and thus was at its core an expression of 'Holocaust envy'.[210]

In this interpretation of history, also favoured by fellow-travelling groups in the Federal Republic, 'Eichmann [stood] for Everyman'.[211] The Nazi genocide thus appeared as a problem of humanity, and theological structures were transposed onto history. The individual fate of victims became embedded in the story of human suffering in general.[212] Such universalization of humanity was part of international discussions and had already become clear with the international success of Anne Frank's *Diary of a Young Girl* (1955), which showed the triumph of universal humanity, art, and spirituality over National Socialist brutality.[213]

Nuclear weapons policies, then, signified the redoubled potency of mass death: 'We used to call Hitler wicked for killing off the Jews, but Kennedy and Macmillan are much more wicked than Hitler…We cannot obey the murderers. They are wicked, they are abominable. They are the wickedest people in the story of man…'.[214] The marchers had taken on the task of expelling the 'wickedness' from their world, but most of them did not want to tumble its foundations. Instead, they emphasized the ways in which they, as persons, could change the world. The threat of nuclear weapons and the desire for security thus led the protesters to discover their sense of self.

[209] *Peace News*, 4 August 1961, 1; *Peace News*, 8 September 1961, 10; C. Wright Mills, *The Causes of World War III* (London, 1958), 34.

[210] Michael Geyer, 'Forum: The Historikerstreit Twenty Years on', *German History*, 24 (2006), 587–607, here 607.

[211] *Peace News*, 25 August 1961, 3; on the fellow-travelling organisations cf. Kraushaar (ed.), *Frankfurter Schule*, i. 212.

[212] Y. Michael Bodemann, 'Eclipse of Memory: German Representations of Auschwitz in the Early Postwar Period', *New German Critique*, 75 (1998), 57–89.

[213] Alvin Rosenfeld, 'Popularization and Memory: The Case of Anne Frank', in Peter Hayes (ed.), *Lessons and Legacies: The Meaning of the Holocaust in a Changing World* (Evanston, IL, 1991), 243–78.

[214] Bertrand Russell, quoted in *Observer*, 16 April 1961, 1.

7

Openings: Politics, Culture, and Activism in the 1960s

In the wake of the 1963 treaty between the United States, the Soviet Union, and the United Kingdom that banned atmospheric nuclear weapons tests, the visual traces of nuclear weapons had been effectively eliminated. Governments 'no longer had to rationalize the constant production of mushroom clouds and the related health concerns over radioactive fallout'. Thus, the arms race also became less visible—official weapons statistics were now the only form of knowledge of the dangers that nuclear weapons still posed. This meant that the 'visual record of the bomb' was frozen 'into what had been created in the period 1945–1963'.[1] The mushroom cloud became a mere token for speaking about nuclear war, but it had less direct resonance, especially as most of the ruins of the Second World War in British and West German city centres had by now been replaced with modern buildings, so that the material traces of the memories of mass destruction were also less directly accessible. In 1966, the West German writer Heinrich Böll reflected on the salience of nuclear weapons by highlighting their 'everydayness': 'we all have it [the Bomb] in our pockets, together with matches and cigarettes; with it, with the bomb, time has gained a new dimension that almost excludes duration.'[2]

By the mid-1960s, peace activists in Britain and West Germany had turned their attention away from the issue of nuclear armaments and focused primarily on the United States' military engagement in Vietnam. Thus, when peace protesters came together in West Berlin in February 1968 to chastise the United States for its military intervention in Vietnam and for the brutality the country used to pursue its aims, their demands sounded quite different from the polite requests developed by the Easter Marchers. In *On Violence*, a reflection on the protests of the 1960s, the

---

[1] Joseph Masco, ' "Survival is your Business": Engineering Ruins and Affect in Nuclear America', *Cultural Anthropology*, 23 (2008), 361–98, here 378.
[2] Heinrich Böll, *Werke: Essayistische Schriften und Reden 2*, ed. Bernd Balzer (Cologne, 1979), 44–5. My translation.

philosopher and cultural critic Hannah Arendt explained the revolutionary potential and some of the pathos of violence among the activists at the
end of the 1960s by recourse to the existential trope of the 'uncanny, sui-
cidal development of modern weapons'. Activists, she argued, had heard
the 'silent ticking of the bombs in the noise of the present'. Nuclear
weapons had turned the idea of progress on its head more generally because they revealed that 'there's no damn thing you can do that can't be
turned into war'.[3] But Arendt's existentialist analysis cannot convincingly
account for the transformation of the politics of security and for the dynamics of historical activism.

Historians of British and West German protests movement have to
account for one fundamental difference in perceptions, however. While
British and West German activists had acquired a sense of being part of
the same and directly connected historical conjuncture in the late 1950s
and early 1960s, they gradually lost this sense over the course of the
1960s. For the cultural critic Jeff Nuttall, the beginning of détente meant
that the 'ban-the-bomb movement' left activists 'stranded in the unbear-
able': while it had destroyed the illusion of security in a world framed by
the nuclear arms race, it had left nothing in its place. Accordingly, the
annual Aldermaston Marches took place, in a smaller format, for the last
time in 1965, until they were rejuvenated in the early 1970s.[4] The West
German Easter March movement continued, by contrast, under a slightly
amended name, highlighting its commitment to 'disarmament' more
generally and becoming part of a larger 'extra-parliamentary opposition'
that incorporated a number of campaigns, ranging from student protests,
to protests against proposed emergency legislation, to the campaign
against the Vietnam War.

Both societies saw a growing importance of subcultural layers of identification that came to be linked with political objectives. Yet the precise
relationships between these layers differed between both countries and
even within each country.[5] The transnational and comparative perspective
adopted here demonstrates especially clearly that the different British and
West German developments did not simply indicate different national
paths. As Alexander Sedlmaier and Stephan Malinowski have argued in a
broader context, there was no one national characteristic, but there were
many different experiences of protest even within individual national

---

[3] Hannah Arendt, *Macht und Gewalt* (1970; Munich, 2006), 17, 21, 20 (my translation; the last phrase appears in English in the German edition).
[4] Jeff Nuttall, *Bomb Culture* (London, 1968), 105.
[5] See conceptually Jakob Tanner, ' "The Times they are A-Changin": Zur subkulturellen
Dynamik der 68er Bewegungen', in Ingrid Gilcher-Holtey (ed.), *1968: Vom Ereignis zum
Mythos* (Frankfurt/Main, 2008), 275–95.

contexts, depending on how activists made sense of the political relevance of culture.[6]

This chapter analyses how the seemingly fundamental differences between West German and British developments in the protesters' politics of security reflected the different nature of the politicization of culture in each movement. Nonetheless, both countries saw the emergence of a new form of the politics of security during this period that focused on the psychological constitution of individuals as the foundation for social and political change. At the same time, this was also a question about the level of organization required to sustain a movement: on one end of the spectrum were those who argued that a movement focused around countercultural developments was sufficient, while others campaigned for a political movement with a sustained organizational structure. For this, the different roles that the social-democratic parties played in each country were of crucial importance.

LOOKING BACK

The peaceful conclusion of the Cuban missile crisis in late autumn 1962 and the Treaty that the United States, the United Kingdom, and the Soviet Union signed in Moscow in August 1963 in order to ban atmospheric nuclear tests meant that nuclear weapons lost their salience for the politics of security in both countries. The scenarios of accidental nuclear war that both movements had developed appeared to be less plausible in a climate of détente, and the Test Ban Treaty removed one of the direct concerns about the dangers from radiation that the protesters had raised. Moreover, above-ground nuclear tests had acted like simulations of nuclear war that made the unthinkable visible, meaning that the ban had made the dangers of nuclear weapons less clear. Not least, the charismatic young American President John F. Kennedy and especially the 'strategy for peace' that he outlined in a speech at American University in Washington, DC on 10 June 1963 fired the imaginations of the mainstream publics in both the United States and Western Europe. Indeed, Kennedy also galvanized the hopes and dreams of most activists in the peace movement.[7]

Kennedy's policies indicated broader transformations in cold war international relations. Around two months before his speech, on 11 April 1963,

[6] Alexander Sedlmaier and Stephan Malinowski, '"1968"—A Catalyst of Consumer Society', *Cultural and Social History*, 8 (2011), 255–74, here 259.
[7] HIS, TEM 300,06: Flyer, 'Zum Tod John F. Kennedys', n.d.; *Sanity* (August 1963), 1.

Pope John XXIII had issued his encyclical *Pacem in terris* and thus indicated that the Catholic Church was willing to participate more actively than before in the politics of peace. On 31 May 1963, the Finnish President Urho Kekkonen called for a nuclear-weapons-free zone in Europe. This followed the declaration of such a zone on 29 April 1963 by Bolivia, Ecuador, Chile, Brazil, and Mexico. All signs, then, appeared to point towards détente and nuclear disarmament.

The peace movements attributed the conclusion of the Partial Test Ban Treaty and the concomitant period of détente to their own campaign efforts, while also applauding the Kennedy administration for its supposed restraint and wisdom. Paradoxically, therefore, they began to accept, at least implicitly, the key parameter of the cold war international system: it rested on a balance of power that was ultimately bought by mutually assured destruction. However, the protest movements in Britain and West Germany did not simply cease their campaigns. Instead, the protesters redefined what they meant by the politics of security. Their experiences of movement success enabled them to develop novel interpretations of the politics of security in the context of international relations.

Fundamentally, the developments in both countries were direct consequences of the ways in which the social-democratic and socialist parties and groups had adapted to the demands of cold war foreign and defence policies. The trajectory of the movements after their peak in the early 1960s was also a direct result of how the organized social-democratic and socialist left proposed to tackle the challenges of international relations. The movements in both countries had opened up a space for discussing these issues beyond the remit of the organized labour parties, as well as beyond the binary logic of the cold war that divided the world strictly into communist and non-communist camps. Nigel Young, one of the founder members of CND, at a conference in June 1963, was quite critical of the campaign's achievements. But he still pointed towards the importance of creating a 'new sort of politics'. While he admitted that CND had failed, in the five years of its existence, to spell out unilateralism to the British public, and while the campaign had failed in its educational activities and in its attempts to organize a central leadership, it had still succeeded in 'creating a "style"—a new kind of politics in which policy is not of paramount importance'. It had thus produced an atmosphere in which the bomb came to be related to other social and political issues, local and international.[8] With hindsight, Sheila Rowbotham, who had made her first experiences with radical politics in the context of CND,

---

[8] Cited in Duff, *Left, Left, Left*, 221–2.

also observed that the campaign made it possible for her and other activists to 'invent an imaginary space out of our sense of displacement' in society and that it 'enlarged the space to be weird' in cold war political culture.[9]

Such developments were even more pronounced and politically important in the highly fractured context of Northern Irish society. The Northern Irish Campaign for Nuclear Disarmament developed forms of political activism that transcended the seemingly straightforward descriptions of politics in religious or ethnic terms. Instead, protests there against the UK naval centre in Clooney near Derry that housed the control centre for nuclear *Polaris* submarines in the Atlantic brought together people from both Catholic and Protestant communities in a pluralistic setting.[10] Although they borrowed, like their friends in mainland Britain, religious forms of campaigning such as silent vigils, they were allowed to enter Derry city centre, which was a proscribed place for nationalist groups. There, on what they called 'Blitz Square', pacifists, Republicans, socialists, and communists protested against the dangers of a repeat of the Second World War bombing campaigns in the nuclear age. This created the networks of activists and the space for campaigning that undergirded the emerging protests against unfair housing policies, rent increases, and the nascent civil rights movement.[11]

Similarly, when he looked back at his experiences in the 'extra-parliamentary opposition' in late November 1967, Klaus Vack, who had come to the Easter Marches through his involvement in socialist youth work, highlighted the transformative potential of the Easter Marches in the context of cold war politics. Reflecting on the role of communists in the Easter March movement, he observed the importance of implementing peaceful coexistence in direct personal relationships. While he entirely rejected the organizational conformism that he observed among communists, he nonetheless saw the life-changing potential of working together with them, implementing some of their ideas in the context of a West German politics of security from below.[12] Other West German activists also recounted how the Easter Marches enabled them to move from previously marginal, if not illicit, groups. For example, the Swabian communist Willy Hoss saw that the movement had allowed him to 'to come into the

---

[9] Rowbotham, *Promise of a Dream*, 13, 71.

[10] John Nagle, 'From "Ban-the-Bomb" to "Ban-the-Increase": 1960s Street Politics in Civil Rights Belfast', *Irish Political Studies*, 23 (2008), 41–58, here 46–53.

[11] Niall Ó Dochartaigh, *From Civil Rights to Armalites: Derry and the Birth of the Irish Troubles* (Basingstoke, 2005), 55.

[12] Note by Klaus Vack, printed in *Tradition heißt nicht, Asche aufheben, sondern die Flamme am Brennen ehalten!*, ed. Komitee für Grundrechte und Demokratie (Sensbachtal, 1985), 181.

open', and to live the life in public that he had previously campaigned for in the context of more clandestine political operations. While the cold war had 'nailed [activists] down in a group' and had endowed them with refutable political identifications, the contacts and networks in the Easter Marches in the context of détente helped to dissolve that compulsion.[13]

This meant that oppositional knowledge now also became available to those who had previously not been involved in protest politics. While Catholics in a society still characterized by confessional boundaries had been more or less absent from the early Easter Marches, they now joined in larger numbers, spurred on by the attempts at Church reform discussed at the Second Vatican Council that met in Rome from autumn 1962 to December 1965. Students, increasingly unhappy with their role in university governance as well as trends towards overcrowding, could also make use of the political space provided by the Easter March. Not least, the Easter Marches appeared to have shown that political mobilization could actually work.

DISAPPOINTMENTS AND POLITICIZATION

These general assessments of the functions of the extra-parliamentary politics of security do not themselves explain the large degree of personal, social, and political continuities in West Germany between the Easter Marches of Atomic Weapons Opponents and what became the extra-parliamentary opposition that campaigned against armaments, emergency legislation, and the Vietnam War, while also campaigning for higher education reform. Herbert Faller, Klaus Vack, Arno Klönne, Andreas Buro, Christel Beilmann, and Heiner Halberstadt continued to be involved in the campaign, and activists like Helmut Schauer provided important contacts to trade unions in the Frankfurt area in the protests against emergency legislation.[14]

These continuities, which did not exist to the same degree in Britain, can be explained only if we consider the dynamic relationship between the social-democratic party organization and some of the Easter March organizers. Rather than accepting the Easter Marches as a campaign that was independent of the party but attracted many *SPD* members and supporters, the mainstream reformist wing in the *SPD* criticized the Easter Marches as being too open towards communist subversion. An

---

[13] Willi Hoss, *Komm ins offene, Freund: Autobiographie*, ed. Peter Kammerer (Münster, 2004), 45; Vack, *Das andere Deutschland nach 1945*, 68–72.
[14] Otto, *Vom Ostermarsch zur APO*, 136–40.

SPD-sponsored brochure called 'Easter March Observations' rivalled official government statements in its condemnation of the protests: while Hans-Konrad Tempel and the other Easter March organizers might have been well-intentioned pacifists, their idealism, the brochure's author argued, had opened the floodgates to communist propaganda.[15]

Whereas the *SPD* never formally declared participation in the Easter Marches incompatible with party membership, its bureaucratic machinery exerted a high level of pressure on individual activists. Party organizers from Herbert Wehner's office visited Hans-Konrad Tempel and others several times to persuade them to abandon the campaign by threatening their eviction from the party. In a political system still dominated by the ideological binaries of the cold war, that eviction from a social-democratic party would have meant being cast outside the boundaries of respectable politics. Since the banning of the German Communist Party in 1956, the political space left of *SPD* was a political no-man's-land, a 'forbidden space'. People who found themselves in it had to fear for their jobs, especially if they worked in the civil service, including at schools and at universities, and for their reputation.[16]

The *SPD*'s pressure on individual activists and organizers led to a gradual process of politicization for most, although some, like Tempel, who could not bear the pressure, took a back seat.[17] The perception that the *SPD*'s organizational power hampered the realization of the Easter Marches' ethico-political aims was given further plausibility by what was happening to the *SPD*'s own student organization, the *SDS*, at around the same time. In 1961, the *SPD* proscribed membership of the *SDS* because of allegations of communist subversion. This amounted to political ostracism, but it also cut the *SDS* off from the party's financial and organizational resources, making it necessary for activists to look for novel forms of political engagement. They continued to find this in the Easter March movement.[18]

It was this constellation of a perception of large organizational pressures exerted by the *SPD* and a social-democratic party that had, by reacting in that way, betrayed its own fundamental values that contributed to the foundation of the gradual politicization of the Easter March movement over the course of the 1960s. Accordingly, activists' critiques of the values

[15] *Vorwärts*, 8 January 1964; *Vorwärts*, 11 March 1964.
[16] Jürgen Seifert in Bernt Engelmann et al. (eds.), *Anspruch auf Wahrheit: Wie werden wir durch Presse, Funk und Fernsehen informiert* (Göttingen, 1987), 65.
[17] HIS, TEM 400,01; Central Committee minutes, 11–12 April 1964, as well as the material in TEM 200,05.
[18] Willy Albrecht, *Der Sozialistische Deutsche Studentenbund (SDS): Vom parteikonformen Studentenverband zum Repäsentanten der Neuen Linken* (Bonn, 1994), 318–39.

that defined the social-democratic party organization took aim at the 'hollowness of the new culture of public civility' that had emerged in West Germany by the early 1960s: while the Easter March activists accepted that there had been demonstrable progress towards a fundamental democratization of West German society, they argued that it had not gone far enough and was merely façade.[19] From this perspective, the Grand Coalition that the *SPD* and the *CDU* formed in 1966 appeared to be the expression of what the activists regarded as a coalition of 'authoritarian forces', where two *SPD* mayors of Berlin, Heinrich Albertz and the former left-winger Klaus Schütz, tried to outbid conservative politicians in their attempts at the policing of public order.[20] With hindsight, Daniel Cohn-Bendit, the French–German activist, identified the core of this quest as one that sought to highlight how 'a society that claimed to be democratic' was made to confront its hidden 'authoritarian structures'.[21]

This constellation prompted Easter March activists to develop a number of approaches to a politics of security that moved decisively beyond the remit of *SPD* party politics. Initially, this meant that the Easter Marches provided a political space in which different strands could exist side by side. Activists agreed that they, rather than the Social Democratic Party, had become the most important protector of the German constitution. The *SPD* and many of the trade unions, they argued, had by contrast become part of the organization of the West German state and were thus also tightly sutured to the 'military–industrial complex'.[22]

What united these interpretations was that they tried to move beyond the organization and bureaucratic confines of 'democracy' that had been established in West Germany after 1945. Instead, they argued that security could be achieved only through the self-organization of society 'from below'. Although Hans-Jürgen Krahl was far from typical, most activists would have accepted his conclusion, in a speech in Frankfurt in 1968, that 'a social democracy lives only from the enlightened self-activity of mature human beings'. Organization then became a form of violence, the 'quotidian violence [*Gewalt*] of bureaucratic paternalism'.[23] Some, like the

[19] Geoff Eley, 'Politics, Culture, and the Public Sphere', *positions*, 10 (2002), 219–36, here 228.
[20] Jacques Schuster, *Heinrich Albertz—Der Mann, der mehrere Leben lebte: Eine Biographie* (Berlin, 1997).
[21] Danny Cohn-Bendit, cited in Ronald Fraser (ed.), *1968: A Student Generation in Revolt* (New York, 1988), 361.
[22] Thomas von der Vring, 'Probleme einer neuen sozialistischen Strategie', *neue kritik*, 5 (1964), 5–15, 12–14; Ursula Schmiederer, 'Rüstung und Abrüstung im Spätkapitalismus', *neue kritik*, 6 (1965), 28–31.
[23] Hans-Jürgen Krahl, 'Römerbergrede', 27 May 1968, in Krahl, *Konstitution und Klassenkampf* (Frankfurt/Main, 1971), 149.

Easter March veteran and SDS member Jürgen Seifert and the *SDS* activist Michael Vester, looked abroad for inspiration, initially to the British New Left, then to the American New Left and civil rights movement.[24] Jürgen Seifert, in particular, argued for a move towards theory in order to gain the analytical tools to address the situation in West Germany.[25] Michael Vester, by contrast, was inspired by the successes of the US civil rights movement and campus revolts that he had experienced first hand as a visiting student there. For him, 'organization' referred not to bureaucratic procedures, but to providing a political space for what he called 'collective learning processes'.[26] Others, like the Marburg *SDS* activist Peter von Oertzen, argued for a more direct engagement with socialist ideas and practices outside the mainstream. Yet others, especially in the Munich and Berlin *SDS*, and most notably Rudi Dutschke, argued less in terms of traditional socialist ideas. Dutschke, in particular, worked through positions of dissident communism (such as Ernst Bloch's and Georg Lucács's ideas) that he had become acquainted with before he left the GDR for West Germany. But he gave them a voluntarist twist by combining them with ideas from Situationism, an international political and artistic movement that emphasized the performative nature of art and culture and sought to use it to develop forms of life beyond capitalism.[27] This implied a strategy of campaigning that, in the words of the Situationist activist Dieter Kunzelmann, disrupted the 'clockwork mechanisms that regulate contemporary living by provoking people into thinking about the meaning of industrial society'. 'Life', Kunzelmann maintained, 'must be the artistic product of the whole of society conceived in terms of human beings capable of communication and pleasure'.[28] The fact that the dissatisfaction with the bureaucratic routines of the social-democratic party organization lay, for many protesters, at the heart of their activism, made such conceptions especially attractive.

Britain did not see a similarly pronounced trend towards politicization. The CND continued to campaign into the late 1960s, now primarily

---

[24] See Michael Schmidtke, *Der Aufbruch der jungen Intelligenz: Die 68er Jahre in der Bundesrepublik und den USA* (Frankfurt/Main, 2003), 46–56.

[25] Jürgen Seifert, 'Die Neue Linke. Abgrenzung und Selbstanalyse', *Frankfurter Hefte*, 1 (1963), 30–40, here 31.

[26] Michael Vester, 'Die Strategie der direkten Aktion', *neue kritik*, 30 (1965), 12–20, here 12–14. On the importance of his US experiences, see Martin Klimke, *The Other Alliance: Student Protest in West Germany and the United States in the Global Sixties* (Princeton, 2010), 40–74.

[27] On this nexus, see Mia Ching Lee, 'Art and Revolution in West Germany: The Cultural Revolution of 1968' (University of Michigan, Ph.D., 2007), especially 193–5.

[28] Quoted in Fraser (ed.), *1968*, 83. On Kunzelmann, see Aribert Reimann, *Dieter Kunzelmann: Avantgardist, Protestler, Radikaler* (Göttingen, 2009).

against the Vietnam War rather than nuclear weapons. Yet, a similar sense of betrayal by the social-democratic left did not exist in Britain, and CND could not emerge as the focus of an extra-parliamentary campaign; nor did any other movement emerge that continued the politics of security within a common cognitive framework. There are several explanations for this. On a purely political level, Britain did not see a grand coalition that would have lent such interpretations plausibility. Rather, in 1964, activists in Britain witnessed the coming-to-power of Harold Wilson's Labour government that had campaigned on a non-nuclear platform. To many contemporary observers, the new government seemed to reassert socialism against reformist trends in the British Labour Party.[29] Moreover, the British politics of the past did not work in the same way as in the Federal Republic: because of the National Socialist regime and many personal continuities within the police, the bureaucracy, and the government, the activists' accusation of witnessing a creeping resurgence of authoritarianism appeared especially acute in the Federal Republic.[30]

And, although Wilson committed his own act of betrayal by not implementing his promise for nuclear disarmament, this did not lead to a fundamental rift between party and activism on the scale that could be observed in West Germany. This was due to the different experiences British activists had with the ways in which the British Labour Party dealt with dissidence. While some reformist politicians and trade unions had voiced their desire to proscribe CND, and while there were moves by Labour's National Executive Committee (NEC) to constrain the pluralism within the party with regard to the contentious areas of social, foreign, and defence policies, the local party organizations never fully implemented the NEC's requests.

The experience of organizational exclusion and suppression of dissident voices was common primarily among the relatively small group of first-generation New Left activists such as E. P. Thompson, John Saville, Peter Worsley, and others. But the growth of a New Left movement out of socialist and social-democratic clubs at several universities made this experience rather marginal overall. For this reason, CND was never the central space for *political* experimentation that the Easter Marches had become in West Germany. It established a *cultural* framework of reference

[29] Ilaria Favretto, ' "Wilsonism" Reconsidered: Labour Party Revisionism 1952–1964', *Contemporary British History*, 14 (2000), 54–80.
[30] Wilfried Mausbach, 'The Present's Past: Recent Perspectives on Peace and Protest in Germany, 1945–1973', *Mitteilungsblatt des Instituts für soziale Bewegungen*, 32 (2004), 67–98.

that filtered into the plurality of protests in 1960s, Britain, rather than establishing one key focal point for debates.[31]

POLITICS AND CULTURE

These organizational developments provided the ground from which activists discussed how *political* culture should be and how *cultural* politics should look. This was the subject of fierce debates over the course of the 1960s. The *SDS* activist Elisabeth Lenk was highly critical of the turn towards cultural politics: 'They already think that they are revolutionary when they sit in jazz cellars and have a hairstyle à la Enzensberger. They already think that they are revolutionary because they smoke Roth-Händle cigarettes, read Konkret or Spiegel and, in order to shock the philistine environment, become members of the SDS.'[32]

With their assessments, Lenk, and others overlooked that the dominant contemporary models for political organization in West German society no longer came from British incarnations of 'middle-class radicalism'. Instead, this form of social bonding reflected a specific blend of popular culture that merged working-class culture with elements of folk and jazz and was personified by bands like the Beatles. Britain remained, also in terms of fashion, a key reference point for the younger generation in Germany before they turned their attention increasingly to US popular culture or home-grown artists who imitated these trends.[33] But its contemporary relevance lay in the fact that it gave expression to a different form of cultural politics. The 'most exciting trait of our social situation', the psychologist Helmut Kentler wrote in 1964, was the fact that 'social initiative and activity no longer emerges to a large and decisive extent from the appropriate public institutions and organizations, but from private circles and privatist movements'.[34] The pluralization of the Easter March movement, together with the loss of organizational coherence within the SDS, accompanied by the emergence of more or less autonomous and highly localized centres of activism with different politics of security, was the functional equivalent to this general trend.

---

[31] Dennis Dworkin, *Cultural Marxism in Postwar Britain: History, the New Left, and the Origins of Cultural Marxism* (Durham, NC, 1997) and the important PhD project by Tom Dowling (Sheffield) on the cultural politics of 'New Leftism'.

[32] Elisabeth Lenk, 'Die sozialistische Theorie in der Arbeit des SDS', *neue kritik*, 13 (November 1962), 7–11, here 8–9.

[33] Siegfried, *Time Is on my Side*, 60.

[34] Helmut Kentler, '"Subkulturen" von Jugendlichen', *Deutsche Jugend*, 12 (1964), 403–12, here 409–10.

This shift also implied a different perception that activists developed of themselves. Rather than regarding themselves merely as rational and disciplined actors, they now also began to stress their sociability and emotions. The perception of conscientious objectors as representing alternative models of masculinity was extremely important for this new culture of political activism—and it was perhaps not a coincidence in this context that some of the key Easter March organizers, such as Klaus Vack, Konrad Tempel, and Andreas Buro, had connections to conscientious objectors' organizations.[35] 'Toughness' and 'endurance' as ideals of masculinity did not disappear entirely, as the self-stylization as revolutionaries of activists like Dutschke showed. But it was now refracted differently, so that an anti-militarist *Sachlichkeit* (rationality) and sobriety went hand in hand with more explicitly emotional forms of bonding.[36]

Such a transformation of the politics and practices of citizenship in the Easter March movements also found expression in the accelerated search for 'authentic' modes of interactions and 'authentic' culture. West German activists were especially fascinated by African Americans and their culture and political activism, as it seemed to reveal especially well the natural other to the tamed and civilized self. Blues, in particular, appeared to them to reveal problems of discrimination and exclusion in the modern civilized world, and African Americans in the black power movement had a particular appeal.[37]

Such new models of an activist masculinity indicated a shift in the politics of security away from conceptions of 'injured citizenship' (Michael Geyer), which had expressed a strong distrust towards the West German state in the wake of the mass violence of the Second World War and thus a fundamental opposition to armaments.[38] By developing a conception of citizenship that contained within it notions of *individual* responsibility for non-violent conduct, activists severed this connection in conceptions

---

[35] Patrick Bernhard, 'An der "Friedensfront": Die APO, der Zivildienst und der gesellschaftliche Aufbruch der sechziger Jahre', in Hodenberg and Siegfried (eds), *Wo 1968 liegt*, 164–200.

[36] For an early reflection on this, see Fritz Vilmar, *neue kritik*, 11 (June 1962), 15. For the general background, see Frank Biess, 'Feelings in the Aftermath: Toward a History of Postwar Emotions', in Frank Biess and Robert Moeller (eds), *Histories of the Aftermath: The Legacies of the Second World War in Europe* (New York, 2010), 30–48, especially 30–3, and Holger Nehring, '"Generation", Modernity and the Making of Contemporary History: Responses in West European Protest Movements around "1968"', in Anna von der Goltz (ed.), *'Talkin' 'bout my Generation': Conflicts of Generation Building and Europe's '1968'* (Göttingen, 2011), 71–94.

[37] APOA, SDS-Gruppen, Frankfurt, 60er Jahre: Sozialistischer Club, n.d. For the general context, see Moritz Ege, *Schwarz warden: 'Afroamerikanophilie' in den 1960er und 1970er Jahren* (Bielefeld, 2007); Klimke, *The Other Alliance*, 108–42.

[38] Geyer, 'Cold War Angst' 385–6.

of citizenship between a 'yes' to military service and a 'no' to (nuclear) armaments. Instead, they developed ideas and practices of citizenship on the demonstrations that rejected military service, but tended to be oblivious to the specificities of nuclear weapons for conceptions of statehood and democratic governance.[39]

The mid- to late 1960s witnessed a plethora of initiatives that sought to undergird the explicitly political work of the Easter March campaign with cultural foundations, and thus moved beyond an idea of politics that was focused on influencing policies alone. Fundamentally, all these attempts were about creating 'third ways', not only on the level of foreign and defence policy, as the previous campaigns had propagated, but to wedge open third spaces within West German society in order to overcome the bipolarities of the cold war from within. In this context, socialist ideas appeared to have the potential to drive this renewal, which could ultimately lead to the breakdown of capitalist democracies in the West and socialist dictatorships in the East. Indeed, the idea had already been explored by the 'non-aligned' powers in world politics whose representatives had met at the 1955 Bandung Conference.[40]

A wide spectrum of such initiatives existed within the wider circles surrounding the Easter March movement, even if the specific relationship between politics and culture varied from group to group. The most overtly political of these was the network of so-called Republican Clubs that flourished across the Federal Republic and West Berlin from spring 1964 in order to provide the Easter March movement with year-long support. By the beginning of 1969, there existed forty clubs across the Federal Republic, also in smaller cities. The initiative for the foundation of such clubs had primarily come from older *SDS* activists, such as Klaus Meschkat and Horst Mahler, who wanted to counter some of the attempts by Dutschke and others to establish a more explicitly cultural politics of security. The groups expanded rapidly when the Grand Coalition between the CDU and *SPD*, which included intellectuals and writers such as Wolfgang Neuss, Hans Magnus Enzensberger, and the young lawyer Otto Schily, was formed in December 1966.[41] The Republican Clubs explicitly sought to broaden the remit of the Easter March movement by incorpo-

---

[39] *konkret*, 8 (August 1968), 22 ff.

[40] R. S. [Rudi Dutschke], 'Zum Verhältnis von Organisation und Emanzipationsbewegung: Zum Besuch Herbert Marcuses', *oberbaumblatt*, 5, 12 June 1967, printed in Kraushaar (ed.), *Frankfurter Schule*, ii. 255–60; Detlef Siegfried, 'Dritte Wege: Konzepte der Emanzpation in den 1960er Jahren', *Jahrbuch des Archivs der deutschen Jugendbewegung*, NF 4 (2007), 17–30.

[41] LAB, B Rep. 002, no. 4346/I: Protokoll der konstituierenden Versammlung des RC, 30 April 1967.

rating questions of democracy into the campaign's arguments, perhaps most famously with a congress on 'Universities and Democracy' that took place in Hanover in June 1967.[42]

An even earlier incarnation of such circles was Club Voltaire in Frankfurt. Carrying the enlightenment principles in its name, the club was set up as 'a site for encounter and information' by a group of activists around Heiner Halberstadt from socialist youth movements and the Easter Marches in the Frankfurt area in December 1962. Many of those who became involved, like Klaus Vack, had also been part of the campaign against French military intervention in Algeria. The groups sought to take some of the work of socialist youth organizations such as the Friends of Nature and the Falcons into new arenas, as the youth organizations were under increasing organizational pressure from the *SPD* to shed their core credentials. Similar clubs subsequently opened across the Federal Republic, with particular strengths in Lower Saxony, the Rhineland, and West-Berlin. The clubs started as reading circles that sought to promote 'practical socialist youth work' by studying the writings of nonconformist Marxists such as Ernst Bloch, Leszek Kołakowski, and Georg Lukács.[43] But when the first Club Voltaire opened its doors in Frankfurt and the sociology student Walmot Falkenberg began to chair the association that provided the financial backing in February 1963, the result was more than a revival of socialist youth movement activities. The club provided a café with a wide range of mainstream and counter-cultural newspapers and magazines. It organized dance events, folksong concerts, and poetry readings as well as theatre performances, especially by artists, poets, playwrights, and actors from East Germany and Eastern Europe, such as the singer-songwriter Wolf Biermann and the Soviet poet Yevgenij Yevtuchenko. In 1965, a similar club was founded in Stuttgart, and, in 1967, clubs emerged in Marburg and Munich, together with a more short-lived venture in Hanover.[44] In early 1967, a similar coffeehouse-cum-cultural venue opened in West Berlin under the name of 'Ça ira'; it was an offspring of the local Falcon youth movement.[45] Its main emphasis was folk music, organizing concerts with Pete Seeger among others. Like the other clubs, it had close links to the Easter March association, providing a venue for networking, meeting, and cultural production besides the demonstrations.[46]

[42] *Lönnendonker, Rabehl and Staadt, Antiautoritäre Revolte*, 347–54.
[43] Nikolaus J. Ryschkowsky, *Die linke Linke* (Vienna, 1968), 38–9.
[44] Paul Gerhard Hübsch, 'Clubs: Zentren der neuen Kultur', in Rolf-Ulrich Kaiser (ed.), *Protestfibel* (Munich, 1968), 128–42.
[45] *Süddeutsche Zeitung*, 17 March 1967.
[46] Brigitte Müller-Bilitza, 'Club ça ira', in Senator für Familie, Jugend und Sport (ed.), *Jugend-Aspekte* (Berlin, n.d.), 14–16.

The Castle Waldeck folk festivals that took place from 1964 until 1969 in a rather remote patch of the Hunsrück area in West Germany highlighted another facet of this productive merger of politics and culture that began to underpin the politics of security from the mid-1960s onwards. Activist Diethart Kerbs was inspired by the life-reform movement of the early twentieth century and by anti-authoritarian paedagogics when he founded these festivals. He saw them as the expression of a movement back to nature into the countryside in order to allow a cultural radicalism to take hold unencumbered by the pressures and norms of city life.[47] Like the clubs, the festivals were a direct product of the cultural work that had accompanied the Easter Marches: the Waldeck festivals were closely linked to the journal *pläne* [plans]. With the journal and later a record company that was directly linked to it, Klönne (the journal's editor between 1959 and 1966), Michael Vester (co-editor of *pläne* and, from 1963 second federal chair of the *SDS*), as well as the activists Karl Hermann Tjaden and Carl and Erdmann Linde, sought to revive, in the context of an explicitly democratic politics of life reform, the quasi-fascist, yet left-wing youth movement d.j.1.11 around Eberhard Köbel 'Tusk' and its journal *Rotgraue Aktion* (Red-Grey Action). Vester, more than his colleagues, was also strongly influenced by E. P. Thompson's and Raymond Williams's work on the relationship between politics and culture with which he had become acquainted during his visit to the United States as an exchange student at Bowdoin College in Maine.[48] Changing the emphasis on the politics of deterrence and nuclear destruction could be successful, they argued, only if some of the key parameters of modern life—such as its emphasis on bureaucratic routines, on everyday rhythms, and on sterile and mediated social interactions—were replaced by more emotional, spontaneous, self-sustained modes of socialization. Their emphasis was primarily on the *production* of politics as a learning process, rather than on the implementation of specific policies on governmental level.

The most culturally-oriented strand of the politics of security that developed around the Easter March movement over the course of the 1960s was made up of those activists who were inspired by the Situationist transgressive practices of a group called 'Subversive Action' around the bohemian Dieter Kunzelmann in Munich. Its activists sought to reveal, through public spectacles and performance art, the manipulative techniques of

---

[47] On the paedagogical underpinnings of the festivals, see Jürgen Oelkers, *Eros und Herrschaft: Die dunklen Seiten der Reformpädagogik* (Weinheim, 2011).
[48] Michael Vester, 'Solidarisierung als historischer Lernprozeß: Zukunftsperspektive systemverändernder Praxis im neueren Kapitalismus', in Diethart Kerbs (ed.), *Die hedonistische Linke: Beiträge zur Subkultur-Debatte* (Neuwied, 1970), 143–98.

consumer society and the oppressive character of capitalist society. They did this also by incorporating mass culture, rather than relying on subcultural strands alone. Rather than seeking to develop a fundamentally different vision of the politics of security and communicate it by means of rational arguments, activists believed that protests could work only if they showed the absurdity of the current power arrangements by using the very same means on which official and mainstream propaganda was based. Here, the politics of security took a form that relied primarily on cultural critique—and on deconstruction—at its central means of communication: the cold war arms race could become real only because of the images of destruction, spread through the mass media, on which it depended. It was, so the argument ran, only by trying to find a world beyond these images that security could be created. Frank Böckelmann singled out Stanley Kubrick's 1964 film *Dr Strangelove* as an ideal example of how this might be done: only through irony and subversion could the general population be made to see the absurdity of the nuclear arms race: people's consciousness had already been manipulated into believing in the avoidability of the cold war arms race and the logic of mutually assured destruction. Direct resistance, by contrast, would merely strengthen the existing power structures.[49] While accepting the arms race almost as an existential reality, Situationists were interested primarily in performative work that would come into its own in the nuclear criticism of the 1980s.[50]

The specificities of this form of the politics of security become even clearer when we compare it with the strand within the Easter March movement that became dominant from 1965–66 onwards: the anti-authoritarian politics theorized and practised by Rudi Dutschke, Hans-Jürgen Krahl, and Bernd Rabehl in the West Berlin *SDS*. Although Rudi Dutschke was very much inspired by the anti-authoritarian elements of this critique and by its emphasis on transgression and playful rule-breaking, he—and most other activists—fundamentally disagreed with its emphasis on cultural critique and deconstruction. Although they could not agree on many other issues, Dutschke and most other Easter March activists still believed that consciousness was autonomous and that activism, carried by the right revolutionary consciousness, had the potential to change the world.[51] Instead of emphasizing the politics

[49] Frank Böckelmann and Herbert Nagel (eds), *Subversive Aktion: Der Sinn der Organisation ist ihr Scheitern* (Frankfurt/Main, 1976), 180, 192.

[50] Cf. Wolfgang Kramer, *Technokratie als Entmaterialisierung der Welt: Zur Aktualität der Philosophien von Günther Anders und Jean Baudrillard* (Münster, 1998).

[51] Rudi Dutschke, *Jeder hat sein Leben ganz zu leben: Die Tagebücher 1963–1979*, ed. Gretchen Dutschke (Cologne, 2003), 21.

of spectacle, Dutschke and others developed voluntarist versions of the politics of security, in which the will of the individual subject was key for political and societal transformation.[52] In his statement on organization (*Organisationsreferat*), student leader Rudi Dutschke argued that state violence (*Staatsgewalt*) in the Federal Republic functioned 'to a totalitarian extent psychologically' through internalized manipulation, so that the real violence remained invisible.[53] Violence at demonstrations appeared, therefore, merely as a symptom of the fundamental problem of the violence applied by government and present in West German society.[54]

Dutschke was not the only one to discuss the phenomenon of structural and cultural violence that did not work solely through the physical attack on human bodies.[55] But Dutschke's suggested response was not cultural deconstruction and playful transgression. Instead, the fundamental problem of organization was that of 'revolutionary existence' that would realize security in a community of revolutionaries.[56] The two male groups that formed in the experimental *Kommune I* in West Berlin—one around Dieter Kunzelmann as the 'revolutionary bridgehead for invasion of everyday life', and the other around a concept of active solidarity in living together, represented these two versions of the most cultural forms of the politics of security.[57] A third model was provided by those with youth movement backgrounds, such as Klaus Vack and Arno Klönne, who wished to create a movement from below that provided a loose organizational context for what they called 'collective learning processes': spaces that allowed for the discussion and working-through of specific issues in order to change individuals through their engagement with each other in a group.[58]

---

[52] Rudi Dutschke, '. . . Professor Habermas Ihr begriffloser Objektivismus erschlägt das zu emanzipierende Subjekt', printed in Kraushaar (ed.), *Frankfurter Schule*, ii. 251, 253.

[53] Rudi Dutschke and Hans-Jürgen Krahl, 'Das Sich-Verweigern erfodet Guerilla-Mentalität', typescript of the sound recording, 5 September 1967 <http://www.glasnost. de/hist/apo/67dutschke.html> (accessed 15 October 2012).

[54] Rudi Dutschke, interview with *konkret*, 3 March 1968.

[55] HStAD, RW 115 443/75–77: 'Freiheit—Revolution—Gewalt—Gewaltlosigkeit. Arbeitspapier des Internationalen Rates der War Resisters' International (WIR) vom 12.–17.–August 1968'.

[56] Printed in Kraushaar (ed.), *Frankfurter Schule*, ii. 287–90.

[57] Aribert Reimann, 'Zwischen Machismo und Coolness: Männlichkeit und Emotion in der westdeutschen "Kulturrevolution" der 1960er- und 1970er-Jahre', in Manuel Borutta and Nina Verheyen (eds), *Die Präsenz der Gefühle. Männlichkeit und Emotion in der Moderne* (Bielefeld, 2010), 229–53.

[58] *apo/IZA*, 54 (1968), 6–7.

In Britain, the ground for what counted as 'political' had itself shifted, too, as the politics of security had become more plural and had moved out of the remit of CND and the surrounding networks of activists. As no one cognitive frame emerged, however, British activists had to lead double lives in juggling cultural hippiedom and their membership in the revolutionary left.[59] But such assessments were also a sign that culture and politics did not fuse around one movement, as they did in West Germany. There was no one focus for a politics of security. In fact, the question of security had more or less faded entirely from discussions of most groups with the exception of CND. A plethora of groups that indicated different conceptions of politics and culture began to exist side by side, although their variety resisted efforts at neat and compact classification.

A first group consisted of novel forms of anti-war protests that wished to move beyond protest marches and towards more concrete forms of campaigning, such as sit-downs and blockades of military installations. The Vietnam Solidarity Campaign, founded in June 1966 at a national conference supported by fifty organizations and groups at the initiative of the Bertrand Russell Peace Foundation and the Trotskyite International Marxist Group, was one of these organizations. A second and closely related group converged around the revolutionary underground newspaper *Black Dwarf* that was edited by Tariq Ali, a former Oxford student from a Pakistani landowning family who wanted to bring the political and alternative left together in order to discuss common themes of the politics of security under the rubric of anti-imperialism. A third strand developed around university protests in the London area. The idea of an 'Anti-University' that sought to break down the divides between teachers and students was particularly appealing. New Left activists within CND tried to cultivate islands of authenticity at a local level, trying to create a new society free from alienation. They attempted to shift the balance of power in society by constructing new centres of power as in and through themselves in order to express their vision of a participatory democracy.

Throughout the 1960s, then, British society saw the emergence of a large variety of counter-cultural groups and trends that understood themselves as political ventures: 'issues of personal life, the way people live, culture, which weren't considered the topics of politics on the Left. We wanted to talk about contradictions of this new kind of capitalist society in which people didn't have a language to express their private troubles, didn't realize that these troubles reflected political and social questions that could be generalized.'[60] Many around the campaigns of the 1960s

---

[59] Rowbotham, *Promise of a Dream*, 160.
[60] Stuart Hall, quoted in Fraser (ed.), *1968*, 30.

began to regard the forms of conventional politics as too limited and goal oriented to promote 'real freedom'. They regarded the participation in artistic experiences or the expansion and transcendence of ordinary consciousness as beneficial social activities. Politics now came to be about friendship and music, mostly between men, with women present only in the background, thus transferring more traditional forms of labour movement sociability into new contexts.[61]

As in West Germany, politics in Britain could be found in many unexpected ways. Skiffle groups, inspired by Acker Bilk, Lonnie Donegan, and other folk musicians with their banjos, guitars, and washboards, as well as other forms of home-made music that had already been regular features at the Aldermaston Marches, now came to stand as symbols that worked against the perceived elitism of the jazz scene and embodied a set of broader egalitarian ideals.[62] But, unlike in the Federal Republic, most of these trends never merged in a public and massmedialized form of campaigning under a common frame of reference, precisely because the pressures towards conformity within organized Labour and cold war political culture had been less pronounced. But many of these developments occurred in highly localized sub- and counter-cultural contexts across the United Kingdom.[63] Activists around the C100 accordingly switched their key orientation towards creating a 'new non-violent society' rather than, like CND originally, campaigning for policy change.[64]

The focus of this cultural politics therefore moved away from explicit political objectives and towards the self-transformation of (male) activists: it was essential to 'establish a new society that [would] allow men to talk about their souls', as the American academic John Gerassi put it at the 'Dialectics of Liberation' conference that took place in Camden Roundhouse, a converted railway depot and one of London's prime countercultural venues, during the 'Angry Arts Week', in July 1967.[65] The driving idea behind the conference was to unite different strands of the politics of

[61] John Charlton, *Don't You Hear the H-Bomb's Thunder? Youth and Politics on Tyneside in the Late Fifties and Early Sixties* (Pontypool, 2009), 88–93; Celia Hughes, 'Young Socialist Men in 1960s Britain: Subjectivity and Sociability', *History Workshop Journal*, 73 (2012), 170–92.

[62] Siegfried, *Time Is on my Side*, 109–10.

[63] Gerd-Rainer Horn, *The Spirit of '68*, 32–5.

[64] BLPES, CND/1/29: 'The Politics of the Committee of 100, 1968'.

[65] Richard Boston, 'Angry Enough about Vietnam', *New Society*, 6 July 1967, 22; David Cooper (ed.), *Dialectics of Liberation* (Harmondsworth, 1968); R. Carrington, 'Cultural and Ideological Challenges of the London Underground Movement, 1965–1971', unpublished PhD thesis, Anglia Ruskin University (2002), 279–325.

culture in order to highlight the systemic constraints and coercion in the absence of the use of material violence.[66]

But the implementation of these politics took place within the highly differentiated context of local and not necessarily connected campaigns, such as the community struggles around housing that George Clark organized.[67] Similarly, Colin Ward's brand of anarchism focused on enhancing already existing practical forms of self-organization by fostering housing and town planning and progressive education from below in forms of 'mutual aid through direct action'.[68] Counter-cultural papers such as *IT* (*International Times*), which was published from October 1966 by the heroin addict Tom McGrath, who had been previously involved with *Peace News*,[69] Richard Neville's *OZ*, which began in January 1967 with a print run of 40,000 copies a week, the Trotskyite *Black Dwarf* and *Red Mole* as well as the Anarchist *Freedom* and *Anarchy* are the main examples for the proliferation of the politics of culture.[70] But many of CND's rank and file worried that this broadening of the agenda might mean losing the campaign's appeal, so that most CND activists did not readily embrace counter-cultural trends.[71] In 1967, the black power activist Stokely Carmichael expressed, to much applause among the audience at the Roundhouse conference, his dissatisfaction with the turn towards psychology and counter-culture: 'I'm not a psychologist or psychiatrist, I'm a political activist and I don't deal with the individual. I think it's a cop out when people talk about the individual.'[72]

Similar debates about the relationship between politics and culture had already been evident within British extra-parliamentary politics since the early 1960s, when they had still focused primarily on the nature of class in an increasingly affluent society and the implications of this for the organization of political campaigns. Raymond Williams, Stuart Hall, and others had drawn the New Left's attention to issues of culture as a key component of politics.[73] In his work on the *Long Revolution*, Williams

---

[66] Jules Henry, 'Social and Psychological Preparation for War', in Cooper (ed.), *Dialects of Liberation*, 50–71.

[67] Rowbotham, *Promise of a Dream*, 69.

[68] Colin Ward, *Anarchy in Action* (London, 1973); David Goodway, *Anarchist Seeds beneath the Snow: Left-Libertarian Thought and British Writers from William Morris to Colin Ward* (Liverpool, 2006), 309–25.

[69] Nigel Fountain, *Underground: The London Alternative Press, 1966–74* (London, 1989), 193; Jonathon Green, *Days in the Life* (London, 1998), 210–11.

[70] Elizabeth Nelson, *The British Counter-Culture, 1966–73: A Study of the Underground Press* (Basingstoke, 1989), 51.

[71] Letter from Geoffrey Strickland, *Sanity* (February 1966), 6.

[72] Stokely Carmichael, 'Black Power', in Cooper (ed.), *Dialects of Liberation*, 150–74, here 150.

[73] Cf. Dworkin, *Cultural Marxism*, ch. 3.

had described a secular shift away from a specific working-class culture over the course of the nineteenth and twentieth centuries. He argued for an understanding of politics that sat oddly with traditional Marxist understandings: his interpretation of social organization assumed not one dominant force—social and economic structures—that drove political and social changes, but argued for the relative autonomy of the four different aspects of society: the levels of decision-making (politics), what he called 'maintenance' (economics), education, and learning, as well as 'generation and nurture'. Economistic understandings simplified, he argued, the complexity of experiences in society.[74] Similarly, Stuart Hall highlighted the importance of 'culture' for understanding contemporary British society and politics, but he faulted Williams for not paying sufficient attention to consumer capitalism, which had 'freed the working class only for new and more subtle forms of enslavement'.[75] E. P. Thompson, however, had been highly critical of this approach to politics: it had replaced, he argued, 'the whole way of struggle' for international and material security and socialism with references to culture as 'the whole way of life'. It therefore had the tendency to weaken the radical thrust of extra-parliamentary campaigns by making power invisible and thus weakening an understanding of 'struggle' and 'confrontation'.[76]

PERFORMANCES

The process of politicization in West Germany was not merely driven by activists' intellectual engagement with their experiences. It was also the result of the practices of protest and the ways in which they framed and reframed the activists' understanding of the politics of security. The process of switching from more general humanitarian objectives to specific political aims had already started in September 1962 when the Easter Marches gave themselves a new name: 'The Easter Marches—Campaign for Disarmament'. The new name meant that its various public interventions no longer merely included a general opposition to nuclear weapons, but listed concrete political demands, such as an end to nuclear testing and the creation of nuclear-weapons-free zones.[77] In line with this politicization, the Easter March movement witnessed a constant rise in support

---

[74] Raymond Williams, *Communications* (Harmondsworth, 1962), 10; Raymond Williams, *The Long Revolution* (London, 1961), x.

[75] Stuart Hall, 'A Sense of Classlessness', *Universities and Left Review*, 5 (1958), 31.

[76] E. P. Thompson, 'The Long Revolution', *New Left Review*, 9 (1961), 24–33, here 30; idem, 'The Long Revolution II', *ibid.*, 10 (1961), 34–9, here 39.

[77] *Informationen zur Abrüstung*, special issue (December 1964).

and membership. In 1964, there were 280 events (up from 130 in 1963) and around 100,000 participants on several rallies and marches (1963: 50,000). In 1965, the campaign organized 300 events with 130,000 participants. In 1966, 145,000 people participated in 600 demonstrations and other events around the country, and in 1967 there were 150,000 people in 800 events.[78]

The fundamental factor in the rise of participation was, initially, the debates in the German parliament about an emergency law. Authority in the case of emergency, such as war or civil war, had, until 195, belonged to the Allied powers. But the Federal Republic's acquisition of at least partial sovereignty with its accession of NATO in that year meant that national legislation became necessary. Discussions about such a law had already begun in the late 1950s. But these plans were controversial when they became public and when it seemed as if the *SPD* would be willing to support at least some form of such legislation. The repercussions of such legislation had become especially clear when the weekly *Der Spiegel* published a leaked report on 10 October 1962 that described, in gruesome detail, the potential consequences of nuclear war on German soil that could result from the NATO combat exercise *Fallex 62*. The publication led to the arrest of several *Spiegel* journalists, including its editor Rudolf Augstein. Chancellor Adenauer called it 'treason'.[79]

Given that several *SPD* politicians had themselves been the target of some of the government's recrimination, their U-turn in support of the emergency laws seemed to many Easter March activists a fundamental betrayal of their social-democratic credentials. Many activists had also diagnosed the growing autonomy of deterrence and security thinking in the West German armed forces, thus removing their democratic accountability.[80] When a novel draft of the emergency bill was discussed in parliament, Easter March activists belonging to the *SDS* detected a 'militarization of the basis', the 'militarization of the production process', and the growth of a 'direct political surveillance apparatus'. The *SPD*, by supporting such measures, would thus turn into a group of 'social fascists'.[81]

It was against this backdrop that 1,200 intellectuals and academics signed a declaration against the emergency legislation in an attempt to avoid the 'total militarization of society'.[82] Shortly before, in November 1964, the

---

[78] Otto, *Vom Ostermarsch zur APO*, 147.

[79] For the most detailed description of governmental attempts to delegitimize the opposition, see Soell, *Schmidt*, 407–38.

[80] Jürgen Seifert, 'Zum Stand der Notstandsdiskussion', *neue kritik*, 17 (July 1963), 5.

[81] *SDS-Korrespondenz*, 6 (May 1966), 45–7.

[82] 'Appell zur Notstandsgesetzgebung an die Vorstände und Fraktionen der Parteien', *Blätter für deutsche und internatioinale Politik*, 10 (1965), 188.

Easter March movement had discussed its participation in some trade unions' campaigns against the legislation. The issue became even more salient when it seemed possible that the bill would be passed by the German parliament in spring 1965.[83] The Easter March campaign thus became, from January 1965, directly linked to the campaign against the proposed emergency law; the very form and shape of democracy had become part of the activists' politics of security: the emergency legislation threatened not only to make a quasi-dictatorship possible during war time; more importantly, it contained within it the 'threat of total militarization in peace time'.[84]

The term 'extra-parliamentary opposition' was not merely a description of an opposition that voiced its claims on the streets rather than through an opposition party in parliament. Its immediate origins as a concept lay in its use by Rudi Dutschke in December 1966 to confront on the streets the Grand Coalition in parliament.[85] Yet, the term also contained a normative assessment. It applied a concept of the practice of democracy that did not see the opposition as part of the state institution, or even as one of its parts, a view that even social-democratic lawyers had developed in the early Federal Republic.[86] The idea of an 'extra-parliamentary opposition' was therefore directly connected to a specific development in the politics of security that had already taken shape in 1965, when some Easter March activists founded the 'Committee "State of Emergency of Democracy"' (*Kuratorium Notstand der Demokratie*) together with a number of academics and intellectuals.[87] Its proponents assumed that the security interests of the state could not merely be played out against pressures coming from the street—such a logic would, they argued, merely replicate the structures of authoritarian thinking that the activists wished to criticize.[88]

The protesters' framing of their activism as a danger to democracy was so persuasive in West Germany because it referred to a common *national*

---

[83] See Michael Schneider, *Demokratie in Gefahr? Der Konflikt um die Notstandsgesetze* (Bonn, 1986), 127–31.

[84] *Informationen zur Abrüstung*, 19 (1964), 73.

[85] *Der Spiegel*, 27 May 1968, 41; Lönnendonker, Rabehl, and Staadt, *Die antiautoritäre Revolte*, 310; with evidence of a slightly earlier mention: Meike Vogel, *Unruhe im Fernsehen: Protestbewegung und öffentlich-rechtliche Berichterstattung in den 1960er Jahren* (Göttingen, 2010), 251.

[86] Carlo Schmid, 'Die Opposition als Staatseinrichtung', *Der Wähler*, 5 (1955), 498–9.

[87] See Boris Spernol, *Notstand der Demokratie: Der Protest gegen die Notstandsgesetze und die Frage der NS-Vergangenheit* (Essen, 2008).

[88] *Demokratie vor dem Notstand: Protokoll des Bonner Kongresses gegen die Notstandsgesetze am 30. Mai 1965* (special issue *neue kritik* (August 1965)), 4; HIS, TEM 400,05: Minutes of Easter March central committee, 22–23 April 1967, 4.

past. The protests' opponents highlighted the similarities with the street battles of the Weimar Republic and saw the forms of activism—highly emotional gatherings as opposed to more orderly demonstrations—as a revival of totalitarian forms of mass mobilization that had the potential to undermine the rational discourse on which democracy should be based.[89] The protesters countered by highlighting, in stark colours and polemical forms, similarities between the US war effort in Vietnam, which the West German government supported, and the Holocaust: 'MURDER. Murder through napalm bombs! Murder through gas? Murder through atomic bombs?...How long will we allow murder to be committed in our name? AMIS GET OUT OF VIETNAM!'[90] The flyer, distributed across the campus of the Free University Berlin on 3 and 4 February 1966 provoked by the new US bombing campaign in Vietnam in January 1966, had been drafted by activists close to Subversive Action and was one of the first attempts to fuse the politics of security with the deconstruction of consciousness through irony and sarcasm that the group propagated. It marked one of the first occasions for a novel politics of security that focused on 'international liberation' and zeroed in on the United States' policies as the main culprit.

The West German politics of the past thus assumed an importance in the politics of the present that they could not have in Britain, as protesters there lacked an awareness of such clear caesuras and ruptures in national history. On 3 April 1967, the *Kuratorium* further escalated its language by warning of the potential 'practice of a dictatorship' and a continuous 'psychological mobilization of the whole population' under a state of emergency.[91] The military putsch in Greece, a NATO country, and the beginning of the Arab–Israeli conflict in June 1967 appeared to lend such an interpretation even more plausibility. In this context, Easter Marchers regarded the eventual support by the Federation of German Trade Unions for the emergency legislation as a further act of betrayal that made more direct and practical steps of resistance necessary.[92] When West German activists engaged with the brutal and violent crushing of the 'Prague Spring' by the Soviet Army on 21 August 1968, they used the very same framework of interpretation. Heinz Beinert of the Falcons exclaimed:

[89] Michael L. Hughes, 'Reason, Emotion, Pressure, Violence: Modes of Demonstration as Conceptions of Political Citizenship in 1960s West Germany', *German History*, 30 (2012), 222–46; Sebastian Ullrich, *Der Weimar-Komplex: Das Scheitern der ersten deutschen Demokratie und die politische Kultur der frühen Bundesrepublik* (Göttingen, 2009).
[90] Cited from Klimke, *The Other Alliance*, 49.
[91] *SDS-Korrespondenz*, 6 (May 1966), 45.
[92] *Extrablatt* (June 1968), cited in Karl A. Otto (ed.), *APO: Die außerparlamentarische Opposition in Quellen und Dokumenten (1960–1970)* (Cologne, 1989), 349–50.

'Who has betrayed us? Red bureaucrats!' ('Wer hat uns verraten, rote Bürokraten!').[93]

Especially those activists who had joined the Easter March movement from the *SDS* argued forcefully that the issue of emergency legislation should become the key focus of the campaign, and they suggested another name change to 'Campaign for Democracy and Disarmament'.[94] The group therefore sought to mobilize more activists and move beyond the traditional marches and demonstrations over the Easter weekend, on Hiroshima Day in August and on Anti-War Day in early September. In a letter to all members of the Campaign's executive committee, Andreas Buro argued in January 1967 for activities all year round, not least to avoid being trumped by the increasingly popular events of the anti-authoritarian wing of the student movement.[95] However, some of the original Easter Marchers like Heinz Kloppenburg and Rudolf Schulz, a doctoral student in theology, disagreed: they sought to continue to alert the West German population of the dangers of nuclear war.[96] Ultimately, however, the reformers won the debate, especially because linking the discussions about the emergency law with general defence policy issues and the politics of NATO was increasingly plausible. When NATO forces participated in the *Fallex* combat exercise on 12 October 1966, the participants simulated the impact of a 'substitution of parliamentary representation in case of war'. This involved scenarios that saw the complete takeover of politics by the executive, the imposition of curfews, and expanded powers for the armed forces for public-order policing.[97]

Conflicts about the precise shape and form of the politics of security in the context of democracy informed discussions at a meeting that the *Kuratorium* had organized in Frankfurt on 30 October 1965 which brought together the representatives from the Easter March movements, trade-union activists from the metal workers' union *IG Metall*, as well as *SDS* activists.[98] Those activists like Michael Vester who advocated a more traditional socialist

---

[93] Tilman P. Fichter and Siegward Lönnendonker, *Dutschkes Deutschland: Der Sozialistische Deutsche Studentenbund, die nationale Frage und die DDR-Kritik von links* (Essen, 2011), 103–04.

[94] HIS, TEM 400,03: Appendix to Central Committee minutes, 17 June 1966.

[95] HIS, TEM 400,05: Andreas Buro to members of the Central Committee, January 1967.

[96] HIS, TEM 400,04: Appendix to Central Committee minutes, 17/18 September 1966.

[97] HIS, TEM 400,04: Press release by *Kuratorium* 'Notstand der Demokratie', 10 October 1966.

[98] Helmut Schauer (ed.), *Notstand der Demokratie: Referate, Diskussionsbeiträge und Materialien vom Kongreß am 30. Oktober 1966 in Frankfurt am Main* (Frankfurt/Main, 1967).

politics were highly sceptical of a strategy of direct action that Dutschke, Krahl, and others advocated. Vester argued that sit-ins and other novel forms of protest would only serve to self-mobilize those who already believe in the cause, rather than tap new groups of supporters. It worked primarily through symbols, Vester pointed out, rather than being based on what he regarded as 'real argumentation'.[99] The editor of the Catholic newspaper *Rheinischer Merkur* Anton Böhm, in a letter to Arno Klönne from April 1963, had already ridiculed protests with 'pushchairs and toy balloons' as 'foolish', while admitting that the boundaries and parameters of politically considerate were about to change.[100] The designer Otl Aicher, one of the key proponents of architectural modernism in the Federal Republic, applied the principles of modernist design to his rather critical analysis of the appearance of the 1966 Easter March: a unified design rather than improvisation should determine the marches' visual appearance in the future, and the youth movement spirit and songs should be replaced by a (one can assume: more rational) model of campaigning around clearly structured jazz music.[101]

The pluralization of the politics of security also had repercussions for actual practices of citizenship on demonstrations and protests. Previous protests had made a point to conform to mainstream expectations by creating a specific image of citizenship as sober, rational, and self-disciplined and that took no explicit note of differences between men and women.[102] Situationists and some *SDS* activists in the Easter March movement were highly critical of the ritualized yearly demonstrations as devices for the stabilization in society.[103] They explicitly sought to link medialization, performance, and action directly as the expression of activists' values.[104] *Kommune I* activists, for example, distributed a leaflet at one of the Easter Marches addressed to the 'Easter marchers and Easter martyrs', thus poking fun at the sombre mood at most of those demonstrations and highlighting that their protests essentially followed the

[99] Michael Vester, 'Die Strategie der direkten Aktion', *neue kritik*, 30 (1965), 12–20, here 12.
[100] AdsD, Christel Beilmann papers, 48: Anton Böhm to Arno Klönne, 16 April 1963.
[101] Report dated 16 April 1966, printed in Beer, *Auf den Feldern von Ulm*, 86–7.
[102] On the general context, see Thomas Lindenberger, 'From the Chopped-Off Hand to the Twisted Foot: Citizenship and Political Violence in Twentieth-Century Germany', in Geoff Eley and Jan Palmowski (eds), *Citizenship and National Identity in Twentieth-Century Germany* (Stanford, CA, 2008), 108–28.
[103] Boris Spix, *Abschied vom Elfenbeinturm? Politisches Verhalten Studierender 1957–1967: Berlin und Nordrhein-Westfalen im Vergleich* (Essen, 2008), 313–15.
[104] Kathrin Fahlenbrach, *Protestinszenierungenm: Visuelle Kommunikation und kollektive Identitäten in protestbewegungen* (Wiesbaden, 2002), 190–9.

mainstream cultural conventions: 'What do you do when the conductor comes? Pay! What are you doing in a self-service shop? Pay!'[105]

Over the course of 1966, 1967, and 1968 such practices of citizenship became more widespread in the movement as a whole. From this angle citizenship lay precisely in the performance of transgression. Referring to a sit-in at the Free University of Berlin, the writer Peter Schneider outlined such a strategy of performative rule-breaking:

We have informed [West Germans] about the war in Vietnam with all matter-of-factness, although we experienced that we could cite the most unthinkable details of American policy in Vietnam without getting our neighbours' imaginations going. But then we found that we only had to step on the lawn where it said "Keep off" to cause sincere, general and lasting horror.[106]

Mass-medialized images were fundamental to this form of transgression: they not only represented the protests, but they constituted them—the logic of the mass media, and television in particular, co-produced this performativity.[107]

Whenever this form of the politics of security was pushed further, as in the commune movement and in some Situationist groups, the boundaries between reality, joking, and phantasy disappeared even more thoroughly, and the nuclear arms race became purely imaginary:

The playful life forces in Europe are suppressed by the culture industry. The value of atomic bombs becomes obvious when used in the struggle against the culture industry...After every shop in a culture supermarket, an atomic bomb is discretely put in together with the product...As soon as the world has become a sea of rubble, the search for experimental life forms can enter a creative stadium.[108]

Britain saw structurally very similar debates, but it did not witness the emergence of one movement around which the different strands converged—there was no single plausible frame under which different sections of the movement could unite. CND as a protest campaign declined and could not write itself into the anti-Vietnam War campaigns and campaigns for university reforms that emerged in Britain over the course of the 1960s. Instead, its activists went elsewhere when they sought to grapple with what they regarded as the fundamental issues of their time. The Old Left remained remarkably strong in

[105] HIS, Sozialistisches Anwaltskollektiv, 03.09: 'Ostermarschierer, Ostermärtyrer', n.d.
[106] Peter Schneider, 'Wir haben Fehler gemacht', in Schneider, *Ansprachen: Reden—Notizen—Gedichte* (Berlin, 1970), 12–14.
[107] Fahlenbrach, *Protestinszenierungen*; Vogel, *Unruhe*.
[108] 'Ritus contra Deprivation', in Böckelmann and Nagel (eds), *Subversive Aktion*, 54–5.

Britain over the course of the 1960s, fundamentally because the Labour Party had never created the fundamental sense of betrayal that the West German activists had sensed with the *SPD*. The New Left, many of whom were active in CND, shared some of the Old Left's ideas, but, unlike the Old Left, supported direct action. CND, therefore, moved away from a general humanitarian towards a more socialist anti-militarist platform. Such a trend was already visible in CND's 1962–63 policy statement that argued that hunger and poverty were the 'real enemies', and that they could not be tackled while the 'reckless waste of arms race' continued.[109] CND and other groups continued to develop this theme further by applying it to the Vietnam War and racial discrimination in the United States.[110] As in West Germany, the US black power movement was attractive to some British protesters, and the origins of a British Campaign against Racial Discrimination (CARD) related directly to the ways in which activists around CND and the C100 engaged with the civil rights movement in the United States. Claudia Jones, the editor of the *West Indian Gazette* who had already taken a role in the 1962 Aldermaston March, organized a march to the American Embassy in London in March 1963 to coincide with Martin Luther King's march on Washington.[111] A number of CND activists, especially Marion Glean, a black West Indian Quaker, Michael Randle (from C100), and Theodore Roszak, the US editor of *Peace News*, played instrumental roles in setting up a meeting with King in London that led to the foundation of CARD.[112]

By the end of the 1960s, then, activists had broadened the scope of the politics of security by embedding the issue of nuclear weapons in more general deliberations about the nature of politics and society around the world: they had developed notions of the world as 'global' that incorpo-rated, but also transcended, previous visions of humanitarian bonds. Activists also accentuated their political commitment by moving from a position of acknowledging the existence of an abstract humanity that had to be preserved against the dangers of nuclear weapons towards a position that emphasized specific and concrete solidarity. Not least, protesters deepened their sense of a politics of security that was rooted not primarily in political processes and procedures, but in themselves as active subjects. They began to reflect on themselves as activists, rather than in terms of

---

[109] BLPES, CND/1/2: Policy Statement 1962–3.
[110] *Sanity* (May 1968), 4–5.
[111] Marika Sherwood, *Claudia Jones: A Biography* (London, 2000), 100–1.
[112] Benjamin W. Heineman, *The Politics of the Powerless: A Study of the Campaign against Racial Discrimination* (Oxford, 1972), 16–19.

other social bonds. Experiences had become essential for them to conceptualize their activism. Throughout the 1960s, changes in the cognitive framing of the contents of a politics of security were linked to the forms in which activists sought to express it. These transformations in the politics of security in both Britain and West Germany meant that 'peace' was no longer defined purely in terms of the absence of war and the arms race or in terms of static ideals of security. Instead, the peace activists now also included social and economic justice as well as personal well-being in the politics of security, although there was no agreement on the exact relationship between the level of politicization of the component elements.

8

Redefining Solidarity

At the International Vietnam Congress, where activists from around the world gathered in West Berlin on 17 and 18 February 1968, participants issued a declaration arguing that the 'military cooperation between the leader of the colonial counter-revolution, the United States, and West European countries, must be broken, and their agency, NATO, must be crushed'.[1] Rudi Dutschke, one the leaders and main organizers of the West German protests, had declared in his address to the Congress that a 'second front' against colonialism and war was needed in West European capitals. At other occasions, he had already called for 'true revolutionary solidarity' and argued that a 'historically open situation' existed that made it possible for activists to succeed with their active resistance to support liberation struggles in the Third World.[2] Things were no longer secure, he pointed out in a TV programme in November 1967: 'they have to be made secure by us.'[3] But at the same time, he vigorously spoke out against what he saw as 'the existing order'. 'Peace', he said, could be realized only as a 'vehement desire' against that order, and it implied an 'almost biological rejection of the total military complex that could neither guarantee peace, nor security nor happiness'.[4] Paradoxically, Dutschke also argued that 'human beings have to become constantly insecure of themselves', so that they can realize all potentialities in the world—human beings had to change, had to become different, for social and political change to be possible.[5] This was, then, the conscious attempt to create an agency of

---

[1] SDS Westberlin, Internationales Nachrichten- und Forschungsinstitut (ed.), *Internationaler Vietnam-Kongreß Februar 1968 Westberlin: Der Kampf des Vietnamesischen Volkes und die Globalisierung des Imperialismus* (Berlin, 1968), 159.

[2] Rudi Dutschke, 'Die geschichtlichen Bedingungen für den internationalen Emanzipationskampf', reprinted in Fichter and Lönnendonker, *Dutschkes Deutschland*, 205–17; Dutschke, *Mein langer Marsch: Reden, Schriften und Tagebücher aus zwanzig Jahren*, ed. Gretchen Dutschke-Klotz et al. (Reinbek, 1980), 20–1.

[3] Reprinted in Dutschke, *Mein langer Marsch*, 20.

[4] *Kursbuch*, 14 October 1967, reprinted in Dutschke, *Mein langer Marsch*, 14–15.

[5] Interview in *Der Spiegel*, 10 July 1967 and contribution to a panel discussion in Hamburg, 24 November 1967, reprinted in Dutschke, *Mein langer Marsch*, 13, 15.

solidarity. Other Western activists had already linked this explicitly to West Germany's post-war history, asserting that the liberation that had taken place in Germany from the outside in 1945 now had to be realized within West German society.[6]

Tariq Ali, the Pakistani Trotskyist who chaired the Vietnam Solidarity Campaign (VSC), was so inspired by the success of the Berlin events that he used his experiences as an argument to organize a British equivalent, plan a demonstration and attempt to occupy the American Embassy on London's Grosvenor Square. His VSC had called for 'complete solidarity with the national liberation movement in Vietnam'. He had also been heavily critical of CND's position that sought to strengthen the United Nations' role in the conflict. The UN, he argued, was part of the power structures of the international system that had to be subverted.[7] The demonstration took place on 17 March 1968 and, to many contemporary observers, seemed to turn London's street into the site of a civil war. Indeed, demonstrators employed tactics of passive resistance when trying to occupy the square and the embassy building. Some hurled stones and other objects at the police. Mounted police were even employed to disperse the protesters—the 'peaceable kingdom' seemed to have come to an end. It apparently inspired the Rolling Stones singer Mick Jagger to write his song 'Street Fighting Man'.[8]

These two episodes demonstrate that the changing relationship between political considerations and culture within British and West German extra-parliamentary politics had resulted in—and had been influenced by—different positions of the role of the international system. The movements in both countries witnessed the protesters' emancipation from the rigid binary cold war system of thinking. This went hand in hand with the realization that it was impossible to discuss the state of world affairs without speaking about 'America'. The increasing focus on events across the Atlantic had profound implications for the mutual perception of the protests, the links between them, and the ways in which they conceptualized their relationship to the world.[9] This chapter traces this transformation in the British and West German protesters' politics of security, which had

[6] Ekkehart Krippendorff, writing in the *Spandauer Volksblatt*, 14 May 1965, cited in his *Lebensfäden: Zehn autobiographische Versuche* (Nettersheim, 2012), 156.
[7] *VSC Bulletin* (April 1967), 1; Nick Thomas, 'Protests against the Vietnam War in 1960s Britain: The Relationship between Protesters and the Press', *Contemporary British History*, 22 (2008), 335–54, here 341.
[8] Tariq Ali, *Street Fighting Years: An Autobiography of the Sixties*, 2nd edn (London, 2005), 300.
[9] For a differently accentuated analysis of the same process, see Oppenheimer, 'Conflicts of Solidarity'.

profound implications for the ways in which they conceived of the subjects and objects of these politics.[10]

Over the course of the 1960s, activists moved increasingly away from positions that assumed that communists were the main danger in world politics. By April 1965, in the wake of the US invasion of the Dominican Republic and while the US war effort in the Vietnam War grew substantially, a *Sanity* editorial called President Lyndon B. Johnson's policies 'wicked, foolish and dangerous' and singled out 'Britain's grotesque subversion to Washington' for a fundamental critique.[11] Such assessments went hand in hand with the increasing realization among some activists that the war in Vietnam, the nuclear arms race, were not single issues but linked to 'American ruthlessness in seeking to maintain and increase its military and economic domination of much of the world'.[12] The International Committee for Disarmament and Peace that had emerged out of the European Federation for Nuclear Disarmament now also campaigned on an anti-Vietnam War platform, organizing meetings not only in Western Europe, but also in non-aligned countries, such as an anti-Vietnam War congress in Ljubljana from 25–28 August 1968.[13]

These changes also transformed the campaigns' relationship to each other and to the world more generally. Whereas the British and West German anti-nuclear-weapons movements had had direct relationships with each other that lay at the root of the kind of political sociability they promoted, the changing relationship between politics and culture meant that the mutual reference points had transformed. While Britain continued to be an important focus for counter-cultural developments, British and West German activists turned increasingly to the United States for inspiration. This included direct networks between activists as well as the more general inspiration activists obtained from observing the civil rights movement and the protests at universities on the other side of the Atlantic. Alongside the relationships between mainstream groups, there existed a plethora of direct links between liberation movements on both sides of the Atlantic as well as in Africa, with the black power movement perhaps being the most prominent example.[14]

---

[10] On this shift in the framing of peace protests towards 'solidarity', see Ziemann, 'A Quantum of Solace?', 372–3; Dorothee Weitbrecht, *Aufbruch in die Dritte Welt: Der Internationalismus der Studentenbewegung von 1968 in der Bundesrepublik Deutschland* (Göttingen, 2012), 15, 38–41.

[11] *Sanity* (April 1965), 1. On the debate about this shift, see the letters by Malcolm Caldwell, *Sanity* (June 1966), and by Tony Hetherington, *Sanity* (July 1966), 7.

[12] Peggy Duff, *Left, Left, Left*, 268.

[13] Klimke, *The Other Alliance*, 100.

[14] Maria Höhn and Martin Klimke, *A Breath of Freedom: The Civil Rights Struggle, African American GIs, and Germany* (Basingstoke, 2010); for 1960s Britain, this (post-)

Activists came to see their 'other alliance' with the better 'other America' as a key plank that was to challenge what they regarded as the United States' militarist dominance in the international system.[15] Throughout their 'internationalism was implicit and simply taken for granted'[16] and therefore did not require personal networks for its operation, but primarily general awareness to be part of a historical and historic movement. Protesters tried to write their own activism into what they regarded as a global movement that was linked to seeing the Third World as a political project. Thus *Black Dwarf*, the paper launched after the violent spring 1968 demonstrations by Tariq Ali and others close to Trotskyite circles and the VSC, exclaimed 'Paris, London, Rome, Berlin. We will fight. We shall win,' and they regarded these European cities as the equivalent to the fights in the Third World.[17] And even the writers of the May Day Manifesto, who sought to revive the New Left of the late 1950s from a more Western-centric angle, highlighted how their own 'ongoing experiment in development of consciousness' related to 'other revolutionary experiments in universities, communities, communes and direct action now taking place in Europe and America'.[18]

THE UNITED STATES AS THE CENTRE OF COLD WAR POLITICS

While most activists had regarded the nuclear arms race as the key symbol for the cold war, this symbolic position now pertained to the United States. While some of these assessments were already present in discussions of the late 1950s and early 1960s, they now assumed a more pivotal position. This had to do with two key transformations in the protesters' politics of security. Both had their roots in the late 1950s, but the different international climate now provided the condition that made it possible for them to be

---

colonial dimension still awaits a more thorough historical investigation. See, however, Anne-Marie Angelo, 'The Black Panthers in London, 1967–1972: A Diasporic Struggle Navigates the Black Atlantic', *Radical History Review*, 103 (2009), 17–35; Stephen Tuck, 'Malcolm X's Visit to Oxford University: US Civil Rights, Black Britain, and the Special Relationship on Race', *American Historical Review*, 118 (2013), 76–103; Ken Keable (ed.), *London Recruits: The Secret War against Apartheid* (London, 2012).

[15] Klimke, *The Other Alliance*, 7.

[16] Rowbotham, *Promise of a Dream*, 172; Vack, *Das andere Deutschland nach 1945*, 60–1.

[17] Jonathon Green, *Days in the Life: Voices from the English Underground, 1961–71* (London, 1998), 266–7.

[18] *May Day Manifesto Bulletin*, 2 (February 1968), 18.

discussed more concretely. First, with the Vietnam War, activists discussed whether US imperialism should replace European colonialism as the central subject for debates, as the search for radical alternatives to the existing world order began and the language of human rights was replaced by that of direct action. While the Marburg section of the *SDS* in particular opposed what they regarded as a move towards merely 'verbal radicalism', a general shift towards this form of campaigning nonetheless transpired.[19] But, by 1966, West German *SDS* activists passed a damning judgement on US politics and policies and stated apodictically that one could no longer argue with the United States and had to move towards more concrete forms of struggle.[20] Klaus Vack, who belonged to the first generation of Easter Marchers, accordingly remembered the protests against the Vietnam War as 'act[s] of patricide' against the United States. The Campaign for Disarmament took up the issue of the Vietnam War for fear of being sidelined by events, so that, 1965/66 saw more than 100,000 people taking the cause to the street in fourteen protest marches. Whereas descriptions of the United States had been rarely heard before, they had now become commonplace.[21]

In Britain, this shift took place, too, but it was accompanied by organizational transformations as well, which meant that 'solidarity' was unable to emerge as a master frame as it did in West Germany. CND and the British Council for Peace in Vietnam (BCPV) that was set up by a group of people close to CND had been the main campaign groups that addressed the Vietnam War until the mid-1960s. They campaigned primarily for the 'implementation of the 1954 Geneva agreements' and 'the holding of national elections in north and south Vietnam' in particular.[22] From 1966 the BCPV was overshadowed by Tariq Ali's VSC, which soon took over from CND as the main protest movement against the Vietnam War. The campaign had been inspired by the turn from civil rights issues towards anti-war protests within the US extra-parliamentary movements a year earlier.[23] Ali had good contacts with the American Students for a Democratic Society (SDS) and personally met US student leader Carl Oglesby in Croydon in 1965.[24] In spring 1966, after some Easter Marchers had ended up at the American Embassy and been arrested, they

---

[19] Frank Deppe und Kurt Steinhaus, 'Politische Praxis und Schulung im SDS', *neue kritik*, 38/9 (1966), 31–9, here 32.

[20] 'SDS Information über Vietnam und die Länder der Dritten Welt' (May 1966), 1.

[21] Quoted in Werner Balsen and Karl Rössel, *Hoch die internationale Solidarität: Zur Geschichte der Dritte-Welt-Bewegung in der Bundesrepublik* (Cologne, 1986), 129.

[22] Thomas, 'Protests against the Vietnam War', 340.

[23] MRC, MSS 189/V, box 1, file 7; MSS 149, box 5, file 2; Ali, *Street Fighting* Years, 48–9.

[24] Ali, *Street Fighting Years*, 46, 61; Taylor and Colin Pritchard, *Protest Makers*, 46–7.

sang 'We Shall Overcome', the song that had become the hymn of the US civil rights movement.[25]

Although CND activists, such as Canon Collins, had highlighted the UK's role as 'an American satellite' within NATO before, this theme now became one of the central themes of VSC campaigns.[26] This transformation had implications for the spaces of activism. The focus of protests now shifted to direct action campaigns at the highly symbolic site of the American Embassy on London's Grosvenor Square. The park in the middle of the square is the site of the memorials to President Franklin Roosevelt's commitment to the US–British alliance and the US Eagle Squadrons who helped to defend the British Isles from Nazi attack from a Lincolnshire airforce base. The memorials demonstrated UK–US cooperation in the Second World War. Protesters, by contrast, were drawn to a different symbol: the post-Second World War modernist embassy building that had been designed by the Finnish–American architect Eero Saarinen as an embodiment of American power: alongside the large golden American Eagle overlooking the square, the fence around the embassy building seemed to suggest the transition from US–UK cooperation to US domination and imperialism.[27]

Already in March 1962, protesters linked to the C100 defaced an abstract painting in an exhibition inside the embassy with the CND symbol.[28] And from March 1965, when a group of six men and one woman chained themselves to the embassy railings in protest against the Vietnam War, there were regular protests on the square, culminating in two major rallies in the spring and autumn of 1968.[29] In summer 1967, someone belonging to a 'Revolutionary Solidarity Movement' fired bullets through the windows of the American Embassy calling for the liberation of 'American negroes' and denouncing racism in the United States, which, the leaflet spelled out, amounted to fascism. In March 1968, a bomb, possibly planted by activists with links to Spanish anarchists fighting Franco's dictatorship, exploded at the American Officers' Club at Lancaster Gate.[30]

Over the course of the 1960s, the conflict between a positive picture of the 'other America' and the preponderance of power by the American government had also filtered through to less radical campaigners of the original New Left who were sceptical of the efficacy of the VSC's direct

[25] *The Times*, 13 April 1966.
[26] Driver, *The Disarmers*, 111.
[27] H. L. Malchow, *Special Relations: The Americanization of Britain?* (Stanford, CA, 2011), 48–52.
[28] *The Times*, 23 March 1962.
[29] *The Times*, 12 March, 6 April, and 18 October 1965; 19 February 1968.
[30] *The Times*, 21 August, 4 September 1967; 5 March 1968.

action campaigns and imagined more of a consciousness-raising intellectual-cum-cultural movement. The May Day Manifesto, to which Michael Barratt Brown, E. P. Thompson, Raymond Williams, Stuart Hall, and others contributed, highlights the transformation of the politics of security quite clearly. While their focus, at the beginning of the 1960s, had been the stifling nature of the cold war as a system of power and knowledge production, they now targeted a particular aspect of that system: the role of the United States as an imperial power that sought to stifle liberation projects around the world and that had a detrimental impact on British political culture in particular: 'Our practical dependence on the United States, expressed in political and military alliances, locked in financial arrangements and the penetration of our economy by United States capital, and supported, as a planned operation, by many kinds of cultural and educational colonisation, makes any attempt at disengagement a fight from the beginning.'[31] At the same time, however, they still regarded the size and strength of anti-war and civil rights campaigns on US campuses as signs of encouragement.

For many more protesters than before, the Third World was a political project and a space in which they could develop political alternatives. The Cuban Revolution and Fidel Castro's coming to power on the Caribbean island in 1959 had already opened up such a space for transformation: it had highlighted the actual and real possibility of a revolution that did not follow the Leninist model to succeed.[32] This transformation unsettled cold war dichotomies, but was also made possible by the development of superpower détente in the first half of the 1960s.[33] These insights opened British activists for a more direct engagement with developments across the Atlantic. And the 1965 Oxford teach-in against the Vietnam War was directly influenced by similar events on the West Coast of the United States.[34] US movements now became examples for British activists in different ways as well: looking across the Atlantic, British activists clarified issues of race and class that were less evident and visible at home and also adopted specific forms of community organizing based on the US example.[35]

---

[31] *New Left May Day Manifesto* (London, 1967), 1–23, 31.
[32] Ruth Glass, 'Cuba Week', *New Left Review*, 17 (1962), 3–8; J. M. Cohen, 'Culture in Cuba', *New Left Review*, 34 (1965), 78–81; 'Che Guevara', *New Left Review*, 46 (1967), 16. On local activities in West Germany, see Weitbrecht, *Aufbruch*, 253–75.
[33] Slobodian, *Foreign Front*, 50.
[34] Ali, *Street Fighting Years*, 50–1.
[35] Rowbotham, *Promise of a Dream*, 24, 57–8, 68, 85, 98–9, 122, 124–5; Ali, *Street Fighting Years*, 216.

THE TRANSFORMATION OF PRACTICES
OF PROTEST

The second opening that undergirded this shift from human rights to active solidarity was the transformation of notions and practices of activism itself: liberation struggles in the Third World became more explicit models for the anti-Vietnam War campaigns in Britain and West Germany. Liberation fighters like Che Guevara became direct examples for the ways in which campaigns should be carried out; only through struggle and fighting could security ultimately be achieved. Only by means of struggle could activists be freed from the shackles of their society and realize their sovereign self. They regarded that sovereign self as the foundation stone of the politics of security.[36] Vietnam appeared as a victim of US imperialism, and the United States was now a perpetrator. Both turned into the main symbols of the West German politics of solidarity that developed over the course of the 1960s and that transformed the politics of security: it was now necessary to attack NATO as the central offspring of global US imperialism in Western Europe, so that the 'ruling apparatus' at home could be broken, too.[37] As Quinn Slobodian's important work has demonstrated, these transformations were not merely driven by discursive shifts, but stemmed from active contact between European and non-European activists. Tariq Ali was a particularly important actor in Britain, whereas the connections between West German protesters and activists who studied in the Federal Republic and came from South Africa, Latin America, and the United States were crucial for establishing awareness there.[38]

This engagement with the extra-European world was not entirely novel. In the early 1960s, the success of the National Liberation Front in Algeria against the French colonial power had served some protesters as an indicator for the success of a socialist politics of solidarity.[39] Some activists, such as Klaus Vack, had been involved in campaigns that sought to highlight practical solidarity by going underground to help Algerian deserters, who had been drafted to fight their own countrymen in the French army, flee to West Germany in order to escape the grip of the French authorities.[40]

---

[36] Leerom Medovoi, *Rebels: Youth and the Cold War Origins of Identity* (Durham, NC, 2005), 323.

[37] Dutschke, 'Die geschichtlichen Bedingungen für den internationalen Emanzipationskampf', 213, 215–16.

[38] Slobodian, *Foreign Front*.

[39] 'Zweimal Zweite Internationale', *Sozialistische Politik*, 8 (1957), 4–5; Vack, *Das andere Deutschland nach 1945*, 59–62; Leggewie, *Kofferträger*, 109.

[40] Ruth Fischer, 'Zur Diskussion über das Problem der unterentwickelten Länder', *neue kritik*, 2 (1964), 3; Herbert Tulatz, 'Nigeria, ein afrikanisches Entwicklungsland', *neue kritik*, 2 (1964), 16.

Yet, unlike the later politics of solidarity, these efforts had been rather small scale and localized and took place in the context of more or less clandestine or at least private initiatives, rather than being shown through direct action. What was crucial for the 1960s was that more traditional anti-militarist groups also embraced these changes and began to combine anti-war rhetoric with efforts to coordinate humanitarian relief. A telling example of this was the 'Assistance Action Vietnam' (*Hilfsaktion Vietnam*) that Heinz Kloppenburg, the trade unionist Walter Fabian, August Bangel, Martin Niemöller, and Gottfried Wandersleb launched in early 1966, which sought to realize peace as a 'true task' rather than as a mere idea.[41] Many now demanded to 'transform struggle against armament into a struggle for a genuine democracy' and to recommend this as a policy to their friends in the American SDS.[42]

The shift was also, at least partly, driven by a more open engagement with ideas of activism from the 'other German state', the GDR, as détente allowed activists to discuss socialist ideas that had previously been taboo more freely. Socialism now re-emerged, after a short period in the late 1940s, as a counter model to affluent society, and its ties to Third World politics also turned this commitment to socialism into a symbol that opened up a space of resistance.[43] To many, the humanitarian commitment that the early Easter Marchers had developed now seemed hypocritical. This had fundamental consequences for the activists' relationship with the GDR—and this was true for British as well as West German protesters. Some saw the East German state as a 'communist Ersatz party' (Christoph Kleßmann), and they regarded reunification not necessarily as the fulfilment of a national agenda, but primarily as a way to realize the transition to socialism in a demilitarized united Germany that was removed from the cold war.[44]

The way in which the memorialization of the German bombing campaign on Coventry was transformed over the course of the 1960s demonstrates the changing frames of resonance especially well and highlights that these developments echoed more widely in political culture as well as the campaigns. In the early 1960s, the GDR government had been

[41] HStAD, RW338, 340: Walter Fabian and Heinz Kloppenburg, 'Die Hilfsaktion Vietnam, ihre Entstehung und Entwicklung'; Herbert Stubenrauch, 'Sittlichkeit—Gewalt—Sexualität', *zivil*, 11 (November 1966), 118–19.

[42] Note to Tom Hayden, n.d., cited in Klimke, *The Other Alliance*, 21–2.

[43] Hans-Ulrich Thamer, 'Sozialismus als Gegenmodell: Theoretische Radikalisierung und Ritualisierung einer Oppositionsbewegung', in Matthias Frese, Julia Paulus, and Karl Teppe (eds), *Demokratisierung und gesellschaftlicher Aufbruch: Die sechziger Jahre als Wendezeit in der Bundesrepublik* (Paderborn, 2003), 741–58.

[44] Cf., for example, Helmut Lindemann, 'Analyse der Deutschlandpolitik in Thesen', *neue kritik*, 25–26 October 1964, 17–23, here 22–3; *Pinx*, 7 (1967), 36.

successful in its attempt to launch a commemorative partnership on the back of the already existing commemorative efforts launched by the British and West German governments in the early 1960s. These efforts had led to plans to rebuild Coventry Cathedral.

From around 1963 onwards, the GDR took a more active interest in more directly framing the ways in which the Coventry and Dresden bombing campaigns were remembered. This came in the context of the GDR attempts to institutionalize British–GDR relations below official diplomatic channels.[45] It developed scenarios of attacks on both cities that portrayed nuclear war as a corollary of capitalism. The memory of the air war thus became part and parcel of a fight against imperialism in the cold war. While such anti-fascist and anti-imperialist arguments had already characterized the activists of the Coventry–Dresden Friendship Society that had been founded by pacifists in 1956, their resonance far beyond the confines of Coventry was novel.[46] The forms of activism linked to the commemorations also had new accents: as part of 'Operation Reconciliation', twenty-five British students travelled to Dresden in March 1965 and attempted to demonstrate their active commitment and solidarity by helping to rebuild a hospital that had been destroyed in the attack.[47] In May 1965, a number of Coventry Christians travelled to Dresden to commemorate the twenty-year anniversary of the end of the Second World War and actively help with a rebuilding effort. This followed an initiative by the historian David Irving, whose book on the destruction of Dresden had come out in 1963.[48]

PROTESTS AND ACTIVISM AS CONSCIOUS SELF-TRANSFORMATION

Many mainstream activists in the West German Easter Marches as well as those activists in the *SDS* in Marburg and Frankfurt did not adhere to an anti-authoritarian ethos, but to more traditionally socialist ideas. They

---

[45] See Stefan Berger and Norman La Porte, *Friendly Enemies: Britain and the GDR, 1949–1990* (New York, 2010), 114–48 (on general cultural relations and exchanges with MPs) and 156–66 (on churches and the peace movement).

[46] Stefan Goebel, 'Coventry und Dresden: Transnationale Netwerke der Erinnerung in den 1950er und 1960er Jahren', in Dietmar Süß (ed.), *Deutschland im Luftkrieg: Geschichte und Erinnerung* (Munich, 2007), 111–120.

[47] 'Coventry Appeal for Dresden', *The Times*, 3 November 1964; 'Dresden Bombing Atonement', *The Times*, 15 March 1965.

[48] HStAD, RW338, 340: Walter Fabian and Heinz Kloppenburg, 'Die Hilfsaktion Vietnam, ihre Entstehung und Entwicklung', and Merrilyn Thomas, *Communing with the Enemy: Covert Operations, Christianity and Cold War Politics in Britain and the GDR* (Oxford, 2005), 220–1.

continued to argue in terms of a more mainstream politics of security, while the anti-authoritarians around Rudi Dutschke and Bernd Rabehl in Berlin and those groups in Munich that adapted Situationist ideas began to conceptualize the role of solidarity with the Third World more clearly. This happened concretely as a consequence of the visit by the Congolese Prime Minister Moishe Tschombé to the Federal Republic, which, according to Dutschke, was 'our cultural revolution'.[49]

Dutschke's assessment highlights the specific ways in which the anti-authoritarian wing of the extra-parliamentary opposition successfully redefined the politics of security towards a very specific blending of cultural resistance and political demonstration. From the Tschombé demonstration onwards, activists pushed even more for a protest strategy that meant that 'authorized demonstrations must be guided into illegality. Confrontation with state power is essential and must be sought out.' Transgression for Dutschke, Rabehl, and others was more than a mere tactic. It was an 'instrument of struggle for creating consciousness' ('Kampfinstrument für Bewußtseinswerdung'), and it allowed the group around Dutschke to bring into the open the hidden powers of manipulation that determined Western societies.[50] Similarly, Jürgen Horlemann, leader of the West-Berlin *SDS*, argued against traditional demonstrations. Describing Vietnam as a 'slaughterhouse', he pointed out that 'mobilizing under liberal democratic demands did damage by preserving the semblance of tolerant civil society': it merely thickened 'the democratic veil... through the whole democratic performance of the splintering of protests, their partial placation, diversion, etc.'. The real challenge was, however, to unveil the hidden structures of power in order to destroy the roots of the arms race, war, and violence.[51]

While there were many different facets of this transformation that make it difficult to generalize, the significant characteristic of the politics of security of the later 1960s and early 1970s was that it moved towards a psychological view of society: activists began to focus on inwardness and singling out individual well-being as the fundamental condition for security, while avoiding individualism and retaining an awareness of the importance of society as a space for social action. From this perspective, demonstrations and other forms of protest turned into more than evidence

[49] Rudi Dutschke, 'Die Widersprüche des Spätkapitalismus, die antiautoritären Studenten und ihr Verhältnis zur Dritten Welt', in Uwe Bergmann et al. (eds), *Rebellion der Studenten oder die neue Opposition* (Reinbek, 1968), 33–57, 36.
[50] Dutschke, 'Widersprüche', in Bergmann et al. (eds), *Rebellion der Studenten*, 36.
[51] Jürgen Horlemann, 'Referat zum Flugblatt "Informationen über Vietnam und Länder der Dritten Welt", May 1966', in Lönnendonker and Fichter (eds), *Hochschule im Umbruch*, v. 311.

of mobilization. They assumed meaning, in a self-reflective turn, as acts of self-enlightenment on the part of the protesters and of society more generally. Within this framing of the politics of security, protesters' direct action appeared rational and emotional at the same time: only through action would protesters turn into true activists and not mere consumers of the unfolding spectacles of demonstrations; but, in order to have an effect, demonstrations themselves had to be spectacular.[52] Dutschke's 'cultural revolution' in the politics of security was, therefore, not merely about highlighting culture, as opposed to political and economic structures, as central elements. It was, fundamentally, about directing protesters' attention towards developing new forms of discussions and everyday forms of interaction and resistance that would undermine bureaucratic and military authority in society. For Dutschke, the root of the politics of security was, therefore, the individual. This also implied an increased attention to psychology and psychoanalysis amongst activists. The place of sociology as the discipline that could allow critical insights into society was supplemented by an attention to psychology and, in some sections of the movements, even turned into its substitute as a 'depersonalized sociology'.[53] The politics of security, so the argument ran, had to begin with the personal conditions for aggression. Only thus could the 'security neurosis' that Germans suffered from be overcome.[54] Security could be achieved primarily through therapy. Self-determination, self-organization, and self-activity were the key words for this new politics of security that the hedonistic left developed in the second half of the 1960s.[55] Some sections of the movement came to this position through active engagement with Christian liberation theology, where they identified face-to-face encounters and practical deeds as fundamental to political renewal.[56] As in

---

[52] Rudi Dutschke at the Hanover congress on the 'Conditions for the Organisation of Resistance', 9 June 1967, cited in Dutschke, *Mein langer Marsch* 89; APOA, 68er Interviews—Berlin, A-H: Interview with Wolfgang Fritz Haug on 27 January 1999 in Berlin.

[53] Anthony D. Kauders, 'Drives in Dispute: The West German Student Movement, Psychoanalysis, and the Search for a New Emotional Order, 1967–1971', *Central European History*, 44 (2011), 711–31, here 720.

[54] See Peter Schneider's diary entry from May/June 1967, cited in Peter Schneider, *Rebellion und Wahn: Mein '68* (Cologne, 2008), 178.

[55] Dutschke, *Mein langer Marsch*, 12; 'Rudi Dutschke zu Protokoll (Interview mit Günther Gaus, 3 December 1967)', cited from *Mein langer Marsch*, 43–4.

[56] Dagmar Herzog, 'The Death of God in West Germany: Between Secularization, Postfascism and the Rise of Liberation Theology', in Michael Geyer and Lucian Hölscher (eds), *Die Gegenwart Gottes in der modernen Gesellschaft: Transzendenz und religiöse Vergemeinschaftung in Deutschland* (Göttingen, 2006), 431–66, here 435; Annegreth Strümpfel, '"Theologie der Hoffnung—Theologie der Revolution—Theologie der Befreiung": Zur Politisierung der Theologie in den "langen sechziger Jahren" in

West Germany, but here primarily inspired by R. D. Laing, psychoanalysis also emerged within sections of the British movements as a key form of exploration of society's ills as well as a security therapy of individual souls.

The transformation of the politics of security into a politics of international solidarity with its specific resonances in each country was key for the radicalization of each movement, as it replaced humanitarian arguments based on rational calculations and statistics with expressly emotional bonds with faraway victims. It converted passive care into active solidarity. In West Germany, this transformation had a specific resonance, as it appealed to more mainstream interpretations of Germans as victims of foreign powers and connected them to the martyrdom of revolutionaries, such as Che Guevara, in the extra-European world.[57] Activists' pronounced turn to international solidarity went hand in hand with a far more explicit visual representation of suffering in the context of the politics of security. This contrasted with both the movements of the early 1960s, which had mostly shied away from showing graphic images of human death in nuclear attacks, and from representation in the mass media. For example, the BBC had officially banned Peter Watkins's film *War Game* because images of nuclear destruction were deemed too horrid to show on television.[58]

EVENTFULNESS

Actual events and the ways in which British and West German activists experienced them further accentuated the differences between the British and West German politics of security. Events had the potential to link active solidarity, the protesters' analysis of the political situation, and their experiences as activists as the basis for a politics of security and led to more sustained requests to forge stronger links between more traditional pacifists and students.[59] In West Germany, two events, in particular, heightened interpretations among activists that their cognitive framing of the politics of security was a true representation of reality: the shooting of

---

globaler Perspektive', in Klaus Fitschen et al. (eds), *Die Politisierung des Protestantismus: Entwicklungen in der Bundesrepublik Deutschland während der 1960er und 1970er Jahre* (Göttingen, 2011), 150–67.

[57] For this interpretation, see Reimann, *Dieter Kunzelmann*, 301.

[58] Tony Shaw, 'The BBC, the State and Cold War Culture: The Case of Televison's *The War Game* (1965)', *English Historical Review*, 121 (2006), 1351–84.

[59] HStAD, RW 115 200/25: August Bangel to SDS, 25 November 1965.

the protester Benno Ohnesorg by a Berlin policeman on 2 June 1967, and the attack on Rudi Dutschke on 11 April 1968 by a paranoid *Bild* reader that left Dutschke with a severe brain injury, were critical for the perception that a politics from below was the only possible response to a state that now appeared as a violent enemy. Activists also interpreted these events as vivid illustrations of what would happen if the emergency legislation were indeed introduced and implemented. It seemed to show the state of emergency in action, which did not leave protesters much time for reaction. Several activists recount how the events on 2 June 1967 lent reality to their theoretical perceptions that West Germany had become a 'fascist' state.[60] 'Comrades! We don't have much time left. In Vietnam, we, too, are crushed [*zerschlagen*] day by day . . . It primarily depends on our will how this period of history will end.'[61] Dutschke's and Krahl's arguments in September 1967 that any creation of security in terms of non-violence would have to start with radical steps to create the conditions for a non-violent society therefore received additional plausibility: the prevention of emergency laws would only paper over attention to the structural conditions in advanced capitalism.[62]

Activists' interpretations of the West German protests as a contestation between democracy and authoritarianism, between activist victims and the all-powerful government machine, meant that a dynamic could emerge that interpreted the Ohnesorg shooting and the attack on Dutschke as the real manifestations of what activists perceived as state violence. The percolation of phantasies of violence in West Germany society as a whole in the wake of the attacks heightened this frame of reference further: the direct action strand of the politics of security contributed to this dynamic of massive perceived insecurities. The Springer press published articles and letters to the editor that imagined bloodbaths against the protesters, and Rudi Dutschke received hundreds of letters with death threats that expressed these feelings.[63] Nonetheless, Dutschke himself,

[60] APOA, Nordrhein-Westfalen, Bonn folder: Volker Rohde, 'Kuratorium Notstand der Demokratie Bonn', *Notstandsinformation*, 1, n.d. (*c.* June 1967); Helmut Lethen, *Suche nach dem Handorakel. Ein Bericht* (Göttingen 2012), 108–9; Schneider, *Rebellion und Wahn*, 192; cf. the analysis of conspiracies and counter conspiracies in Nick Thomas, *Protest Movements in 1960s West Germany. A Social History of Dissent and Democracy* (Oxford, 2003), ch. 10 and Hanshew, *Terror and Democracy*, 88–107.
[61] Dutschke, 'Die geschichtlichen Bedingungen für den internationalen Emanzipationskampf', 216.
[62] Rudi Dutschke and Hans-Jürgen Krahl, 'Das Sich-Verweigern fordert Guerilla Mentalität (Organisationsreferat auf der 22. Delegiertenkonferenz des SDS, September 1967', in Rudi Dutschke, *Geschichte ist machbar: Texte über das herrschende Falsche und die Radikalität des Friedens*, ed. Jürgen Miermeister (Berlin, 1992), 89–95, here 91.
[63] *Briefe an Rudi D.*, ed. Stefan Reisner, Voltaire Flugschrift, 19 (Berlin, 1968); Dutschke, *Mein langer Marsch*, 123–37.

Herbert Marcuse, and Oskar Negt developed their own phantasies of violence by equating the power of the law with real physical violence, and by broadening their understanding of violence to encompass not merely direct physical injuries but potentially all forms of power relationships within society.[64] This further deepened activists' understandings of solidarity with the Third World, as they now regarded themselves as equivalent to Third World revolutionaries who were subject to state violence. In this context, Ohnesorg became a martyr who symbolized this victimhood.[65] This led to what Quinn Slobodian has called 'corpse polemics', whereby Third World activism was 'transformed into speechless and mutilated bodies', as protesters sought to heighten their own sense of agency.[66] Oskar Negt recognized the dynamic potential within this novel semantics of violence when he commented sarcastically on the conditions that made the attack on Ohnesorg possible, alluding to the so-called pudding attack against US Vice-President Hubert H. Humphrey on 2 April 1967 that a few members of *Kommune I* carried out: while pointing to the 'state apparatus with its compact forms of violence', he excoriated the mainstream press for 'turning pudding into knives' and thereby creating the conditions of possibility of real violence.[67]

As in West Germany, spring and summer 1967 in Britain saw the 'lightning crackling behind the sunshine of the psychedelic movement'.[68] Two of the largest demonstrations in Britain since the Chartist movement in the nineteenth century took place on 17 March and 27 October 1968, with 10,000 and 20,000 protesters appearing respectively. When the occupation of the American Embassy on Grosvenor Square in March 1968 led to clashes between protesters and police, no comparable interpretative frame existed that would have enabled British protesters to see themselves as the victims of an authoritarian government.[69] This did not mean that the British police was necessarily less brutal than its West German counterparts, or that no violence occurred at the demonstrations.

---

[64] See, for example, Oskar Negt, 'Politik und Gewalt' [speech in Frankfurt/Main, 13 April 1968], *neue kritik*, 47 (1968), 10–23; Negt, 'Strategie der Gegengewalt', *Die Zeit*, 26 April 1968, 4.

[65] Klaus Vack, cited in Balsen and Rössel, *Hoch die internationale Solidarität*, 181; 'Die Studenten', *Arbeitskreis Hannoverischer Kriegsdienstverweigerer DFG IDK VK* (August 1967), 1–2.

[66] Slobodian, *Foreign Front*, 135; Otto Köhler, 'Kongo-Müller oder die Freiheit die wir verteidigen', *Pardon* (February 1967), 33.

[67] Oskar Negt, 'Benno Ohnesorg ist das Opfer eines Mordanschlags', *Frankfurter Rundschau*, 12 June 1967; Sara Hakemi, *Anschlag und Spektakel: Flugblätter der Kommune I, Erklärungen von Ensslin/Baader und der frühen RAF* (Bochum, 2008).

[68] Jeff Nuttall, *Bomb Culture* (London, 1968), 69.

[69] Paul Baker, 'Portrait of a Protest', *New Society*, 318, 31 October 1968, 631–4.

The tabloid *Sun* developed phantasies of violence similar to the ones endorsed by the West German Springer press, evoking scenes of public disorder in the 1930s. Violence was, its journalist wrote, 'the horror that comes with something akin to mass hysteria and leaves in its wake a trail of battered bodies, pummelled and trampled and kicked and bruised and bloodied in the countless "incidents" which leave a nasty taste in the mouth'.[70] But, after the October demonstrations that went more or less peacefully, interpretations changed and painted a far less radical picture of the protests, writing them into the *longue durée* of British history, focusing on their counter-cultural components rather than political meanings and thus pacifying them.[71] *The Guardian* had already set the tone in March 1968 by asking whether 'the British student' was a 'democrat' or merely a 'layabout' and identified a small minority as politically committed radicals who were bent on using violence.[72] The VSC nonetheless declared the October demonstration a victory: 'that the demonstration did not become a riot was due to the fact that the authorities conceded our right to occupy the whole street unhindered.'[73]

The recollections of British protesters, therefore, had an air of playfulness, of the ritual cat-and-mouse game between protesters and authorities, which West German activists would have been hard pushed to evoke. Manchester student Dave Clark's testimony about his participation in the violent March 1968 protests in Ronald Fraser's oral history of 1968 is, in its difference from the West German sources collected in the same volume, remarkable. He recalls how he and a fellow demonstrator tried to drag a police horse to the ground:

We had worked out in advance how it could be done. There were theories around that lion's dung would scare police horses, and there was even an expedition planned to Manchester zoo to get some. But I and a bloke from Sheffield University planned that, as the horse charged, one of us on each side would grab the reins and pull down...After we'd done it the police went absolutely barmy, and I took a real beating from their fists, knees and boots.[74]

[70] *The Sun*, 18 March 1968; Thomas, 'Protests against the Vietnam War', 342; on parallels with the inter-war period, see Tony Aldgate, 'The Newsreels, Public Order and the Projection of Britain', in James Curran, Anthony Sith, and Pauline Wingate (eds), *Impacts and Influences: Essays on Media Power in the Twentieth Century* (London, 1987), 145–56.
[71] See Thomas, 'Protests against the Vietnam War', 341–9.
[72] *The Guardian*, 7 March 1968; Thomas, 'Protests against the Vietnam War', 351.
[73] 'Editorial', *VSC Bulletin*, 19 November 1968, 1; Thomas, 'Protests against the Vietnam War', 349.
[74] Fraser (ed.), *1968*, 161–2.

Protests at some British universities continued into 1969, and some, like Warwick and Sheffield, saw their main protest activities only in the 1970s. One of the most spectacular protests at an institution that had already been the focus of student unrest earlier was the decision on 24 January 1969 by the LSE to build iron fences in order to protect its buildings against an occupation by students who wanted more direct representation in the School's governance. The LSE had to close for a month after a contested vote ended with 242 in favour of more action and 236 students against, with 76 abstentions.[75]

But there were no 'critical events' (Pierre Bourdieu) similar to the ones in West Germany in Britain. The actual protest movement was smaller and, more importantly, the mass media did not consistently identify the individual protest events as part of a larger movement. Protesters' understanding of their activism therefore found little resonance in British political culture at large. Not least, the different relationship between culture and politics in the multiple movements in Britain meant that the Situationist idea of regarding protests as performances, on which the assessment of an event as 'critical' rested, was far less plausible to activists in Britain than it was in West Germany. Most British activists around the various campaigns agreed on defining 'revolution as a way of life', and thus continued to emphasize local cultural projects in the politics of security.[76] In West Germany, by contrast, the eventfulness of 1967 and 1968 meant that it took until the 1970s for this turn towards a conceptualization of politics as one primarily defined by cultural projects to take hold.[77] Activists could now look back and consider their individual activism as part of 'the collective "we" of the movement'.[78]

[75] Ralf Dahrendorf, *LSE. A History of the London School of Economics and Political Science 1895–1995* (Oxford, 1995), 465–6; Helen Mathers, *Steel City Scholars. The Centenary History of the University of Sheffield* (London, 2005), 251–7; E. P. Thompson, *Warwick University Ltd.* (Harmondsworth, 1970).

[76] David Fernbach, 'Strategy and Struggle', *New Left Review*, 53 (1969), 41.

[77] Autorenkollektiv 19, 'Beitrag zur Organisationsdebatte (I)', in Lutz Schulenburg (ed.), *Das Leben ändern, die Welt verändern! 1968. Dokumente und Berichte* (Hamburg, 1998), 433–6, here 433.

[78] Anna von der Goltz, 'Generations of 68ers: Age-Related Constructions of Identity and Germany's "1968"', *Cultural and Social History*, 8 (2011), 473–90, here 477.

Epilogue: Redefining Experiences

The dynamic interaction between events and the ways West German and British activists made sense of them was the condition that made it possible for activists to gain novel experiences of the cold war, and to reinterpret their agency. But British and West German developments differed in terms of the concrete links that activists made between their broader counter-cultural engagements and their political activism. This had consequences for the ways in which activists reflected upon their activism and developed their experiences from the end of the events around 1968 to the 1970s.

In West Germany, the specific dynamics between international relations, concrete events, and activism lent the cognitive framework that linked an international politics of security with questions of the concrete forms of democracy, and the cultural practices that accompanied it added plausibility. In fact, it was primarily because of the unifying force of the events of 1967 and early 1968 that the diverse plurality of groupings that had emerged around the Easter March movement could be held together in one movement as an 'extra-parliamentary opposition': the lines between protesters and authorities appeared to be clearly drawn, and the Nazi past of some of the key players, such as Chancellor Kurt Georg Kiesinger, gave added relevance to an interpretation of the present that was fearful of the return of the Nazi past. In February 1967, the activist Helmut Schauer, in a paper distributed amongst Easter March activists, therefore, argued for a thoroughly new form of opposition that lay completely out of the left/right divisions of organizational politics, in particular because the *SPD* had stopped being a reliable partner for any politics aiming at furthering 'democratic and progressive tendencies'.[1] Accordingly, the Easter March in 1968 already happened without the traditional public announcement in the winter. Instead, the Easter March committee developed an explicitly political platform that was discussed at a separate gathering in

---

[1] HIS, TEM 400, 05: Helmut Schauer, 'Arbeitsthesen über die Probleme der Opposition', Easter March Central Committee, minutes, 18–19 February 1967.

Essen in January 1968. There, those activists who had long argued for a politics of security that combined attention to international relations and domestic issues formally won the day: it was decided to rename the 'Easter Marches—Campaign for Disarmament' as 'Campaign for Democracy and Disarmament'.[2] There was, however, no agreement about how to take these general principles forward. The *SDS* activist K. D. Wolff argued for an explicitly anti-parliamentary politics, whereas Klaus Meschkat, a member of the Republican Club, argued in favour of a model of *Räte-demokratie*, a form of democracy from below through delegated councillors modelled upon the workers' and soldiers' councils of the early twentieth century.[3] For some activists, the events around 1968 brought experiences of personal insecurity and fear—for example, because their personal relationships broke down, as they committed themselves fully to political campaigning: the complete merger between politics and private emotion therefore left little space for intimacy. The result was a yearning for the warmth of personal belonging and community.[4]

Britain, where the boundaries of the political were already less starkly drawn in the early 1960s, did not see the same kind of productive and public merger of culture and politics around a single movement, while the British politics of security saw essentially the same developments as the West German movement—a pluralization of groupings, together with a sustained and intensive discussion about the relationship between politics and culture. Although 1967 and 1968 were similarly eventful, and although many activists engaged constructively and adapted the cognitive frameworks of their European and especially West German counterparts, the protests remained seemingly localized: no single frame emerged that could have tied these different strands together by making the issues under discussion more generally relevant politically. The discussions about student participation in university government, though often seen as a general trend, still remained by and large issues that mattered differently for different institutions.[5] And, although some commentators linked the local protests to a larger pattern of protests worldwide, the seeming peacefulness of the events of 1967–68 appeared to corroborate interpretations that British developments were peculiar: protests had not led to a breakdown of public order, and there was a relative lack of violence. This

[2] HIS, TEM 400,05: Easter March Central Committee, minutes, 16–17 September 1967; *Extradienst*, 17 January 1968, 3–4.

[3] Cited in *apo/IZA*, 54 (1968), 11, 12.

[4] Citing from his diary: Schneider, *Rebellion und Wahn*, 13, 285. Cf. also Lethen, *Handorakel*, 75.

[5] Nick Thomas, 'Challenging Myths of the 1960s: The Case of Student Protest in Britain', *Twentieth Century British History*, 13 (2002), 277–97.

encouraged a framing of protests as primarily local and worked against a sustained framing, by the mass media, of these protests as part of a larger social movement.

Unlike in West Germany, most British protests in the 1960s unfolded not within a national political frame of reference, but within the remit of university-specific issues. It was therefore possible for each strand to 'keep reinventing itself at the grass roots without ever becoming effectively integrated into wider political alliances'.[6] The first protests broke out at the London School of Economics (LSE) in 1966 when the school announced that Walter Adams, who had been director of University College, Rhodesia, and had backed the apartheid regime at his home institution, would become the new director of the school. This happened without proper consultation of the student body, so that issues of intra-university democracy were linked to issues of the lingering imperialism of British politics and culture.[7]

Students at the LSE drew parallels with the Berkeley sit-ins in 1964, and the presence of Marshall Bloom at the LSE, an American student who had been involved in the US civil rights movement, helped to cement these networks more tangibly.[8] Over the course of 1968, student protests also took place at Sussex, where fifty students burned a US flag. Moreover, there was a sit-in at Leeds 'against the visit of the right-wing conservative MP Patrick Wall' to the campus, and students at Oxford occupied the Clarendon Building.[9] Similarly, around 500 students occupied the administration building at Hull, and a number of students came out to heckle Secretary of Defence Denis Healey when he visited Cambridge University. Leicester and Hornsey Arts School also saw protests.[10] The VSC organized a number of increasingly violent demonstrations in London over the course of 1967 and 1968 to respond to the escalation and intensification of the US war effort. Some 5,000 people attended the rally on 2 July 1967, and there were thirty-one arrests after small-scale

[6] Alistair J. Reid, 'The Dialectics of Liberation: The Old Left, the New Left and the Counter-Culture', in David Feldman and Jon Lawrence (eds), *Structures and Transformations in Modern British History* (Cambridge, 2011), 261–80, here 280.

[7] See the overview in Ralf Dahrendorf, *LSE: A History of the London School of Economics and Political Science 1895–1995* (Oxford, 1995), 443–71; Tessa Blackstone et al., *Students in Conflict: L.S.E. in 1967* (London, 1970).

[8] Ben Brewster and Alexander Cockburn, 'Revolt at the LSE', *New Left Review*, 43 (May–June 1967), 11–25.

[9] *The Times*, 4 May 1968, 1; Nick Thomas, 'Challenging Myths of the 1960s: The Case of Student Protest in Britain', *Twentieth Century British History*, 13 (2002), 277–97, here 284.

[10] David Triesman, 'Essex', *New Left Review*, 50 (July–August 1968), 70–2; Tom Fawthrop, 'Hull', *New Left Review*, 50 (July–August 1968), 59–64; *The Times*, 8 and 9 March 1968.

fights with the police.[11] Another demonstration took place on 22 October that attracted between 4,000 and 8,000 protesters with forty-seven arrests made.[12] The largest and most violent protest took place in front of the American Embassy in London on 17 March 1968 and was inspired directly by a similar protest in West Berlin a few weeks before.[13] Of the 10,000–20,000 activists, 300 were arrested, and thirty-six were injured by baton charges and mounted police.[14] Protesters themselves noted the variety of aims behind the façade of the anti-Vietnam War protests in London in spring and autumn 1968, and some were worried to be seen as making common cause with violent factions within the movement.[15] Media representations of the protests worked further to diminish such an interpretation: unlike in West Germany or in the United States, the mass media did not interpret the British protests as part of a global revolution. Rather, they diagnosed a spot of 'me-too-ism' among British students, who were merely 'looking for a grievance' to protest against.[16]

The anti-imperialist theme never developed into a master frame for all protests, as debates at the arts schools at Hornsey and Guildford focused on student representation and specific conditions at those institutions, whereas discussions at Hull and Essex tried to connect a generally anti-imperialist agenda with specific local issues.[17] In May 1968, for example, a group of Essex students disrupted lectures by T. A. Inch, a specialist in germ warfare, in order to highlight the 'militarization' of British universities and demonstrate how British research might be related to the conduct of the Vietnam War.[18]

Given that they could not develop a common framing of their activities, the protests remained more or less isolated incidents that could not generate a general thrust or momentum. Another factor was that activists continued to be, on balance, less sceptical towards party politics, with most of them still supporters of the Labour Party.[19] Not least, there was no fundamental sense, as there existed in West Germany, among extra-parliamentary protesters that Harold Wilson's policies of technocratic

[11] *VSC Bulletin*, 6 (July–August 1967), 1.
[12] Thomas, 'Myths', 289.
[13] Ali, *Street fighting Years*, 239–46.
[14] *The Guardian*, 18 March 1968, 1, 3.
[15] MRC, MSS 21/3369/29: October 27 Ad Hoc Committee, 'Briefing to all Demonstrators: "Street Power"' [printed leaflet].
[16] *The Guardian*, 10 June 1968, 8.
[17] Lisa Tickner, *Hornsey 1968: The Art School Revolution* (London, 2008).
[18] Triesman, 'Essex', 70–1.
[19] *Student Demonstrations: A Gallup Poll Inquiry with Students at two Universities, Cambridge and Sussex, Undertaken for the Daily Telegraph Magazine* (May 1968), questions 8 and 9.

planning would lead to the establishment of an authoritarian regime that would violate the viability of democracy and the moral integrity of the individual: Britain's lack of a recent authoritarian (albeit not necessarily unblemished) past and the lack of a simultaneous sustained discussion of the militarization of British society in the context of emergency legislation worked against the emergence of such a framework of interpretation.[20] The dynamics of events in Britain worked further against a more large-scale mobilization. The protests in May 1968 appeared to indicate to British activists that demonstrations could be a powerful means for overthrowing the political system. But this motivation occurred at a time when the French movement was already in decline, so that it could provide no further inspiration.[21]

Some British activists interpreted this seeming lack of a movement as an expression of political apathy: 'virtually all intelligent and worthwhile debate . . . still takes place among relatively small groups in an atmosphere of comparative privacy.'[22] Others, like E. P. Thompson, reacted by using the standard tropes of cultural critique and by classifying the transformation of the politics of security away from more expressly political aims as 'psychic self-mutilation . . . self-absorbed, self-inflating and self-dramatising. *Very* like Methodist revivalism.'[23] Some reacted by wishing to awaken students' revolutionary consciousness. By the mid-1960s, there were still thousands of activists in the revolutionary left who looked for socio-economic roots of the arms race.[24] Factions such as the International Marxist Group (IMG) replaced the metaphysics of labour with an emphasis on students as 'the new revolutionary vanguard'.[25] Accordingly, IMG activists joined some *New Left Review* activists in establishing the Revolutionary Socialist Students' Federation (RSSF) in June 1968 in order to instil the spontaneity of student activism with some revolutionary consciousness.[26]

---

[20] Sylvia Ellis, '"A Demonstration of British Good Sense?" British Student Protest during the Vietnam War', in Gerard J. de Groot (ed.), *Student Protest: The Sixties and after* (London, 1998), 54–69. Cf., by contrast, 'Notstand—Ende aller Sicherheit', *Der Spiegel*, 11 April 1966, 37–61.

[21] Sheila Rowbotham, *Woman's Consciousness, Man's World* (Harmondsworth, 1973), 24.

[22] *Ripple*, 12 January 1967, 3, cited from Thomas, 'Myths', 282.

[23] In a letter to Sheila Rowbotham in March 1968, cited in Rowbotham, *Promise of a Dream*, 169.

[24] John Callaghan, *The Far Left in British Politics* (Oxford, 1987); Avishai Zvi Ehrlich, 'The Leninist Organisations in Britain and the Student Movement 1966–1972' (PhD, University of London, 1981), especially 52.

[25] *Black Dwarf*, 5 July 1968, 1; *Black Dwarf*, 15 October 1968, 1; Gareth Stedman Jones, 'The Meaning of the Student Revolt', in Alexander Cockburn and Robin Blackburn (eds), *Student Power: Problems, Diagnosis, Action* (Harmondsworth, 1969), 25–56.

[26] Cf. Marcus Collins and Willie Thompson, 'The Revolutionary Left and the Permissive Society', in Marcus Collins (ed.), *The Permissive Society and its Enemies: Sixties British Culture* (London, 2007), 155–68.

Hence, when activists in Britain reflected on their experiences in extra-parliamentary politics after 1968, they did not see a future determined by a series of social movements in key areas. Instead, they argued, like the authors of the May Day Manifesto (with contributions from Michael Barratt Brown, Raymond Williams, and others) that was written by a number of New Left activists in 1968: 'The key to our future, I firmly believe, is the extension of politics beyond the routines of the parliamentary process, as CND, more than any other movement has already shown to be possible.'[27] Thus, the key idea to come out of the British politics of security was to try to implement the kinds of politics that the New Left had started in the early 1960s.[28]

But by spring 1969, the 'euphoria of May '68 had metamorphosed into "the past"', and the memory of the experiences of the late 1960s became a driving force for the campaigns of the 1970s.[29] Activists sought to do this by working in local campaigns to fight poverty or to work for affordable housing in the big cities, campaigns that were coordinated by the national convention of the left that was set up in April 1969. The most significant of these new departures was, however, a regrouping of the feminist movement, and the emergence of gay and lesbian activism: as women participated in the politics of culture over the course of the 1960s and gradually discovered their selfhood, they also became aware of the gendered structure of extra-parliamentary politics where they were responsible for specifically female tasks, such as typing, cooking, and some of the organizational work, but were more or less ignored by their male counterparts when they wished to participate in discussions about ideology and strategy.

These moves, especially among feminists and gay activists, sought to redefine the politics of security in terms of a politics of individual liberation as the root for societal transformation. In Britain, whereas many previous campaigns had posited a model of society that was characterized by a dialectic between the socio-economic base and the political and ideological superstructure, these movements now argued, following the psychological insights of R. D. Laing and others and reflecting on the new culture of subjectivity in counter-culture that had emerged over the course

[27] Cited in Alan O'Connor, *Raymond Williams: Writing, Culture, Politics* (London, 1989), 20.
[28] Fred Inglis, *Raymond Williams* (London, 1995), 196–209; John Davis and Anette Waring, 'Living Utopia. Communal Living in Denmark and Britain', *Cultural and Social History*, 8 (2012), 513–30, especially 520–4.
[29] Rowbotham, *Promise of a Dream*, 224; on the variety of movements in Britain, see Adam Lent, *British Social Movements since 1945: Sex, Colour, Peace and Power* (Basingstoke, 2002).

of the 1960s, that individual and society were superimposed upon, and read through, one other. Therapeutic activism was now the appropriate form of politics, prompting individuals to analyze how enmeshed they were both structurally and ideologically within the structures of power and violence in their society.[30] The movements that emerged in Britain from the 1960s were, therefore, no longer campaigns or pressure groups, but worked primarily in the cultural field.

In West Germany, the period after 1968 saw the break-up of the extra-parliamentary opposition. The events alone could no longer conceal the growing rifts between the different sections of the movement.[31] In October 1969, the former socialist Willy Brandt, who had to flee Nazi Germany and take exile in Norway, became the first social democrat to lead the federal government in West Germany. Although most activists had not reconciled themselves with the *SPD*, Brandt's election and his commitment, expressed in his inaugural address, to 'dare more democracy' made interpretations of a gradual re-Nazification of West German politics implausible.[32]

As the organizational coherence had already suffered before 1967, there now emerged a plethora of small groups that sought to continue the work of the sections of the extra-parliamentary opposition.[33] The most tangible effect was the growth of a women's movement when, at the Federation's 23rd delegate conference in September 1968, Helke Sander put forward a fundamental critique of the male structure of authority within the *SDS*. Hans-Jürgen Krahl, who chaired the discussion, simply ignored her. When Sander hurled six tomatoes at him, calling him a counter-revolutionary, a separate women's caucus was formed. This was the origins of the West German women's movement.[34]

What united all these groupings was that they rested on a novel conception of the political: the creation of spaces that enabled critical thinking and action. Politics itself now appeared to be both a productive process

---

[30] R. D. Laing, 'The Obvious', in David Cooper (ed.), *Dialects of Liberation* (Harmondsworth, 1968), 13–33; Lucy Robinson, 'Three Revolutionary Years: The Impact of the Counter Culture on the Development of the Gay Liberation Movement in Britain', *Cultural and Social History*, 3 (2006), 445–71, here 455.

[31] *Extradienst*, 17 January 1968, 3–4.

[32] On the Brandt government's democratic agenda, see Bernd Faulenbach, *Das sozialdemokratische Jahrzehnt: Von der Reformeuphorie zur Neuen Unübersichtlichkeit: Die SPD 1969–1982* (Bonn, 2011), 39–79.

[33] Rainer Paris, 'Der kurze Atem der Provokation', *Kölner Zeitschrift für Soziologie und Sozialpsychologie*, 41 (1989), 33–52.

[34] Kristina Schulz, *Der lange Atem der Provokation: Die Frauenbewegung in der Bundesrepublik und in Frankreich 1968–1976* (Frankfurt/Main, 2002), 81; Sarah Haffner, 'Die Kunst als Weg zu sich selbst', in Ute Kätzel (ed.), *Die 68erinnen: Porträt einer rebellischen Frauengeneration* (Berlin, 2002), 141–60, here 151.

and a process of production, where the representation of experiences rather than political opinions was paramount.[35] Spaces here were not merely geographical locations, but also relational networks between people.[36] The Young Socialists' 1969 slogan 'Don't leave politics to the politicians' summed up this sentiment.[37] In their very different ways, these groupings carried the ethico-political objectives that had driven the Easter Marchers into the 1970s. While some organizations, such as the Red Army Faction and some hard-core communist groups, sought to develop revolutionary and even violent forms of bonding, most of these groups advocated ideals of authenticity and autonomous life forms as key.[38] They focused on practices of living together in the present, rather than on creating the conditions where this might happen after a revolutionary transformation of society.[39] For example, a movement sprang up to organize children's nurseries away from the churches and the state sector in order to practise such novel ways of engagement from early childhood. First tried out spontaneously at the West Berlin International Vietnam Congress in 1968, the movement is an especially good example of this transformation towards framings and conceptualizations of democracy as a form of 'intimacy'. Till van Rahden has identified this transformation as a key shift in the culture of politics in post-war West Germany.[40] The *Sozialistisches Büro* (*SB*, Socialist Office) is one of the clearest examples for this redefinition of the political within the politics of security. The *SB* had come out of attempts by a group of Easter March organizers and activists with socialist youth movement backgrounds, such as Klaus Vack, Herbert Stubenrauch, Heiner Halberstadt, Arno Klönne, and Christel Beilmann. The group sought to redefine the ground on which extra-parliamentary politics would take place after the Easter March movement had been abandoned following the last marches over Easter 1969. In July 1970, these activists therefore agreed to dissolve the central Easter March committee and create a

---

[35] 'Kurzprotokoll über die Sitzung des Zentralen Ausschusses der KfDA', 29–30 June 1968, 2, cited in Otto (ed.), *APO*, 357.

[36] Ingrid Gilcher-Holtey, *1968: Eine Zeitreise* (Frankfurt/Main, 2008), 100–2; Oskar Negt, *Achtundsechzig: Politische Intellektuelle und die Macht* (Göttingen, 2001), 158.

[37] Johano Strasser, *Als wir noch Götter waren im Mai: Erinnerungen* (Munich, 2007), 129–30.

[38] Andreas Buro, *Gewaltlos gegen den Krieg:. Lebenserinnerungen eines Pazifisten* (Frankfurt/Main, 2011), 127–8.

[39] Sven Reichhardt and Detlef Siegfried, 'Das Alternative Milieu. Konturen einer Lebensform', in Reichhardt and Siegfried (eds), *Das Alternative Milieu: Antibürgerlicher Lebensstil und linke Politik in der Bundesrepublik Deutschland und Europa 1968–1983* (Göttingen, 2010), 9–24.

[40] Berliner Kinderläden, *Antiautoritäre Erziehung und sozialistischer Kampf*, 2nd edn (Cologne, 1970) 15–17; for the general context, see Rahden, 'Clumsy Democrats'.

new forum for a range of different forms of political engagement.[41] As protest activity had moved elsewhere, the Aldermaston Marches in Britain took place in a different format in 1964 and 1965 and were then discontinued. They were revived again in 1972 in the context of campaigns for a final US withdrawal from Vietnam.

Such an 'organization' was no longer oriented towards creating an efficient mass base for revolutionary transformation, but instead provided a loose *forum* for exchanges and encounters that would allow the free discussion of different social and political interests from below and outside bureaucratic routines and restrictions. Its focus was not on creating a collective *identity* of interests. Instead, it was to provide a space from which a 'political morality of action' could be realized—and where Max Weber's distinction between an 'ethics of responsibility', as practised by politicians in the context of governmental bureaucracies, and an 'ethics of intention', as practised by those who wanted to do good outside these restrictions, were no longer opposed to each other. Instead, activists began to conceptualize these two ideal types as two sides of the same coin, as they reflected on the ways in which they quite literally produced their politics and as the form of organization would reflect the moral intentions—the self-organized politics from below was, therefore, both the form of this new politics, but also its main moral and political purpose. Instead of trying to channel experiences through an organization, groups such as the *SB*, wanted to accept experiences as given and deal creatively with their plurality.[42] Such groups became part of one densely networked milieu, with 11,500 alternative projects existing across West Germany by the early 1980s.[43] Within these groups, the cipher '1968' became a code through which the former activists could discuss the meaning of their activism as well as their experiences of hopes and disappointments in achieving security.[44]

In Britain and West Germany, the politics of security had now come full circle. It now encompassed both international relations and issues of

---

[41] Letter cited in Vack, 'Versuch, Geschichte und Erfahrung darzustellen: Mehr als biographische Daten, weniger als eine Lebensgeschichte', in Komitee für Grundrechte und Demokratie (ed.), *Tradition heißt nicht, Asche aufheben, sondern die Flamme am Brennen ehalten!* (Sensbachtal, 1985), 151–225, here 194. On the historical genealogies of these debates, see the pathbreaking study by Karrin Hanshew, *Terror and Democracy in West Germany* (Cambridge, 2012), ch. 4.

[42] Oskar Negt, *Keine Demokratie ohne Sozialismus: Über den Zusammenhang von Politik, Geschichte und Moral* (Frankfurt/Main, 1976), 11, 300–12.

[43] Sven Reichhardt and Detlef Siegfried, 'Das Alternative Milieu. Konturen einer Lebensform', in Reichhardt and Siegfried (eds), *Das Alternative Milieu*, 11.

[44] Detlev Claussen, 'Chiffre 68', in Dietrich Harth and Jan Assmann (eds), *Revolution und Mythos* (Frankfurt/Main, 1992), 219–28; Wolfgang Kraushaar, *1968 als Mythos, Chiffre und Zäsur* (Hamburg, 2000).

social security, as well as security against terrorists and personal security. The former activists had begun their 'long march through the institutions' in which they tried to make 'subversive use of the contradictions and possibilities in and outside the state–social apparatus as a whole, in order to destroy it within a long process'.[45] Yet, state institutions reacted by developing broader notions of security that resembled those of the activists by resting on perceptions of selfhood and on self-control.[46] In the guise of 'human security', such ideas are used in the early twenty-first century to justify military interventions outside Europe in the name of 'humanitarian' values and goals.[47] The mass violence and the bombing warfare of the Second World War were no longer the key reference points for comprehending the cold war arms race. Attention had now shifted towards one key feature of the cold war: the United States. It appeared to be the root cause for the origins and continuation of the cold war, and the use of its military highlighted the real violence of the cold war. From this perspective, the United States *was* the cold war. The multiple endings of the politics of security that had begun in 1945 in the shadow of the violence of the Second World War were also new beginnings.

[45] Dutschke, *Mein langer Marsch*, 22–3; Belinda Davis, 'Jenseits von Terror und Rückzug: Die Suche nach politischem Spielraum und Strategien im Westdeutschland der siebziger Jahre', in Klaus Weinhauer, Jörg Requate, and Heinz-Gerhard Haupt (eds), *Terrorismus in der Bundesrepublik: Medien, Staat und Subkulturen in den siebziger Jahren* (Frankfurt/Main, 2006), 154–86.

[46] Holger Nehring, 'The Era of Non-Violence: "Terrorism" in West German, Italian and French Political Culture, 1968–1982', *European Review of History*, 14 (2007), 343–71; Christoph Gusy and Gerhard Nitz, 'Vom Legitimationswandel staatlicher Sicherheitsfunktionen', in Hans-Jürgen Lange (ed.), *Kontinuitäten und Brüche: Staat, Demokratie und Innere Sicherheit in Deutschland* (Leverkusen, 1999), 335–54.

[47] Christopher Daase, 'Sicherheitskultur: Ein Konzept zur interdisziplinären Erforschung politischen und sozialen Wandels', *Sicherheit und Frieden*, 29 (2011), 59–65.

Conclusion

In his essay on *Bomb Culture*, the British cultural critic Jeff Nuttall contrasted the European and the Japanese post-war: 'The world of the European victory was a brown, smelly, fallible, lovable place, and old-fashioned, earthy, stable place, a place in which there was considerable sure and common ground between men on issues of morality, where good was good and bad was bad...'. By contrast, 'the world of the Japanese victory was a world in which an evil had been precipitated whose scope was immeasurable, the act being, in itself, not an event, but a continuum, not an occasion, but the beginning of a condition'.[1] The tension between the two conceptions of the post-war, and the ways in which the two overlapped, also formed the two poles between which the British and West German politics of security unfolded. Despite their entirely different experiences and memories of the Second World War and its aftermath, British and West German activists participated in the same historical conjuncture. And, although most West Germans did not necessarily regard the Allied victory as 'lovable', they certainly regarded the end of the war, like their British counterparts, as a moral and political watershed 'where good was good and bad was bad', just that most Germans would have excluded themselves from 'the bad'.[2]

British and West German activists thus participated in the contestations of what 'security' might have meant in the post-Second World War world, which was, at the same time, the world of the nuclear arms race. This book has told the story about how the activists wrestled with this problem and what their actions meant for the various conceptions of 'the political' that undergirded post-war British and West German politics. The quest for some form of security in two post-war societies lay at the root of the contestations that characterized the extra-parliamentary politics in Britain and West Germany. Although the campaigns were connected through networks of activists and although they shared the same historical conjuncture, their resonance and meaning differed. The interactions and the eventfulness of the campaigns reveal the very specific

---

[1] Jeff Nuttall, *Bomb Culture* (London, 1968), 18.
[2] Dan Diner (ed.), *Zivilisationsbruch: Denken nach Auschwitz* (Frankfurt/Main, 1988).

processes of politicization and depoliticization in post-war Britain and West Germany through the ways in which they conceptualized, thought about, discussed, and actively produced politics.

This 'politics' started out primarily, but not exclusively, as politics in the narrow sense. But it turned into a more general contestation about the relationship between politics and culture. It thus involved a discussion about 'the political' as the very space in which 'politics' could be made and produced, and about the agency of those who made politics. The protests might have been marginal in their respective political systems. But what matters is not their marginality, but their liminality: their existence at the borderlands of politics, in the spaces 'betwixt and between' the centre of government, of nation states, of public and privates lives, of foreign and domestic politics, of the global and the local, and of cold war political ideologies. It is the activists' liminality that offers us important insights into the making and the dialectics of cold war protest politics from the end of the Second World War into the late 1960s.[3]

By framing their campaigns in terms of 'security', which seemed to reflect broader contemporary discussions, rather than in terms of the more utopian idea of 'peace', activists wrote and acted themselves into the cold war. 'Security', defined as 'national security', was one of the key ideologies of defence and foreign policy. By contrast, 'peace' was regarded as a tool of communist propaganda. But, it was also through their acceptance of the hegemonic terms of the debate that the activists were able to open up new vistas for social and political organization. Indeed, they proposed 'alternative futures' to the ones advocated by governments, which allowed the activists to create their own histories and to produce novel possibilities for political agency.[4] Defence and foreign policymakers, by using 'security', sought to evoke the importance of constant preparedness for war. By engaging with their own experiences and memories of violence and warfare, however, the activists in both countries read safety from external violence together with the possibility of military attack. They connected with the aim of internal stability, unity, and concord, as well as with a good life guaranteed by the welfare state. In West Germany, this connection had a particular resonance, as it accompanied and vouched for the transformation of a nation defined by violence to one defined by

---

[3] Cf. Victor Turner, 'Betwixt and Between: The Liminal Period in Rites of Passage', in Melford E. Spiro (ed.), *Symposium on New Approaches to the Study of Religion* (Seattle, 1964); Turner, *The Ritual Process: Structure and Anti-Structure* (Piscataway, NJ, 2008), 94–130.

[4] The term 'alternative futures' is from Arif Dirlik, 'There is More in a Rim than Meets the Eye: Thoughts on the "Pacific Idea"', in Dirlik (ed.), *What is in a Rim? Critical Perspectives on the Pacific Region Idea* (Lanham, MD, 1998), 351–69, here 365.

peace, from dictatorship to democracy, from a country divided within to one divided through its outside borders.

These processes were controversial, contested, and involved quests for political representation. These quests were about representation not merely in terms of the politics of a pressure or interest group. At the core, they involved representing the nuclear arms race as a problem for politics and therefore for public debate. Activists revealed the dangers of the arms race and nuclear radiation stemming from nuclear weapons tests. They thus revealed what had previously been invisible and thus made the topic negotiable within politics. By focusing on the issue of nuclear weapons, activists touched upon the core and essence of statehood and sovereignty in the cold war. It was through the symbol of nuclear weapons that cold war states sought to show their power. And it was in the 'geopolitical privacy' that the *arcana imperii* were kept under lock and key.[5]

This book has therefore highlighted a crucial feature that historians of social movements in the context of domestic political, social, and cultural history often forget: the importance of assumptions about both countries' *international* role in politics, the way in which international relations came to matter to people, and how they wrestled with the dangers and political challenges they saw as threatening to their world. Highlighting the importance of international relations for individual lives in this way more than merely breaks the division between international and domestic politics. It enables us to comprehend the cold war as a war in very immediate and direct, rather than diffuse and symbolic, ways.

Indeed, those Britons and West Germans active in the protests against nuclear weapons sought to highlight the dangers of the nuclear arms race as dangers that would surpass those of recent conflicts. While they communicated this knowledge to their respective populations, they also lost an awareness of the very threat of the arms race, because they came to focus on different components of the cold war, and especially the real violence that the cold war meant for countries outside the United States and Europe. For the campaigners in both countries, the cold war was a constant pre-war situation. Understood from the perspective of the arms race, my study has shown how cold war events played an active role in producing the movements that campaigned against its central characteristic, the nuclear arms race. And the cold war also played a role in un-making and remaking these connections. Social connections and

---

[5] Eva Horn, *Der geheime Krieg: Verrat, Spionage und moderne Fiktion* (Frankfurt/Main, 2007). For the concept 'geopolitical privacy', see Michael Mann, *States, War and Capitalism* (Oxford, 1988), 32.

relations, social order as such, are highly unlikely and fragile. It was primarily by reference to the warlike elements of the cold war and by working through the implications of the politics of security that the foundations for these social movements could be built. The activists' interpretations of the world as well as their very actions made visible the political and the social in whose name the activists claimed to act. The cold war nuclear arms race thus provided the conditions for its own critique.[6]

There existed, of course, a fundamental difference between Britain and West Germany: Britain was a sovereign country with its own arsenal of nuclear weapons that had come out of the Second World War victorious. By contrast, West German politics were, in the words of James N. Rosenau and Wolfram Hanrieder, a 'penetrated system' in which 'nonmembers of a national society participate[d] directly and authoritatively, through actions taken jointly with the society's members, in either the allocation of its values or the mobilization of support on behalf of its goal'. Thus, international politics were, by definition, part of domestic politics; even the government could not make sovereign decisions about the use of nuclear weapons.[7] In West Germany, international politics appeared to hold almost existential importance. As Michael Geyer has put it, the 'deadly intimacy with international relations turned grand questions of power politics into very personal concerns'.[8]

But this stark difference can be overdrawn. Within the context of NATO, it was far from clear that the UK government could always exercise its national sovereignty vis-à-vis the policies of the United States. Combining a transnational and connective approach with the methods of comparative history, this book has been able to query such straightforward conclusions that most structuralist and systemic explanations would favour. Indeed, the problem with such systemic postulations is that they lead to 'the neutralisation of the problem of aggression'. As a consequence, they deprive political systems of any domestically derived responsibilities 'outside of what the system imposes as a system'.[9]

---

[6] Cf., conceptually, Ernesto Laclau, 'The Impossibility of Society', in Laclau, *New Reflections*, 92.

[7] James N. Rosenau, 'Pre-Theories and Theories of Foreign Policy', in Rosenau (ed.), *The Scientific Study of Foreign Policy* (New York, 1971), 127; Wolfram F. Hanrieder, *West German Foreign Policy, 1949–1963: International Pressure and Domestic Response* (Stanford, CA, 1967), 230.

[8] Geyer, 'Cold War Angst', 378; cf. also Michael Geyer and Konrad H. Jarausch, *A Shattered Past: Reconstructing German Histories* (Princeton, 2002), 351.

[9] Anders Stephanson, 'Offensive Realism', *boundary 2*, 27 (2000), 181–95, here 186–7.

This book has, therefore, highlighted the multiple and complex ways in which existing structures were confronted by individual experiences. It has focused on the 'creative moments where the individual struggling to make sense of him- or herself and the world will bend, select, recombine, amend, transform the sources of meaning' in order to bring historical contingency and structural contexts together.[10] The actual practice of protesting on the basis of existing structures introduced new visions of the world, utopias in the original sense of the word as 'non-places', places away from existing political and social imaginaries that were nonetheless sutured tightly to the conditions in which they were produced.[11] Thus, the British and West German protesters whose stories this book has told were dialectically related to official renderings of the politics of security: as the dominant and oppositional groups interacted, their struggles thus constantly clarified the political–cultural field of the cold war rather than being proof for its demise. As William Sewell has argued with regard to the French Revolution, 'the act of contesting dominant meanings itself implies a recognition of their centrality.'[12]

The protesters' radical potential did not only lie in challenging governmental authority *tout court*, as much of the recent scholarship on the location of protests in cold war history has assumed.[13] Such a perspective merely reproduces rather than analyses and deconstructs contemporary perspectives. Rather, the British and West German protests' radical potential lay precisely in making visible those assumptions of governments, and they provided the methods, means, and potential for the critique of these assumptions. Discussing nuclear weapons offered activists ways of debating and working through the violence of the Second World War and of grappling with the threat of new violence on a potentially unprecedented scale. Their politics of security therefore worked in three interconnected ways: in reading memories of the Second World War into the reality of the cold war; in demanding specific forms of political engagement related to these memories; and in connecting their campaigns beyond the level of nation states as 'decision and identity spaces' (Charles S. Maier), while nonetheless staying moored within local and national frames of understanding.

Activists thus made the cold war world comprehensible as a space of potential and real destruction. The central element of stability in cold war

---

[10] James Hinton, *Nine Wartime Lives: Mass-Observation and the Making of the Modern Self* (Oxford, 2010), 19.

[11] Cf. conceptually Sahlins, *Islands of History*, xiv; Sahlins, *How 'Natives' Think: About Captain Cook, for Example* (Chicago, 1995), 9.

[12] William H. Sewell, *The Logics of History: Social Theory and Social Transformation* (Chicago, 2005), 173.

[13] Cf. Suri, *Power and Protest*; Klimke, *The Other Alliance*.

international relations, namely the strategy of mutually assured destruction that had been established by the end of the 1950s and lasted into the
1980s, did not depend on the material reality of devastation. Instead, it
was based on the hypotheses that the opposing parties developed about
their behaviour in the future. In short, the cold war arms race depended
on the scenarios that societies developed to make sense of it. It was this
fiction of the arms race that made it real.[14] The British and West German
protesters played a key role in creating this knowledge of the cold war and
in making it politically relevant. It was through this image of destruction
that British and West German activists gained access to multiple forms of
knowledge of political and social transformation that undermined the
very assumptions on which the binary structure of the arms race rested.

Fundamentally, discussing nuclear weapons enabled protesters to speak
about the Second World War in ways that made its violence tangible at a
time when the British and West German societies did not always thematize
these memories openly.[15] Well into the early 1960s, for the protesters, the
cold war was essentially the threat of a repeat of the Second World War.
But, although these memories and experiences looked similar and mir-
rored general West European patterns, the consequences of war assumed
different temporalities and resonances in Britain and West Germany. Total
defeat accentuated the German post-war more strongly.[16] To a much
greater extent than in Britain, West German protesters' experiences were
shot through with nightmares of violence and shock, and the history of the
alleged normality of the increasingly affluent society was also the 'history
of the imagination of horror'.[17] British protesters shared an uneasy awareness that the unity of their nation and the patriotic community that had
been created in the Second World War was linked to murderous violence
that was incompatible with the kind of society they wished to preserve.[18]

But the meanings of this awareness were fundamentally different in
West Germany, which meant that it had a different resonance there among
both the protesters and the general public. While discussions in other
areas led to strategies 'that sought to erase the consequences of German
violence *and* of violence against Germans', discussing the bombing war

[14] Claus Pias, 'Abschreckung denken: Hermann Kahns Szenarien', in Claus Pias (ed.), *Abwehr. Modelle—Strategien—Medien* (Bielefeld, 2009), 169–88.
[15] Geoff Eley, 'Finding the People's War: Film, British Collective Memory, and World War II', *American Historical Review*, 106 (2001), 818–38; Moeller, *War Stories*.
[16] Frank Biess and Robert W. Moeller (eds), *Histories of the Aftermath: The Legacies of the Second World War in Europe* (New York, 2010).
[17] Svenja Goltermann, *Die Gesellschaft der Überlebenden: Deutsche Kriegsheimkehrer und ihre Gewalterfahrungen im Zweiten Weltkrieg* (Munich, 2009), 17, 29.
[18] Hinton, *Nine Wartime Lives*, 13.

conjured up these memories in different ways: it conjured up memories of victimhood during the bombing war, while, nevertheless, showing a modicum of awareness for German crimes. The symbolic linkage between the Bergen-Belsen camp and the British missile base Bergen-Hohne that protesters established on the first German Easter March highlights this most clearly. It worked towards developing 'redemptive transformations' and thus, in paradoxical ways, allowed them to read their own activism not only into the cold war but also into the young West German democracy.[19]

Protesters' implicit and explicit references to their 'injured citizenship' (Michael Geyer) highlighted this aspect of their politics of security explicitly, although this injury had normally remained silent: protesters shared a profound distrust of the use of the military by the German state, while they approved of the security provided by the welfare state and while they might even have agreed to serving in the West German army.[20] This meant that the West German protests against nuclear weapons appeared, at first, less mainstream and therefore more controversial. However, it was precisely the fact that West German activists expressed widely shared, yet not publicly discussed, fears about their sovereignty as citizens and their country's sovereignty in the international arena that made them so controversial. While Britain saw a variety of protest movements over the course of the 1960s, the West German Easter Marches transformed themselves into an 'extra-parliamentary opposition' that profoundly shifted the ground for what the politics of security meant.

In the wake of the crisis over the building of the Berlin Wall in August 1961, when Soviet and US tanks faced each other in Berlin, and following the Cuban missile crisis in autumn 1962, when the world seemed to have come to the brink of a nuclear war, a geostrategic modus operandi was established in Europe between the United States and the Soviet Union. It established a mutual agreement about the use of nuclear weapons for deterrence in a system of 'mutually assured destruction'.[21] The new status quo found expression in the banning of atmospheric nuclear weapons tests through an international treaty between the United States, the Soviet Union, and the United Kingdom in 1963 and the continuous improvement of the direct relations between the major powers. In this constellation, the British and West German governments successfully

---

[19] The quotations are from Frank Biess, *Returning POWs and the Legacies of Defeat in Postwar Germany* (Princeton, 2005), 7.

[20] Geyer, 'Cold War Angst', 385–6.

[21] Marc Trachtenberg, *A Constructed Peace: The Making of the European Settlement, 1945–1963* (Princeton, 1999).

managed to uncouple the link between the dangers of radioactivity and the arms race. They successfully replaced the dangers of the arms race with an understanding of nuclear energy as the harbinger and key symbol of modernity, focusing on health and safety measures to combat radio-activity and thus winning back people's trust in this form of energy. From around 1963, therefore, and until the mid- to late 1970s, the politics of security no longer primarily revolved around the cold war as characterized by an arms race.[22]

This meant that the visual arsenal of the real and tangible dangers of the arms race that nuclear weapons tests had provided had disappeared, so that nuclear weapons no longer appeared to many to assume the central importance for making sense of the cold war. Instead, protesters now increasingly focused on the real violence practised by the United States in the Vietnam War, and they highlighted what they regarded as specifically American ideologies, such as a specific brand of consumer culture, as the essence of the invisible cold war. Whereas, for the protesters of the late 1950s and early 1960s, the cold war had essentially been about nuclear weapons interpreted in the light of the Second World War's aerial bomb-ing campaigns, by the mid-1960s the cold war had a different shape and structure for most activists. The United States and what activists regarded as its 'imperialism' had, for most protesters, become the symbol and incarnation of the cold war, as it threatened to suppress the projects for liberation that people in the developing world had promoted. Activists' previous debates about security now enabled them to discuss their aim as 'liberation'.

In West Germany, this theme could be tied to the more general con-cerns of individual and national sovereignty that protesters had discussed before. Their campaigns gained plausibility because 'high' politics—the Grand Coalition of the two major political parties *CDU* and *SPD* in 1966 as well as a number of ex-National Socialists in government and exposed civil-service positions—seemed to highlight the need for such a campaign. 'Liberation' for West German activists therefore also meant liberation from the past, providing security from a return of the past. The Easter Marches therefore transformed themselves into a campaign for disarmament and for democracy. Because of the different meanings and repercussions of activists' politics of security, such common cognitive framework could not develop in Britain. As a consequence, the politics of security broke up into separate and different movements with no clearly identifiable centre,

---

[22] Lawrence S. Wittner, 'The Nuclear Threat Ignored: How and Why the Campaign against the Bomb Disintegrated in the late 1960s', in Carole Fink, Philipp Gassert, and Detlef Junker (eds), *1968: The World Transformed* (Cambridge, 1998), 439–58.

although separate movements, ranging from CND to anarchist and Trot-skyte groups, represented aims that were similar to the ones assembled in West Germany's single 'extra-parliamentary opposition'.

The different histories of protest and contestation in 1950s and 1960s Britain and West Germany were, therefore, the outcome of the ways in which British and West German protesters tried to write themselves—and their societies—into the cold war within the specific conditions of their countries. They were not simply the outcome of different traditions of radicalism in both countries or of different political systems. Nor were they merely responses to their countries' different geostrategic positions within cold war international relations.

But the politics of security was not merely about an active engagement with cold war international relations per se. Protesters' analysis of the international system offered the ground and conditions from which British and West German activists developed their arguments and their campaigns. The disruption of the ethico-political order across Europe during the Second World War remained a strong influence on political imaginaries well into the post-war period, as contemporaries sought to address the foundational question of how a 'workable ethics of democracy' should look.[23] Debates about this issue were profoundly shaped by the almost existential feelings of disorder about politics that people knew, as it seemed to them that history's continuum had been broken and had to be reassembled again. This meant that a complex multitude of different temporalities influenced the ways in which activists sought to turn security into their topic politically. Manifold reappropriations of the past were necessary and also guaranteed that the past had an enormous discursive appeal. Coming to terms with the past had a profound impact on the contest of the boundaries that were supposed to separate politics from non-politics, the resources on which protesters could draw to make their argument.

This theme had different resonances in Britain and West Germany and therefore provided different local and nationally specific contexts that help explain the different protest histories of the 1950s and 1960s. The protests in both countries participated in forging cold war political cultures. This confrontation in which British and West German activists engaged opened up new spaces of political action. Both campaigns grew out of a deep dissatisfaction with the organization and politics of the parliamentary left—in West Germany the *SPD* and in Britain the Labour and Communist Parties.

---

[23] Geoff Eley, 'A Disorder of Peoples: The Uncertain Ground for Reconstruction in 1945', in Jessica Reinisch and Elizabeth White (eds), *The Disentanglement of Populations: Migration, Expulsion and Displacement and Post-War Europe, 1944–9* (Basingstoke, 2011), 291–314, here 304.

CND in Britain and the Campaign against Nuclear Death and the Easter Marches in West Germany thus provided spaces of political experimentation in which politics and culture could merge in novel ways. These spaces facilitated an engagement with political traditions in the context of concrete events and circumstances. The ways in which extra-parliamentary politics became enmeshed with culture, and the ways in which subcultures became political and were transformed into counter-cultures thus differed between Britain and West Germany in important ways. In West Germany, culture was more readily politicized because the *SPD* was more pronouncedly a cold war party and tried to suppress protests outside its organizational framework more fiercely than the British Labour Party. The feelings of disappointments connected with this were therefore much greater, not least because the hopes that had been tied to the *SPD* as the progressive party of democratization had been so much larger.

Moreover, although the specific *contents* of the politics of security that the West German protests developed—their emphasis on the memories of the Second World War in the context of Germany's post-National Socialist society—had more resonance with mainstream public opinion than its British counterpart, the same could not be said for the *forms* they developed to express these politics. As West Germany was a divided country at the front line of the cold war, as anti-communist and anti-socialist sentiments continued to linger, and as memories of the street battles of the Weimar Republic as destabilizing forces in Germany's first democracy continued to loom, the boundaries of politics were much more tightly drawn in West Germany than in Britain. All activism that came to be seen left of the *SPD* was regarded as inherently dangerous for political stability. This was also true for activities that involved cultural engagement with artists, music, and theatre that was regarded as 'socialist' and 'communist'. Hence, mainstream popular culture was gradually depoliticized over the course of the 1960s precisely because it could be presented as the outward symbol of democratic affluence. By contrast, since they seemingly furthered the case of the 'other Germany', the cultures of activism that underpinned the extra-parliamentary protests of the late 1950s and the 1960s remained highly politicized.[24] This meant that the West German extra-parliamentary movement retained its dynamics and unifying cognitive framework beyond the issue of nuclear weapons. In Britain, by contrast, culture itself became a substitute for politics more readily than in West Germany: while sub- and counter-cultures were often tied to political projects, they were not directly linked to political campaigns.

---

[24] On mainstream popular culture, see Uta G. Poiger, *Jazz, Rock and Rebels: Cold War Politics and American Culture in a Divided Germany* (Berkeley and Los Angeles, 2000).

The New Left activist Perry Anderson attributed this lack of continuity in British protests of the 1960s, and the lack of a more sustained protest movement that rivalled the ones in continental Europe, to the *longue durée* of British history and the importance of 'traditions' in British political culture. In particular, he faulted protesters of the late 1950s and early 1960s for not moving beyond these traditions and for not engaging more actively with continental European theories of societal transformation. Observing France and West Germany in particular, Anderson diagnosed a special path in British radical politics, arguing that British radicalism had never been quite radical enough. Anderson came to this assessment through an engagement with Antonio Gramsci's notions of (cultural) 'hegemony', which he discovered through his friend Tom Nairn, who had learned of the Italian's work during a stint at the *Scuola Nuova Superiore* in Pisa in the early 1960s. Anderson argued, therefore, that it was necessary to shift attention within the politics of security towards undermining hegemony within culture by developing a revolutionary consciousness through intellectual and theoretical engagement.[25]

Although Anderson's diagnosis was already hotly debated at the time, it has been more or less unquestioningly transferred into the historiography on the British 1960s, albeit mostly without attention to its Gramscian roots: most historians and commentators highlight the importance of cultural changes over the course of the 1960s, while failing to engage with the political repercussions and the specific social and political locations of these cultural shifts.[26] They have, therefore, tended to subscribe to Anderson's diagnosis in slightly different ways by highlighting the 'conservative nature of British modernity'.[27] The comparative and transnational perspective applied here demonstrates, however, that West German protesters equally relied on traditions to anchor their protests. Indeed, Germany saw 'multiple restorations' similar to those in Britain, and it would be difficult to place the protests on scales of different degrees of conservatism and progressivism.[28]

---

[25] Perry Anderson, 'Origins of the Present Crisis', *New Left Review*, 23 (1964), 26–53.

[26] Of these, Nick Thomas's work is the most precise: Thomas, 'Challenging Myths of the 1960s'; Arthur Marwick, *The Sixties: Cultural Revolution in Britain, France, Italy, and the United States, c.1958–c.1974* (Oxford, 1998).

[27] Cf., for example, Jon Lawrence, 'Pioneers of Modernity' [review essay], *History Workshop Journal*, 73 (2012), 330–8; Black, *Redefining British Politics*; Stephen Brooke, *Sexual Politics: Sexuality, Family Planning and the British Left from the 1880s to the Present Day* (Oxford, 2011).

[28] Jeffrey Herf, 'Multiple Restorations: German Political Traditions and the Interpretation of Nazism, 1945–1946', *Central European History*, 26 (1993), 21–55.

Conversely, one of the standard works on the history of the New Left, following more or less Anderson's line of direct theoretical engagement, fails to take account of the cultural dimensions of politics altogether.[29] Yet, these interpretations that have dominated the historiography on protests in the British 1960s are themselves in need of historicization. Anderson argued from a specific political position that entailed a commitment primarily to cultural theorizing rather than the concrete solidarity practised by the VSC, and he was also quite sceptical of those groups that sought to develop the politics of security as a politics of authenticity under the auspices of counter-culture. Moreover, Anderson's *longue durée* explanation and diagnosis of hegemony have entered the historiography of the period in a way that was oblivious to the interaction between cultural politics and concrete events. His thinking highlights the move towards counter- and subcultures while forgetting the concrete political debates that accompanied that transition.

But the comparison of the British and West German extra-parliamentary protests shows how their politics of security cannot be slotted easily into the functionality of modernist political terminology and of the models of politics these terms connote, especially as far as the nature of political change and categorization of political actors are concerned. The dynamic, rather than linear, pattern of politico-cultural transformation in which activists in both countries were engaged is lost in straightforward models of resistance, repression, and response. It also sits uneasily in straightforward interpretations of social and cultural change such as 'liberalization' and 'the growth of permissiveness'.[30]

Importantly, these transformations of activism also shaped the multiple experiences that activists were able to share and express as part of their protests. Activists' experiences highlighted the ways in which the international, social, and personal were imbricated in one another, but activists developed different degrees of awareness as to the boundedness of their experiences. Some also developed different assessments of the political relevance of their campaigns that joined the existing parameters of interpretation. Whereas CNDers and early Easter Marchers stressed the rationality of their campaign as the key feature of a meaningful politics of security, their engagement in the campaign and the contestations they took part in gave rise to a view that highlighted the role of individual

---

[29] Chun, *The British New Left*.
[30] Cf. Davis, 'What's Left?', versus Herbert (ed.), *Wandlungsprozesse in Westdeutschland*, and Paul Addison, *No Turning Back: The Peaceful Revolutions of Post-War Britain* (Oxford, 2010).

convictions within the context of a given political and social context as the necessary precondition for creating security: security, therefore, had to start with the conversion of individuals and their emotions, as opposed to the reform of society at large and of governmental machinery.

Activists remained, however, almost entirely immune to recognizing the authenticity and political relevance of experiences that women voiced in terms that were similar to those of men. The late 1950s and early 1960s saw a revival of a specifically female discourse about security and peace as a specifically female and motherly responsibility, and male campaigners did not accept a genuine and explicit political role for female campaigners: mostly, women were backroom organizers, but only rarely public speakers. Although many women participated in the campaigns, male activists did not treat them as equal partners. But, for many women, their participation in the protest campaigns was an opening too: by involving them in protest organizations that did not represent their own feelings and interests, they developed different ways of thinking through politics and challenged the hegemony of male concepts of citizenship, first in the privacy of their campaign offices, and then publicly in their own campaigns for women's rights and through a series of cultural initiatives. They thus highlighted the fact that the very experiences male activists claimed for themselves as authentic expressions of their political demands depended on the 'emotions' that they had previously claimed to be female.[31] The conceptions of agency that activists developed were therefore themselves transformed over the course of their activism, as they sought to create a world for themselves that was not determined by the anonymous structures of government but that happened between people.

Protesters acted at the boundaries of the cold war and thereby produced conceptions of the political that came to lie outside the established forms of politics. They did this in the context of networks and frames of thinking that transcended the boundaries of the nation state. They thus purported to challenge the ethico-political force of the national state as the key organizing principle of the international system. Martin Klimke has powerfully argued for the connections between American and West German students that 'activists from different geographical, economic, political, and cultural frameworks imagined themselves as part of a global revolutionary movement', which allowed them to develop collective protest identities with shared political and cultural reference points.[32]

---

[31] Cf. for similar developments in different contexts: Steedman, *Landscape for a Good Woman*.

[32] Klimke, *The Other Alliance*, 2.

But a closer and more detailed analysis of the networks and perceptions that carried such links between British and West German protesters highlights the fundamental paradoxes and ambiguities of these processes. Even as activists made claims of their transnational connections, they drew on resources, networks, and opportunities of the societies they lived in. More specifically, the transnational transfer of forms and methods of protest as well as cognitive frameworks always involved complicated processes of translation that the notion of 'transfer' can capture only incompletely. Knowledge was rarely transferred in packages by specific actors within the different transnational networks. Rather, the ways in which activists made sense of each other—and in which they assessed other activists around the world—influenced the transnational connections directly. As the transnational actors engaged with each other, they therefore always also compared themselves with each other and with third parties. This meant that their relationship to each other was rarely on equal terms and was very often competitive.

This has important conceptual implications for our study of transnational social movement activism: instead of following the border-crossing networks of a few elite activists, historians should remain attuned to an awareness to the everyday relevance of such interactions within protest campaigns. Just as scholars should beware of taking the distance between movement organizations and mainstream political cultures at face value, they should also not, within a transnational perspective, reify the distance between border-crossing activists and the national, and often very local, contexts in which they operated. Instead, scholars should, in turn, historicize these patterns of interactions by embedding them within concrete and lived experiences. Transnational and comparative history should be creatively combined in order to highlight how images of transnational connections were already formed at the time, as activists in different locations compared and contrasted their experiences as they interacted with and observed each other.

For the protests in the late 1950s and early 1960s, CND held an almost absolute 'epistemological sovereignty' in the relationship between the two movements.[33] CNDers not only saw their campaign as the original anti-nuclear-weapons movement, but also regarded its activities as part of a non-violent, liberal, and ultimately beneficial British civilizing mission that would help hold together and fortify the decolonizing British Empire in a novel and mutually beneficial Commonwealth. This

---

[33] Thomas W. Laqueur, 'Bodies, Details, and the Humanitarian Narrative', in Lynn Hunt (ed.), *The New Cultural History* (Berkeley and Los Angeles, 1989) 176–204, here 188.

interpretation wrote the crucial role that activists' observation of Gandhi's campaign in India had played in forming these policies out of history and thus reified CND's position of 'epistemological sovereignty', although individual activists continued to refer to it. West Germans in the Easter Marches replicated this self-understanding of the British campaign by likewise interpreting CND as an example to follow and emulate: what they regarded as British traditions of peacefulness, radicalism, and individual freedom resonated especially strongly.

This meant that, for the Easter Marches, Britain provided the models for civic organization that West German protesters sought to translate into the West German context. British ideas of middle-class sociability and civility, and their seeming emphasis on rational debates rather than populist rallies, played a key role for the translation of British activism to the West German context. Within the contexts of their politics of security, British and West German activists therefore engaged in, adapted, and transformed what the sociologist Andreas Reckwitz has termed 'subject cultures', the ways in which individuals and societies make sense of their subjectivity in terms of both the one that is subjected to something (*subiectum*) and the one that subjects others.[34] This was essentially the subject culture based around middle-class/bourgeois civility that worked through the medium of morality, which could be generalized to gain the status of an acceptable public doctrine, and self-regulation through conscience and reasonable public engagement through (dominantly male) social groups within which participants regarded themselves as naturally equal.[35]

The shift of the politics of security away from nuclear weapons towards perceptions of US imperialism and the question of affluence from the mid-1960s also entailed different assessments of 'epistemological sovereignty'. Most protesters in both Britain and West Germany now assumed that US society, in the shape of the 'other America' of activists as well as of those groups opposing US imperialism worldwide, provided foundational knowledge on which protest politics could be built, although US activists themselves had been influenced by their British-inflected engagement with Gandhian politics of direct action and civil disobedience.[36] They now spelled out more clearly than they had done before that this also meant highlighting the importance of the Third World as a political project unconstrained by the binary features of the cold war that had the

[34] Andreas Reckwitz, *Das hybride Subjekt: Eine Theorie der Subjektkulturen von der bürgerlichen Moderne zur Postmoderne* (Weilerswist, 2006), 10–11.
[35] Reckwitz, *Subjekt*, 242–74.
[36] Sean Chabot, *Transnational Roots of the Civil Rights Movement: African American Explorations of the Gandhian Repertoire* (Lanham, MD, 2012).

potential to open up spaces from which political radicalism could be thought and acted out, and that brought with it a new form of ethico-political engagement that transcended those of the rational citizen subject.[37]

The subject culture that activists engaged in from the mid-1960s was one that fused elements of the artistic avant-garde of the 1920s with those of sub- and counter-cultural trends that emerged over the course of the 1960s. Their historical specificity lay in their appropriation of culture—and counter-culture—as an antidote to the social control, technical rationality, and routine that they regarded as the key features of governance during this time period.[38] It was not a little ironic that the technocratic GDR played a key role as a reference point for some protesters in both countries, as its foreign political propaganda emphasized elements of socialist subcultures that developments in the West seemed to have overlooked.

From this point of view, which developed over the course of the 1960s, with roots among pacifists in the 1950s, structures appeared as 'structural violence' and the rationalism of the external order as a power that forced the subject's self to embrace it. The solution for some protesters to this problem was to invert the normative coding of the difference between 'rational' and 'irrational'/'emotional' from positive/negative to negative/positive, from the principle of a rational reality towards playfulness, from the form of protest marches that sought to represent the rationality of the claims in a relatively sombre atmosphere through forms of direct action that aimed to subvert normality through playful practices.[39] This transformation was never complete and always contested, but it fundamentally reoriented the protesters' mutual frame of reference towards a global scope. Throughout, British and West German activists differed, both between and among themselves, as to how to weight the different elements of this subject culture. There were, therefore, never two entirely separate national paths within this transnational conjuncture, although British political culture was generally characterized by a lower level of politicization than its West German counterpart.

The shift in transnational relations from a bourgeois to an avant-gardist/counter-cultural subject culture was accompanied by a transformation of the ways in which activists made sense of the world. In line with the

---

[37] For general overviews, cf. Klimke, *The Other Alliance*, and Slobodian, *Foreign Front*.
[38] Reckwitz, *Subjekt*, 456.
[39] Reckwitz, *Subjekt*, 452–99.

middle-class model of sociability whose proponents regarded their own
activism as universally valid because it was based on reason, transnational
perceptions in both countries until the early 1960s characterized the
world as one fundamentally influenced by the struggle between life and
death. Protesters therefore spoke of mass death, not in historically specific, but in universal terms. This had special consequences for the politics of the past in West Germany, as it helped activists there to talk about
mass death without directly mentioning their own involvement in the
millionfold mass death of the Second World War. This 'universalist scope
of identification' with the world enabled activists to highlight the warlike
character of the cold war.[40] Yet it also enabled them to emphasize a community of humanity that looked like 'the family of man'. Within that
large family, a metaphor that evoked the intimacy and closeness of this
community, potential differences of age, genders, social class, and
ethnic belonging were subsumed within a general anthropological
understanding.

    With the shift towards more ideologically oriented understandings
geared towards models of protest focused on direct action and the transformation of the activists' cultures of subjectivity, this anthropological
understanding of world politics as a 'family of man' underwent an important transformation. The focus was now on political solidarity with those
suffering from oppression. This solidarity was not only an ideal, a frame
of understanding, or a social formation. Rather, 'solidarity' by definition
implied the activity of showing the solidarity in order to bridge the gap
between protests here and the object of solidarity there—the 'family of
man', by contrast, had been an existing condition. This transformation
was by no means a history of gains, as the British and West German activists' attempts to adopt the politics of solidarity turned the subjects of liberation into passive victims of oppression that often served as fetishized
icons of protest politics.[41]

    The transnationality of the campaigns therefore always implied a sense,
furthered by mutual observations often through the mass and movement
media, that the protest movements shared a common historical conjuncture that protesters from Britain and West German activists interpreted
differently in the late 1960s from how they had done in the late 1950s.
This transformation of the mutual reference points of the campaigns was
behind many of the contestations about extra-parliamentary politics and
it framed the multiplicity of protests that was drawn together under the

[40] Oppenheimer, 'West German Pacifism', 372.
[41] Slobodian, *Foreign Front*.

heading of '1968'.[42] We cannot understand these debates if we do not bear in mind their genealogies in the earlier politics of security. When the West German Frankfurt School philosopher Jürgen Habermas criticized Rudi Dutschke and other activists as 'left-wing fascists', he was unable to detect this transformation in the transnational dimensions of the politics of security.[43]

Habermas had developed his arguments in his book on the structural transformation of the public sphere that first appeared in German in the early 1960s: interpreting developments in nineteenth-century Britain, Habermas regarded the rational discussion among (male) members of the middle class as the core of politics. Rational argumentation lay at the core of this model of democracy; consumer society, the mass media, and the emotions they provoked could only distort what Habermas assumed was a discourse among equals.[44] Dutschke, Krahl, Wolfgang Lefèvre, and others in the *SDS*, but also activists in the Easter March movement more generally, however, believed that democracy also had to be based on the fearlessness of conviction, and the voluntarist belief that individual actions could provoke social and political change, and that these actions could transcend the existing political order only if they developed the Situationist idea of transgression and playfulness in novel ways.[45] In short, in this Protestant inflection of Marxist ideas, the world could and would only change if individuals changed and were converted to a better life.[46] The counter-publics and counter-cultures that undergirded the extra-parliamentary campaigns in both Britain and West Germany, though to different degrees and with different agglomerations, did not easily align with Habermas's straightforward ideas. Situationism, the local protest cultures oriented towards 'anti-authoritarian' subversive practices, socialist youth cultures, the jazz and folk scenes, poetry slams in pubs, the art school movements, and the counter-cultural magazines with their playful cultural engagement of serious political themes as well as the aesthetic radicalism and stylistic dissidence in the art and literary world in

---

[42] Cf. Christopher Booker, *The Neophiliacs: Revolution in English Life in the Fifties and Sixties* (London, 1992), for Britain; and Wolfgang Kraushaar, *1968 als Mythos, Chiffre und Zäsur* (Hamburg, 2000) for Germany.

[43] Jürgen Habermas, 'Rede über die politische Rolle der Studentenschaft in der Bundesrepublik', in Kraushaar (ed.), *Frankfurter Schule*, ii. no. 126, 246–9, 250–1; cf. also Habermas, 'Scheinrevolution und Handlungszwang', *Der Spiegel*, 10 June 1968, 57–8.

[44] On the historicization of Habermas's thoughts, see Hodenberg, *Konsens und Krise.*

[45] Rudi Dutschke, '. . . Professor Habermas, Ihr begriffloser Objektivismus erschlägt das zu emanzipierende Subjekt . . .' (9 June 1967), reprinted in Kraushaar (ed.), *Frankfurter Schule*, ii, no. 129, 251–3, here 251 and 253.

[46] On the Protestant context, see Dagmar Herzog, *Sex after Fascism: Memory and Morality in Twentieth-Century Germany* (Princeton, 2005), 154–62.

Britain did not make sense from the perspective of Habermas's normative orientation towards a perspective of the early nineteenth-century British public sphere. He saw 'fascism' and inflections of revolutionary existentialism where he might instead have seen a constructive engagement with other 1920s avant-garde traditions.[47]

Ironically, both mainstream (male) protesters who focused on direct action and Habermas and his supporters in the movements and elsewhere ignored one crucial opening that their movements had produced. Probably the most important range of activism for which the movements of the 1960s provided a crucial space was feminism. But even that feminist activism was still inflected with echoes of the cold war politics of security from earlier periods—for example, when some feminists emphasized their war community of direct personal interactions to the anonymous structures of the cold war. Some feminists' emphasis on liberation and individual subjectivity therefore was another product of the dialectic of cold war protest politics: the ideas of personal liberation and gender identities directly replicated and dialectically reproduced from below the emphasis on freedom and personal independence in mainstream Western cold war propaganda.[48]

Through their existence, then, the campaigns in both countries expanded the space of what could be said and what could be done in politics in both countries, but they never did this in isolation from mainstream political cultures. Indeed, they enabled the integration of activists who had previously been excluded from legitimate political activities. However, by making this form of politics more legitimate, the marches enabled an ever larger pool of activists to emerge who challenged central parameters of the respective political systems. This was particularly important in the Federal Republic. There, the West German Easter Marches worked towards both strengthening and weakening political integration. While Easter March activists had previously been keen to avoid any allegations of working together with communists, they gradually adopted a position that regarded activities that consciously bridged the bipolar political divides of the cold war as key for the effectiveness of their protests. The Easter Marches were, therefore, constantly able to reinvent themselves as adequate responses to the relevant issues in international relations at the time—the interpretation of the Nazi past in the context of US hegemony provided an adequate master frame for the campaigns. The

---

[47] Cf. Geoff Eley, 'Politics, Culture, and the Public Sphere', *positions*, 10 (2002), 219–36.
[48] Cf. the key conceptual work by Leerom Medovoi, *Rebels: Youth and the Cold War Origins of Identity* (Durham, NC, 2005), especially 30.

different resonances of the British and West German movements meant that the stories activists have told with hindsight are structured differently: where many British activists write about awakenings and self-fulfilment in terms of an education of (cultural and political) sensibilities and sentiments and, at times, heroic agency, West German activists tend to stress the ruptures and discontinuities that the events of 1967 and 1968, in particular, implied.[49] British and West German activists thus endowed the concept 'experience' with different and specific meanings that reflected these different perceptions.

As the issue of nuclear weapons appeared to become less pressing, British and West German activists began to focus on questions of cold war ideology and forms of governance. On the one hand, their politics of security began to transcend the cold war binaries much more radically than before. On the other hand, this move had the tendency to take the nuclear arms race more readily for granted as one of many political problems. The bomb gradually became secondary.[50] Both British and West German activists, each in their specific ways, produced their own history by appropriating elements of hegemonic frameworks of interpretation and understanding, and they turned these back against governments and parties. They did this by applying the past to the present and thus produced their own *contemporary* history. They continued to move on.

---

[49] See Ali, *Street Fighting Years*, and Rowbotham, *Promise of a Dream*, in comparison with Ute Kätzel, *Die 68erinnen: Porträt einer rebellischen Frauengeneration* (Munich, 2008); Lethen, *Handorakel*, and Schneider, *Rebellion und Wahn*. On the background, see Joseph Maslen, 'Autobiographies of a Generation? Carolyn Steedman, Luisa Passerini and the Memory of 1968', *Memory Studies*, 6 (2013), 23–36.

[50] Wittner, 'Nuclear Threat'.

Bibliography

1. MANUSCRIPT AND ARCHIVAL SOURCES

Archiv der sozialen Demokratie, Bonn (AdsD)
Archiv Aktiv, Hamburg
Archiv APO und soziale Bewegungen, Free University Archives, Berlin (APOA)
Bodleian Library, Oxford
British Library for Political and Economic Science, London (BLPES)
University Archives, Brynmor Jones Library, University of Hull (BJL)
Bundesarchiv, Koblenz (BAK)
Bundesarchiv–Militärarchiv, Freiburg (BA–MA)
Hamburger Institut für Sozialforschung (HIS)
Evangelisches Zentralarchiv, Berlin (EZA)
Hauptstaatsarchiv Düsseldorf (HStAD)
Internationaal Instituut voor sociale Geschiedenis, Amsterdam (IISG)
Institut für Zeitgeschichte, Munich (IfZ)
J. B. Priestley Library, Commonweal Collection, University of Bradford
Labour History Archive and Study Centre, Manchester (LHASC)
Landesarchiv Berlin (LAB)
Manchester Archive and Local Studies Unit (MALSU)
Mass Observation Archive, University of Sussex, Falmer, Brighton (M-OA)
Modern Records Centre, University of Warwick, Coventry (MRC)
The National Archives, Kew (TNA)
Politisches Archiv des Auswärtigen Amtes, Berlin (PolArchAA)
Sammlung Archiv Partei- und Massenorganisationen im Bundesarchiv, Berlin
   (SAPMO-BArch)
Stiftung Archiv Akademie der Künste Berlin-Brandenburg, Berlin
Working Class Movement Library, Salford (WCML)

2. INTERVIEWS

Carl Amery, Munich; Andreas Buro, Grävenwiesbach; Arno Klönne, Paderborn;
   Erdmann Linde, Dortmund; John Saville, Hull; Hans-Konrad Tempel,
   Ahrensburg; Dorothy Thompson, Worcester; Klaus Vack, Sensbachtal; Peter
   Worsley, London.

3. PRINTED PRIMARY SOURCES

a. Newspapers and periodicals
Das Argument
Blätter für deutsche und internationale Politik

Bulletin des Presse- und Informationsamtes der Bundesregierung
Bulletin of the Atomic Scientists
CND Bulletin
Christian Action
colloquium
Coracle
Daily Mail
Daily Telegraph
Deutsche Friedensgesellschaft—Informationsdienst
Die Zeit
Diskus—Frankfurter Studentenzeitung
Frankfurter Allgemeine Zeitung
Frankfurter Hefte
Frankfurter Rundschau
Friedensrundschau
The Friend
Das Gewissen
Informationen zur Abrüstung
The Junction
Junge Kirche
Kongreßdienst
konkret
konsequent
Kursbuch
The Listener
Manchester Guardian/The Guardian
Methodist Recorder
New Leader
New Reasoner
neue kritik
Neue Politik
New Left Review
Non Violence
Peace News
pläne
Parlamentarisch-Politischer Pressedienst
Reasoner
Sanity
Socialist Register
Solidarität
Solidarity
Stimme der Gemeinde
Studentenkurier
Süddeutsche Zeitung
The Times

The Tribune
Universities & Left Review
Vorwärts
Welt der Arbeit
Werkhefte katholischer Laien/werkhefte. zeitschrift für probleme der gesellschaft und des katholizismus
Wir sind jung

b. Published primary sources

20. Juli 1944. Ein Drama des Gewissens und der Geschichte. Dokumente und Berichte (Freiburg, 1963).

Abrams, Philip, and Little, Alan, 'The Young Voter in British Politics', *British Journal of Sociology*, 16 (1965), 95–110.

Abrams, Philip, and Little, Alan, 'The Young Activist in British Politics', *British Journal of Sociology*, 16 (1965), 315–33.

Abrams, Philip, and Rose, Richard, *Must Labour Lose?* (Harmondsworth, 1960).

Accidental War: Some Dangers in the 1960s: The Mershon Report (London, 1962).

Ali, Tariq, *Street Fighting Years: An Autobiography of the Sixties*, 2nd edn (London, 2005).

Amery, Carl, *Die Kapitualtion oder Deutscher Katholizismus heute* (Reinbek, 1963).

Anders, Günther, *Die Antiquiertheit des Menschen* (2 vols; Munich, 1956, 1980).

Anders, Günther, 'Theses for the Atomic Age', *Massachusetts Review*, 3/3 (1962), 493–505.

Anders, Günther, *Hiroshima ist überall* (Munich, 1982).

Arnott, D. G., *Our Nuclear Adventure* (London, 1957).

Atomwaffen und Ethik: Der Deutsche Protestantismus und die atomare Aufrüstung 1954–1969. Dokumente und Kommentare, ed. Christian Welther (Munich, 1981).

Baade, Fritz, *Weltenergiewirtschaft: Atomenergie—Sofortprogramm oder Zukunftsplanung?* (Hamburg, 1958).

Beer, Klaus, *Auf den Feldern von Ulm: In den wechselnden Winden von Adenauer bis Brandt* (Blaubeuren, 2008).

Beilmann, Christel, *Eine katholische Jugend in Gottes und dem Dritten Reich: Briefe, Berichte, Gedrucktes 1930–1945: Kommentare 1988/89* (Wuppertal, 1989).

Bell, George, Bishop of Chichester, *Nuclear War and Peace* (Peace Aims Pamphlet, no. 60) (London, 1955).

Bergmann, Uwe, et al. (eds), *Rebellion der Studenten oder die neue Opposition* (Reinbek, 1968).

Berlin 1958: Bericht über die Tagung der zweiten Synode der EKD (Hanover, 1959).

Bernal, John D., *Science in History* (London, 1954).

Bernal, John D., *World without War* (London, 1958).

BIKINI. Die Fünfziger Jahre. Kalter Krieg und Capri-Sonne. Fotos-Texte-Comics-Analysen, ed. Eckhard Siepmann (Berlin, 1981).

Bloch, Ernst, *Das Prinzip Hoffnung* (3 vols; Frankfurt/Main, 1959).

Böckelmann, Frank, and Nagel, Herbert (eds), *Subversive Aktion: Der Sinn der Organisation ist ihr Scheitern* (Frankfurt/Main, 1976).

Bonham, John, 'The Middle Class Revolt', *Political Quarterly*, 23 (1962), 238–46.

Boulton, David (ed.), *Voices from the Crowd* (London, 1964).

Brandt, Leo, *Die Zweite industrielle Revolution* (Bonn, 1956).

British Council of Churches, *The Era of Atomic Power* (London, 1946).

British Council of Churches, *The British Nuclear Deterrent* (London, 1963).

British Council of Churches, *The Search for Security: A Christian Appraisal* (London, 1973).

Brockway, Fenner, *Outisde the Right* (London, 1963).

Burning Conscience, ed. Robert Jungk (London, 1961).

Buro, Andreas, *Gewaltlos gegen den Krieg: Lebenserinnerungen eines Pazifisten* (Frankfurt/Main, 2011).

Butler, D. E., and Rose, Richard, *The British General Election of 1959*, new edn (London, 1999).

Butler, D. E., and King, Anthony, *The British General Election of 1964*, new edn (London, 1999).

Cadogan, Peter, 'From Civil Disobedience to Confrontation', in Robert Benwick and Trevor Smith (eds), *Direct Action and Democratic Politics* (London, 1972), 169–70.

'Cambridge Communism in the 1930s and 1940s: Reminiscences and Reflections', *Socialist History*, 24 (2003), 29–77.

Charlton, John, *Don't you Hear the H-Bombs Thunder? Youth and Politics on Tyneside in the Late Fifties and Early Sixties* (Pontypool, 2009).

The Church and the World: The Bulletin of the British Council of Churches (June/July 1959), 1–2.

Cmnd 124: *Defence: Outline of Future Policy* (London, 1957).

Collins, L. John, *Faith under Fire* (London, 1966).

Cooper, David (ed.), *Dialectics of Liberation* (Harmondsworth, 1968).

De Ligt, Bart, *The Conquest of Violence* (London, 1938).

Die Denkschriften der Evangelischen Kirche in Deutschland, vol. 1/2: *Frieden, Versöhnung, Menschenrechte* (2 vols; Gütersloh, 1978).

Dirks, Walter, 'Ein "anderer" Katholizismus?', in Norbert Greinacher and Heinz Theo Risse (eds), *Bilanz des deutschen Katholizismus* (Mainz, 1966), 326–59.

Diski, Jenny, *The Sixties* (London, 2009).

Driver, Christopher, *The Disarmers: A Study in Protest* (London, 1964).

Duff, Peggy, *Left, Left, Left: A Personal Account of Six Protest Campaigns* (London, 1971).

Dutschke, Rudi, *Mein langer Marsch: Reden, Schriften und Tagebücher aus zwanzig Jahren*, ed. Gretchen Dutschke-Klotz et al. (Reinbek, 1980).

Dutschke, Rudi, *Geschichte ist machbar: Texte über das herrschende Falsche und die Radikalität des Friedens*, ed. Jürgen Miermeister (Berlin, 1991).

Dutschke, Rudi, *Jeder hat sein Leben ganz zu leben: Die Tagebücher 1963–1979*, ed. Gretchen Dutschke (Cologne, 2003).

Dutschke, Rudi, 'Die geschichtlichen Bedingungen für den internationalen Emanzipationskampf', reprinted in Tilman Fichter and Siegward Lönnendonker, *Dutschkes Deutschland: Der Sozialistische Deutsche Studentenbund, die nationale Frage und die DDR-Kritik von links* (Essen, 2011), 205–17.

Dutschke, Rudi, Krahl, Hans-Jürgen, 'Das Sich-Verweigern erfordet Guerilla-Mentalität', typescript of the sound recording, 5 September 1967 <http://www.glasnost.de/hist/apo/67dutschke.html> (accessed 15 October 2012).

The Effects of Atomic Bombs at Hiroshima and Nagasaki: Report of the British Mission to Japan, published for the Home Office and Air Ministry (London, 1946).

Es geht ums Leben: Der Kampf gegen die Bombe 1945–1965. Eine Dokumentation. Stimmen des Gewissens aus aller Welt zur Atomgefahr. Zur Vorgeschichte des Moskauer Teststoppabkommens, ed. Günther Heipp (Hamburg, 1965).

Evanston to New Delhi 1954–1961: Report of the Central Committee to the Third Assembly of the World Council of Churches, New Delhi (Geneva, 1961).

Fall Out: Radiation Hazards from Nuclear Explosions, incl. a report on the Windscale Disaster and an Analysis of the United States Congress Report on Radioactive Fall out and its Effects in Man, ed. Antoinette Pirie (London, 1958).

The Family of Man: The Greatest Photographic Exhibition of All Time, created by Edward Steichen for the Museum of Modern Art (New York, 1955).

Fraser, Ronald (ed.), *1968: A Student Generation in Revolt* (New York, 1988).

Friedenskomitee der Bundesrepublik Deutschland (ed.), *Blaubuch über den Widerstand gegen die atomare Aufrüstung der Bundesrepublik* (Düsseldorf, 1957).

Fyvel, T. R., *The Troublemakers: Rebellious Youth in an Affluent Society* (New York, 1964).

Gallup, George H. (ed.), *The Gallup International Public Opinion Polls, Great Britain, 1937–1975* (2 vols; New York, 1976).

Goldthorpe, John H., and Lockwood, David, 'Affluence and the British Class Structure', *Sociological Review*, NS 11 (1963), 134–6, 148–56.

Gollwitzer, Helmut, *Forderungen der Freiheit: Aufsätze und Reden zur politischen Ethik* (Munich, 1957).

Gollwitzer, Helmut, *Die Christen und die Atomwaffen*, 4th edn (Munich, 1958).

Green, Jonathon, *Days in the Life: Voices from the English Underground, 1961–1971* (London, 1988).

Green, Jonathon, *All Dressed up: The Sixties and the Counter-Culture* (London, 1998).

Gregg, Richard, *The Power of Non-Violence* (London, 1936).

Grodzins, Morton, and Rabinowitch, Eugene (eds), *The Atomic Age: Scientists in National and World Affairs. Articles from the Bulletin of the Atomic Scientists* (New York, 1963).

Halberstadt, Heiner, 'Protest gegen Remilitarisierung, "Kampagne Kampf dem Atomod" und Ostermarschbewegung in Westdeutschland', in Ulrich Herrmann (ed.), *Protestierende Jugend: Jugendopposition und politischer Protest in der deutschen Nachkriegsgeschichte* (Weinheim and Munich, 2002), 313–27.

Hamblett, Charles, and Deverson, Jane, *Generation X* (London, 1964).

The Hazards to Man of Nuclear and Allied Radiations, ed. Medical Research Council (London, 1956).

Heinemann, Gustav W., 'Christus ist für uns alle gestorben', *Friedensrundschau*, 12/3 (1958), 16–22.

Heuer, Kenneth, *The End of the World: A Scientific Enquiry* (London, 1953).

Hey, Ian (ed.), *80th Birthday Book for Ernest Darwin Simon: Lord Simon of Wythenshawe, b. 9th October 1879* (Stockport, 1959).

Hindell, Keith, and Williams, Philip, 'Scarborough and Blackpool: An Analysis of Some Votes of the Labour Party Conferences of 1960 and 1961', *Political Quarterly*, 33 (1962), 306–20.

Hobsbawm, Eric, 'The Historians' Group of the Communist Party', in Maurice Cornforth (ed.), *Rebels and their Causes: Essays in Honour of A. L. Morton* (London, 1978), 21–47.

Hobsbawm, Eric, *Interesting Times: A Twentieth-Century Life* (London, 2002).

Hoher Meißner 1913: Der Erste Freideutsche Jugendtag in Dokumenten, Deutungen und Bildern, ed. Winfried Mogge and Jürgen Reulecke (Cologne, 1988).

Howe, Günther (ed.), *Atomzeitalter, Krieg und Frieden* (Witten and Berlin, 1959).

Jahrbuch der öffentlichen Meinung 1947–1955, ed. Elisabeth Noelle and E. Peter Neumann, 2nd edn (Allensbach, 1956).

Jahrbuch der öffentlichen Meinung 1958–1964, ed. Elisabeth Noelle and Erich Peter Neumann (Allensbach and Bonn, 1965).

Jaspers, Karl, *Die Atombombe und die Zukunft des Menschen* (Munich, 1957).

Jenke, Robert, *Ostermarsch-Betrachtungen* (Cologne, 1964).

Jenke, Robert, *Ostermarsch-Nachbetrachtungen* (Cologne, 1964).

Jones, Mervyn, *Freed from Fear* (London, 1961).

Jones, Mervyn, *Chances* (London, 1987).

Jungk, Robert, *Die Zukunft hat schon begonnen. Amerikas Allmacht und Ohnmacht* [1952], 8th edn (Stuttgart and Hamburg, 1953).

Jungk, Robert, *Heller als Tausend Sonnen* (Frankfurt/Main, 1956).

Jungk, Robert, and Mundt, Hans Josef (eds), *Deutschland ohne Konzeption? Am Beginn einer neuen Epoche* (Munich et al., 1964).

Kätzel, Ute, *Die 68erinnen: Porträt einer rebellischen Frauengeneration* (Munich, 2008).

Keable, Ken (ed.), *London Recruits: The Secret War against Apartheid* (London, 2012).

Kennan, George F., *Russia, the Atom, and the West* (London, 1958).

Kirst, Hans Hellmut, *Keiner kommt davon: Bericht von den letzten Tagen Europas* (Munich et al., 1957).

Kliefoth, Werner, 'Atomrundschau', *Atomkernenergie*, 2 (1957), 50.

Kliefoth, Werner, *Sind wir bedroht? Ein sachliches Wort zur Atomfrage* (Mosbach/Baden, 1956).

Klönne, Arno, and Reulecke, Jürgen, ' "Restgeschichte" und "neue Romantik". Ein Gespräch über Bündische Jugend in der Nachkriegszeit', in Franz-Werner Kersting (ed.), *Jugend vor einer Welt in Trümmern: Erfahrungen und Verhältnisse der Jugend zwischen Hitler- und Nachkriegsdeutschland* (Weinheim and Munich, 1998), 87–103.

Komitee für Grundrechte und Demokratie e.V. (ed.), *Geschichten aus der Friedensbewegung: Persönliches und Politisches*, collected by Andreas Buro (Cologne, 2005).

Kraushaar, Wolfgang (ed.), *Die Protest-Chronik 1949–1959: Eine illustrierte Geschichte von Bewegung, Widerstand und Utopie* (4 vols; Hamburg, 1996).

Kraushaar, Wolfgang (ed.), *Frankfurter Schule und Studentenbewegung: Von der Flaschenpost zum Molotowcocktail 1946–1995*, 2nd edn (3 vols; Hamburg, 1998).

Krippendorff, Ekkehart, *Lebensfäden: Zehn autobiographische Versuche* (Nettersheim, 2012).

Labour Party, *Proceedings of the 30th Annual Conference* (Bournemouth, 1937).

Labour Party, *Proceedings of the 59th Annual Conference* (Scarborough, 1960).

Lethen, Helmut, *Suche nach dem Handorakel: Ein Bericht* (Göttingen, 2012).

Lönnendonker, Siegward, and Fichter, Tilman (eds), *Freie Universität Berlin: 1948–1973. Hochschule im Umbruch*, (6 vols; Berlin, 1974).

The Macmillan Diaries: The Cabinet Years, 1950–1957, ed. and with an introduction by Peter Catterall (London, 2004).

The Macmillan Diaries II: 1959–1966, ed. and with an introduction by Peter Catterall (London, 2012).

Mass Observation, *Peace and the Public* (London, 1947).

Masters, Dexter, and Way, Katharine (eds), *One World or None: A Report on the Full Meaning of the Atomic Bomb* (New York, 1946).

Methodist Church, *Declarations of Conference on Social Questions* (London, 1959).

Michaltscheff, Theodor, *Gewissen vor dem Prüfungsausschuß* (Hamburg, 1962).

Mills, C. Wright, *The Causes of World War III* (London, 1958).

Ministry of Supply (ed.), *Harwell, the British Atomic Energy Research Establishment, 1946–1951* (London, 1952).

Minnion, John, and Bolsover, Philip (eds), *The CND Story: The First Twenty-Five Years of CND in the Words of the People Involved* (London, 1983).

NATO Strategy Documents, 1949–1969, ed. Gregory W. Pedlow (Brussels, 1997).

Niemeier, Gottfried (ed.), *Evangelische Stimmen zur Atomfrage* (Hanover, 1958).

Niemöller, Martin, *Martin Niemöller zu atomaren Rüstung: Zwei Reden* (Darmstadt, 1959).

Niemöller, Martin, *Reden 1958–1961* (Frankfurt/Main, 1961).

Noelle, Elisabeth, and Neumann, Erich P. (eds), *The Germans: Public Opinion Polls 1947–1966* (Allensbach, 1967).

Otto, Karl A. (ed.), *APO: Die außerparlamentarische Opposition in Quellen und Dokumenten, 1960–1970* (Cologne, 1989).

Oxford University Socialist Discussion Group (ed.), *Out of Apathy: Voices of the New Left 30 Years On* (London, 1989).

Protokoll der 4. ordentlichen Jugendkonferenz der IG Metall für die Bundesrepublik Deutschland, Berlin, 8. und 9. Mai 1958 (Frankfurt, 1958).

Protokolle des Rates der Evangelischen Kirche in Deutschland, ed. Carsten Nicolaisen and N. A. Schulze (4 vols; Göttingen, 1995).

Redgrave, Vanessa (ed.), *Pussies and Tigers* (London, 1963).

Reulecke, Jürgen, 'Waren wir so? Zwanzigjährige um 1960: Ein Beitrag zur "Ich-Archäologie", in Jürgen Reulecke, *"Ich möchte so einer werden so wie die . . ." Männerbünde im 20. Jahrhundert* (Frankfurt/Main, 2001), 249–66.

Richter, Hans Werner (ed.), *Bestandsaufnahme: Eine deutsche Bilanz 1962* (Munich, 1962).

Richter, Hans Werner, *Briefe*, ed. Sabine Cofalla (Munich, 1997).

Riehl-Heyse, Herbert, *Ach, du mein Vaterland: Gemischte Erinnerungen an 50 Jahre Bundesrepublik* (Munich, 2000).

Rienow, Robert, and Rienow, Leona, *Our New Life with the Atom* (New York, 1958).

Röhl, Klaus Rainer, *Fünf Finger sind keine Faust* (Cologne, 1974).

Rothstein, Andrew, *Peaceful Co-Existence* (Harmondsworth, 1955).

Rowbotham, Sheila, *Promise of a Dream: Remembering the Sixties* (Harmdonsworth, 2000).

Russell, Bertrand, *Has Man a Future?* (Harmondsworth, 1961).

Russell, Bertrand, *Unarmed Victory* (London, 1963).

Russell, Bertrand, *The Autobiography of Bertrand Russell* (3 vols; London, 1978).

Saville, John, *Memoirs from the Left* (London, 2003).

Schelsky, Helmut, *Die skeptische Generation: Eine Soziologie der deutschen Jugend* (Cologne and Düsseldorf, 1957).

Schmidt, Helmut, *Defense or Retaliation: A German Contribution to the Consideration of NATO's Strategic Problem* (London, 1962).

Schneider, Peter, *Rebellion und Wahn: Mein '68* (Cologne, 2008).

Schoenmann, Ralph (ed.), *Bertrand Russell: Philosopher of the Century* (New York, 1967).

Schönhoven, Klaus, and Weber, Hermann (eds), *Quellen zur Geschichte der deutschen Gewerkschaftsbewegung im 20. Jahrhundert* (13 vols; Bonn, 2005).

Schwab, Günther, *Der Tanz mit dem Teufel: Ein abenteuerliches Interview* (Hanover, 1958).

SDS Westberlin, *Der Kampf des vietnamesischen Volkes und die Globalstrategie des Imperialismus: Internationaler Vietnam-Kongress 17./18. Februar 1968* (West-Berlin, 1968).

Seifert, Jürgen (ed.), *Die Spiegel Affäre* (2 vols; Freiburg, 1963).

Shute, Nevil, *On the Beach* (London, 1957).

Skriver, Ansgar, 'Von der Schülermitverwaltung zur Kampagne "Kampf dem Atomtod": Der Berliner Studentenkongreß gegen Atomrüstung 1959 und die Auseinandersetzung des "Gespräche"-Kreises mit der "konkret"-Gruppe', in Ulrich Herrmann (ed.), *Protestierende Jugend: Jugendopposition und politischer*

Protest in der deutschen Nachkriegsgeschichte (Weinheim and Munich, 2002), 387–403.

Speier, Hans, *German Rearmament and Atomic War: The Views of German Military and Political Leaders* (Evanston, IL, 1957).

Die Spiegel Affäre, ed. Jürgen Seifert (2 vols; Freiburg, 1963).

Stein, Walter (ed.), *Nuclear Weapons and Christian Conscience* (London, 1961).

Stocks, Mary, *Ernest Simon of Manchester* (Manchester, 1963).

Szczesny, Gerhard, *Als die Vergangenheit Gegenwart war* (Frankfurt/Main, 1990).

Taylor, A. J. P., *The Trouble Makers: Dissent over Foreign Policy, 1792–1939* (London, 1957).

Taylor, A. J. P., *The Origins of the Second World War* (London, 1961).

Taylor, A. J. P., 'Accident Prone, or What Happened Next', *Journal of Modern History*, 49 (1977), 1–18.

Taylor, A. J. P., *A Personal History* (London, 1983).

Tempel, Hans-Konrad, and Tempel, Helga, 'Ostermärsche gegen den Atomtod', in Christoph Butterwegge et al. (eds), *30 Jahre Ostermarsch: Ein Beitrag zur politischen Kultur der Bundesrepulik Deutschland und ein Stück Bremer Stadtgeschichte* (Bremen, 1990), 11–14.

Tempel, Helga, and Tempel, Hans-Konrad, 'Anfänge gewaltfreier Aktion in den ersten 20 Jahren nach dem Krieg', *Gewaltfreie Aktion. Sonderband* (Berlin, 1997), 63–88.

Thayer, George, *The British Political Fringe: A Profile* (London, 1965).

Thielicke, Helmut, 'Der Christ und die Verhütung des Krieges im Atomzeitalter', *Zeitschrift für Evangelische Ethik*, 1 (1957), 1–6.

Thielicke, Helmut, *Die Atomwaffe als Frage an die Christliche Ethik* (Tübingen, 1958).

Thompson, Edward P. (ed.), *Out of Apathy* (London, 1960).

Thompson, Edward P., *The Making of the English Working Class* (London, 1961).

Thompson, Edward P., *Witness against the Beast: William Blake and the Moral Law*, ed. Dorothy Thompson (Cambridge, 1993).

Tjaden, Kay, *rebellion der jungen: die geschichte von tusk und von dj. 1.11* (Frankfurt/Main, 1958).

Uhlig, Werner A., *Atom, Angst oder Hoffnung? Die Lehren des ersten Atommanövers der Welt*, 2nd edn (Munich, 1956).

Unruh, Fritz von, *Wir wollen Frieden: Die Reden und Aufrufe, 1960–61* (Düsseldorf, 1961).

Vack, Klaus, 'Blick zurück ohne Zorn?—Einige politisch-persönliche Auskünfte über Engagement und Organisation sozialer Bewegungen', *Forschungsjournal Neue Soziale Bewegungen*, 2 (November 1989), 131–9.

Vack, Klaus, *Das andere Deutschland nach 1945: Als Pazifist, Sozialist und radikaler Demokrat in der Bundesrepublik Deutschland. Politisch-biographische Skizzen und Beiträge* (Cologne, 2005).

Vincent, Revd J. J., *Christ in a Nuclear World* (Manchester, 1962).

Was Niemöller sagt—wogegen Strauß klagt: Niemöllers kasseler Rede vom 25. Januar 1959 im vollen Wortlaut (Darmstadt, 1959).

Weizsäcker, Carl Friedrich von, *Die Verantwortung der Wissenschaft im Atomzeitalter* (Göttingen, 1957).

Weizsäcker, Carl Friedrich von, *Der bedrohte Frieden: Politische Aufsätze 1945–1981* (Munich, 1983).

Widgery, David (ed.), *The Left in Britain, 1958–1968* (Harmondsworth, 1976).

Wilhelm, Theodor, *Pädagogik der Gegenwart* (Stuttgart, 1960).

Wodehouse, P. G., 'Bingo bans the bomb', in Wodehouse, *Plum Pie* (London, 1966), 119–36.

Wolf, Ernst, and Schmauch, Werner, *Die Königsherrschaft Christi und der Staat* (Munich, 1958).

Wolf, Ernst, Schmauch, Werner, et al., *Christusbekenntnis im Atomzeitalter?* (Munich, 1959).

Young, Wayland, *Strategy for Survival: First Steps in Nuclear Disarmament* (Harmondsworth, 1959).

Zweig, Ferdynand, *The Worker in an Affluent Society: Family Life and Industry* (London, 1961).

Zweig, Ferdynand, *The Student in the Age of Anxiety* (London, 1963).

4. PRINTED SECONDARY WORKS

Albrecht, Willy, *Der Sozialistische Deutsche Studentenbund (SDS): Vom parteikonformen Studentenverband zum Repräsentanten der Neuen Linken* (Bonn, 1994).

Angelo, Anne-Marie, 'The Black Panthers in London, 1967–1972: A Diasporic Struggle Navigates the Black Atlantic', *Radical History Review*, 103 (2009), 17–35.

Appelius, Stefan, *Pazifismus in Westdeutschland: Die Deutsche Friedensgesellschaft 1945–1968* (2 vols; Aachen, 1991).

Arnold, Jörg, *The Allied Air War and Urban Memory: The Legacy of Strategic Bombing in Germany* (Cambridge, 2011).

Bald, Detlef, *Die Atombewaffnung der Bundeswehr: Militär, Öffentlichkeit und Politik in der Ära Adenauer* (Bremen, 1994).

Ballistier, Thomas, *Straßenprotest: Formen oppositioneller Politik in der Bundesrepublik Deutschland* (Münster, 1996).

Balsen, Werner, and Rössel, Karl, *Hoch die internationale Solidarität: Zur Geschichte der Dritte-Welt-Bewegung in der Bundesrepublik* (Cologne, 1986).

Behrenbeck, Sabine, *Der Kult um die toten Helden: Nationalsozialistische Mythen, Riten und Symbole 1923 bis 1945* (Vierow, 1996).

Beinert, Heinz et al. (eds), *Zwischen Anpassung und politischem Kampf. Schriftenreihe der SJD—Die Falken. Dokumente 5* (Bonn 1974).

Berger, Stefan, 'A Return to the National Paradigm? National History Writing in Germany, Italy, France and Britain from 1945 to the Present', *Journal of Modern History*, 77 (2005), 629–78.

Berger, Stefan, and La Porte, Norman, *Friendly Enemies: Britain and the GDR, 1949–1990* (Oxford, 2010).

Berger, Stefan, and Lilleker, Darren, 'The British Labour Party and the German Democratic Republic during the Era of Non-Recognition, 1949–1973', *Historical Journal*, 45 (2002), 433–58.

Bernhard, Patrick, *Zivildienst zwischen Reform und Revolte: Eine bundesdeutsche Institution im gesellschaftlichen Wandel 1961–1982* (Munich, 2005).

Bess, Michael, 'E. P. Thompson: The Historian as Activist', *American Historical Review*, 98 (1993), 18–38.

Bessel, Richard, and Schumann, Dirk (eds), *Life after Death: Approaches to a Cultural and Social History of Europe during the 1940s and 1950s* (Cambridge, 2003).

Bethge, Horst, '"Die Bombe ist böse": Wie der Ostermarsch in Hamburg entstand', in Jörg Berlin (ed.), *Das andere Hamburg: Freiheitliche Bestrebungen in der Hansestadt seit dem Spätmittelalter* (Cologne, 1981), 357–68.

Betts, Paul, 'Germany, International Justice and the Twentieth Century', *History & Memory*, 7 (2005), 45–86.

Betts, Paul, and Crowley, David, 'Introduction', *Journal of Contemporary History*, 40 (2005), 213–36.

Betts, Paul, and Eghigian, Greg (eds), *Pain and Prosperity: Reconsidering Twentieth-Century German History* (Stanford, CA, 2003).

Biess, Frank, *Homecomings: Returning POWs and the Legacies of Defeat in Postwar Germany* (Princeton, 2006).

Biess, Frank, '"Everybody Has a Chance": Civil Defense, Nuclear *Angst*, and the History of Emotions in Postwar Germany', *German History*, 27 (2009), 215–43.

Biess, Frank, 'Feelings in the Aftermath: Toward a History of Postwar Emotions', in Biess and Moeller (eds), *Histories of the Aftermath: The Legacies of the Second World War in Europe* (New York, 2010), 30–48.

Biess, Frank and Moeller, Robert (eds), *Histories of the Aftermath. The Legacies of the Second World War in Europe* (New York, 2010).

Biltz, Fritz, 'Die Protestbewegungt gegen Remilitarisierung und Atomwaffen am neuen Bundeswehrstandort Köln', in Jost Dülffer (ed.), *Köln in den 50er Jahren. Zwischen Tradition und Modernisierung* (Cologne, 2001), 305–19.

Bingham, Adrian, *Family Newspapers: Sex, Private Life, and the British Popular Press 1918–1978* (Oxford, 2009).

Bingham, Adrian, '"The Monster"? The British Popular Press and Nuclear Culture, 1945–Early 1960s', *British Journal for the History of Science*, 45 (2012), 609–24.

Black, Lawrence, *The Political Culture of the Left in Affluent Britain, 1951–64: Old Labour, New Britain?* (Basingstoke, 2003).

Black, Lawrence, *Redefining British Politics: Culture, Consumerism and Participation, 1954–70* (Basingstoke, 2010).

Bock, Hans Manfred, *Geschichte des 'linken Radikalismus' in Deutschland: Ein Versuch* (Frankfurt/Main, 1976).

Bodemann, Y. Michael, 'Eclipse of Memory: German Representations of Auschwitz in the Early Postwar Period', *New German Critique*, 75 (1998), 57–89.

Bogdanor, Vernon, and Skidelsky, Robert (eds), *The Age of Affluence 1951–1964* (London, 1970).

Boll, Friedhelm, 'Von der Hitler-Jugend zur Kampagne "Kampf dem Atomtod": Zur politischen Sozialisation einer niedersächsischen Schüler- und Studentengruppe', in Ulrich Herrmann (ed.), *Protestierende Jugend: Jugendopposition und politischer Protest in der deutschen Nachkriegsgeschichte* (Weinheim and Munich, 2002), 357–85.

Boll, Friedhelm, 'Die Werkhefte katholischer Laien 1947–1963: Jugendbewegung—Gesellschaftskritik—Pazifismus', in Michel Grunewald and Uwe Puschner (eds), *Le Milieu intellectuel catholique en Allemagne, sa presse et ses reseaux (1871–1963)* (Berne, 2006), 505–36.

Booker, Christopher, *The Neophiliacs: Revolution in English Life in the Fifties and Sixties* (London, 1992).

Bourdieu, Pierre, *Language and Symbolic Power* (Cambridge, 1992).

Bourdieu, Pierre, *Soziologische Fragen* (Frankfurt/Main, 1993).

Boyens, Armin, 'Das Stuttgarter Schuldbekenntnis vom 19. Oktober 1945—Entstehung und Bedeutung', *Vierteljahrshefte für Zeitgeschichte*, 19 (1971), 374–97.

Brandstetter, Thomas, 'Wie man lernt die Bombe zu lieben: Zur diskursiven Konstruktion atomarer Gewalt', in Günther Friesinger, Thomas Ballhausen, and Johannes Grenzfurthner (eds), *Schutzverletzungen: Legitimation medialer Gewalt* (Berlin, 2010), 25–54.

Braun, Hans, 'Das Streben nach "Sicherheit" in den 50er Jahren: Soziale und Politische Ursachen und Erscheinungsweisen', *Archiv für Sozialgeschichte*, 18 (1978), 279–306.

Breines, Wini, *Community and Organization in the New Left, 1962–1968: The Great Refusal* (New Brunswick, NJ, 1982).

Briem, Jürgen, *Der SDS: Die Geschichte des bedeutendsten Studentenverbandes der BRD seit 1945* (Frankfurt/Main, 1976).

Brown, Andrew, *Keeper of the Nuclear Conscience: The Life and Work of Joseph Rotblat* (Oxford, 2012).

Brown, Callum, *The Death of Christian Britain* (London, 2000).

Brubaker, Rogers, and Cooper, Frederick, 'Beyond "Identity"', *Theory and Society*, 29 (2000), 1–47.

Buchan, Jane, and Buchan, Norman, 'The Campaign in Scotland', in John Minion and Philip Bolosver (eds), *The CND Story: The First 25 years of CND in the Words of the People Involved* (London, 1983), 52–5.

Buchanan, Tom, *East Wind: China and the British Left, 1925–1976* (Oxford, 2012).

Burk, Kathleen, *Troublemaker: The Life and History of A. J. P. Taylor* (New Haven and London, 2000).

Burkett, Jodi, 'Re-Defining British Morality: "Britishness" and the Campaign for Nuclear Disarmament 1958–1968', *Twentieth Century British History*, 21 (2010), 184–205.

Burkett, Jodi, 'The Campaign for Nuclear Disarmament and Changing Attitudes towards the Earth in the Nuclear Age', *British Journal for the History of Science*, 45 (2012), 625–39.

Butterwegge, Christoph, *Friedenspolitik in Bremen nach dem Zweiten Weltkrieg* (Bremen, 1989).

Butterwegge, Chistoph (ed.), *30 Jahre Ostermarsch: Ein Beitrag zur politischen Kultur der Bundesrepublik Deutschland und ein Stück Bremer Stadtgeschichte* (Bremen, 1990).

Butterwegge, Christoph, *Bremen im Kalten Krieg: Zeitzeug(inn)en berichten aus den 50er und 60er Jahren: Westintegration—Wiederbewaffnung—Friedensbewegung* (Bremen, 1991).

Buzan, Barry, *People, States and Fear: An Agenda for International Security Studies in the Post-Cold War Era* (Boulder, CO, 1991).

Byrne, Paul, *Social Movements in Britain* (London and New York 1997).

Calhourn, Craig, *Roots of Radicalism: Tradition, the Public Sphere, and Early Nineteenth-Century Social Movements* (Chicago, 2012).

Callaghan, John, 'The Left and the "Unfinished Revolution": Bevanites and Soviet Russia in the 1950s', *Contemporary British History*, 15 (2001), 63–82.

Callaghan, John, *Cold War, Crisis and Conflict: The CPGB 1951–68* (London, 2003).

Campbell, John, *Nye Bevan and the Mirage of British Socialism* (London, 1987).

Cannadine, David, *Class in Britain* (London, 2000).

Canning, Kathleen, 'Introduction: The Politics of Symbols, Semantics, and Sentiments in the Weimar Republic', *Central European History*, 43 (2010), 567–80.

Canning, Kathleen, and Rose, Sonya O., 'Gender, Citizenship and Subjectivity: Some Historical and Theoretical Considerations', *Gender & History*, 13 (2001), 427–43.

Carson, Cathryn, *Heisenberg in the Atomic Age: Science and the Public Sphere* (Cambridge, 2010).

Carter, April, *Peace Movements: International Protest and World Politics since 1945* (London, 1992).

Castoriadis, Cornelius, *The Imaginary Institution of Society* (Cambridge, MA, 1998).

Ceadel, Martin, *Semi-Detached Idealists: The British Peace Movement and International Relations, 1854–1945* (Oxford, 2000).

Chabot, Sean, *Transnational Roots of the Civil Rights Movement: African American Explorations of the Gandhian Repertoire* (Lanham, MD, 2012).

Chandler, Andrew, 'The Church of England and the Obliteration Bombing of Germany in the Second World War', *English Historical Review*, 108 (1993), 920–46.

Chun, Lin, *The British New Left* (Edinburgh, 1993).

Cioc, Mark, *Pax Atomica: The Nuclear Defense Debate in West Germany during the Adenauer Era* (New York, 1988).

Clark, Ronald William, *The Life of Bertrand Russell* (London, 1975).

Collini, Stefan, *Public Moralists: Political Thought and Intellectual Life in Britain 1850–1930* (Oxford, 1991).

Conze, Eckart, 'Sicherheit als Kultur: Überlegungen zu einer "modernen Politikgeschichte" der Bundesrepublik Deutschland', *Vierteljahrshefte für Zeitgeschichte*, 53 (2005), 357–80.

Conze, Eckart, *Die Suche nach Sicherheit: Eine Geschichte der Bundesrepublik von 1949 bis zur Gegenwart* (Berlin, 2009).

Crowson, Nick, Hilton, Matthew, and McKay, James (eds), *NGOs in Contemporary Britain: Non-State Actors in Society and Politics since 1945* (London, 2009).

Daase, Christopher, 'National, Societal, and Human Security: On the Transformation of Political Language', *Historical Social Research*, 35/4 (2010), 22–37.

Daase, Christopher, 'Sicherheitskultur – Ein Konzept zur interdisziplinären Erforschung politischen und sozialen Wandels', *Sicherheit und Frieden*, 29/2 (2011), 59–65.

Daase, Christopher, 'Die Historisierung der Sicherheit. Anmerkungen zur historischen Sicherheitsforschung aus politikwissenschaftlícher Sicht', *Geschichte und Gesellschaft*, 38, 3 (2012), 387–405.

Damberg, Wilhelm, *Abschied vom Milieu? Katholizismus im Bistum Münster und in den Niederlanden 1945–1980* (Paderborn et al., 1997).

Davie, Grace, *Religion in Britain since 1945: Believing without Belonging* (Oxford, 1994).

Davis, Belinda, 'Jenseits von Terror und Rückzug: Die Suche nach politischem Spielraum und Strategien im Westdeutschland der siebziger Jahre', in Klaus Weinhauer, Jörg Requate, and Heinz-Gerhard Haupt (eds), *Terrorismus in der Bundesrepublik: Medien, Staat und Subkulturen in den siebziger Jahren* (Frankfurt/Main, 2006), 154–86.

Davis, Belinda, 'Violence and Memory of the Nazi Past in 1960s–70s West German Protest', in Phillip Gassert and Alan Steinweis (eds), *Coming to Terms with the Past in West Germany: The 1960s* (New York, 2006), 245–86.

Davis, Belinda, 'What's Left? Popular Participation in Postwar Europe', *American Historical Review*, 113 (April 2008), 363–90.

Davis, John, and Waring, Anette, 'Living Utopia: Communal Living in Denmark and Britain', *Cultural and Social History*, 8 (2012), 513–30.

Della Porta, Donatella, and Diani, Mario, *Social Movements: An Introduction* (Oxford, 1999).

Donnelly, Mark, *Sixties Britain* (Harlow, 2005).

Dülffer, Jost, 'The Movement against Rearmament 1951–55 and the Movement against Nuclear Armament 1957/59 in the Federal Republic: A Comparison', in Maurice Vaïsse (ed.), *Le Pacifisme en Europe des années 1920 aux années 1950* (Brussels, 1993), 417–34.

Dutschke, Gretchen, *Rudi Dutschke: Wir hatten ein barbarisches, schönes Leben. Eine Biographie* (Cologne, 1996).

Dworkin, Dennis, *Cultural Marxism in Postwar Britain: History, the New Left, and the Origins of Cultural Marxism* (Durham, NC, 1997).

Echternkamp, Jörg, ' "Verwirrung im Vaterländischen"? Nationalismus in der deutschen Nachkriegsgesellschaft 1945–1960', in Echternkamp and Sven Oliver Müller (eds), *Die Politik der Nation: Deutscher Nationalismus in Krieg und Krisen 1760–1960* (Munich, 2002), 219–46.

Eckert, Michael, 'Die Anfänge der Atompolitik in der Bundesrepublik Deutschland', *Vierteljahrshefte für Zeitgeschichte*, 37 (1989), 115–43.

Edgerton, David, *Warfare State: Britain, 1920–1970* (Cambridge, 2006).

Eitler, Pascal, 'Politik und Religion: Semantische Grenzen und Grenzverschiebungen in der Bundesrepublik Deutschland 1965–1975', in Ute Frevert and Heinz-Gerhard Haupt (eds), *Neue Politikgeschichte: Perspektiven einer historischen Politikforschung* (Frankfurt/Main and New York, 2005), 268–303.

Eley, Geoff, 'Labour History, Social History, *Alltagsgeschichte*: Experience, Culture, and the Politics of the Everyday—a New Direction for German Social History?', *Journal of Modern History*, 61 (1989), 297–343.

Eley, Geoff, 'Is All the World a Text? From Social History to the History of Society Two Decades Later', in Terrence J. McDonald (ed.), *The Historic Turn in the Human Sciences* (Ann Arbor, 1996), 193–243.

Eley, Geoff, *Forging Democracy: The History of the Left in Europe, 1850–2000* (Oxford, 2002).

Eley, Geoff, and Nield, Keith, *The Future of Class in History: What's Left of the Social?* (Ann Arbor, 2007)

Engels, Jens Ivo, 'Vom Subjekt zum Objekt: Naturbild und Naturkatastrophen in der Geschichte der Bundesrepublik', in Dieter Groh et al. (eds), *Naturkatastrophen: Beiträge zu ihrer Deutung, Wahrnehmung und Darstellung in Text und Bild von der Antike bis ins 20. Jahrhundert* (Tübingen, 2003), 119–42.

Eyerman, Ron, and Jamison, Andrew, *Social Movements: A Cognitive Approach* (Cambridge, 1991).

Fahlenbrach, Kathrin, *Protestinszenierungenm: Visuelle Kommunikation und kollektive Identitäten in protestbewegungen* (Wiesbaden, 2002).

Favretto, Ilaria, '"Wilsonism" Reconsidered: Labour Party Revisionism, 1952–1964', *Contemporary British History*, 14 (2000), 54–80.

Fichter, Tilman, *SDS und SPD: Parteilichkeit jenseits der Partei* (Opladen, 1988).

Fichter, Tilman, and Lönnendonker, Siegward, *Dutschkes Deutschland: Der Sozialistische Deutsche Studentenbund, die nationale Frage und die DDR-Kritik von links* (Essen, 2011).

Fielding, Steven, *Labour and Cultural Change* (Manchester and New York, 2003).

Fink, Carole, Gassert, Philipp, and Junker, Detlef (eds), *1968: The World Transformed* (Cambridge, 1998).

Freedman, Lawrence, *Britain and Nuclear Weapons* (London and Basingstoke, 1980).

Gallus, Alexander, *Die Neutralisten: Verfechter eines vereinten Deutschlands zwischen Ost und West, 1945–1990* (Düsseldorf, 2001).

Gerster, Daniel, 'Von Pilgerfahrten zu Protestmärschen? Zum Wandel des katholischen Friedensengagements in den USA und der Bundesrepublik Deutschland 1945–1990', *Archiv für Sozialgeschichte*, 51 (2011), 311–42.

Gerster, Daniel, *Friedensdialoge im Kalten Krieg: Eine Geschichte der Katholiken in der Bundesrepublik* (Frankfurt/Main, 2012).

Geyer, Michael, *Deutsche Rüstungspolitik 1860–1980* (Frankfurt/Main, 1984).

Geyer, Michael, 'Der kriegerische Blick: Rückblick auf einen noch zu beendenden Krieg', *SoWi* 19 (1990), 111–17.

Geyer, Michael, 'Das Stigma der Gewalt und das Problem der nationalen Identität in Deutschland', in Christian Jansen, Alf Lüdtke, and Bernd Weisbrod (eds), *Von der Aufgabe der Freiheit: politische Verantwortung und bürgerliche Gesellschaft im 19. und 20. Jahrhundert: Festschrif für Hans Mommsen zum 5. November 1995* (Berlin, 1995), 673–98.

Geyer, Michael, 'Cold War Angst: The Case of West-German Opposition to Rearmament and Nuclear Weapons', in Hanna Schissler (ed.), *The Miracle Years: A Cultural History of West Germany, 1949–1968* (Princeton and Oxford, 2001), 376–408.

Gilcher-Holtey, Ingrid, *'Die Phantasie an die Macht'. Mai 68 in Frankreich* (Frankfurt/Main 1995).

Gilcher-Holtey, Ingrid (ed.), *1968—Vom Ereignis zum Gegenstand in der Geschichtswissenschaft* (Göttingen, 1998).

Gilcher-Holtey, Ingrid, '"Askese schreiben, schreib: Askese": Zur Rolle der Gruppe 47 in der politischen Kultur der Nachkriegszeit', *Internationales Archiv für Sozialgeschichte der deutschen Literatur*, 25 (2000), 134–67.

Gildea, Robert and Mark, James, 'Introduction: Voices of Europe's 68', *Cultural and Social History*, 8 (2011), 441–8.

Gleadle, Kathryn, *Borderline Citizens: Women, Gender and Political Culture in Britain, 1815–1867* (Oxford, 2009).

Gleason, Philip, 'Identifying Identity: A Semantic History', *Journal of American History*, 69 (1983), 910–93.

Goebel, Stefan, 'Coventry und Dresden: Transnationale Netwerke der Erinnerung in den 1950er und 1960er Jahren', in Dietmar Süß (ed.), *Deutschland im Luftkrieg: Geschichte und Erinnerung* (Munich, 2007), 111–120.

Goldstein, David M., 'Toward a Critical Anthropology of Security', *Current Anthropology*, 51 (2010), 487–99.

Goltz, Anna von der, 'Generations of 68ers: Age-Related Constructions of Identity and Germany's "1968"', *Cultural and Social History*, 8 (2011), 473–90.

Gowing, Margaret, *Independence and Deterrence: Britain and Atomic Energy, 1945–1952* (2 vols; London, 1974).

Grant, Matthew, *After the Bomb: Civil Defence and Nuclear War in Britain* (Basingstoke, 2009).

Grayzel, Susan R., *At Home and under Fire: Air Raids and Culture in Britain from the Great War to the Blitz* (Cambridge, 2012).

Greschat, Martin, *Protestantismus im Kalten Krieg: Kirche, Politik und Gesellschaft im geteilten Deutschland* (Paderborn, 2010).

Groh, Dieter, and Brandt, Peter *'Vaterlandslose Gesellen': Sozialdemokratie und Nation 1860–1990* (Munich, 1992).

Gröschel, Roland, *Zwischen Tradition und Neubeginn: Sozialistische Jugend im Nachkriegsdeutschland: Entstehung und historische Wurzeln der Sozialistischen Jugend Deutschlands—Die Falken* (Hamburg, 1986).

Grünewald, Guido, *Zwischen Kriegsdienstverweigerergewerkschaft und politischer Friedensorganisation: Der Verband der Kriegsdienstverweigerer 1958–1966* (Hamburg, 1977).

Grünewald, Guido, *Die Internationale der Kriegsdienstgegner (IdK): Ihre Geschichte 1945–1968* (Cologne, 1982).

Gunn, Simon, and Vernon, James, 'Introduction', in Simon Gunn and James Vernon (eds), *The Peculiarities of Liberal Modernity in Imperial Britain* (Berkeley and Los Angeles, 2011), 1–18.

Habermas, Jürgen, *The Structural Transformation of the Public Sphere: An Inquiry into a Category of Bourgeois Society* (Cambridge, 1989).

Hakemi, Sara, *Anschlag und Spektakel: Flugblätter der Kommune I, Erklärungen von Ensslin/Baader und der frühen RAF* (Bochum, 2008).

Hamilton, Scott, *The Crisis of Theory: EP Thompson, the New Left and Postwar British Politics* (Manchester, 2011).

Hanshew, Karrin, *Terror and Democracy in West Germany* (Cambridge, 2012).

Harrison, Brian, 'Oxford and the Labour Movement', *Twentieth Century British History*, 2 (1991), 226–71.

Harrison, Brian, *Seeking a Role: The United Kingdom 1951–1970* (Oxford, 2009).

Hasenöhrl, Ute, *Zivilgesellschaft und Protest: Eine Geschichte der Naturschutz- und Umweltbewegung in Bayern 1945–1980* (Göttingen, 2011).

Hastings, Adrian, *A History of English Christianity 1920–1990* (London, 1991).

Hauswedell, Corinna, *Friedenswissenschaften im Kalten Krieg: Friedensforschung und friedenswissenschaftliche Initiativen in der Bundesrepublik in den achtziger Jahren* (Baden-Baden, 1997).

Heigl, Richard, *Oppositionspolitik: Wolfgang Abendroth und die Entstehung der Neuen Linken* (Hamburg, 2008).

Henderson, Ian (ed.), *Man of Christian Action: Canon John Collins—the Man and his Work* (Guildford, 1976).

Hennessy, Peter, *The Secret State: Preparing for the Worst 1945–2010* (Harmondsworth, 2010).

Herbert, Ulrich (ed.), *Wandlungsprozesse in Westdeutschland: Belastung, Integration, Liberalisierung 1945–1980* (Göttingen, 2002).

Herms, Michael, *Hinter den Linien: Westarbeit der FDJ 1945–1956* (Berlin, 2001), 262–75.

Herzog, Dagmar, *Sex after Fascism: Memory and Morality in Twentieth-Century Germany* (Princeton, 2005).

Heuser, Beatrice, *NATO, Britain, France and the FRG: Nuclear Strategies and Forces for Europe, 1949–2000* (Basingstoke and London, 1998).

Heuser, Beatrice, *Nuclear Mentalities? Strategies and Belief-Systems in Britain, France and the FRG* (Basingstoke and New York, 1998).

Hewison, Robert, *In Anger: Culture in the Cold War 1945–60* (London, 1981).

Hilton, Matthew, 'Politics is Ordinary: Non-Governmental Organisations and Political Participation in Contemporary Britain', *Twentieth Century British History*, 22 (2011), 230–68.

Hinton, James, *Protests and Visions: Peace Politics in 20th Century Britain* (London, 1989).

Hinton, James, *Nine Wartime Lives: Mass-Observation and the Making of the Modern Self* (Oxford, 2010).

Hodenberg, Christina von, *Konsens und Krise: Eine Geschichte der westdeutschen Medienöffentlichkeit 1945–1973* (Göttingen, 2006).

Hodenberg, Christina von, and Siegfried, Detlef (eds), *Wo '1968' liegt: Reform und Revolte in der Geschichte der Bundesrepublik* (Göttingen, 2006).

Hoefferle, Caroline, *British Student Activism in the Long Sixties* (London, 2012).

Höhn, Maria and Klimke, Martin, *A Breath of Freedom: The Civil Rights Struggle, African American GIs, and Germany* (Basingstoke, 2010).

Hogg, Jonathan and Laucht, Christoph, 'Introduction: British Nuclear Culture', *British Journal for the History of Science*, 45 (2012), 479–93.

Holmes Cooper, Alice, *Paradoxes of Peace: German Peace Movements since 1945* (Ann Arbor, 1996).

Horn, Eva, *Der geheime Krieg: Verrat, Spionage und moderne Fiktion* (Frankfurt/ Main, 2007).

Horn, Gerd-Rainer, *The Spirit of '68: Rebellion in Western Europe and North America, 1956–1976* (Oxford, 2007).

Howe, Stephen, *Anticolonialism in British Politics: The Left and the End of Empire, 1918–1964* (Oxford, 1993).

Howell, David, ' "Shut your Gob!": Trade Unions and the Labour Party, 1945–64', in Alan Campbell, Nina Fishman, and John McIlroy (eds), *British Trade Unions and Industrial Politics*, i. *The Post-War Compromise, 1945–64* (Aldershot et al., 1999), 117–44.

Hudson, Kate, *CND—Now More Than Ever. The Story of a Peace Movement* (London, 2005).

Iriye, Akira, *Global Community: The Role of International Organizations in the Making of the Contemporary World* (Berkeley and Los Angeles, 2002).

Jarausch, Konrad H., and Geyer, Michael, *Shattered Past: Reconstructing German Histories* (Princeton, 2003).

Jochheim, Gernot, *Antimilitaristische Aktionstheorie, Soziale Revolution und Soziale Verteidigung: Zur Entwicklung der Gewaltfreiheitstheorie in der europäischen antimilitaristischen und sozialistischen Bewegung 1890–1940, unter besonderer Berücksichtigung der Niederlande* (Frankfurt/Main, 1977).

Juchler, Ingo, *Die Studentenbewegungen in den Vereinigten Staaten und der Bundesrepublik Deutschland der sechziger Jahre: Eine Untersuchung hinsichtlich ihrer Beeinflussung durch Befreiungsbewegungen und -theorien aus der dritten Welt* (Berlin, 1996).

Jung, Matthias, *Öffentlichkeit und Sprachwandel: Zur Geschichte des Diskurses über die Atomenergie* (Opladen, 1992).

Jureit, Ulrike, and Wildt, Michael (eds), *Generationen: Zur Relevanz eines wissenschaftlichen Grundbegriffs* (Hamburg, 2005).

Kaufmann, Franz-Xaver, *Sicherheit als soziologisches und sozialpolitisches Problem* (Stuttgart, 1970).

Keck, Margaret E., and Sikkink, Kathryn, *Activists beyond Borders: Advocacy Networks in International Politics* (Ithaca, NY, and London, 1998).

Kenny, Michael, 'Communism and the New Left', in Geoff Andrews, Nina Fishman, and Kevin Morgan (eds), *Opening the Books: Essays on the Social and Cultural History of British Communism* (London and Boulder, CO, 1995), 195–209.

Kenny, Michael, *The First New Left: British Intellectuals after Stalin* (London, 1995).

Kenny, Michael, 'Socialism and the Romantic "Self": The Case of Edward Thompson', *Journal of Political Ideologies*, 5 (2000), 105–27.

Kirby, Dianne, 'The Church of England and the Cold War Nuclear Debate', *Twentieth Century British History*, 4 (1993), 250–83.

Kittsteiner, Heinz Dieter, *Die Entstehung des modernen Gewissens* (Frankfurt/Main, 1995).

Kittsteiner, Heinz Dieter, 'Das deutsche Gewissen im 20. Jahrhundert', in Richard Faber (ed.), *Politische Religion—Religiöse Politik* (Würzburg, 1997), 227–42.

Klein, Maria, Müller, Gerhard, and Schlaga, Rüdiger, *Politische Strömungen in der Friedensbewegung 1966–1974: Diskussionen, Auseinandersetzungen und Veränderungen in der Deutschen Friedensgesellschaft (DFG), der Internationale der Kriegsdienstgegner (IdK) und dem Verband der Kriegsdienstverweigerer (VK) bis zu deren Vereinheitlichung zur Deutschen Friedensgesellschaft/Vereinigte Kriegsdienstgegner (DFG/VK)* (Frankfurt/Main, 1978).

Klimke, Martin, *The Other Alliance: Student Protest in West Germany and the United States in the Global Sixties* (Princeton, 2009).

Klimke, Martin and Scharloth, Joachim (eds), *1968. Handbuch zur Kultur- und Mediengeschichte der Studentenbewegung* (Stuttgart, 2007).

Klimke, Martin and Scharloth, Joachim (eds), *1968 in Europe. A History of Protest and Activism* (New York, 2008).

Klönne, Arno, *Blaue Blumen in Trümmerlandschaften: Bündische Jugendgruppen in den Jahren nach 1945* (Witzenhausen, 1990).

Klönne, Arno, 'Kampagnen im Ruhrgebiet gegen die Rüstungspolitik: Erinnerungen und Reflexionen eines Zeitzeugen', in Jan-Pieter Barbian and Ludger Heid (eds), *Die Entdeckung des Ruhrgebiets: Das Ruhrgebiet in Nordrhein-Westfalen 1946–1996* (Essen, 1997), 107–12.

Klotzbach, Kurt, *Der Weg zur Staatspartei: Programmatik, praktische Politik und Organisation der deutschen Sozialdemokratie 1945–1965* (Bonn, 1996).

Knoch, Habbo, *Die Tat als Bild: Fotografien in der deutschen Erinnerungskultur* (Hamburg, 2001).

Koonz, Claudia, *The Nazi Conscience* (Cambridge, MA, and London, 2003).

Kosek, Joseph Kip, 'Richard Gregg, Mohandas Ghandi, and the Strategy of Nonviolence', *Journal of American History*, 91 (2005), 1318–48.

Koss, Stephen E., *Nonconformity in Modern British Politics* (London, 1975).

Kössler, Till, 'Zwischen militanter Tradition und Zivilgesellschaft. Die Kommunisten in Westdeutschland 1945–1960', in Thomas Kühne (ed.), *Von der Kriegskultur zur Friedenskultur? Zum Mentalitätswandel in Deutschland seit 1945* (Hamburg, 2000), 210–41.

Kössler, Till, *Abschied von der Revolution: Kommunisten und Gesellschaft in Westdeutschland 1945–1968* (Düsseldorf, 2005).

Kraushaar, Wolfgang, *1968 als Mythos, Chiffre und Zäsur* (Hamburg, 2000).

Kritidis, Gregor, *Linkssozialistische Opposition in der Ära Adenauer: Ein Beitrag zur Frühgeschichte der Bundesrepublik Deutschland* (Hanover, 2008).

Kruke, Anja, *Demoskopie in der Bundesrepublik Deutschland: Meinungsforschung, Parteien und Medien 1949–1990* (Düsseldorf, 2007).

Kühne, Thomas, *Kameradschaft: Die Soldaten des nationalsozialistischen Krieges und das 20. Jahrhundert* (Göttingen, 2006).

Laclau, Ernesto, *New Reflections on the Revolution of our Time* (London, 1990).

Laucht, Christoph, 'Atoms for the People: The Atomic Scientists' Association, the British State and Nuclear Education in the Atom Train Exhibition, 1947–1948', *British Journal for the History of Science*, 45 (2012), 591–608.

Lawrence, Jon, 'Forging a Peaceable Kingdom: War, Violence and the Fear of Brutalization in Post-First World War Britain', *Journal of Modern History*, 75 (2003), 557–89.

Leggewie, Claus, *Die Kofferträger: Das Algerien-Projekt der Linken im Adenauer-Deutschland* (Berlin, 1989).

Lehnert, Detlef, *Sozialdemokratie zwischen Protestbewegung und Regierungspartei 1848–1983* (Frankfurt/Main, 1983).

Lilleker, Darren G., *Against the Cold War: The History and Political Traditions of Pro-Sovietism in the British Labour Party 1945–89* (London, 2004).

Lindenberger, Thomas, 'From the Chopped-off Hand to the Twisted Foot: Citizenship and Political Violence in Twentieth-Century Germany', in Geoff Eley and Jan Palmowski (eds), *Citizenship and National Identity in Twentieth-Century Germany* (Stanford, CA, 2008), 108–28.

Linse, Ulrich, *Ökopax und Anarchie: Eine Geschichte der ökologischen Bewegungen in Deutschland* (Munich, 1986).

Lönnendonker, Siegward (ed.), *Linksintellektueller Aufbruch zwischen 'Kultur-revolution' und 'kultureller Zerstörung': Der Sozialistische Deutsche Studenten-bund (SDS) in der Nachkriegsgeschichte (1946–1969). Dokumentation eines Symposiums* (Opladen, 1998).

Lönnendonker, Siegward, Rabehl, Bernd, and Staadt, Jochen, *Die Antiautoritäre Revolte: Der Sozialistische Deutsche Studentenbund nach der Trennung von der SPD* (Wiesbaden, 2002).

Lorenz, Robert, *Protest der Physiker: Die 'Göttinger Erklärung' von 1957* (Bielefeld, 2011).

Mah, Harold, 'The Predicament of Experience', *Modern Intellectual History*, 5 (2008), 97–119.

McAdam, Doug, McCarthy, John D., and Zald, Mayer N. (eds), *Comparative Perspectives on Social Movements* (Cambridge, 1996).

McAdam, Doug, Tarrow, Sidney, and Tilly, Charles, *Dynamics of Contention* (Cambridge, 2001).

McCarthy, Helen, 'Democratising British Foreign Policy: Rethinking the Peace Ballot, 1934–5', *Journal of British Studies*, 49/2 (2010), 358–87.

McCarthy, Helen, *The British People and the League of Nations: Democracy, Citi-zenship and Internationalism, c.1918–1945* (Manchester, 2011).

McCarthy, John D. and Zald, Mayer N., 'Resource Mobilization and Social Movements: A Partial Theory', *American Journal of Sociology*, 82 (1977), 1212–41.

Major, Patrick, *The Death of the KPD: Communism and Anti-Communism in West Germany, 1945–1956* (Oxford, 1997).

McKibbin, Ross, *Classes and Cultures: England 1918–1951* (Oxford, 1998).

McKibbin, Ross, *Parties and People: England 1914–1951* (Oxford, 2010).

McLeod, Hugh, 'The Religious Crisis of the 1960s', *Journal of Modern European History*, 3 (2005), 205–29.

Mandler, Peter, and Pedersen, Susan, 'Introduction: The British Intelligentsia after the Victorians', in Peter Mandler and Susan Pedersen (eds), *After the Victorians: Private Conscience and Public Duty in Modern Britain* (London and New York, 1994), 1–28.

Marwick, Arthur, *The Sixties: Cultural Revolution in Britain, France, Italy, and the United States, c.1958–c.1974* (Oxford, 1998).

Maslen, Joseph, 'Autobiographies of a Generation? Carolyn Steedman, Luisa Passerini and the Memory of 1968', *Memory Studies*, 6 (2013), 23–36.

Masters, Brian, *The Swinging Sixties* (London, 1985).

Mausbach, Wilfried, 'The Present's Past: Recent Perspectives on Peace and Protest in Germany, 1945–1973', *Mitteilungsblatt des Instituts für soziale Bewegungen*, 32 (2004), 67–98.

Mercer, Paul, *'Peace' of the Dead: The Truth behind the Nuclear Disarmers* (London, 1986).

Mergel, Thomas, 'Der mediale Stil der "Sachlichkeit". Die gebremste Amerikanisierung des Wahlkampfs in der alten Bundesrepublik', in Bernd Weisbrod (ed.), *Die Politik der Öffentlichkeit—die Öffentlichkeit der Politik: Politische Medialisierung in der Geschichte der Bundesrepublik* (Göttingen, 2003), 29–53.

Mergel, Thomas, *Propaganda nach Hitler: Eine Kulturgeschichte des Wahlkamps in der Bundesrepublik* (Göttingen, 2010).

Moeller, Robert G., 'The "Remasculinization" of Germany in the 1950s: Introduction', *Signs*, 24 (1998), 101–6.

Moeller, Robert G., *War Stories: The Search for a Usable Past in the Federal Republic of Germany* (Berkeley, 2001).

Moeller, Robert G., 'Germans as Victims? Thoughts on a Post-Cold War History of World War II's Legacies', *History and Memory*, 17 (2005), 147–94.

Moeller, Robert G., 'On the History of Man-Made Destruction: Loss, Death, Memory, and Germany in the Bombing War', *History Workshop Journal*, 61 (2006), 103–34.

Möller, Ulrich, *Im Prozeß des Bekennens: Brennpunkte der kirchlichen Atomwaffendiskussion im deutschen Protestantismus 1957–1962* (Neukirchen-Vluyn, 1999).

Monk, Ray, *Bertrand Russell: The Ghost of Madness 1921–1970* (London, 2000).

Morgan, Kenneth O., *Labour People: Leaders and Lieutenants, Hardie to Kinnock* (Oxford, 1987).

Morgan, Kenneth O. *The People's Peace: British History 1945–1989* (Oxford, 1990).

Mort, Frank, 'The Ben Pimlott Memorial Lecture 2010: The Permissive Society Revisited', *Twentieth Century British History*, 22 (2011), 269–98.

Moses, A. Dirk, 'The Forty Fivers: A Generation between Fascism and Democracy', *German Politics and Society*, 17 (1999), 94–125.

Müller, Jan-Werner, *Another Country: German Intellectuals, Unification and National Identity* (New Haven and London, 2000).

Myers, Frank E., 'Civil Disobedience and Organizational Change: The British Committee of 100', *Political Science Quarterly*, 86 (1971), 92–112.

Naumann, Klaus (ed.), *Nachkrieg in Deutschland* (Hamburg, 2001).

Nehring, Holger, 'The National Internationalists: Transnational Relations and the British and West German Protests against Nuclear Weapons, 1957–1964', *Contemporary European History*, 14/4 (2005), 559–82.

Nehring, Holger, 'The Era of Non-Violence: "Terrorism" in West German, Italian and French Political Culture, 1968–1982', *European Review of History*, 14/3 (2007), 343–71.

Nehring, Holger, ' "Generation" as Political Argument in West European Protest Movements in the 1960s', in Stephen Lovell (ed.), *Generations in Twentieth-Century Europe* (Basingstoke, 2007), 57–78.

Nehring, Holger, ' "The long, long night is over": The Campaign for Nuclear Disarmament, "Generation" and the Politics of Religion (1957–1964)' in Jane Garnett et al. (eds), *Redefining Christian Britain* (London, 2007), 138–47.

Nehring, Holger, ' "Generation", Modernity and the Making of Contemporary History: Responses in West European Protest Movements around "1968" ', in Anna von der Goltz (ed.), *'Talking 'bout my Generation': Conflicts of Generation Building and Europe's '1968'* (Göttingen, 2011), 71–94.

Nehring, Holger, 'Technologie, Moderne und Gewalt. Günther Anders, *Die Antiquiertheit des Menschen* (1956)', in Uffa Jensen et al. (eds), *Gewalt und Gesellschaft: Klassiker modernen Denkens neu gelesen* [FS Bernd Weisbrod] (Göttingen 2011), 238–47.

Newman, Michael, *Ralph Miliband and the Politics of the New Left* (London, 2002).

Norman, E. R., *Church and Society in England, 1770–1970* (Oxford, 1976).

Oakes, Guy, 'Managing Nuclear Terror: The Genesis of American Civil Defense Strategy', *International Journal of Politics, Culture, and Society*, 5 (1992), 361–403.

Oertzen, Peter von, 'Behelfsbrücken: Linkssozialistische Zeitschriften in der Ära der "Restauration" 1950–1962', in Michael Buckmiller and Joachim Perels (eds), *Opposition als Triebkraft der Demokratie: Bilanz und Perspektiven der zweiten Republik* (Hanover, 1998), 80–97.

Oppenheimer, Andrew, 'West German Pacifism and the Ambivalence of Human Solidarity, 1945–1968', *Peace & Change*, 29 (2004), 353–89.

Oppenheimer, Andrew, 'Air Wars and Empire: Gandhi and the Search for a Usable Past in Postwar Germany', *Central European History*, 45 (2012), 669–96.

Ormrod, David, 'The Churches and the Nuclear Arms Race, 1945–1985', in Richard Taylor and Nigel Young (eds), *Campaigns for Peace: British Peace Movements in the Twentieth Century* (New York, 1987), 175–95.

Osgerby, Bill, *Youth in Britain since 1945* (Oxford, 1998).

Otto, Karl A., *Vom Ostermarsch zur APO: Geschichte der ausserparlamentarischen Opposition in der Bundesrepublik 1960–1970* (Frankfurt/Main and New York, 1982).

Paris, Michael, *Warrior Nation: Images of War in British Popular Culture, 1850–2000* (London, 2000).

Parkin, Frank, *Middle Class Radicalism: The Social Bases of the British Campaign for Nuclear Disarmament* (Manchester, 1968).

Paul, Gerhard, '"Mushroom Clouds". Entstehung, Struktur und Funktion einer Medienikone des 20. Jahrhunderts im interkulturellen Vergleich', in Gerhard Paul (ed.), *Visual History* (Göttingen, 2006), 243–64.

Pedersen, Susan, 'Roundtable: Twentieth-Century British History in North America', *Twentieth Century British History*, 21 (2010), 375–418.

Pettenkofer, Andreas, *Radikaler Protest: Zur soziologischen Theorie politischer Bewegungen* (Frankfurt/Main, 2010).

Phythian, Mark, 'CND's Cold War', *Contemporary British History*, 15 (2001), 133–56.

Pias, Claus (ed.), *Abwehr. Modelle—Strategien—Medien* (Bielefeld, 2009).

Poiger, Uta G., *Jazz, Rock, and Rebels: Cold War Politics and American Culture in a Divided Germany* (Berkeley and Los Angeles, 2000).

Polletta, Francesca, ' "Free Spaces" in Collective Action', *Theory and Society*, 28 (1999), 1–38.

Prynn, David, 'The Woodcraft Folk and the Labour Movement 1925–70', *Journal of Contemporary History*, 18 (1983), 79–95.

Rahden, Till van, 'Clumsy Democrats: Moral Passions in the Federal Republic of Germany', *German History*, 29 (2011), 485–504.

Reckwitz, Andreas, *Das hybride Subjekt: Eine Theorie der Subjektkulturen von der bürgerlichen Moderne zur Postmoderne* (Weilerswist, 2006).

Reichardt, Sven, and Detlef, Siegfried (eds), *Das Alternative Milieu: Antibürgerlicher Lebensstil und linke Politik in der Bundesrepublik Deutschland und Europa 1968–1983* (Göttingen, 2010).

Reid, Alistair J., 'The Dialectics of Liberation: The Old Left, the New Left and the Counter-Culture', in David Feldman and Jon Lawrence (eds), *Structures and Transformations in Modern British History* (Cambridge, 2011), 261–80.

Reimann, Aribert, *Dieter Kunzelmann. Avantgardist, Protestler, Radikaler* (Göttingen, 2009).

Robinson, Lucy, *Gay Men and the Left in Post-War Britain: How the Personal Got Political* (Manchester, 2007).

Rowlands, Peter, and Attwood, Vincent (eds), *War and Peace: The Life and Work of Sir Joseph Rotblat* (Liverpool, 2006).

Rucht, Dieter (ed.), *Protest in der Bundesrepublik. Strukturen und Entwicklungen* (Frankfurt/Main and New York, 2001).

Rupp, Hans Karl, *Außerparlamentarische Opposition in der Ära Adenauer: Der Kampf gegen die Atombewaffnung in den fünfziger Jahren. Eine Studie zur innenpolitischen Entwicklung der Bundesrepublik* (Cologne, 1970).

Rusinek, Bernd-A., ' "Kernenergie, schöner Götterfunken!" Die "umgekehrte Demontage". Zur Kontextgeschichte der Atomeuphorie', *Kultur & Technik*, 4 (1993), 15–21.

Ruston, Roger, *A Say in the End of the World: Morals and British Nuclear Weapons Policy 1941–1987* (Oxford, 1989).

Sahlins, Marshall, *Islands of History* (Chicago, 1985).

Scalmer, Sean, *Gandhi in the West: The Mahatma and the Rise of Radical Protest* (Cambridge, 2011).

Schmidt, Fritz (ed.), *tusk: Versuche über Eberhard Köbel* (n.p. [Witzenhausen], 1994).

Schmidtke, Michael, *Der Aufbruch der jungen Intelligenz: Die 68er Jahre in der Bundesrepublik und den USA* (Frankfurt/Main, 2002).

Schmidtmann, Christian, *Katholische Studierende 1945–1973: Ein Beitrag zur Kultur- und Sozialgeschichte der Bundesrepublik Deutschland* (Paderborn, 2005).

Schneider, Michael, *Demokratie in Gefahr?: Der Konflikt um die Notstandsgesetze: Sozialdemokratie, Gewerkschaften und intellektueller Protest* (1958–1968) (Bonn, 1986).

Schönfeldt, Rolf, 'Die Deutsche Friedens-Union', in Richard Stöss (ed.), *Parteien-Handbuch: Die Parteien der Bundesrepublik Deutschland 1945–1980* (Opladen 1983), 848–76.

Schrafstetter, Susanna, 'The Long Shadow of the Past: History, Memory and the Debate over West Germany's Nuclear Status, 1954–69', *History & Memory*, 16 (2004), 118–45.

Schwartz, David N., *NATO's Nuclear Dilemmas* (Washington, 1983).

Schwarz, Bill, ' "The People" in History: The Communist Party Historians' Group, 1946–56', in Richard Johnson et al. (eds.), *Making Histories: Studies in History, Writing and Politics* (London 1982), 15–43.

Schwarz, Bill, ' "Claudia Jones and the *West Indian Gazette*": Reflections on the Emergence of Post-Colonial Britain', *Twentieth Century British History*, 14 (2003), 264–85.

Schwarz, Hans-Peter, 'Adenauer und die Kernwaffen', *Vierteljahrshefte für Zeitgeschichte*, 37/4 (1989), 567–93.

Sedlmaier, Alexander, and Malinowski, Stephan, ' "1968"—A Catalyst of Consumer Society', *Cultural and Social History*, 8 (2011), 255–74.

Siegfried, Detlef, ' "Don't trust anyone older than 30?" Voices of Conflict and Consensus between Generations in 1960s West Germany', *Journal of Contemporary History*, 40 (2005), 727–44.

Siegfried, Detlef, 'Demokratie und Alltag: Neuere Literatur zur Politisierung des Privaten in der Bundesrepublik Deutschland', *Archiv für Sozialgeschichte* 46 (2006), 737–50.

Siegfried, Detlef, *Time Is on my Side: Konsum und Politik in der westdeutschen Jugendkultur der 60er Jahre* (Göttingen, 2006).

Sisman, Adam, *A. J. P. Taylor: A Biography* (London, 1994).

Slobodian, Quinn, *Foreign Front: Third World Politics in Sixties West Germany* (Durham, NC, 2012).

Snow, David A., et al., 'Frame Alignment Processes, Micromobilization, and Movement Participation', *American Sociological Review*, 51 (1986), 464–81.

Soell, Hartmut, *Helmut Schmidt: Vernunft und Leidenschaft* (Munich, 2003).

Somers, Margaret, *Genealogies of Citizenship: Markets, Statelessness, and the Right to Have Rights* (Cambridge, 2008).

Spernol, Boris, *Notstand der Demokratie: Der Protest gegen die Notstandsgesetze und die Frage der NS-Vergangenheit* (Essen, 2008).

Spix, Boris, *Abschied vom Elfenbeinturm? Politisches Verhalten Studierender 1957–1967: Berlin und Nordrhein-Westfalen im Vergleich* (Essen, 2008).

Staadt, Jochen, *Die geheime Westpolitik der SED 1960–1970: Von der gesamtdeutschen Orientierung zur sozialistischen Nation* (Berlin, 1993).

Stankowski, Martin, *Linkskatholizismus nach 1945: Die Presse oppositioneller Katholiken in der Auseinandersetzung für eine demokratische und sozialistische Gesellschaft* (Cologne, n.d. [1976]).

Steedman, Carolyn, *Landscape for a Good Woman* (London, 1986).

Steedman, Carolyn, *Dust: The Archive and Cultural History* (Manchester, 2002).

Steedman, Carolyn, *Master and Servant: Love and Labour in the English Industrial Age* (Cambridge, 2007).

Steinberg, Marc W., 'The Talk and Back Talk of Collective Action: A Dialogic Analysis of Repertoires of Discourse among Nineteenth-Century English Cotton Spinners', *American Journal of Sociology*, 105 (1999), 736–80.

Steinmetz, Willibald, 'Anbetung und Dämonisierung des "Sachzwangs": Zur Archäologie einer deutschen Redefigur', in Michael Jeismann (ed.), *Obsessionen: Beherrschende Gedanken im wissenschaftlichen Zeitalter* (Frankfurt/Main, 1995), 293–333.

Stephanson, Anders, 'Offensive Realism', *boundary 2*, 27 (2000), 181–95.

Stoehr, Irene, 'Phalanx der Frauen? Wiederaufrüstung und Weiblichkeit in Westdeutschland 1950–1957', in Christiane Eifler and Ruth Seifert (eds), *Soziale Konstruktionen—Militär und Geschlechterverhältnisse* (Münster, 1998), 187–204.

Stoehr, Irene, 'Frieden als Frauenaufgabe? Diskurse über Frieden und Geschlecht in der bundesdeutschen Friedensbewegung der 1950er Jahre', in Jennifer A. Davy, Karen Hagemann, and Ute Kätzel (eds), *Frieden—Gewalt—Geschlecht: Friedens und Konfliktforschung als Geschlechterforschung* (Essen, 2005), 184–204.

Stölken-Fitschen, Ilona, *Atombombe und Geistesgeschichte: Eine Studie der fünfziger Jahre aus deutscher Sicht* (Baden-Baden, 1995).

Suri, Jeremi, *Power and Protest: Global Revolution and the Rise of Détente* (Cambridge, MA, and London, 2005).

Steege, Paul, *Black Market, Cold War: Everyday Life in Berlin, 1946–1949* (Cambridge, 2007).

Steege, Paul, Bergerson, Andrew Stuart, Healy, Maureen, and Swett, Pamela E., 'The History of Everyday Life: A Second Chapter', *Journal of Modern History*, 80 (2008), 358–78.

Süß, Dietmar, *Tod aus der Luft: Kriegsgesellschaft und Luftkrieg in Deutschland und England* (Munich, 2010).

Sywottek, Arnold, ' "Wohlstand"—"Sicherheit"—"Frieden": Beobachtungen zur westdeutschen Entwicklung', in Thomas Kühne (ed.), *Von der Kriegskultur zur*

Friedenskultur? Zum Mentalitätswandel in Deutschland seit 1945 (Hamburg, 2000), 243–61.

Tarrow, Sidney, *Power in Movement: Social Movements and Contentious Politics* (Cambridge, 1998).

Tarrow, Sidney, *Strangers at the Gates: Movements and States in Contentious Politics* (Cambridge, 2012).

Taylor, Miles, 'Patriotism, History and the Left in Twentieth-Century Britain', *Historical Journal*, 33 (1990), 971–98.

Taylor, Richard, *Against the Bomb: The British Peace Movement 1958–1965* (Oxford, 1988).

Taylor, Richard, and Pritchard, Colin, *The Protest Makers: The British Nuclear Disarmament Movement of 1958–1965, Twenty Years On* (Oxford, 1980).

Thießen, Malte, *Eingebrannt ins Gedächtnis. Hamburgs Gedenken an Luftkrieg und Kriegsende 1943 bis 2005* (Munich, 2007).

Thoß, Bruno, *NATO-Strategie und nationale Verteidigungsplanung: Planung und Aufbau der Bundeswehr unter den Bedingungen einer massiven atomaren Vergeltungsstrategie 1952–1960* (Munich, 2006).

Thomas, Merrilyn, *Communing with the Enemy: Covert Operations, Christianity and Cold War Politics in Britain and the GDR* (Oxford et al., 2005).

Thomas, Nick, 'Challenging Myths of the 1960s: The Case of Student Protest in Britain', *Twentieth Century British History*, 13 (2002), 277–97.

Thomas, Nick, *Protest Movements in 1960s West Germany: A Social History of Dissent and Democracy* (Oxford, 2003).

Thomas, Nick, 'Will the Real 1950s Please Stand up? Views of a Contradictory Decade', *Cultural and Social History*, 5 (2008), 227–36.

Thomas, Nick, 'Protests against the Vietnam War in 1960s Britain: The Relationship between Protesters and the Press', *Contemporary British History*, 22 (2008), 335–54.

Thompson, William, 'The New Left in Scotland', in Ian MacDougall (ed.), *Essays in Scottish Labour History: A Tribute to W. H. Marwick* (Edinburgh, 1978), 207–24.

Tilly, Charles, 'Social Boundary Processes', *Philosophy of the Social Sciences*, 34 (2004), 211–36.

Tuck, Stephen, 'Malcolm X's Visit to Oxford University: US Civil Rights, Black Britain, and the Special Relationship on Race', *American Historical Review*, 118 (2013), 76–103.

Veldman, Meredith, *Fantasy, the Bomb, and the Greening of Britain: Romantic Protest, 1945–1980* (Cambridge, 1994).

Verheyen, Nina, *Diskussionslust: Eine Kulturgeschichte des "besseren Arguments" in Westdeutschland* (Göttingen, 2010).

Vogel, Meike, *Unruhe im Fernsehen: Protestbewegung und öffentlich-rechtliche Berichterstattung in den 1960er Jahren* (Göttingen, 2010).

Walker, Mark, 'Legenden um die deutsche Atombombe', *Vierteljahrshefte für Zeitgeschichte*, 38 (1990), 45–74.

Waters, Chris, '"Dark Strangers" in Our Midst: Discourses of Race and Nation in Britain, 1947–1963', *Journal of British Studies*, 36 (1997), 207–38.

Waters, Chris, 'J. B. Priestley 1894–1984: Englishness and the Politics of Nostalgia', in Susan Pedersen and Peter Mandler (eds), *After the Victorians: Private Conscience and Public Duty in Modern Britain* (London and New York, 1994), 209–24.

Weart, Spencer R., *Nuclear Fear: A History of Images* (Cambridge, MA, 1988).

Webster, Wendy, *Englishness and Empire 1939–1965* (Oxford, 2005).

Weinhauer, Klaus, *Schutzpolizei in der Bundesrepublik. Zwischen Bürgerkrieg und Innerer Sicherheit: Die turbulenten sechziger Jahre* (Paderborn, 2003).

Weisbrod, Bernd, 'Der englische Sonderweg in der neueren Geschichte', *Geschichte und Gesellschaft*, 16 (1990), 233–52.

Weisbrod, Bernd, 'Generation and Generationalität in der Neueren Geschichte', *Aus Politik und Zeitgeschichte*, B8/2005 (21 February 2005), 3–9.

Weitbrecht, Dorothee, *Aufbruch in die Dritte Welt: Der Internationalismus der Studentenbewegung von 1968 in der Bundesrepublik Deutschland* (Göttingen, 2012).

Weitz, Eric D., 'The Ever-Present Other: Communism in the Making of West Germany', in Hanna Schissler (ed.), *The Miracle Years: A Cultural History of West Germany, 1949–1968* (Princeton and Oxford, 2001), 219–32.

Wernecke, Günter, and Wittner, Lawrence S., 'Lifting the Iron Curtain: The Peace March to Moscow of 1960–1961', *International History Review*, 21 (1999), 900–17.

Williams, Philip, *Hugh Gaitskell* (Oxford, 1982).

Wittner, Lawrence S., *One World or None: A History of the World Nuclear Disarmament Movement through 1953* (Stanford, CA, 1993).

Wittner, Lawrence S., *Resisting the Bomb: A History of the World Nuclear Disarmament Movement 1954–1970* (Stanford, CA, 1997).

Wittner, Lawrence S., 'The Nuclear Threat Ignored: How and Why the Campaign against the Bomb Disintegrated in the late 1960s', in Carole Fink, Philipp Gassert, and Detlef Junker (eds), *1968: The World Transformed* (Cambridge, 1998), 439–58.

Wittner, Lawrence, 'Gender Roles and Nuclear Disarmament Activism, 1954–1965', *Gender & History*, 12 (2000), 197–222.

Young, Nigel, *An Infantile Disorder? The Crisis and Decline of the New Left* (London, 1977).

Zahn, Robert von (ed.), *Folk und Liedermacher an Rhein und Ruhr* (Münster, 2002), 77–127.

Ziemann, Benjamin, ' "Vergesellschaftung der Gewalt" als Thema der Kriegsgeschichte seit 1914: Perspektiven und Desiderate eines Konzeptes', in Bruno Thoß and Hans-Erich Volkmann (eds), *Erster Weltkrieg—Zweiter Weltkrieg: Ein Vergleich* (Paderborn, 2002), 735–58.

Ziemann, Benjamin (ed.), *Peace Movements in Western Europe, Japan and USA since 1945: Historiographical Reviews and Theoretical Perspectives* (Essen, 2004).

Ziemann, Benjamin, 'Situating Peace Movements in the Political Culture of the Cold War: Introduction', in Ziemann (ed.), *Peace Movements in Western Europe, Japan and the USA during the Cold War* (Essen, 2007), 13–38.

Ziemann, Benjamin, 'The Code of Protest: Images of Peace in the West German Peace Movements, 1945–1990', *Contemporary European History*, 17 (2008), 237–61.

Ziemann, Benjamin, 'A Quantum of Solace? European Peace Movements during the Cold War and their Elective Affinities', *Archiv für Sozialgeschichte*, 49 (2009), 351–89.

Zimmer, Jochen, 'Das Abseits als vermiedener Irrweg: Die Naturfreundejugend in der westdeutschen Friedens- und Ökologiebewegung bis zum Ende der APO', in Heinz Hoffmann and Jochen Zimmer (eds), *Wir sind die grüne Garde: Geschichte der Naturfreundejugend* (Essen, 1986), 93–170.

5. UNPUBLISHED THESES

Carrington, R., 'Cultural and Ideological Challenges of the London Underground Movement, 1965–1971' (unpublished PhD thesis, Anglia Ruskin University, 2002).

Ehrlich, Avishai Zvi, 'The Leninist Organisations in Britain and the Student Movement 1966–1972' (unpublished PhD thesis, University of London, 1981).

Lee, Mia Ching, 'Art and Revolution in West Germany: The Cultural Revolution of 1968' (unpublished PhD thesis, University of Michigan, 2007).

Myers, Frank E., 'British Peace Politics: The Campaign for Nuclear Disarmament and the Committee of 100, 1957–1962' (unpublished PhD thesis, Columbia University, 1965).

Oppenheimer, Andrew, 'Conflicts of Solidarity: Nuclear Weapons, Liberation Movements, and the Politics of Peace in the Federal Republic of Germany, 1945–1975' (unpublished PhD thesis, University of Chicago, 2010).

Index